THE DUAL TRUTH

Studies on Nineteenth-Century
Modern Religious Thought and Its Influence
on Twentieth-Century Jewish Philosophy

Studies in Orthodox Judaism

Series Editor

Marc B. Shapiro (University of Scranton, Scranton, Pennsylvania)

Editorial Board

Alan Brill (Seton Hall University, South Orange, New Jersey)
Benjamin Brown (Hebrew University, Jerusalem)
David Ellenson (Hebrew Union College, New York)
Adam S. Ferziger (Bar-Ilan University, Ramat Gan)
Miri Freud-Kandel (University of Oxford, Oxford)
Jeffrey Gurock (Yeshiva University, New York)
Shlomo Tikoshinski (Jerusalem)

Books in This Series

Fundamentals of Jewish Conflict Resolution: Traditional Jewish Perspectives on Resolving Interpersonal Conflicts
Howard Kaminsky

Hybrid Judaism: Irving Greenberg, Encounter, and the Changing Nature of American Jewish Identity
Darren Kleinberg
Preface by Marc Dollinger

Modern Orthodoxy in American Judaism: The Era of Rabbi Leo Jung
Maxine Jacobson

My Father's Journey: A Memoir of Lost Worlds of Jewish Lithuania
Sara Reguer

The Middle Way: The Emergence of Modern-Religious Trends in Nineteenth-Century Judaism, Volumes I & II
Ephraim Chamiel
Edited by Dr. Asael Abelman
Translated by Dr. Jeffrey Green

Her Glory All Within: Rejecting and Transforming Orthodoxy in Israeli and American Jewish Women's Fiction
Barbara Landress

The Pillar of Volozhin: Rabbi Naftali Zvi Yehuda Berlin and the World of Nineteenth Century Lithuanian Torah Scholarship
Gil Perl

THE DUAL TRUTH

Studies on Nineteenth-Century
Modern Religious Thought and Its Influence
on Twentieth-Century Jewish Philosophy

EPHRAIM CHAMIEL

Translated by Avi Kallenbach

Volume I

Boston
2019

Library of Congress Cataloging-in-Publication Data

Names: Chamiel, Ephraim, author. | Kallenbach, Avi, translator.

Title: The dual truth : studies on nineteenth-century modern religious thought and its influence on twentieth-century Jewish philosophy / Ephraim Chamiel; translated by Avi Kallenbach.

Other titles: Emet ha-kefulah. English

Description: Boston : Academic Studies Press, 2018. | Series: Studies in Orthodox Judaism | "This book, The Dual Truth, was originally published by Carmel Publishing House in Hebrew in 2016" — Foreword to the English edition. | Includes bibliographical references.

Identifiers: LCCN 2018048880 (print) | LCCN 2018053238 (ebook) | ISBN 9781618118691 (ebook) | ISBN 9781618118820 (hardcover) Subjects: LCSH: Jewish philosophy—19th century. | Jewish philosophy—20th century. | Judaism—History—Modern period, 1750- | Hirsch, Samson Raphael, 1808-1888. | Luzzatto, Samuel David, 1800-1865. | Bible. Old Testament—Criticism, interpretation, etc.—History—19th century. | Bible. Old Testament—Criticism, interpretation, etc.—History—20th century.

Classification: LCC B5800 (ebook) | LCC B5800.C43313 2018 (print) | DDC 181/.06—dc23

LC record available at https://lccn.loc.gov/2018048880

©Academic Studies Press, 2019
ISBN 9781644696118
ISBN 9781618118691 (electronic)

Book design by Kryon Publishing Services (P) Ltd.
www.kryonpublishing.com

On the cover: Torah crown, Alessandria, Italy, 1849 (Silver and gilded silver cut, chased, engraved). U. Nahon Museum of Italian Jewish Art.

Published by Academic Studies Press
28 Montfern Avenue
Brighton, MA 02135, USA
press@academicstudiespress.com
www.academicstudiespress.com

Dedicated to My Children
Noam and Michal, Nitzan and Tehilah, Itay-Jacob and Vered, Liad

Table of Contents

Translator's Note   vii

Foreword to the English Edition   viii

Introduction   ix

Chapter One: Samson Raphael Hirsch: The Neo-Orthodox, Neo-Romantic Educator, and his Approach of Neo-Fundamentalist Identicality   1

Chapter Two: Interpretations of Hirsch's Thought from the Right and the Left   27

Chapter Three: "Heavenly Reward"—Samuel David Luzzatto's Doctrine of Divine Providence—between Revelation and Philosophy   73

Chapter Four: Development of Halakhah: Luzzatto's Evolving Views   105

Chapter Five: The *Peshat* is One, Because the Truth is One: Luzzatto between Interpretation and Thought   132

Chapter Six: Luzzatto and Maimonides: "Accept Truth from Whoever Speaks It"   149

Chapter Seven: Luzzatto on Theosophical Kabbalah: Harmful Invention with Worthy Intentions   186

Chapter Eight: Between Reason and Revelation: The Encounter between Rabbi Tsvi Hirsch Chajes and Nahman Krochmal   219

Translator's Note

Dr. Chamiel's book is a study of past and present—an exploration of how the echoes of nineteenth-century Jewish philosophy continued to reverberate in the minds and thoughts of Jewish thinkers in the twentieth century and today. Translating a study with such an ambitious scope—covering a wide spectrum of thinkers, speaking different languages in different time periods, from nineteenth-century Germany, Italy and Poland to modern-day Israel and the United States—was not always simple. Perhaps the greatest challenge was translating excerpts from nineteenth- and early twentieth-century Hebrew writers such as Samuel David Luzzatto, Rav Kook, and Jehiel Jacob Weinberg, who wrote in forms of Hebrew that are far from the expressions and norms of modern Hebrew. More than modern Hebrew, their vocabularies are filled with the ancient terminology of the Bible and rabbinic literature which they skillfully—and sometimes subtly—use to discuss the issues of the modern world; I can only hope that my translation did their prose justice.

Excerpts from Rabbi Hirsch, Hermann Cohen and Franz Rosenzweig were taken from existing English translations (with our emphasis) and excerpts from Eliezer Berkovits were taken from the English originals.

My gratitude to Dr. Jeffrey Green whose translation of Dr. Chamiel's previous book served as a model for imitation and inspiration; my thanks to Avi Staiman, CEO of Academic Language Experts, and Professor Marc Shapiro, who reviewed and corrected the translation as I proceeded; and of course, my many thanks to Dr. Chamiel, who took an active part in the translation process, offering insightful comments throughout.

Avi Kallenbach
Academic Language Experts

Foreword to the English Edition

This book, *The Dual Truth*, was originally published by Carmel Publishing House in Hebrew in 2016. Ever since then, I have aspired to translate it into English. With the founding of the translation company Academic Language Experts, the idea of translating the book began to take shape. The translation was carried out in partnership with the CEO of the company, Avi Staiman, and its chief academic translator Avi Kallenbach who did the actual, wonderful work. We began working on the project more than a year ago, and we have now completed it in the best possible way. It was proofread by Academic Studies Press, but any remaining errors are, of course, my responsibility; any feedback is much appreciated. The book was produced by ASP which served also as the publisher of my previous translated work *The Middle Way*, providing an edition of the work for those wishing to read and study it in English. Both productions were carefully reviewed by Professor Marc Shapiro, the series editor for *Studies in Orthodox Judaism*, who provided me with important comments on the translation and also saved me from duplicating some mistakes I made in the Hebrew original. I would like to thank all the aforementioned people for their contribution. I hope that presenting this book to the English-speaking scholars and public will help increase its circulation and serve to promote the study of Jewish thought in the modern era.

Ephraim Chamiel
October 2017, Jerusalem

Introduction

> It is best that you grasp the one
> Without letting go of the other
> For one who fears God will do his duty by both
> (Ecclesiastes 7:18 according to Ibn Ezra and Sforno)

> Science without religion is lame,
> Religion without science is blind.
> (*The Expanded Quotable Einstein*, 213)

Since the publication of my first book on modern religious Jewish thought in the nineteenth century,[1] in which I discussed in depth the philosophies of Samson Raphael Hirsch (1808–1888), Samuel David Luzzatto (1800–1865) and Tsvi Hirsch Chajes (*Maharats*, 1805–1855), I have had the opportunity to delve deeper into the worldviews of these three figures and to examine whether their legacy left any lasting mark on the landscape of modern, religious Jewish thought. During my research, it became clear to me that none of these men bequeathed their philosophies to any notable protégés. While it is often said that Hirsch founded Jewish neo-Orthodoxy, his neo-Orthodox successors expressed views very different than his own. Although R. Jacob Reines (1839–1915),

---

1   E. Chamiel, *The Middle Way* (Brighton, MA, 2014). My first book was largely a reworking of my doctorate at Hebrew University from 2006, on the subject of "Life in Two Worlds—the 'Middle Way': Religious Responses to Modernity in the Philosophy of Z.H. Chajes, S. R. Hirsch, and S. D. Luzzatto" (Hebrew). It can be read for free, in Hebrew, on my website www.echamiel.com. I discuss the "dual truth" in the English translation of the aforementioned book on pages 482–490. This current research relies on conclusions and insights from my last book, and most of its chapters appeared as articles in various academic journals from 2010 to 2014, or were prepared for the purpose of lectures and conferences (see the list at the end of the book). Therefore, there may occasionally be short repetitions and duplications.

R. Avraham Yitshak Kook (1865–1935) and R. Joseph B. Soloveitchik (1903–1993) all integrated both tradition and modernity into their worldviews—out of a belief in the Sinaitic origins of both the Written and Oral Torah, never foregoing even one *halakhah*—their systems were very different from that of Hirsch. Reines's point of view was one of a Zionist realist, Rav Kook's that of a Zionist-mystical-Messianist and Soloveitchik's that of a dialectical-Zionist-existentialist. Hirsch's immediate disciples and descendants failed to preserve his complex system. Some veered towards Haredism, repudiating the fundamental importance of European culture and secular studies, while others turned to a form of modern, realistic religion, separating religious and secular studies, and assigning them to different spheres of life. Thus Hirsch's original Romanticist system of *Torah im Derekh Erets* ("Torah with the 'way of the world'") vanished, replaced by the educational system of nationalist, religious Zionism. It was actually religious, non-Orthodox thinkers such as Hermann Cohen (1842–1918) Franz Rosenzweig (1886–1929) and Yeshayahu Leibowitz who while refusing to adopt the alienating views of the Reform movement, espoused important parts of Hirsch's thought and bequeathed them, albeit in a different garb, to succeeding generations. There were however also a few important halakhists and rabbis such as David Tsvi Hoffman (1843–1921), Yehiel Yaakov Weinberg (1884–1966), and his disciple Rabbi Professor Eliezer Berkovits (1908–1992) who considered themselves Orthodox, were active for many years in Germany, and who also adopted important Hirschian ideas. Luzzatto did have students but none of them could compare to their teacher's unique stature and none were capable of emulating his impressive personality, or of sustaining his complex system which was exceedingly difficult to implement on a larger, public scale. A few of his followers joined the American Conservative movement (Sabato Morais [1823–1897]) implementing certain aspects of his system. Moshe David Cassuto (1883–1951) was one of the most prominent of all Italian scholars who adopted parts of Luzzatto's teachings, especially in biblical scholarship. Chajes left no successors and mentored no students. In this book I will present before the reader three schools of exciting, outstanding, and virtuous scholars who held the distinction of being both modern and observant of Halakhah: two schools in Germany, the third in Italy, all of them absorbing the Jewish and non-Jewish cultures of their homelands. One school includes rabbis—biblical interpreters and halakhists—beginning with Jacob Ettlinger (1798–1871) and ending with Berkowitz. The second includes Jewish philosophers and thinkers beginning with Ḥakham Isaac Bernays (1793–1850) and ending with Leibowitz. Both schools revolve around the thought of Hirsch.

The third school was one of biblical interpreters beginning with Luzzatto and ending with Cassuto. These three systems of study prevailed until the establishment of the State of Israel.

In the first chapter of this book I will once again present the main principles of Hirsch's philosophy based on the discussions in my first book. In the second chapter, I will deal with different interpretations of Hirsch's thought, by his students and by scholars, to the left and to the right. From chapter three to seven, I will present the main points of Luzzatto's views on philosophy, biblical exegesis (especially his treatment of Maimonides's and Ibn Ezra's methods of interpretation), rabbinic literature and Kabbalah, also based on discussions in my first book. The eighth chapter will be dedicated to Maharats Chajes and the philosophical connection between him and Naḥman Krokhmal (1785–1840). In the ninth chapter, I will discuss the influence of Hirsch's thought on non-Orthodox thinkers in the twentieth century, and in the tenth and eleventh chapters, I will trace the influence of Hirsch's thought on rabbis and halakhists in the twentieth century. In the twelfth chapter, I will show the surprising influence of Hirsch and his successors on a young Rav Kook. In the thirteenth chapter, I will discuss the influence of Luzzatto's system of biblical interpretation on the twentieth-century Cassuto. In the final chapter, I will briefly deal with modern religiosity in the post-modern age, beginning with the second half of the twentieth century, showing how its roots lie in the dialectical Jewish thought of the preceding century, especially that of Luzzatto.

My research has led me to the conclusion that two critical issues occupied the middle trend of Jewish thought in the nineteenth and twentieth centuries. The first is the difficulty in harmonizing the statements of the Torah, which was considered divine revelation, with the statements of modern science, which sometimes reach conclusions that contradict the biblical text. Because these thinkers believed that these two realms were extremely important for the modern Jew, they offered solutions to this problem hoping to establish religion on reliable foundations. I discussed this issue in detail in my first book, and will continue to do so in the current one.

The attempt to deal with difficulties encountered by those who believe in God and revelation, but who at the same time wish to maintain a connection with western culture and its philosophy and accept the conclusions of scientific research, is a common theme running through the philosophies discussed in this book. Its title "The Dual Truth" reflects the centrality of this dilemma. The figures described in this book deal with this issue on a variety of different levels ranging from fundamentalism to liberalism, from apologetics to head-on confrontation. They juggle two sources of knowledge, each one claiming exclusive sovereignty over the truth, forcing them to determine the relationship between the two.

I have used the model of Shalom Rosenberg in his book *Torah Umada* who says that two extreme points of views should be excluded from discussion—the view that denies revelation entirely, that believes nothing exists except the material world, and that only science can serve as a source of knowledge, and the opposite view that claims that reason is misleading, leaving us to rely entirely upon revelation. If we look at other views along the spectrum, we can say that Moses Mendelssohn (1729–1786) held the compartmental approach (religion and science) arguing that each area deals with different issues and that there is no contradiction between them. Naḥman Krochmal adopted the resolvable dialectical approach (based on Friedrich Hegel 1770–1831). Tsvi Hirsch Chajes essentially adopted Judah Halevi's approach (identicality of science/philosophy with religion), which curbs the claims of science when it contradicts revelation. Samson Rafael Hirsch adopted an inconsistent form of neo-fundamentalism, oscillating between the view of Judah Halevi and that of Maimonides—identicality of science with religion and interpreting the Torah in-line with science. R. Avraham Kook and Joseph B. Soloveitchik advanced the dialectical approach which can be resolved rarely. Luzzatto advocated the approach of the "dual truth" (based on Eliyahu Delmedigo, 1458–1493) also known as the irresolvable dialectical approach. In my opinion, this is the preferred option because it is rooted in tradition but not delusional, even if it is exceedingly difficult. According to this view one should maintain, *simultaneously*, the validity of both human intellect and the religious tradition of Scripture and Rabbinic literature, both suitable means of arriving at the truth and the virtue, even if at times these truths directly contradict each other, at least in the world of man. The contradiction is both challenging and painful; however, making peace with it allows one to continue studying and experiencing the world without delusions, and allows the thinking religious person to subsist in this world.

The second issue is the reliability of the chain of tradition emanating from Sinai, which at the beginning of the modern period began to be challenged. I have used the models of Moshe Halbertal and Shalom Rosenberg to argue that Jewish positions on this issue are spread across a spectrum extending from right to left: on the right edge of the spectrum lie those who radically adopt the traditional approach, opposing any suggestion that the Sages innovated *halakhot* at all. This is the view of kabbalists and mystics such as

Nachmanides and his disciples—Rabbi Yom Tov Ishbili (the *Ritba*) and Rabbenu Nissim (the *Ran*). They believe that at Sinai Moses received the entire Torah—that is the Written Torah as well as the entire range of differing opinions contained in the Oral Torah. The role of the Sages was to uncover, select and establish the relevant Halakhah for us, based on these preexisting traditions, but without creating anything themselves. To the left of this, one can find the Ge'onim, Ibn Daud and other fundamentalists—the Haredim, Orthodox, and neo-Orthodox such as Hirsch—who believe that the Written Torah and rulings in the Oral Torah were all given to Moses at Sinai. The role of the Sages was to use the methods of halakhic *midrash* to retrieve certain *halakhot* that were lost or forgotten due to the travails and persecutions of exile, which are also the cause of Rabbinic dispute. This recovery is accomplished using the thirteen hermeneutic principles which were also revealed at Sinai. Over the course of the twentieth century, there was a leftward shift among some Neo-Orthodox thinkers, in the direction of more liberal views. They borrowed from classic Conservative thinkers arguing for a historical conception of halakhic development. To the left of the Orthodox is the position of Judah Halevi. He believes that the Written Torah and only some laws of the Oral Torah were revealed at Sinai. The remaining *halakhot* comprising the Oral Torah, were transmitted gradually to the Sages in subsequent acts of revelation—a sort of continuous theophany of Sinai. To the left of him are R. Yosef Albo, Krochmal, and Tsvi Hirsh Chajes. They too believe that both the Written Torah and some laws of the Oral Torah were transmitted to Moses at Sinai. However, other aspects of the Oral Torah while transmitted to Moses, were only revealed in potential. The role of the Sages was to use their intellect (aided by the thirteen hermeneutical principles) to enact these other *halakhot*, actualizing them with majority rulings based on *Midrash Halakhah*. To the left of this position is the concept of an accumulative halakhic codex, the view of Maimonides, according to which the 613 commandments enumerated in the Written Torah were revealed to Moses at Sinai. Other laws, however, were created by the Sages who were aided by their own reasoning, the methods of *Midrash Halakhah* and the thirteen hermeneutical principles which were revealed at Sinai. To the left of Maimonides lies Luzzatto and classic Conservative thinkers. They believe that the Written Torah was originally revealed at Sinai. However, the Oral Torah constitutes a series of enactments and rulings made by the Sages aided by the thirteen principles which they themselves invented in order to anchor their own laws in the text of Torah as scriptural reference (*asmakhta*) but not as a primary reading.

The Sages were men of gigantic spiritual stature, and used their own reasoning and objective vision to understand the needs of their time and the place of their generation, tailoring new laws which sometimes contradict the biblical commandments and sometimes add to them. In the middle of the twentieth century most Conservative Jewish thinkers shifted even further to the left towards a belief that the Written Torah is also a human creation, severely weakening their dedication to Halakhah as a result. At the far left of the spectrum, which completely denies the traditional view, is the view of Reform Judaism. The Reform argue that divine revelation to man is not, nor ever was, possible. The Written Torah is a human creation, the invention of men. The Oral Torah likewise is the human legislation of the Sages. The Reform went even further in their treatment of the Sages and their laws, arguing that while the Sages sometimes established laws with wisdom, at other times they did so with guile, in order to consolidate their complete control over the people by encumbering them with oppressive laws. Consequently, we, today, must abolish significant parts of this extraneous burden.

This book deals with the views of Hermann Cohen, Franz Rosenzweig, Yeshayahu Leibowitz, David Tsvi Hoffman, Yehiel Yaakov Weinberg, Rav Kook, Eliezer Berkowitz and Moshe David Cassuto regarding these issues. Similarly it will present my claim that these thinkers, who differ regarding these two issues, shared a common influence, the thought of Rav Samson Raphael Hirsch, which left an imprint on important elements of their philosophies.

In the wake of the variety of new Neo-Orthodox, Conservatives—classic and new—and Reform positions in the last few decades, a new stance has developed to the right of the Reform, primarily in academic circles, a position I designate Orthoprax, "Conservadox," or post-Orthodox, a position held by Cassuto (influenced by Luzzatto) as well as myself. This is the "dual truth," a position maintained by traditional academic scholars. It is the position of those who do not believe in the possibility of a real, historical revelation of God to man, and who as men of science and reason, think that any text, by definition, is a human work. However, as believing, sentimental intellectuals, they aspire to observe all the laws dictated in the *Shulḥan Arukh* as well as later Halakhah developing after it up until this day, and hope that it will continue to develop, shaping itself to fit to changing times as well as to the renewed Jewish sovereignty in the State of Israel following the spirit of the Torah. This is all out of an understanding that the narrative of "The Jewish People," constructed by the Sages and the spiritual giants of the nation over the centuries, is extremely important to their lives as ethical, thinking people in need of a sacred, supernatural, spiritual space which anchors them to their past and tradition, a foundation upon which an experiential and real future can be built. I discussed this issue in my first book and will continue to do so in the current book.

I will conclude with a methodological note. I know that cataloguing and pigeonholing people in a simplistic fashion following a set of criteria is imprecise and even daunting. Humans are complex creatures with complicated minds and intricate reasoning; no system of classification can encapsulate their views in their entirety. Nevertheless, I think that in order to undertake any comparative scholarship of worth, it is difficult to avoid simplistic definitions and categories, which so effectively highlight the differences and similarities between different figures for the reader's benefit. At the same time, it is important to cautiously note the fact that reality, at times, can be complex and far from simple.

CHAPTER ONE

Samson Raphael Hirsch: The Neo-Orthodox, Neo-Romantic Educator, and his Approach of Neo-Fundamentalist Identicality

Rabbi Samson (the son of) Raphael Hirsch[1] lived and was active in the midst of the polemical turmoil of the mid-nineteenth century, situated in the eye of the storm. He was born during Romanticism's rise in Germany, following the decline of Rationalism and metaphysics. From his youth, he experienced the ongoing Orthodox struggle with the Reform movement—afterwards with the positivist-historical school (which would later become the Conservative movement)—as well as the weakening of Jewish community autonomy. In his youth in Hamburg, during which he experienced the powerless Orthodox struggle against the Reform temple, he decided to devote himself to the protection of Torah and tradition using modern methods. His education was structured according to the curriculum of Naftali Hirz

---

1 Information about the time period and biography of Hirsch can be found in the introduction to my book *The Middle Way*. In this book the reader will also find his responses to Bible criticism (and his Neo-Fundamentalism), to religious reformation movements (and his polemics surrounding the divinity of the Torah) to the Haskalah and secular studies (and his Neo-Romanticism), to the return to the Land of Israel (and his humanist universalism), to progress towards the improvement of the status of women and to modern Jewish life in Christian neighborhoods.

Wessely (1725–1805), which integrated religious and secular studies. Jewish philosophy from Isaac Bernays based on the teachings of Judah Halevi and Talmud studies from Rabbi Ya'akov Ettlinger molded his conception of a middle way with which he hoped to rejuvenate the Torah. He called this method "Torah im Derekh Erets" ("Torah with the way of the world"), and it became the basis of the movement known as Modern Orthodoxy, or Neo-Orthodoxy. To Hirsch's left were religious reformers and Bible critics, deniers of the Torah's divinity, to his right Orthodox zealots eschewing anything new or innovative. He believed that his new system, the middle way, was not a compromise but Judaism's true path, the way of its golden era. He writes about the pious:

> The richer the minority's cause, the more will the minority treasure it. But then it may easily come to regard all other knowledge in "outside" domains as unnecessary, or even as utterly worthless. It may reject all intellectual activity in any field outside its own as an offense against its own cause, as an inroad upon the devotion properly due to that cause and an infringement on its prerogatives. Such a one-sided attitude does not stop at mere disregard for other intellectual endeavors. Once this attitude has taken hold in a Jewish minority, that minority will be unable to form a proper judgment and a true image of those intellectual pursuits which are not cultivated in its own ranks but pursued mainly by its opponents. Then, as a result of simple ignorance, the minority will begin to fear that which at first it merely neglected out of disdain. Consequently, the minority will begin to suspect the existence of an intrinsic close relationship between these "outside" intellectual pursuits and those principles to which the Jewish minority stands in opposition... Rather, it has cause to regard all truth, wherever it may be found on the outside, as a firm ally of its own cause, since all truth stems from the same Master of truth.[2]

Hirsch devoted himself to the community rabbinate, emphasizing his ideological struggles and his educational system. He also briefly familiarized himself with the academic world and, on his own, experienced and studied the speculative philosophy of his time.

---

2   *Writings*, 2:247–248. The "Writings" originally appeared in German in Hirsch's journal *Jeschurun* from 1855 onwards in Frankfurt, and were subsequently collected in his *Gesammelte Schriften*. My quotations are from the English translation entitled *The Collected Writings*. See there also 387–388. See E. Stern, *Ishim Vekivunim* (Ramat Gan, 1987), 52–53; see also Hirsch, *Writings*, 1:322–325; 4:176–177; 5:312, 326–327; Hirsch, Num. 25:12.

BASIC CHARACTERISTICS OF HIRSCH'S THOUGHT

This chapter is dedicated to some basic characteristics of Hirsch's thought. It is commonly known that Hirsch was the central pillar of the Neo-Orthodox movement. For our purposes, Orthodoxy refers to the worldview which maintains that God—a being possessing personality, choice and will—created the world and man in a process lasting six days, occurring approximately six thousand years ago. God appeared to the Children of Israel at Mount Sinai after bringing them out of Egypt, and through Moses, gave them the Written Torah and the laws of the Oral Torah. Hirsch's innovation lies in his attempt to integrate the truth, beauty and good of modernity—its culture, science and philosophy—into Jewish tradition, without abandoning even one commandment. He affirms that revelation and reason, science and religion, are actually identical, because they both stem from the same source—God. Being Orthodox, he completely disavows Bible criticism. He assesses well the danger to Orthodoxy posed by the Reform position that denies the Torah's divinity, and therefore, opposes on principle the use of the academy's philological-historical method to analyze the Holy Scripture. Hirsch categorically maintains that the Torah is nothing less than the word of God, authentic and uniform, and it should only be studied from within and as it presents itself—as the word of God. The Torah is immaculate and inerrant and it encapsulates truths that were unknown and incomprehensible to the generation of its recipients. One's duty is to ascend towards the Torah, not to lower it to one's level as demanded by religious reformers. Therefore, all criticism—higher source criticism and lower textual criticism—is impossible. Hirsch acquired his Neo-Orthodox views after he had already assimilated important ideas from the Jewish *Haskalah* movement of Moses Mendelssohn and Naftali Hirz Wessely. Consequently, universalism, humaneness, human rights, the centrality of the individual, and freedom and equality for all mankind—were absorbed into his doctrine, especially his ethics. These Neo-Orthodox views led to the two revolutions he initiated.

EDUCATIONAL REVOLUTION

His first revolution was the implementation of a "Torah im Derekh Erets" curriculum in the school he founded in Frankfurt, inspired by the "Science of Man" (*Torat Ha-Adam*) and the "Divine Teaching" (*Torat ha-Elohim*) of Wessely's *Divrei Shalom Ve-Emet*. In this school both boys and girls were instructed from a young age using a curriculum which combined religious and secular studies. Internalizing the educational revolution of the Haskalah in its entirety, Hirsch believed that one should teach secular studies to young children in formal educational institutions, albeit using an integrative method which teaches from the Torah's perspective. This integration was not successful even in the school he himself founded. Nevertheless, the principle of demanding secular education for all young students was firmly established for generations to come as a result of his efforts. Hirsch maintained that the integration of religious and secular studies was not a concession to circumstance; Judaism has always believed in accepting external truths, and always accorded these truths inherent value. Loyal to tradition, Hirsch defended this method of education, arguing that it had always occupied a place in Judaism, and it was only exile which had damaged it, erasing it from Jewish memory. Hirsch boldly asserted that this integrative combination of Torah studies with secular education would produce a result which would be dialectically greater than the sum of its parts. He says about this combination:

> In keeping with its educational program, our school accords the same serious and devoted attention to subjects of general studies as it does to what is commonly regarded as specifically Jewish education. From the very beginning, our school has been aware that, in carrying out the task it has set for itself, it has combined two distinct elements that are considered mutually exclusive by prejudiced outsiders with a superficial point of view. One, they claim, must of necessity limit the other by virtue of the time and energy required to do justice to both. Our school, by contrast, has been of the opinion from the outset that these two elements, although commonly viewed as mutually limiting antitheses (and even considered by some as nullifying one another), are, in fact, two closely related, mutually complementary part of one greater, integrated educational unity. In practical life, this unity produces a Jew with moral and spiritual training in the general culture of the mankind, a man and citizen with a moral and spiritual education in the values of Judaism. As a consequence, the school, which should be the nursery for practical life, should promote both these elements in such a manner that they will complement and support one another to form one harmonious whole.[3]

---

3   Hirsch, *Writings*, 7:63, in the essay "The Role of Hebrew Study in General Education," from 1866.

I regard it important to dispute the view of some who consider themselves Hirsch's successors (including scholars)—that the decision to combine secular education with religious studies was a compromise, designed to meet the needs of Germany's Jewry at the time, or that Hirsch never accorded inherent value to secular studies, and never affirmed that they could contribute valuably to Jewish education. In respect to compromise, Hirsch says explicitly in his essay "The Relevance of Secular Studies to Jewish Education":

> There are proponents of Jewish studies who view any attempt to give our youth a secular education as a sacrifice of time and energy that should be devoted to things Jewish. They may sanction this sacrifice as a concession to the demands of the present day, but they will deplore it and will feel deeply concerned about the influence that an educational element they consider alien to Judaism will have on the future Jewish attitude and lifestyle of our youth. In view of the fact that our institution gives the same earnest and devoted attention to general education as it does to Jewish studies. . . It would be important to demonstrate to the Jewish friends of our institution the close connection between these two fields of education and the significant benefits which secular studies have to offer to the future philosophy and lifestyle of our Jewish youth. . . The question whether a school embraces all fields of study with equal enthusiasm out of a deep inner conviction, or because it is forced to do so by circumstances beyond its control, certainly cannot be a matter of indifference to those whose trust the school hopes to obtain for its endeavors. Only ideas rooted in genuine conviction will be received with enthusiasm. Products of compromise can expect no more than grudging acceptance forced by considerations of expediency.[4]

I will return to this topic in the following chapter.

REVOLUTION IN THE STATUS OF WOMEN

Hirsch's second revolution is the position that in Judaism the woman is always considered superior to the man intellectually and ethically. Hirsch argues that the reason that women are exempt from positive time bound commandments is because they have no need for them. Although the commandments are meant

---

4   Hirsch, *Writings*, 7:81–82.

to rescue the observant from the sensuality of the flesh and the deception of impulse, women, by their very nature, are secure from such threats. Women fulfill their role in the home. They are tasked with ensuring that their husbands and children will study and observe the Torah, which will guarantee them ethical purity and sanctity safeguarded from the desires of flesh, and the desires for wealth and fame. Loyal to tradition, Hirsch claims, in contrast to most biblical and rabbinic sources, that this was Judaism's position from ancient times, an approach kept in all generations.

Hirsch writes about the exemption of women from positive time-bound commandments:

> The most likely reason the Torah does not obligate women in these *mitsvos* is that *women do not need them.* For the whole purpose of מצוות עשה שהזמן גרמא [positive time-bound commandments] is to represent—through symbolic actions—certain truths, ideas, principles, and resolutions, and to bring these values afresh to our minds, from time to time, so that we take them to heart and put them into practice. The Torah takes it for granted that woman has great fervor and faithful enthusiasm for her calling, and that the temptations awaiting her in the sphere of her calling pose but little danger to her. Hence, it was not necessary to impose on her all the *mitzvos* that are imposed on man. For man requires repeated exhortation to remain true to his calling, and it is necessary to repeatedly caution him against any weakness in the fulfillment of his mission. . . Women's exemption from ראייה and from חגיגה [*reiya* and *hagiga*—different types of sacrifices at the Temple during the pilgrimage festivals], however, is apparently to be explained differently: The public national representation of the Torah—which is what summons the nation to the Sanctuary—belonged primarily to the calling of the men.[5]

Hirsch writes about female superiority in the last essay of his series about the woman in Judaism, appearing in *Jeschurun* and dedicated to the subject of "the Jewish Woman in the Talmud":

> Even though the Sages of Judaism fully appreciate that women, because of their nature, are basically different from men, they regard women as full intellectual equals of the male sex. . . Our Sages consider *women*

---

5   Hirsch on Lev. 23:43.

intellectually superior to men. The Creator has given greater intellectual gifts to the woman than to the man [BT Niddah 45b]; that is why women attain intellectual maturity earlier than men (נדה מה). This, too, is why the Sages of the Jewish people regard the matriarchs, women such as Sarah and Rebecca, as no less inspired by the spirit of God and no less capable of communicating with Him than the patriarchs... In general, the view of the Sages of Judaism is that every human being, regardless of class, sex, or nationality, is capable of intellectual and moral perfection.[6]

---

6 Hirsch, *Writings* 8:134–135. Emphasis added. In the Talmud, in Niddah, the well-known teaching by Rav Hisda appears, explaining Rav's reason for stating in the Mishnah that a woman's vows are valid from the age of twelve, whereas those of a man only from the age of thirteen. "'And God built the rib' teaches that the Holy One, blessed be He, gave more intelligence to the woman than to the man" (BT Niddah 45b). Cf. Breuer, *Edah*, 116. Breuer represents the approach of twentieth-century Modern Orthodoxy, and he therefore admires greatly the "reversal" that Hirsch performed, without criticizing it. Ross, *Armon*, 89–91, 101–105, also took note of the reversal in Hirsch's words, but for some reason she does not cite this source, which is the most explicit of all. She is also disturbed by the refusal of Hirsch and those like him to acknowledge the element of women's inferiority in the Jewish tradition. Her further, post-modern criticism is of Hirsch's apologetics, which, even if it is sincere, is no longer persuasive in many circles. She sees a flaw in the modern conservative approaches that rejected the historical conception of religion and preferred a single, eternal meta-program. In my opinion, it is hard to blame Hirsch for not being a post-modern pluralist, so that his approach no longer pleases us. His choice of a meta-narrative of a super-historical Judaism, entirely derived from Sinai, is understandable in its time. He prefers his meta-program to those proposed by others. He explains with great clarity that it is not possible to accept the historicism of the Halakhah that was proposed by the Reform movement and the historical positivists. For, in his opinion, if the Oral Law and the written Torah are not from heaven, there is no longer any basis to obligate us to observe them as they are and to prevent us from making corrections in them as our hearts desire, which is what others did, to his regret. My critique is different. I present a wide variety of sources and show that Hirsch's selective apologetics, even if they are sincere, leads to difficulties and contradictions, making it difficult to maintain the meta-narrative that he so cherishes. Interestingly, Breuer, *Edah*, n. 111, 364, points out that the Rabbi Judah Loew (the *Maharal*) had a similar idea regarding the superiority of women. Examination of the source he quotes and other places in the Loew produces, in my opinion, a picture of the status of women entirely different from the reversal that Hirsch presents. Loew discusses there an Aggada in BT Brakhot 17a on a verse which at face value portrays women negatively, referring to them as: "women that are at ease" and "confident daughters," (Isaiah 32:9) and warns them of their impending destruction. The Aggada, however, interprets the verse positively, promising a larger reward for women than for men (this why they are at ease and confident) explaining that their reward is greater because they are concerned to have their sons and husbands study Torah. According to Loew, based on Aristotle and his followers, the woman is matter, and the man is form. The man is active, and the woman is passive. Only the man is the essence of reality, and the woman is defective reality. The woman—even the whole part in her is not removed from inferiority. True, this inferiority gives her an advantage in one area. Since matter needs

NEO-ROMANTICISM

Neo-Romanticism is another feature of Hirsch's approach. For our purposes, Romanticism refers to the philosophical and cultural ideas which conquered Europe in the wake of idealist philosopher Immanuel Kant (1724–1804) who maintained that man's pure reason is incapable of comprehending things in themselves and, therefore, God is certainly beyond reason's powers of apprehension. Kant, then, proffers man's practical reason as adjudicatory. The Romantics, on the other hand, choose instead human experience obtained from the nation's past. Anchored in emotion and transmitted through tradition, it supports the individual and the nation as a whole and constitutes a source of law. The Romantics wished to return to nature and the past, and were drawn to emotionalism and mysticism. Hirsch is a Romantic. He disqualifies rationalist, speculative philosophy based on Maimonides, Benedict (Baruch) de Spinoza (1632–1677) and Mendelssohn who believe that truth and morality belong only to reason. Hirsch, by contrast, argues that Scripture contains no hidden philosophical layer of allegory, and that intellectual study does not constitute a Jew's ultimate purpose. He uses Kant's philosophical revolution to argue that the failure of pure reason leaves us with only the historical experience of divine revelation as our standard for the true and good. Therefore, the highest form of morality is not an autonomous system adjudicated by man's practical reason

---

form and easily clings to it, it is easy for a woman, who is herself a passive creation, quiet and at ease, "being matter ready for this, then she unites and connects with the Torah [which is form] completely in the most marvelous eagerness... But men in this respect must work and take pains with the Torah without rest night and day." This advantage enables the woman to receive a greater reward from the study of Torah. However, she is not permitted to study Torah, but her activity to assist and encourage her husband and sons to study Torah, which is an act less important than study itself, is enough for that. See Judah Loew, *Drush 'Al Hatorah Vehamitsvot*. (Pieterkov, 1914), 3–31; Judah Loew, *Kitvei Hamaharal Miprag, Mivḥar*, A. Kariv (ed.) (Jerusalem, 1960), Vol. 2, 340. In Rav Kook as well—and the Maharal was one of his spiritual teachers—there is a position that appears to be close to that of Hirsch, but its source is in a kabbalistic position which also holds woman to be inferior. The man legislates and conquers, and she is legislated and conquered, he is like the spirit, and she is like the soul, and therefore she also has an advantage, in that sanctity is natural to her and does not need to observe a large part of the commandments or to learn the Torah of the men. See Rozenak, *Hanevuit*, 246–251 and nn. 149, 161 there. Chertok, in his book *Diyuqan Haisha Hayehudit beHaguto shel Rabbi Shimshon Rafael Hirsch* (Jerusalem, 2006) did not discern that Hirsch maintains that the woman always possesses intellectual and ethical superiority over the man, and was very forgiving of his apologetics and his selective use of the words of the sages. The same can be said of his book *Qanqan Yashan Male Ḥadash* (Bnei Brak, 2000), chapter 2. For an extensive development of Hirsch's stance regarding the status of the woman in Judaism and the internal difficulties it entails see Chamiel, *Middle Way*, chapter 5.

which suffers from the limits of the flesh. The highest morality is a heteronomous system—a morality received from a transcendental, external source, a supernatural power, unfettered by matter's sensual bonds. In terms of man's purpose, and the lesson the Torah means to teach, Hirsch determines, in line with his Romantic post-rationalist approach, that the Torah contains no esoteric philosophy or secret mysticism. It is a codex of divine, ethical norms, which if accepted will bring mankind redemption. Man's end-goal is ethical sanctity, a non-elitist goal, and Torah's morality is the exclusive means of achieving it. True morality is divine and it is free of the hindrances and restrictions of any sensuality which can prevent reason from overcoming human will and hinder the observance of morality in its pristine form. Concerning the importance of returning to nature and its beauty, and the connection between nature and morality, Hirsch states:

> How utterly different is the spirit of Judaism where it can unfold itself freely! It transports us into the open country, where the brooks trickle and the meadows bloom, where the seeds ripen and the trees blossom and the herds pasture, where man exercises his powers in close contact with nature and places his exertions immediately under the protection and blessing of God. Nature meant us to be men of the fields and flocks. The *Galuth* has made us into wandering traders. Oh, that we could turn our backs on this occupation which has been artificially imposed on us, that with our children we might flee away to the simplicity of a country life infused with the Divine Jewish spirit! Then would simplicity and peace, temperance and love, humanity and joy, enthusiasm and happiness dwell with us; David's harp would sound again and Ruth would again find the ears of corn on the field of Boaz.[7] Clearly, the Torah considers it crucial that we see the Divine Lawgiver in the organic life of nature.[8] Man is the only creature endowed with a capacity for enjoying beauty. This shows the importance of the aesthetic sense for the moral mission of man.[9] Beauty's effect on the soul is as radiance, as breath of air.[10]

---

7   *Writings*, 2:318. Praise of romanticism and proper emotionality is found in one of his essays on Hanukkah, *Writings*, 2:261–264.
8   Hirsch on Gen. 1:11–13.
9   Hirsch on Gen. 2:9.
10 Hirsch on Gen. 39:6–7.

Hirsch does not subscribe however to classical romanticism represented in non-Jewish philosophy by the likes of Friedrich Schleiermacher (1768–1834) and in Judaism by the kabbalists and their modern interpreters, the Hasidic masters. I consider Hirsch a Neo-Romantic for two reasons. Firstly, as one who internalized the Haskalah, he eschewed mysticism like fire. He had nothing to do with theosophy, ecstasy, asceticism, meditative seclusion, theurgy, and sentimentality, seeing in all of these a pagan-Christian approach, playing on man's emotions in order to obtain unbefitting, short-term achievements, an approach the Reform movement tries to emulate. Consequently, he rejects Kabbalah and Hasidism as well.

He expresses his objection to being swept away by emotion in a number of places. Discussing Reform Rabbis, he writes in an essay on the High Holidays:

> Indeed, any era of religious restoration based on religious sentiment and "belief" tends to produce also a growth of beliefs in clairvoyance, spiritism and even downright satanic cults. Indeed, where could the line be drawn if our emotional life were not to remain under the control of our clear good sense and intellect?[11]

In a sharp piece directed against Christian priests, whom the leaders of Reform Judaism wish to imitate, he writes that they radically employ emotion, sorrow and weeping, cheaply manipulating these feelings in order to promote religious fanaticism (the Hebrew word for non-Jewish priests, "Kemarim," derives from the expression "נכמרו רחמיו" [his mercy was stirred, play of words on the root כמר]; cf. his commentary there). Jewish priests (Kohanim), on the other hand, employ pure reason to improve man's powers of judgment:

> The Jewish כהן [Kohen] is not dependent on devotion, emotion. Jewish Divine service is not designed to excite dark mysterious feelings. The Jewish Sanctuary appeals *primarily to the intellect*: התפלל [to pray] means to rectify one's *judgment* and to make clear to oneself one's relationship to things in general, one's duties. Feelings are very cheap. One can weep copiously before God in prayer, and then get up and be no better than one was before! The כומר [komer] counts on exciting the emotions. The כהן, however, has to be כן [honest] with himself and מכין [preparing], provide others with firm direction and a firm basis. Heathenism works on

---

11 *Writings*, 2:140–141.

the emotions and thereby shackles the intellect. The emotions, however, are like a clock mechanism without hands, restless movement that knows not whence or whither, which can be exploited for any purpose. The כומר fans the flames of hell and arouses fanaticism; he celebrates his triumph when נכמרו רחמיו, when the innards of the believers reach a point of total ferment.[12]

In his first book *The Nineteen Letters* (English translation 1898, p. 187), Hirsch criticizes the corruption of Kabbalah, arguing that it has deviated from its pristine form and has become "a magical mechanism, a means of influencing or resisting theosophical worlds or anti-worlds." However, as a loyalist to tradition, and because Kabbalah is directly linked by tradition to the *Tanna* Rabbi Shimon Bar Yohai, he could not completely dismiss it. He therefore avoided the discussion, claiming he did not understand esoteric matters, and that in any case extant Kabbalah is inauthentic.

Secondly, while Hirsch opposes speculative philosophy, he does not disqualify the importance of reason, maintaining that emotion should be restricted by healthy logic. According to Hirsch, Judaism does not support coercion. It teaches man to use his reason and to freely choose to follow the Torah's morality which, as mentioned, is the greatest morality possible. It is a morality received in a divine revelation, experienced by the nation in an empirical, historical theophany. Its authenticity is affirmed by the event's publicity and its subsequent transmission from father to son. Intellect receives the facts of revelation and formulates them and this formulation combined with free will is linked to the performance of a chosen way of life through the medium of emotion. Hirsch writes:

> What is required for the practice of God's commandments is not hazy and excited emotion and imagination, but a clear mind and a sharp and sober intellect. The symbols of the Sanctuary speak not to the imagination, but to the clear and lucid mind. For only the mind—which comprehends clearly, reaches accurate conclusions, and places every detail in its proper category—is capable of guiding us to carry out God's commandments.[13]

---

12 Hirsch on Gen. 43:30. Hirsch's explanation of prayer as directed toward the person praying and not to God with the expectation of influencing Him, penetrated deeply into Jewish thought after him. One prominent proponent of this view was Leibowitz.

13 Hirsch on Lev. 10:9–11. On Hirsch's opposition to Kabbalah, see Katz, "Hirsch," 19–21. Katz states that in his criticism Hirsch refers to "the magical mechanism for influencing theosophical worlds or to defend against Satanic worlds," in the Kabbalah of the "Ari"

NEO-FUNDAMENTALISM

A third feature of Hirsch's thought is Neo-Fundamentalism. Fundamentalism is the view that the words of God, transmitted in writing or orally, cannot contain error, and everything they tell truly happened in real time and space. Any historical, geographical or scientific information appearing in the Holy Scripture is therefore absolutely true, and in the event of contradiction between religious texts and historical, scientific or philological research, truth lies with revelation and the statements of science should be restricted. This definition was formulated by James Barr,[14] who stresses in his book that he is exclusively discussing Christian Evangelicalism and not Judaism. In his opinion, Judaism has no distinct form of fundamentalism as it possesses a virtually uniform version of Scripture, and lacks internal contradictions unlike the New Testament's divergent descriptions of Christianity's beginnings in the gospels. That being said, I think that Hirsch's struggle against historical, philological Bible criticism as well as his struggle against the positivist-historical movement (which claimed that the Oral Torah developed within history and did not originate from God at Sinai) can both be considered fundamentalist. His struggle against religious reforms, initiated by the Reform movement at the beginning of the second decade of the nineteenth century, occupied almost the entirety of Hirsch's literary and educational enterprise. When the positivist-historical school appeared on the stage mid-century, he quickly discerned the danger posed to Orthodoxy by this position. The view that the Oral Torah is the independent creation of the Sages was, in Hirsch's opinion, an undermining of Judaism's very foundations, because it implied that we too, like the Sages, can continue to change Halakhah according to our own understanding and in accordance with the changing needs of our times.

Hirsch adopted the fundamentalist position of the Geonim and Nachmanides, that the entire Torah, both the written Pentateuch and the oral halakhic *midrash*, originate from Sinai, and are both divine (though Nachmanides's claim, that all halakhic disputes were also of Sinaitic origin, never occurred to him). The Torah's account of the public theophany at Sinai, and the Sages' testimony concerning the chain of tradition—that all of Halakhah stems from Sinai and that they simply played the part of transmitters—are all proof of

---

(Rabbi Isaac Luria). Horvitz, "Haqedusha," concurs. To the best of my understanding, these areas of theurgy and duality in the Kabbalah were already present in the Zohar. See Tishby, *Hazohar*, 105–107, 287–301. Yehuda Liebes and Moshe Idel have shown that these pursuits were already known in talmudic times. See Chapter Seven below.

14 J. Barr, *Fundamentalism* (Philadelphia, 1978).

this. In order to distance the position of reformers as much as possible, Hirsch initiated an additional, third revolution, adopting a position beyond that of Nachmanides and the Geonim, as already shown by Jay Harris in his book *How Do We Know This?* Hirsch asserts that at first the entire Torah was transmitted orally, from God, at Sinai or in the wilderness of Sinai, and it is this transmission which constitutes the law code of the Jewish people. It was only at a later stage, during or at the end of the sojourn in the wilderness, that a second stratum was added to this: Moses received a written book of codes summarizing the Oral Torah in the most efficacious way, as well as the thirteen hermeneutical principles, the key to deciphering the Written Torah and a means of reconstituting forgotten laws. Such a code book is important for its ethical and educational messages, its explication and emphasis of less common cases, and its focus on commandments related to the Land of Israel.

This code book was intended to ensure that Halakhah would never be forgotten and would be easy to study and memorize, as well as to preserve the link between Halakhah and the revelation at Sinai. This revolutionary view assists Hirsch in his struggle against Bible critics, who argue that Scripture contains allusions to later events, which indicate, in their opinion that it was written only subsequent to them. For example, the Sabbath is already mentioned in the creation account even though it was only taught to Israel at Sinai. The role of celestial bodies in establishing holidays is also mentioned there even though this process is only known from the Oral Torah. The emphasis on "according to their kind" (*le-minehu*) mentioned in the creation account is basically the prohibition of crossbreeding, a commandment only appearing in *Parashat Qedoshim*. Bible critics claimed that such cases prove that the Nation of Israel developed traditions, which crystalized into documents and eventually into the Torah, a process continuing hundreds of years after Moses. Only after all of this was the Oral Torah developed by the *Tannaim* and *Amoraim*. Hirsch, however, argued the opposite. At first, Moses received from the Almighty the entire halakhic codex of the Oral Torah as a single unit, and it was only afterwards that he received the Written Torah, as a secondary stratum, containing allusions to the previously transmitted laws. The Sages innovated nothing, and only recovered forgotten *halakhot* from this book of codes, assisted by the thirteen principles. Hirsch thus elevated the Oral Torah's status from its usual secondary position, and with characteristic fundamentalism transformed it into the Torah's primary layer, delegating the Written Torah to second tier. The main source of Hirsch's views on this subject appears at the beginning of his commentary on *Parshat Mishpatim*. There he explains (according to his position) that the transcription of the commandments specifically began from the marginal laws of male and female Hebrew slaves, in order to emphasize the importance the Torah accords to the well-being and prosperity of the nation's weakest classes.

Following this answer, he writes about the respective statuses of oral and written Torah:

> The primary source of Jewish law is not the written word, the "Book," but the living teachings of the oral tradition: the "Book" serves only as an aid to memory and a resource when doubts arise. The Book itself establishes the fact that the whole Torah had already been transmitted to the people and impressed upon them and lived by them for forty years, before Moshe—just before his death—turned over to them the Book of the Torah. . .
>
> On the whole, the "Book" records not principles of law, כללים, but individual concrete cases, and they are recorded in such an instructive manner that one can easily deduce from them the principles that were entrusted to the living consciousness of the oral tradition. The language of this "Book" was so skillfully chosen that in many instances an unusual term, a change in sentence structure, the position of a word, an extra or missing letter, and so forth can imply a whole train of legal concepts.
>
> This Book was not intended as a primary source of the Law. It was meant for those who were already well-versed in the Law, to use as a means of retaining and reviving, ever anew, the knowledge that they had already committed to memory. It was intended as a teaching aid for teachers of the Law, as a reference to confirm the Oral Law, so that the students should find it easy, with the aid of the written text before them, to reproduce in their minds, ever anew, the knowledge they received by word of mouth.
>
> The relationship between תורה שבבתב [the Written Torah] and תורה שבעל פה [the Oral Torah] is like that between brief written notes taken on a scientific lecture, and the lecture itself. Students who attended the oral lecture require only their brief notes to recall at any time the entire lecture. They often find that a word, a question mark, a period, or the underscoring of a word is sufficient to bring to mind a whole series of ideas, observations, qualifications, and so forth. But for those who did not attend the instructor's lecture, these notes are not of much use. If they try to reconstruct the lecture solely from these notes, they will of necessity make many errors. Words, marks, and so forth, that serve the students who listened to the lecture as most instructive guiding stars for the retention of

the truths expounded by the lecturer appear completely meaningless to the uninitiated. The non-initiate who will attempt to use these same notes in order to construct (as opposed to *reconstruct*) for himself the lecture he did not attend will dismiss what seems unclear as baseless mental gymnastics and idle speculations leading nowhere.[15]

In any event, it is clear that according to Hirsch it is the morality of the Torah, encapsulated in its oral and written components, which represents the highest form of morality and the only ethic that can redeem mankind. Nothing else can elevate man to sanctity: a state of control over one's sensual desires (as much as this is possible), and a closeness to the spiritual God.

As mentioned, Hirsch had internalized important principles of the Haskalah. Universalism, the equality of humans—possessors of reason, and the integration of the "Science of Man" (*Torat ha-Adam*) with the "Divine

---

15 Hirsch on Ex. 21:2, italics in original. This is not the first time that traditionalists have taken extreme positions against those wishing to undermine the Sinaitic origins of the Oral Torah. Saadya Gaon, in his struggle with the *Karaites*, preceded Hirsch. He maintained that God taught Moses the entire Torah and then selected parts of it to be written and transmitted by Moses to the Jewish people. The rest of it was transmitted as an oral tradition. He thus accorded the Oral Torah equal status with the Written Torah. See H. Ben Shammai, 'al-mudawin, in *Orekh Sifrei Hamiqra, Beparshanut Hamiqra Haaravit Hayehudit Rishonim Veahronim, Meḥqarim Betoldot Yisrael Mugashim Leavraham Grosman*, ed. Y. Hacker et al. (Jerusalem 2009), 73–110. Hirsch is also not the last to give the Oral Torah precedence. His revolutionary stance recalls that of Rabbi Joseph B. Soleveitchik and Yeshayahu Leibowitz with respect to the status of the Halakhah in the Oral Law, discussed by A. Sagi, "Leibowitz: Hagut Yehudit Lenokhaḥ Hamoderna," in idem, ed. *Yeshayahu Leibowitz Olamo Vehaguto* (Jerusalem 1995). According to Sagi, they state that the Oral Law takes preference over the written Torah. However, he is wrong in stating that they were the first to do so. However, their revolution was different both in meaning and motivation. As Sagi explains, their revolution was a more modern one, deriving from understanding that the written Torah—as the word of God—is transcendental and not subject to understanding, whereas the Oral Law is a human creation and therefore it is relevant to people, and it is what gives the divine dimension to the written Torah. According to Leibowitz, the obligatory status of this human creation derives from its not emerging from reality or determined by it, but that it turns outward from within human reality, and it is entirely contrary to human nature, demanding that people must rise above their nature, needs, and values. Among those values one must include ethics, so that obedience to a commandment because of its ethical value is not worship for its own sake. This approach is clearly entirely different from Hirsch's fundamentalism, which maintains that the Oral Law is also from heaven as the word of God, and its transcendental and obligatory status derives therefrom, and it is the goal of the Torah to teach us ethics, and this is the inner meaning of the commandments. Hirsch's motivation, as I show, was to distance himself from the phenomenon of modernity—historical research, Bible criticism, and the trend of reforming the Halakhah.

Teaching" (*Torat ha-Elohim*), were all important foundations of his thought. However, unlike his contemporaries—Luzzatto and Chajes—who shared his desire to combine Torah and science, he rejected *Wissenschaft des Judentums* in its entirety because in his opinion it reflected aspiration for religious reform in accordance with the modern Zeitgeist. He especially opposed the invalid principle of using modern, textual research tools to understand the divine text of the Torah and on similar grounds rejected the historical-evolutionary approach to Halakhah. Hirsch considered both components of the Torah, written and oral, supra-historical and beyond time and place, and saw the Sages not as legislators but as transmitters and restorers of laws which had originated from Sinai. He therefore disputed at length the views of Heinrich Graetz (1817–1891) and Rabbi Zacharias Frankel (1801–1875) from the historical-positivist school, who saw the Sages as creators and innovators of the Oral Torah. The view that the Sages were brilliant individuals, creating *halakhot* according to their own human leanings and based on their deep insights into the needs of the nation and time, was seen by Hirsch as a diminution of the Sages' status, and a legitimization of halakhic reform. Hirsch therefore debates at length with the theories of Graetz and Frankel as reflected in their works.

I believe that Hirsch clearly proves that one cannot conclude on the basis of tannaitic and amoraic texts that the Sages were split into a group of traditionalists opposed by a group of creative legal innovators. Similarly, there is no basis for the claims that Shammai and Rabbi Eliezer did not engage in exegesis, relying only on tradition, while others Sages such as Hillel (who formulated seven hermeneutical principles), Rabbi Yohanan ben Zakkai, Rabbi Yehoshua and Rabbi Akiva, marginalized the centrality of tradition and advocated independent innovation in order to justify their creation of new laws. The claim that Rabbi Yishmael was moderate and rational in his reading of the text ("the Torah spoke in the language of man") and in his halakhic rulings and that Rabbi Akiva was a radical innovator and a strict legislator is a generalization. Hirsch demonstrates that Graetz's entire typological approach is based on an erroneous reading of the midrashic text. His proofs are sweeping, superficial, tendentious and selective; they embed the arrow and draw a target around it. Looking back retrospectively, I think it is fair to say that both sides were wrong and right at the same time. On the one hand, one can generally agree with Hirsch's textual criticism of Graetz and Frankel, while not agreeing with his conclusions regarding the unity of Halakhah and its divine origins from Sinai. Conversely, it is necessary, in my opinion, to agree with the conclusions of Graetz and Frankel regarding the historical development of Halakhah and its origins in rabbinic innovation without agreeing with their specific reading of the text.

Generally speaking, Hirsch's keen observations about the words of the Sages as recorded in the Mishna and Talmuds are superior to the interpretations of Graetz and Frankel. I believe that the objective difficulty in demonstrating the historical development of Halakhah from canonical texts reinforces Hirsch's interpretation. Such a procedure is mistaken in my opinion, leading to tendentious and selective scholarship, as Hirsch indeed demonstrated. The protagonists, writers, and editors, of canonical texts, were infused with a consciousness of Halakhah's Sinaitic origins, and believed in a chain of tradition stretching back to Moses himself. Consequently it is very difficult to extract evidence of the human origins of the oral Halakhah or of its historical development from their texts. Even creative exegetes such as Hillel, Rabbi Yehoshua and Rabbi Akiva did not operate with a consciousness that they were creating a new *halakhah* using their own reasoning, even if this is what they actually did. The Sages for the most part were imbued with a consciousness that their activity was an act of reconstructing lost or forgotten *halakhot* (R. Abahu in BT Temurah 15a; R. Eliezer in BT Hagiga 3b) of revealing laws from Sinai which were not given to Moses or which he never transmitted further for a variety of reasons (Rav Huna as quoted by R. Tanḥuma in *Bereshit Rabbah* 1, 14; R. Akiva in BT Eruvin 21b) or an act of establishing and determining Halakhah from a number of possibilities conveyed to Moses at Sinai (R. Elazar ben Azarya, *Tosefta Peah*, 3:2 and in BT Hagigah 3b; R. Yannai in *Midrash Shoher Tov* and R. Tanḥum ben R. Hanilai in *Pesiqta Rabbati* 21). One cannot conclude from an author infused with such a consciousness that his activity or the activity of his colleagues constituted an act of new, original legislation deriving from the character and personal motives of its adjudicators.

That being said, Hirsch's conclusion that it is possible and permitted to demonstrate the divinity of the Bible from the text itself is patently unscientific. The argument that this is what the text, its protagonists, and its bearers claim, or the logic that it can be demonstrated from the words of the Sages themselves that they were not Halakhah's innovators, only its transmitters and reconstitutors, do not stand up to historical-philological criticism which is conducted on the basis of comparative research and close readings of the text, or upon rising above the text and beyond its content. For example, Graetz and Frankel's argument that it was Hillel who first formulated the seven hermeneutical principles is not based on the actual statements of Hillel or the sons of Beteira but rather on the fact that before them nobody discussed these principles or their existence.

Consequently, it can be argued against Hirsch's approach (that the principle of a Torah dictated from God himself is based on the Torah's own self-reference) that this single and non-objective testimony of a text about a public revelation at Sinai cannot be relied upon if we wish to prove its real occurrence in time and space. That being said, one must be extremely careful when searching for evidence in the statements of Moses or the text's other protagonists, its author or editor, all of whom are imbued with a consciousness of revelation, in order to support the argument that Sinai is nothing more than a later myth. The arguments of Bible criticism do not depend on the content of the text but rather on subtle inference and delicate philological analysis, which demonstrate the existence of variations between different parts of the text—differences in names, titles, language and style and in cosmological and theological worldviews. No *naïve* traditional belief in a truly real, public revelation at Sinai can compete with what philological and hermeneutical scholarship understands today about the manner in which texts and religions are produced, about the authors of texts, whose worlds and traditions are reflected in the text, and about commentators, whose interpretations are heavily influenced by their native culture and birthplace and by their worldviews and personalities. Similarly, one cannot demonstrate based on the words of halakhic Sages, who are permeated with an awareness of revelation and continuity, that their activity is innovation and not transmission, as done by Graetz and Frankel. Conversely, one cannot demonstrate that their laws truly did originate at Sinai, as done by Hirsch.

Graetz and Frankel's correct conclusions about the development of Halakhah led a portion of the modern scholarship on rabbinic exegesis to cling to arguments which attempt to base themselves on the contents of the text, an effort which Hirsch showed to be a failure. Graetz's typology, followed by later scholars, to greater or lesser extents, beginning with Rabbi David Tsvi Hoffman and after him Abraham Joshua Heschel (1907–1972), Isaac Dov Gilat, Yisrael ben Shalom and Rabbi Binyamin Lau, was criticized from the left and right. Religious fundamentalists on the right criticize it following the manner of Hirsch, arguing that the Sages only transmitted laws, and that their personal beliefs and opinions had no impact. The left of academic scholarship, represented by Ephraim Elimelech Urbach (1912–1991), argues that rabbinic *midrashim* should be studied and classified according to topics not personalities. Extant Rabbinic literature cannot be pigeonholed according to one specific thesis, as this entails ignoring certain scriptural interpretations or modifying them. Similarly, different *midrashim* belong to different time periods and many scriptural interpretations have been revised over the generations, sometimes over the course of several generations, according to the different worldviews of their editors, and therefore do not represent a sage's original words. Likewise, humans change their opinions over the course of their lives and even contradict themselves. Therefore, it is impossible to arrive at consistent conclusions about the personal views of any given sage.

I tend to agree with Urbach's claims and with Hirsch's textual criticism. In my opinion, the typologists clinging to Graetz and Frankel's arguments, were mistaken, in that they believed that the contents of tannaitic texts yield arguments which, in my opinion, the Sages of Halakhah never intended: that Hillel formulated the seven hermeneutical principles, and that Rabbi Yishmael broadened them further; that Shammai was a traditionalist who opposed *midrash halakhah*; that Rabbi Eliezer was a follower of Shammai on this issue and rejected all innovative exegesis; that Rabbi Eliezer's excommunication was due to his worldview which diverged from that of his colleagues (and not because he did not accept the ruling of the majority); that Rabbi Yehoshua was a creative innovator; that Rabbi Akiva was a brilliant innovator deriving laws from minute textual details (like particles *et* and *raq*); that his rival and polar opposite was Rabbi Yishmael whose views included the principle "the Torah spoke in the language of man"; about Rabbi Yishmael's anger at Rabbi Akiva who wanted to execute a betrothed daughter of a Cohen by fire based solely on a seemingly redundant letter *vav* ("and") in the word *va-bat* ("and the daughter").

I will not reiterate Hirsch's textual analysis on these issues but I invite the interested readers to look at the English translation of Hirsch's writings, *Collected Writings* (vol. 5, Feldheim Press) and judge for themselves. I will only add that a precise reading of BT Sanhedrin 51b indicates that even Rabbi Yishmael condemned the promiscuous betrothed maiden to death, albeit by stoning (which according to the Sages in Mishna Sanhedrin 7:1; 9:3—is the most severe court sentence) and not by fire. Rabbi Yishmael does not ignore Rabbi Akiva's superfluous *vav* based on the principle "the Torah spoke in the language of man"; he simply uses it to derive another ruling as the dispute whether or not the "Torah speaks in the language of man" only applies to repeated words. Truth be told, this dispute appears many times in the Babylonian and Jerusalem Talmuds and in the halakhic *midrashim*; it is clear that many Sages took part in it, and that it did not represent the exclusive view of Rabbi Yishmael. An extensive Tosafot in the Babylonian Talmud (Sota 24a, *s.v.* "ve-rabbi Yonatan") makes sense of the issue. It maintains that Rabbi Yishmael and Rabbi Akiva's views are indeed consistent but that other Sages modify their stances on a case by case basis. Although our text (BT Berakhot 31b) suggests that Rabbi Akiva maintains the principle of "the Torah spoke in the language of men," the same source appears in BT Sota 26a, reversing the opinions; the aforementioned Tosafot seemed to possess a textual variant, which fitted the consistent views of Rabbi Akiva and Rabbi Yishmael. In any case, Hirsch remarks, correctly in my opinion, that Rabbi Yishmael's principle is only applied in cases of a repeated word and is not used to describe any other linguistic phenomenon. Urbach shares this view.[16] Rabbi Akiva, the creative exegete and "innovator of *halakhot*," expresses his own thoughts on the issue explicitly in the *Midrash Sifra* on Lev. 26:46: "Rabbi Akiva said [. . .] 'at Sinai through Moses', this teaches that the Torah was given with its laws, interpretations and minutiae, by God through Moses at Sinai".

It is important to note that Hirsch's position towards Aggada is more daring. He decisively states that Aggada does not originate from Sinai, only reflects accepted scientific knowledge in the time of the Sages, that in such matters they too could err and that therefore no halakhic rulings should be based on it.

Hirsch's fundamentalist view is connected to his stance regarding the relationship between reason and revelation. Hirsch disputes Mendelssohn's view that reason and revelation occupy two important but separate realms in Judaism and that universal reason is a standard for eternal truths and morality

---

16   On the stances of the Sages see S. Rosenberg, *Lo Bashamayim Hi* (Alon Shvut, 1997) 12–21, 69–70. On the stance of scholarship see Hoffman, *Mesilot Letorat Hatanaim* (Tel Aviv, 1988); A. Heschl, *Torah Min Hashamayim Beaspaqklaria Shel Hayahadut*, vol. 1 (Jerusalem, 1962); I. D. Gilat, *Mishnato Shel R. Eli'ezer Ben Horqanos* (Tel Aviv 1968); idem, *Peraqim Behishtalshelut Hahalakhah* (Ramat Gan, 1992); I. Ben Shalom, *Beit Shammai Umaavaq Haqanaim Neged Romi* (Jerusalem 1994). See also B. Lau, *Hakhamim*, vol. 1 (Jerusalem, 2006), 153, 166–167, 188, vol. 2 (Jerusalem 2007), 45–46, 62, 83, 98–106, 188, 193, 198–199, 201, 205. On Urbach's position see *Hazal Pirqei Emunot Vede'ot* (Jerusalem 1969), 2, 13–14, and n. 26. In my opinion the source of the personal typological system is in Krochmal, and it is also found in Luzzatto (his commentary on Ex. 12: 44). On this see also A. Shinan, "Qodem Kol Sifrut," introduction to B. Lau, *Hakhamim*, vol. 3, *Yemei Hagalil* (Jerusalem 2008), 20–21. On Rabbi Akiva's position see Silman, *Qol Gadol*, 26–31. He states that Rabbi Akiva was a traditionalist—who took a position that he calls *shlemutit* [a neologism that might be translated as "holistic"], according to which both of the Torahs are entirely from Sinai, and there is no place for innovation. On pp. 40 and 48 he explains that the attitude of traditionalists to innovation that they themselves created derives from deep conviction that these innovations existed from time immemorial. In contrast, M. Fish, *Ladaat Hokhma: Mada, Ratsionaliut Vetalmud Torah* (Tel Aviv, 1994), 89–90 states that the Sages purposely concealed the innovation in their words, consciously donning a cloak of traditionalism. According to him, these Sages were pretending. I prefer Silman's approach.

(as stated by Maimonides). According to Mendelssohn, revelation constitutes a particularistic code of laws given to the Jews and encompasses no historical truths.

Hirsch however, aided by Kant (the thing in itself cannot be known) argues that reason (even practical reason) based on sense experience cannot be used as a standard for truth and good. Although natural sciences, philosophy and revelation, at least in their unadulterated forms, all lead to identical conclusions, the decisive standard in cases of difficulties and contradictions, is—as maintained by Judah Halevi—revelation. One who rejects this identicality is a heretic because nature, reason and the Torah are all rooted in God:

> The God who commands man is none other than the Lawgiver and Director of nature.[17]
>
> The identicality of the one and only God in nature and in history is the basis of our God-consciousness and self-knowledge... He gives and upholds the law by which the sun and the earth run their course, the seasons alternate, and all living things happily and hopefully begin and eventually complete their life cycles; so, too, He gave us the Law under which we are to develop our own character and all its potential for goodness and truth.[18]

Hirsch, therefore, maintains a fundamentalist view that the Written and Oral Torah cannot be mistaken, and reflect the highest and most absolute truth. In my opinion, Hirsch developed a neo-fundamentalist view as per the definition of James Barr.[19] In his book, Barr maintains that the classic fundamentalist clings to the belief in the superiority of the Holy Scripture over every other statement, whereas the neo-fundamentalist will change his stance in step with the establishment of scientific truths which contradict the truth of revelation, and is loyal to only one principle: the inerrancy of the holy text. Hirsch is indeed inconsistent in his "identicality approach," oscillating back and forth between the "the restrictive (of science) position" (based on Judah Halevi) and the "interpretative (of Scripture) position" (based on Maimonides, according the model of Shalom Rosenberg).[20] As long as the scientific theories under

---

17 Hirsch on Gen. 7:9.
18 Hirsch on Deut. 16:1. See also on Lev. 25:18–19.
19 Barr, *Fundamentalism*.
20 Shalom Rosenberg, *Torah Umada' Bahagut Hayehudit Hahadasha*. Jerusalem, 1988. See Chamiel, *The Middle Way*, vol. 1, 351–357. Judah Halevi summarizes his view in the *Kuzari*, 1, §67.

discussion have not been satisfactorily proven, and still seem to be nothing more than speculative science or philosophy, he adopts the "restrictive approach" which modifies science in accordance with the Torah, based on the argument that scientific theories are constantly changing and are nothing more than hypotheses. However, in matters of empirical science, already demonstrated beyond a reasonable doubt (such as the age of the Earth and the date of creation, the Copernican revolution, and even Darwin's theory of evolution if adequately proven) methods of interpretation were not exhausted, and he was willing to employ the "interpretative approach" and to harmonize the Torah with science, as long as he was not forced to admit that the information in the Torah or in the halakhic *midrashim* of the Sages contained errors. As far as he is concerned, if the Creator formed all of creation from one cell, imbuing it with the necessary potential for the world to evolve into all the wonder and diversity before our eyes, this would be sufficient to establish the claims of Judaism and to guarantee its ethical superiority.

The sources of Hirsch's neo-fundamentalist attitude towards the relationship between the achievements of science and the statements of the Torah also appear in his essay "The Educational Value of Judaism," written in 1873 and enclosed with invitations that were sent to the annual graduation ceremony of his educational institutions, and which was also intended for a non-Jewish audience. The essay was published in a book of his collected writings, *Jeschurun*, only in 1937. In the introduction to the book Mordechai Breuer notes that the essay was not included in the first publication of collected writings by Hirsch's sons between 1902 and 1912. He does not explain why but apparently they had what to hide.

Hirsch writes about speculative science which cannot compete with the statements of revelation:

> Only in the halls of academe does it become clear to us how many hypotheses of our era lack the support of reality, and how many of these hypotheses can be viewed only as possibilities or, at best, probabilities, even though everyone acts as if they had already been proven correct beyond the shadow of a doubt. Only in the halls of academe do we discover that there is hardly a phenomenon in nature not subject to widely divergent interpretations and that particularly the most common phenomena pose problems for which an explanation has yet to be found. Only in the halls of academe do we find out that any formula employed to compute the various aspects of a given phenomenon reflects no more than an accurate observation of the facts in a given process, but

this formula is still very far from giving us an insight into the essence, the real "whence" and "wherefore" of the fact. Only in the halls of academe can we truly see how scientific theories are subject to change and how the amazing progress of science in our era demonstrates that assumptions which today are proclaimed as truth triumphant, and are accepted by the minds of the masses with a blind faith that only unscientific minds can muster, may well be made obsolete by further scientific discoveries a decade hence. The halls of academe have seen many a "scientific theory" discarded as just another notion that has been proven erroneous and outdated. . . Judaism has survived so many of these theories; Judaism has been able to live with some of them, but it has never mandated any of them to be incorporated into its own belief system. On the other hand, Judaism is most anxious to make its adherents aware that all the phenomena of nature are subject to certain unchanging laws. Since Judaism itself is a system of laws through and through, it attaches a profound ethical value to the study of the natural sciences. Judaism considers it vitally important for its adherents to become aware that their entire universe is governed by well-defined laws, that every creature on earth becomes what it is only within the framework of fixed laws, and that every force in nature can operate only within specified limits . . . Judaism should certainly be permitted to cite the existence of such a theory [i.e., evolution] as proof that so many of the theories confidently advanced by science to disprove the Jewish concept of God and man are subject to change at any time. How many decades ago was the variety of the human races known today cited as an argument against the Biblical account which traces the descent of all mankind to one single human couple? And yet, today's science would brand as an ignoramus anyone who would dare discount the thesis that all living creatures, not only man and the orangutan. . . are descended from one single living creature![21]

He also writes about proven scientific theories, which should be used to interpret the statements of revelation:

Judaism is not frightened even by the hundreds of thousands and millions of years which the geological theory of the earth's development bandies

---

21 *Writings*, 7:261–265, from 1873. Interestingly, both Hirsch and Luzzatto use the same argument against scientific theories, which constantly refute their predecessors. See Luzzatto, *Meḥqerei Hayahadut*, vol. 1, pt. 2, 244.

about so freely. Judaism would have nothing to fear from that theory even if it were based on something more than mere hypothesis, on the still unproven assumption that the forces we see at work in our world today are the same as those that were in existence, with the same degree of potency, when the world was first created. Our Rabbis, the Sages of Judaism, discuss (Midrash Rabbah 9; Tractate Haggigah 16a) the possibility that earlier worlds were brought into existence and subsequently destroyed by the Creator before He made our own earth in its present form and order. However, the Rabbis have never made the acceptance or rejection of this and similar possibilities an article of faith binding on all Jews. They were willing to live with any theory that did not reject the basic truth that "every beginning is from God." In fact, they were generally averse to speculations about what was in the past and what will be in the future, because, in their view, such questions transgressed the limits of that which is knowable to man, or, at best, they did not enhance man's understanding of his moral function. In the view of our Rabbis, the Book of Books was intended to be mankind's guide for life on earth as it is at present... Anything beyond that simply did not exist for our Sages.[22]

What Judaism does consider vitally important is the acceptance of the premise that all the hosts of heaven move only in accordance with the laws of the one, sole God. But whether we view these laws from the Ptolemaic or Copernican vantage point is a matter of total indifference to the purely moral objectives of Judaism. Judaism had never made a credo of these or similar notions... This will never change, not even if the latest scientific notion that the genesis of all the multitude of organic forms on earth can be traced back to one single, most primitive, primeval form of the life should ever appear to be anything more than what it is today, a vague hypothesis still unsupported by fact. Even if this notion were ever to gain complete acceptance by the scientific world, Jewish thought, unlike the reasoning of the high priest of that notion, would nonetheless never summon us to revere a still extant representative of this primal form as the supposed ancestor of us all. Rather, Judaism in that case would call upon its adherents to give even greater reverence than ever before to the one, sole God Who, in His boundless creative wisdom and eternal omnipotence, needed to bring into existence no more than one single, amorphous nucleus and one single law of "adaption and heredity" in order to bring

---

22 *Writings*, 7:265–266.

forth, from what seemed chaos but was in fact a very definite order, the infinite variety of species we know today, each with its unique characteristics that sets (sic) it apart from all other creatures. This would be nothing else but the actualization of the law of *le-mino*, the "law of species" with which God began His work of creation. This law of *le-mino*, upon which Judaism places such great emphasis in order to impress upon its adherents that all of organic life is subject to Divine laws, can accommodate even this "theory of the origin of species."[23]

NEUTRALIZING THE RETURN TO ZION, ASSIGNING IT TO A UTOPIAN FUTURE OUTSIDE OF HISTORY

When it comes to the subject of the Land of Israel and the Return to Zion, Hirsch adopts Mendelssohn's neutralizing approach. In my opinion, a close reading of his texts indicates that Hirsch should not be considered a precursor to Zionism. On this issue, he expresses coherent views, both in terms of a Return to Zion in his own time as well as in a distant messianic future, and not as claimed by Pinchas Rosenblit and Rivka Horowitz.[24] The Jews, who are obligated by the three oaths, maintain loyalty to their homelands of residence, and the Return to Zion is vision of a utopian, supra-historical future. In Hirsch's system, exile becomes an ideal which allows the Jewish people to serve as a light to the nations, teaching them the morality of the Torah, preparing them for redemption. Hirsh, who generally dissents from Maimonidean views, actually adopts Maimonides's position on this issue, arguing that there is no unique, immanent sanctity to the Land of Israel or to the Jewish people. As a universalist who had internalized many ideas of the Haskalah, who sought to integrate into general culture and who demanded emancipation, he affirms (with a large dose of apologetics) that unlike his cultural hero Judah Halevi, the Jewish people are only first among equals, and the Land of Israel is only an instrument for observing the Torah—an instrument which has so far disappointed. He maintains that the Land of Israel is a dangerous as a tool: in the past, the abundant good it bestowed upon the people, when they kept the Torah in the land, ultimately led to their moral corruption. That being said, loyal to tradition, and unlike the Reform movement, Hirsch writes that indeed at the end

---

23 *Writings* 7:263–264.
24 See P. Rosenblit, "*Galut Veerets Yisrael 'Al Pi S.R Hirsch Uvnei Doro*," in S. Schmidt (ed.), *Sefer Zikaron Lemordekhai Viser Pirqei Ma'as Vehagut. Qevutsat Yavna*, 1981, 160–169; R. Horowitz, "Hirsch," 446–447. For details see next chapter.

of real history the Jewish people will return to its land and state, although he expressed little excitement at this eventuality. The integration of a redeemed Jewish religious community, conducting itself according to the norms of the Torah, into an acculturated and flourishing Germany, was far more alluring to him. He also did not point to any inherent advantage to the separate national existence of the Jewish people in its land in this utopian end of days.

In summary, I have presented in this chapter Hirsch's three "neo"s which reflect the novelty in his Orthodoxy, Romanticism and fundamentalism and the three apologetic revolutions he initiated within Orthodoxy: in Jewish education, the status of women, and the status of the Oral Torah. This is opposed to his more classically conservative views on Bible criticism and the Return to Zion. I have shown that when it comes to religion and science, Hirsch maintains that at least theoretically, and in terms of their true and pristine statements, these two sources of knowledge should be identical. Practically speaking however, when difficulties and contradictions arise, revelation should be seen as the ultimate standard of the true and good. But when science proves its claims, and continues to be at odds with revelation, it is revelation which should be reinterpreted and harmonized with science as long as no harm is done to the inerrancy of the Holy Scripture. This is a patently incoherent point of view which I have designated Neo-Fundamentalism. I elaborate on all these topics in the following chapter.

CHAPTER TWO

Interpretations of Hirsch's Thought from the Right and the Left

Ceremonies marking Hirsch's 200th birthday re-raised controversies between his interpreters on sensitive aspects of his thought. At a *qiddush* in honor of the event, in the Breuer K'hal Adath Jeshurun Synagogue in Washington Heights, a descendant of Hirsch delivered a speech in which he accused the synagogue of abusing its status by failing to educate using Hirsch's approach of "Torah im Derekh Erets," and for not studying his philosophy from his writings and his commentary on the Torah. This infuriated the rabbi of the synagogue, Yisroel Mantel, who considers the *Haredi* system of Lakewood the ideal approach for our times. Hirsch is no longer with us, he claimed, and without his personal guidance we, by ourselves, cannot successfully implement his system.

Many scholars and interpreters have written about Hirsch's thought, and many of them have failed to read it with the requisite level of objectivity. While an interpreter is inevitably captive to his own personal landscape—projecting his personal views onto his writings, readings and interpretations—sometimes this bias transcends the reasonable and in such cases the truth cries out and deserves to be heard. In Hirsch's case, erroneous readings hail both from his right and left. His left-wing interpreters include Natan Rotenstreich, Eliezer Schweid, Noah Rosenbloom, Rivka Horwitz, Pinhas Rosenblit, Shalom Rosenberg, Ismar Schorsch, David Ellenson, Yehoyada Amir and Shlomo Chertok. Some wish to disassociate themselves from Hirsch, and to downplay his importance, ascribing to him exaggerated Haredism or compromising rationalism. Others seek to draw him closer to their own views, overstating his importance and ascribing to him exaggerated leanings towards secularism, liberal humanism or mysticism. Right wing interpreters include rabbis such as Judah Leib Orlean, Jehiel Jacob Weinberg, Isaac Breuer and Eliyah Meir Klugman as well as Jacob Rosenheim. They all attribute excessive Haredism to Hirsch, seeking to draw him closer to themselves. Balanced interpreters include Mordechai Breuer, Isaac Heineman, Jacob Katz, Eliezer Stern, Robert Liberles, Michael Meir, Benjamin Ish Shalom and Lawrence Kaplan, scholars who read Hirsch as he is: a man of the middle path, not seeking to draw his views closer to their own, neither to the left nor to the right.

In this chapter, I will present Hirsch's different interpreters according to their attitudes towards him and his philosophy, showcasing a sampling of interpretations, some of which openly incline towards the personal leanings of the interpreter or scholar in question. This should serve as a warning sign to any researchers or scholars who wish to genuinely understand the views of a philosopher: to be cognizant of their own leanings and weaknesses, and to defer passing judgment until they have studied the majority of a philosopher's writings with as much objectivity as possible. I myself will choose the balanced interpretation of Hirsch and on the basis of textual analysis will argue for a distinction between the theoretical principles of Hirsch's method as opposed to his proposal for practical action.

Researchers and interpreters are divided over Hirsch's attitude towards two major issues. The first is his system of "Torah im Derekh Erets" and whether or not it represents absolute truth or merely a compromise. The second is the question of Hirsch's position on the spectrum between particularism and universalism, and whether or not Hirsch can be considered a precursor of Zionism.

I will try to demonstrate that this debate often stems from interpreters' personal positions, and I will take this opportunity to try and clarify my own views on Hirsch's attitudes to these two controversial issues.

Haredi interpreters legitimately considered Hirsch an opponent of Zionism, or more precisely, an opponent of an organized return to Zion in the real world. It was because of this and because of his determined battle to rescue Orthodoxy and combat religious reformers in Western Europe that they sought to appropriate him for their camp. To accomplish this they were forced to ignore his emphatic advocacy of incorporating secular studies into the Jewish educational system, as well as his esteem for all that is true, beautiful and good in European culture, an attitude he considered the true philosophy of Judaism. His opposition to kabbalistic mysticism, Hasidism, and the speculative rationalism of Maimonides, did not please defenders of the faith who considered Kabbalah and Maimonides's *Mishneh Torah* sacred. This phenomenon compelled them to not only interpret Hirsch in the spirit of their own thought, but also to censor his writings or at the very least revise and "improve" them, in order to better suit their purposes. Academic research also makes errors (although it at least strives to read Hirsch's writings with a measure of objectivity), allowing the personal, subjective attitudes of researchers to creep in.

"TORAH IM DEREKH ERETS"—OPTIMAL TRUTH OR COMPROMISE AFTER THE FACT

The Haredi Position

Before Hirsch's rabbinical disciples, and apparently even in his own lifetime, his system was the subject of European rabbinic criticism. Rabbi Israel Salanter (1810–1883) founder of the Lithuanian *Mussar* movement, is credited with the view that Hirsch's system is only appropriate post-factum, suited only for the specific time and place of Germany—its *yeshiva* system already destroyed—a last ditch effort to save a generation already imprisoned by the chains of the Haskalah. In Russia, however, where the strongholds of Torah were more solid, Torah study should not be reduced at the expense of any other discipline, a measure that could lead to destructive results. Nevertheless, Salanter was excited about Hirsch's *Nineteen Letters* and looked favorably on the idea of translating it into Russian to allow Russian yeshiva students to study it.[1]

Following this approach, the Haredi world eventually developed two attitudes towards Hirsh's "Torah im Derekh Erets." Some read Hirsch's writings in depth, grasping his serious approach to the subject, agreeing that Hirsch did not consider his system a compromise. When interpreting the significance of this system, however, they divest it of its revolutionary sting. Eliyahu Meir Klugman explains that in Hirsch's system the Torah retains total sovereignty over any Derekh Erets, as has been and will always be:

> Torah study is primary, and the study of the wonders of creation (science) and God's providence and orchestration of the world (history) is subordinate. Comparing them or giving them equal status, in any form or under

---

[1] See I. Etkes, *R. Yisrael Salanter Vereshita Shel Tenu'at Hamussar* (Jerusalem, 1984), 305–309 and note 118 there. See also A. Klugman, "Quntres Vayehi Biyeshurun Melekh," introduction to S. R. Hirsch, *Sefer Shemesh Marpe* (New York, 1992), idem (ed.), 281–282 and note 40 there.

> any name, leads a person directly to heresy. [...] It is therefore clear, that no "Derekh Erets" and no wisdom has the right to be accepted on its own merits. [...] The situation in Germany at that time was very similar to the current situation in Western Europe and the United States. Consequently, there was also a need to immunize the youth against the temptations of the world, temptations which were enormous.

In the past, he argues, secular education was studied for practical purposes only and never to understand the world or man's obligations within it, and serious secular studies were only the pursuit of a small elite. This was mainly due to a fear of secular studies' negative influence and a concern for wasting time that could be better spent on Torah study.[2]

This historical analysis of Judaism's approach to secular education may be correct, but it is not what Hirsch thinks. He maintains that as long as it was still possible, all Jews studied secular subjects alongside Torah, treating them as a value and a necessity. Persecution and oppression made this impossible during the majority of Exile.[3] However, now that it is once again feasible, it is incumbent upon us to restore our former glory and to properly combine these two disciplines, in an institutional curriculum intended for all students from a young age. Klugman disregards passages in which Hirsch stresses the importance of secular studies and their equal footing with religious education, two realms stemming from God. Obviously, reason resides in a material body subject to sensuality, and is liable to err (and even does so quite often) and therefore external philosophies which conflict with the Torah are to be summarily dismissed. Nevertheless, Hirsch still maintains that everything true, good and beautiful from European culture—as long as it does not contradict the Torah, or can be reinterpreted in its light—should be willingly accepted, serving to enhance the structure of the *Mensch-Jisroel* (Man-Israel). The revelation encapsulated in the Torah represents absolute, all-encompassing truth. However, parts of it were forgotten due to oppression and persecution, it was interpreted poorly, and it contains sections which are unclear to us. Philosophy and natural sciences, fruits of distilled reason, reach conclusions identical to the truth of revelation. However, the path to this understanding is long and beset by many obstacles. When purified, the Torah and the natural sciences and philosophy represent one identical truth, deriving from the same divine source.

---

2   See ibid., 328–334.
3   See Hirsch, *Writings*, 7:12–13.

Integrating them into a student's education allows him to overcome the obstacles present in the study of Torah and the natural sciences. This combination refines both areas of study, and molds a student with a synthetic personality, dialectically greater than the sum of its parts. As I have shown in the first chapter, this revolutionary position, which only professes to be traditional, is largely based on the notion that the doors of interpretation always remain open, even going so far as to allow the acceptance of Darwin's theory of evolution. Below I will elaborate upon this view further.

Klugman's stance is based on the views of Isaac Breuer as well as Jehiel Jacob Weinberg. Like Klugman and Breuer, Weinberg interprets Hirsch's view so that it will accord with the Haredi position. He devotes a special essay to Hirsch's thought, which, among other things, attempts to explain the system of "Torah im Derekh Erets." He writes:

> Truth be told, Rabbi Samson Raphael Hirsch sought in good faith, a *mixture* (*meziga*) of "Torah im Derekh Erets" and understood the concept "Derekh Erets" in its broader sense. [...] Judaism and culture are not contradictory elements and principles. On the contrary, they mutually complement each other. Not only does Judaism permit and tolerate culture in its domain, it itself constitutes the highest form of culture.

It is important to read this carefully: I am not sure that Weinberg's use of the word "mixture" (*meziga*) refers to a synthesis. A mixture implies a combination of two things, not the creation of a new substance from two ingredients. The words mixture and synthesis do not imply the identity discussed by Hirsch. However, Weinberg also expresses reservations:

> Does Judaism require augmentation from general culture? Perhaps Judaism itself must serve as augmentation to this culture? Needless to say, the need for this kind of question devalues Torah. No observant Jew will agree to the view that even though he has studied much Torah, from a cultural perspective he is still incomplete, and must seek culture outside of the Torah to enrich his personality. Indeed there is nothing in Rabbi Hirsch's writings, not even one word, to make room for the notion that he believed that Judaism and general culture complement each other. There is not even a hint of the idea that Judaism must tolerate another culture. [...] The Torah is therefore according to Rabbi Hirsch the power which creates "form"—Aristotle's term for essence—and Derekh Erets is but

the matter upon which the Torah's [form] acts. [. . .] They claimed that Rabbi Hirsch felt special admiration for German culture, as if he admitted to modern philosophy's right to exist as complementary to Jewish culture, serving as intellectual inspiration. I have found no support for such a view in all of Rabbi Hirsch's writings.[4]

Concluding his discussion of this matter, he cites as an authority Isaac Breuer, who claims that, according to Hirsch, "Torah im Derekh Erets" does not mean that Torah needs Derekh Erets, but rather that the Torah dominates Derekh Erets.

Yaakov Rosenheim proposes a position more rightwing and less sophisticated than that of Klugman. He writes: "Rabbi Samson Raphael Hirsch, may his memory be a blessing, understood the concept of Derekh Erets [...] as a person's overall activeness in the system of business and work." Similarly, Rosenheim believes that in his vulnerable generation, Hirsch considered it important to teach students secular studies as a defense mechanism against heresy—"know what to say to a heretic." Rosenheim is also selective in his citations, underpinning his entire case from passages appearing in Hirsch's commentary on Lev. 18:4, where Hirsch affirms that the sciences should be cultivated only as disciplines ancillary and subordinate to Torah study. Rosenheim explains that "it is

---

4   J. J. Weinberg *ha-more ha-gadol* (1951), in *Kitvei Hagaon Rabbi Yaakov Weinberg*, vol. 2, ed. M. Shapiro (Scranton, 1951), 340–349. Shapiro in his book, Between the Yeshiva World and the Modern Orthodoxy, The Life and Works of Rabbi Jehiel Jacob Weinberg: 1884–1966 (Oxford-Portland, Oregon, 1999) 154–157 writes that Weinberg shifted from sharp opposition to Hirsch's education system to agreement after his move to Berlin to head the Rabbinical Seminary there. He believes that Weinberg had a synthesis in mind but emphasizes that Weinberg's interpretation of Hirsch even when he accepted and defended it was conservative, on the basis of this source. See M. Breuer, "Shitat Tora 'Im Derekh Erets Bemishnato Shel Harav S. R. Hirsch," Hamaya'an, Tevet 1969, 10–29. In the second pamphlet, 25–28, Breuer enumerates the interpretations of Hirsch's system by Rabbis and Torah scholars who maintain that it was intended post-factum and only in Germany, and he argues that they are mistaken. In the first pamphlet on p. 2 he quotes Weinberg (whom he considers the only Rabbi to understand Hirsch) as saying "Torah im Derekh Erets is like the form on matter. There is no existence to the one without the other, they rely on each other and mix together." On p. 14 Breuer quotes a passage from Hirsch which seems to have been Weinberg's source "not only do they [Torah and Derekh Erets] not annul one another, they rely on each other, and mutually complement and complete each other, and only when they have been united and bound and been tightly mixed together—will they give birth the good and fortuitous, which we must strive for all our days on this earth." Comparing the source to the quote it is easy to note the addition of "form and matter" and Weinberg's significant omissions. For a detailed discussion of Weinberg's approach to Hirsch's Torah im Derekh Erets see below Chapter Eleven.

possible to arm oneself with sufficient valor and spiritual might to designate the wisdom of the nations as *raqahot ve-tabahot* [handmaidens; lit. perfumers and cooks] serving the molding of a perfect Jewish personality."[5] He thus demotes secular studies from assistants to slaves in Hirsch's esteem.

In contrast to the aforementioned approach, a second Haredi approach maintains that Hirsch's position was always intended as compromise or at the very least that it is doubtful he would continue to maintain it in different circumstances. In their opinion, Hirsh was aware that his position did not optimally mesh with tradition. Nevertheless, he was forced to take action in order to rescue Judaism from ruin as an emergency injunction—"a time to act for God, they have annulled your Torah."

Once Hirsch was successful in Western Europe, and Torah study had stabilized there (as well in the United States, and afterwards in Israel), the advocates of this position decided that his system was no longer necessary and that a curriculum of exclusive Torah studies should be resumed.

The spokesperson of this view is Judah Leib Orlean. In his opinion, Hirsch knew that his system of "Torah im Derekh Erets" was appropriate only for a small minority of the Jewish people:

> This is a system only suitable for the decayed and frozen part of the nation. It was conceived as a rescue anchor to save Western Judaism in the tumultuous struggles of that time, in the wake of the "Haskala." [...] It would be a mistake on our part if we were to ignore the absolute truth, which Rabbi Hirsch (may his memory be blessed) did not ignore, a truth upon which he stated his opinion: that great danger lies in this system which has the potential to create new obstacles for the faithful Judaism in other countries.[6]

---

5   J. Rosenheim "Rashar Hirsch—Mevaser Umagshim Ḥazon Hayahadut Hanitsḥit," introduction to *Ma'aglei Shana Kitvei Rabbi Shimshon Rafael Hirsch*, vol. 1.)Bnei Brak, 1965(, 9–41. Rosenheim also maintains that Hirsch expresses no opposition to Kabbala and that Kabbala completes and serves as the basis of Hirsch's symbolic interpretation of the commandments and their particularities. He ignores many sources in which Hirsch rejects mysticism and the panentheism of Hasidism considering them part of a new paganism spreading throughout the world, alongside materialism, Spinozan pantheism and Christian Hegelianism. Hirsch opposes ecstasy, theurgy, divine stratification, kabbalistic symbolism and the existence of satanic worlds. See, for example, Hirsch, *The Nineteen Letters of Ben Uziel*, trans. Bernard Drachman (New York and London: Funk and Wagnalls, 1899) letter 18, 187; Hirsch Ex. 20:20; Lev. 10:9–11. Cf. also J. Katz, *Hahalakhah Bameitsar* (Jerusalem, 1992) 234–236; Breuer, *Eda* 71–73.

6   J. Orlean, "Zemana u-Meqoma shel Shitat Rashar Hirsch" introduction to *Ma'aglei Shana Kitvei Rabbi Shimshon Rafael Hirsch*, vol. 4 (Bnei Brak, 1966), 15–29. Cf. also J. Orlean,

Therefore, in Orlean's opinion, Hirsch's system should not be adopted in Israel, Eastern Europe, or anywhere else, and focus should be concentrated exclusively on Torah study. Even trade schools are superfluous and those disabled in spiritual matters, can resolve their situation without institutional intervention, learning a trade on their own. This position also justifies the censorship, correction and revision of Hirsch's texts in order to make them more suitable for a new Haredi readership. This is what the Haredi publisher Netsaḥ did in its Hebrew translation of *The Nineteen Letters*, and its essay collections *Bema'aglei Shana* and *Yesodot Haḥinnukh*. These translations are essentially rewritings, revising and "improving" Hirsch's words as needed. Hirsch's criticisms of Maimonides and Kabbalah in letter eighteen of the *Nineteen Letters*, were censored and erased altogether, and the essay collections published by *Netsaḥ* did not include all the material relevant to their stated subject matter. In their collection of essays translated from Jeshurun and included in two volumes entitled *Yesodot Haḥinnukh, Kitvei Rabbi Shimshon Rafael Hirsch*[7] the publishers did not hide their omissions. They explained, in the introduction to the second volume, that they omitted essays containing unambiguously positive portrayals of the system of "Torah im Derekh Erets" because it is doubtful that in our day, Hirsch would continue to maintain his method which would compete with today's flourishing Torah education system.

Even the English translations published by Feldheim, though invaluably preferable to those of Netsah, are not free of "improvements." I did not methodically compare Feldheim's translation to the source text, but came across discrepancies during my study, when a certain wording in the translation did not seem to reflect Hirsch's views. In the English translation, I found such an "improvement" in the essay "Ḥazaq Venitḥazaq" at the end of the eighth volume of Hirsch's Collected Writings. In this paragraph, Hirsch writes that the circumstances of religious students are more difficult today than in the past. In the German original Hirsch writes that these students study in the academy and in *yeshivot* and are occupied by their Jewish *Bildung* ("education"), assailed from left and from right. The English translation omits Jewish "Bildung" and instead writes about students "who devote themselves to their Jewish studies

---

"Ha-Ḥinnukh ha-Yehudi ve-Yesodotav be-Avar u-ba-Hove" introduction to *Yesodot Ha-Ḥinnukh*, vol. 2 (Bnei Brak, 1968), 25–42.

7   Volume one lists the publication date as 1980, whereas in volume two is listed as 1968. It seems the year 1980 in volume one is a second print as it is unlikely that the first volume was published in 1980 and the second volume in 1968. According to the editor's introduction to volume two it seems that volume one was published in 1958.

at Talmudical academies or yeshivoth."[8] The source text legitimizes university studies, which the translator was unable to accept. This is a fundamental and significant change.

In the new Hebrew translation of *Horeb* I found a revision in a chapter discussing the commandments of education. Hirsch writes there, in the German original, that one should teach a child natural sciences and history but should be careful that these studies only be ancillary to Torah studies. The translator writes "However, all of this [secular studies] should be for the child only *raqaḥot vetabaḥot* [handmaidens]."[9] This expression is commonly used in traditional texts and by Haredim (such as Orlean as cited above) to lower the status of external disciplines to the level of maidservants. However, Hirsch—whose lexicon does not contain any such expression—would not agree. With little difficulty, one can use the same symbolism to explain Hirsch's true view: Hirsch would compare these disciplines to the matron of the house, her husband's helpmate, equal to him in her value and rights. Just as the husband brings his wife into his house, sheltering her under his wing, so the Torah serves as the touchstone for examining and purifying the statements of science and philosophy.

The Academic Stance

A review of academic studies on Hirsch's system of "Torah im Derekh Erets" reveals three basic trends: scholars who distance themselves from his views, regarding them with disapproval; scholars who admire his views and tailor them to draw them even closer to their own; and scholars with a balanced approach, who admire some of his positions and disagree with others, but read him with as much objectivity as possible.

Disapproval of Hirsch

Nathan Rotenstreich, Ismar Schorsch, Yehoyada Amir and Noah Rosenbloom belong to the group of researchers who disapprove of Hirsch's views. Rotenstreich sees no significant difference between Hirsch and the Haredim. According to him, the combination of "Torah im Derekh Erets" proposed by Hirsch is limited to practical day-to-day life. In his theoretical philosophy

---

8   Hirsch, *Writings*, 8:320.
9   Hirsch, *Ḥorev*, trans. Y. Friedman (Jerusalem and New York, 2007), 384.

Hirsch wished to preserve Judaism's seclusion within its own boundaries.[10] Rotenstreich argues that the contradiction between Torah on one hand and Derekh Erets (in the sense of the sum of practical knowledge) on the other, is in fact the contradiction between Judaism—as it materialized over the course of the centuries from its own internal sources—and daily life in the Hirsch's time. According to Rotenstreich, Hirsch admits that Jews in his time can no longer confine themselves to Judaism's internal world and as a compromise to the needs of the era, must include Derekh Erets, which as an element of day-to-day life only does not shape Judaism's content. Unlike Rotenstreich, I believe that Hirsch denies any contradictions between Torah and Derekh Erets, maintaining their identicality on a theoretical and philosophical level. Practically speaking also, it is important to combine them, though here one must be more cautious, assessing the achievements of culture using the Torah as a litmus test. It seems that Hirsch's dialectical approach, which considers general culture valuable in molding a complete Jew (as I will explain below), is far beyond what Rotenstreich attributes to him.

Ismar Schorsch and Yehoyada Amir reject Hirsch's worldview based on their dissapproval of Modern Orthodoxy,[11] but I disagree with their interpretations. Schorsch generalizes that Hirsch rejected science as a foreign method of thought. Amir claims that Hirsch did not dare to bring secularism into the domain of Torah, and did not accord it an equal status with religious study. In my opinion, Hirsch believed that purified religion and purified science must be identical, and anyone who thinks otherwise is a heretic! Torah study is incomplete without its secular counterpart, and a perfect Torah Jew is one who has internalized, integratively and dialectically, the very best of European cultural wisdom. I will try to demonstrate this below.

Rosenbloom rejects Hirsch from the right, due to (what he considers) Hirsch's exaggerated religious moderation and his proclivities for rationalism.[12] He claims that Hirsch tries to emulate Maimonides—a strange statement considering Hirsch's explicit disagreements with Maimonides, and his choice of Judah Halevi as his cultural hero. Mordechai Breuer sharply criticizes Rosenbloom's research on Hirsch, rejecting many of his claims and arguing that Rosenbloom harbored prejudices against Hirsch's personality, leading him

---

10 Cf. Rotenstreich, *Hamaḥshava Hayehudit Ba'et Haḥadasha* (Tel Aviv, 1987), 104.
11 See Schorsch, *From Text to Context the Turn to History in Modern Judaism* (Hanover and London,1994) 314; Amir, *Qol Demama Daqa* (Jerusalem, 2009), 131.
12 See N. Rosenbloom, Tradition in an Age of Reform: the Religions Philosophy of Samson Raphael Hirsch (Philadelphia, 1976).

to dismiss and alter proven historical and biographical facts to better fit his preconceptions.[13] Breuer argues that Rosenbloom's comparison of Hirsch to Maimonides is mistaken and is based on a speculative psychoanalytical process. He rejects, among other things, Rosenbloom's claims that Hirsch borrowed the term "Mensch-Jisroel" from Mendelssohn and that Hirsch in his educational curriculum primarily emphasized secular studies. As Breuer correctly points out, Mendelssohn considered these two realms separate whereas Hirsch considered them dynamically linked. Moreover, Hirsch considered religious studies at the very least equal to secular studies. Many new studies are not reflected or simply ignored in Rosenbloom's work either because he was unaware of them or because they did not suit his thesis. Rosenbloom also relies on Netsaḥ publishers' tendentious and distorted Hebrew translation of Hirsch's collected writings. All in all, his book is not objective and his facts and arguments are constructed around his biases, tailored to prove his thesis.

Admiration of Hirsch

I include among Hirsch's admirers the scholars Eliezer Schweid, Rivka Horwitz, Pinhas Rosenblit, Shalom Rosenberg, David Ellenson, and Shlomo Chertok. With the exception of Rosenberg, these researchers draw Hirsch to the left of the middle way he had advocated. In *The Nineteen Letters*,[14] Hirsch compares Torah research to inquiry into natural laws and phenomena in which a hypothesis which contravenes even one factual phenomenon is rejected; the conclusions of research based on a researcher's assumptions and proposals must accord with a factual phenomenon. Similarly, no research can lead to a conclusion entailing the abolishment of God's teachings—the commandments—factual phenomena, requiring no corroboration. Hirsch emphasizes that inquiry into nature and the Torah's commandments is necessary in order to reveal their immanent divine wisdom. However, such research must be conducted using the correct tools and its results cannot alter facts contained in revelation. Consequently Hirsh invalidates the use of historical-philological tools to study the divine text of the Torah.

Cultural Jewish humanist, Jewish humanist, Eliezer Shweid, considers Hirsch a positive figure, one whose views approach a notion of cultural

---

13 See M. Breuer, "'Tradition in the Age of Reform' by Rosenbloom, Noah H." *Tradition* 16, 4 (1977), 140–149.
14 See *Nineteen Letters*, letter 18, 194, note 1. For an explanation of Hirsch's position see Breuer, *Eda*, 160–162.

universalism, at least as much as Orthodoxy can allow itself. He therefore maintains that "Samson Raphael Hirsch was no less sensitive than the philosophers of the Reform movement to the positive values of contemporary humanistic culture, and he, no less than they, wished to find harmony between the worlds of pure Judaism and pure humanism". It should be noted that while Hirsch is humane (that is one who loves humanity), he is not an advocate of humanism (the authority of human consciousness). Wherever the commandments of the Torah, as interpreted by the Sages, distinguish between Jew and gentile, Hirsch does not seek to blur these lines and at the heart of his thought always stands a commanding, sovereign God, to whom an obedient mankind is subordinate.

Schweid gives a liberal interpretation of Hirsch's opposition, in *The Nineteen Letters*, to the scientific and critical research of the biblical text. He explains that Hirsch demands objectivity from Bible critics, and expects them not to exclude the possibility that the Torah truly is divine:

> Objective criticism requires that we assume, if only hypothetically, that Scripture is what it says it is [divine]. We must first study its contents according to that assumption and only then decide if they pass the test of reason. [...] Just as the researcher of natural science removes any preconceptions about the plausibility of facts, opening himself to the experience, that is to say to nature's self-revelation, so too a researcher of the Holy Scripture must remove all his preconceptions and open himself to the experience unfolding during the learning process. [...] Hirsch believes in Torah study's indirect powers of persuasion, as long as a person does not defend himself with pre-suppositions.[15]

I believe that Schweid's interpretation is mistaken. As far as Hirsch is concerned, the Torah's divine origins and the obligation to observe its commandments are not assumptions open to inquiry. They are factual truth, which like natural phenomena require no validation. The assumption that the Torah derives from a human source is false and forbidden. The "assumptions" which Hirsch permits a scholar to make are related to the rationales of the commandments and the overarching connections between them, not to the commandments themselves and their divine origins. Researching the commandments is an obligation. But this is only on the condition that factual truth not be harmed by one's conclusions. If such damage does occur then it is a sign of error, and

---

15 See Schweid, *Toledot Hehagut Hayehudit ba'et Haḥadasha* (Jerusalem 1978), 297.

at that point one should resume one's research. Abraham Geiger (1810–1874), the father of Reform ideology, also does not share Schweid's reading. In his book reviews of *The Nineteen Letters* and *Horeb*, Geiger attacks Hirsch's antiscientific and dogmatic removal of the Torah's divine origins from the purview of scientific research, striking it from the roster of legitimate questions which can be asked about Judaism.[16]

Ellenson also attempts to garner signs of secularization from Hirsch to draw him closer to his own views, offering his own explanation as to why Hirsch wished to secede from the larger Jewish community and create a purified Neo-Orthodox breakaway.[17] He sees this separation as part of a process of secularization underwent by Neo-Orthodoxy, which included an understanding that unity between all segments of the community was no longer possible. I was unconvinced that secularization can be discussed in a Hirshian context, and Ellenson fails to anchor his statements in any kind of source.

The views of Horwitz, Rosenblit, Rosenberg and Chertok are related to a dispute about another subject: anticipation of Zionism, which I will discuss in the following section.

Balanced Reading of Hirsch

Reading all of Hirsch's writings unselectively allows a balanced interpretation of his position, a reading that does not shy away from pointed criticism. This type of reading takes account of the fact that Hirsch's writings include two tendencies. The first considers secular studies subordinate to Torah studies—ancillary disciplines subject to the litmus test of the divinely transmitted Torah. The second considers secular studies a necessity, according them inherent value equal to that of Torah studies. When incorporated into a curriculum, secular studies are the only way to build a complete "Mensch-Jisroel," dialectically greater than the sum of its parts. In order to find a common denominator between these two tendencies one is forced to say the following: in principle, Hirsch maintains that these two realms, science and Torah, are identical in terms of their conclusions and theoretical statements; both derive from God, one from divine

---

16 See M. Seidler "Le'fitron Haba'ayot Hamerkaziot Beyoter Shel Hatoda'a Hayehudit, Hasimboliqa Shel Harav Shimshon Rafael Hirsch 'Al Reqa' Tequfato," in B. Ish Shalom (ed.), *Bedarkhei Shalom* (Jerusalem, 2007), 325–327, and note 20 and 21 there.

17 See D. Ellenson, "Ha-Dogma be-Tguvot Masortiot la-Reforma ha-Modernit: Ha-Paradigma shel Ha-Ortodoqsia ha-Germanit," in *Ortodoqsia Yehudit Hebetim Ḥadashim*, ed. Y. Salmon et al. (Jerusalem 2006), 345–366.

revelation, the other from God's gift to man—reason. The problem begins when we try to implement this principle in practice. At this point, it becomes clear that these two realms have their problems. Reason is limited by the sensuality of the flesh, hindering its ability to independently maintain ethical norms which oppose desire and egoism. Furthermore, it certainly cannot arrive at the symbolic commandments offered by the Torah. Revelation is not always clear and although meant to be all-encompassing, it does not always provide enough detail to cover all aspects of life. Moreover, it was misinterpreted by specious commentators in the past and parts of its oral component were even forgotten due to persecution and exile. Therefore, to be cleansed and purified, these two realms must be adjoined already in the first stages of education, allowing them to mutually complement each other. In Hirsch's opinion, the limits of reason are far greater than those of revelation and therefore we must give priority to the revelation afforded to us by the Torah. We must examine the ideas of reason and to reject them as false if they contradict revelation. Accordingly, Hirsch prefers Judah Halevi's notion of identicality—revelation as the standard of truth—to Maimonides's notion of identicality—reason as the standard of truth.[18] Hirsch adds that only when the theories of science and reason have been proven beyond a doubt, and cleansed of human shortcomings, is it (apologetically) necessary to reinterpret revelation, suiting it to the scientific theory in question, resolving any contradictions which remain. This is because contradiction is impossible between these two identical realms and the information provided by the Torah is the inerrant word of God. Whoever does not believe in this identicality denies that God is the giver of the Torah and the creator of man. This inconsistent position I have dubbed "neo-fundamentalism."

SUPPORTING THE BALANCED READING

Below are some citations from Hirsch's writings which support a balanced reading of his thought.

---

18 See I. J. Gutmann, *Dat Umada* (Jerusalem, 1979), 16–21, 66–70, 86–89; idem, *Hafilosofia Shel Hayahadut* (Jerusalem, 1989), 115–129, 145. Shalom Rosenberg's view on Judah Halevi's identicality approach is similar, see *Be'iqvot Hakuzari* (Jerusalem, 1991), 104–105. For Binyamin Ish-Shalom's point of view see his "'Al Mada' Ushlemut Haruaḥ—Biqoret Hamoderniut Vehapostmoderniut, R. Y. D. Soloveitchik Vehagut Haneo-Ortodoqsit," in *Emuna Bizmanim Mishtanim*, ed. A. Sagi (Jerusalem, 1996), 352–353. In terms of the opinions of Judah Halevi and Maimonides, his views are similar to Gutman's.

In Chapter One, I already cited Hirsch's statements about the identicality of the laws of nature and the laws of Torah due to their shared divine source (according to the second tendency) as well as his statements about God's orchestration of history.[19]

Hirsch maintains that human reason, like the wonders of nature, is also a form of divine revelation:

> Judaism is probably the only religion that does not declare extra me nulla salus [there is no salvation outside myself], that happily welcomes any intellectual or moral advance, no matter what its origin. Indeed, the timeless words of the Jewish prophets look with firm assurance to the ever-growing, ever-spreading spiritual and moral ennoblement not only of the Jews but of all mankind. Judaism is probably the only religion that teaches its followers to view not only the early light of dawn, the blossoms of springtime, the darkness of thunder, the flashes of lightning, not only the sight of anything beautiful, sublime, powerful or beneficial in nature, but also the sight of any human being great in wisdom or knowledge, no matter what his nationality or religion, as a revelation of the Divine. Whenever Jews behold such an individual, they must pronounce a blessing in praise of God Who has "given of His wisdom to mortals."[20]

In contrast, Hirsch's first tendency emphasizes the caution that should be exercised before adopting foreign culture: evaluating culture according to the principles of Judaism and refraining from employing Bible criticism which uses human research tools. He says about this:

> We are to be careful not to introduce into the sphere of the Torah foreign ideas that were developed on the basis of other premises. Rather, we should always be mindful of the superiority of the Torah which differs from all other scientific knowledge through its Divine origin. We should not imagine that it is based on mere human knowledge and accordingly is on the same level as other human sciences. [...] One should occupy himself with this knowledge only from the Torah's perspective, for only in this

---

19 Notes 17–18.
20 *Writings*, 7:86, in the essay on "The Relevance of Secular Studies," and see also ibid., 416.

way will this knowledge be beneficial to us, and they warn us that neglecting this perspective will jeopardize our intellectual life.[21]

However, in principle, and at the end of the human educational journey, purified culture and Torah are identical, a position noted by Mordechai Breuer and Binyamin Ish Shalom. Hirsch writes: "Culture beings the education of mankind and the Torah completes it... In the case of *Israel*, ארץ דרך [Derekh Erets, lit. "the way of the earth," here: civility] and Torah are tied together. In the House of Israel, the perfect human being and the perfect Jew are identical concepts."[22]

According to Hirsch's apologetic approach, once we have attained knowledge through the mediums of science and philosophy—knowledge which, at first glance, was lacking in revelation—we can subsequently find this knowledge in the Torah itself upon second review:

> Where among the spiritual treasures of modern nations and modern civilizations is there anything true and noble, good and beautiful, anything truly conduce to human happiness that cannot be traced back, directly or indirectly, to this sacred literature? Modern European civilization is the child of Hebrew and classic antiquity. Wherever we behold truth clothed in the beauty of form, we behold a joined product of Hebrew thought and Hellenic sensibility, Hebrew truth and Hellenic esthetics.[23]

---

21 Hirsch, Deut. 6:7.
22 Hirsch on Gen. 3:24. E. Schweid, "Two Neo-Orthodox Responses to Secularization—Samson Raphael Hirsch," *Immanuel* 19 (1984–85), 116, argues that for Hirsch the world of Torah and the world of culture beyond it are separate—adjoining but never uniting; they live together in peace, and the demand for definite boundaries limits any attempt to unite them. A. Ravitzky *Ḥerut 'al Haluḥot* (Tel Aviv, 1999), 167, 169 also states that the relationship between modernity and tradition in Hirsch's thought is one of cultural dualism and coexistence. I disagree. According to Hirsch, the relationship between Torah and culture is one of identicality in which the tradition is the standard for purifying modernity of its errors, and it is obligatory to educate for an integrated personality that unites, dialectically, Torah and refined culture. The term "co-existence" is more appropriate to Mendelssohn and Hildesheimer. On Hirsch's identicality approach and its ideological basis see Breuer, "Shitat Tora 'Im Derekh Erets." On pp. 2–3 of the first pamphlet he explains Hirsch's concept of *Torah Im Derekh Erets* and on p. 10 of the second pamphlet he distinguishes between Hirsch's theoretical worldview of *Torah Im Derekh Erets* and its practical application. On pp. 15–18 he discusses true knowledge and science and true Troah. See also Breuer, *Eda*, 73–77, and his citations in notes 80–77. See Ish-Shalom "'Al Mada' Ushlemut Haruaḥ," 356–361.
23 *Writings*, 7:76, in the essay, "Hebrew Study in General Education." See Ravitzky, *ḥerut*, 169. E. Stern, *Ishim Vekivunim* (Ramat Gan, 1987) 20–21, 28, puts more emphasis on this

Interpretations of Hirsch's Thought from the Right and the Left • CHAPTER TWO

In an essay for the month of Kislev (Hanukah, December 1856) dedicated to "Hellenism and Judaism,"[24] Hirsch writes that the two sources of human knowledge, the information received from revelation and the attainments of human reason embodied in philosophy, science and culture (the wisdom of Greece) are identical. Both have inherent value and, by using revelation as a standard to examine the attainments of reason, reason can be purified, and apparent discrepancies between these two realms will disappear. In an essay on "the classical principle of Jewish education" Hirsch once again emphasizes this identicality:

> The laws of nature are simply another commentary on the truths of Judaism. [...] Only the Jewish concept of God, that is, the concept of one God, can be the foundation for the scientific study of nature and the basic premise for the student of the natural sciences. For the scientist is in search of the thought behind nature, the law that governs the world order, the law of nature that appears to be an interplay of accidents. He regards the world as one entity, and he happily anticipates the moment when he will succeed in recapitulating all the concepts of nature in terms of one single concept, all the laws that govern the world in terms of one single law.[25]

The true Jew is the complete Jew: someone who has purified for himself these two realms. Such a person will certainly rejoice at the prospect of cultural progress:

> If our religion indeed required us to renounce what men call civilization and culture, we would be ready to do so without hesitation. [...] But is this really necessary? Judaism was never alien to *genuine civilization and culture*. [...] The more the Jew is a Jew, the more universalist will be his views and aspirations, the less alien will he be to anything that is noble and good, true and upright in the arts and sciences, in civilization and culture. [...] The more the Jew is a Jew, the more gladly will he give himself to all that is *true progress* in civilization and culture—provided that in this new circumstance he will not only maintain his Judaism but will be able

---

conservative side of his position. Nevertheless he acknowledges that Hirsch accords inherent value to European culture, and agrees that his position is one of identicality.
24 Cf. Hirsch, *Writings*, 2:200–204.
25 Hirsch, *Writings*, 7:293–294.

> to bring it to ever more *glorious fulfilment*. A Jew who remains steadfast amidst the seductive, derisive voices of his thoughtless contemporaries, who remains sufficiently firm to sacrifice to God's holy Will his personal inclinations and prospects of material gain, displays far greater moral strength and thus a far more worthy culture than the thoughtless son of the present century whose principles melt away at the first glance of ridicule or at the first tempting prospect of personal gain...[26]

With his characteristically apologetic and neo-fundamentalist revolutionism, Hirsch argues that from Judaism's perspective the modern era has introduced nothing novel. Judaism has always accepted culture in its purified form, and it is only persecution which separated them: "In almost every era, its [Judaism's] followers stood at the very height of the culture of their day. [. . .] If in recent centuries, the German Jews remained more or less alien to European culture, the fault lay not in their religion but in coercion, the tyranny from the outside that forcibly confined them to the alleys of their ghettos and shut them off from communication with the outside world..."[27]

Hirsch believes that every new and pure contribution to culture enhances and complements man's service of God. That being said, he constantly preaches that in practice the Torah is the standard for evaluating and purifying science and culture:

> The Jew is heartened to develop all his energies in the service of God. He welcomes each new truth as a valuable contribution to the ever more penetrating revelation of God in nature and history. In each new art form, in each new science, he sees a welcome addition to the means for perfecting the service and worship of God.
>
> Hence, the Jew will not be opposed to any science, any art form, any culture that is *truly* ethical, *truly* moral, *truly* contributing to the welfare and progress of man. He will measure everything by the eternally inviolable yardstick of the teachings of his God. Nothing will exist for him that cannot stand up before the Divine Will. The more firmly he stands on the rock of his Judaism, the more conscious he becomes of his Jewish destiny, the more he will be inclined to accept and gratefully absorb all knowledge,

---

26 Hirsch, *Writings*, 6:120–123, in the essay "Religion Allied with Progress." On "true science and enlightenment," see Breuer, *Eda*, 74, note 77.
27 Ibid., 120.

Interpretations of Hirsch's Thought from the Right and the Left • CHAPTER TWO | 45

wherever he will find it, לקבל האמת ממי שאמרה [to accept truth from whoever speaks it] (Maimonides, Introduction to the *Ethics of the Fathers*).[28]

In an open letter responding to Isaac Dov (Seligman Baer) Bamberger (1807–1878) about secession from the Reform community (whose leaders Hirsch considered absolute heretics), Hirsch happily identifies with Maimonides's criticism of heretics and apostates, citing him as an authority. In that essay Hirsch concludes that one who claims a contradiction between religion and science is a heretic. He cites Maimonides's essay on martyrdom which interprets the talmudic account of Rabbi Eliezer and the Babylonian governor (BT Avoda Zara 16b). In this account the governor criticizes Rabbi Eliezer for engaging in idle pursuits such as Torah study. Maimonides explains that Rabbi Eliezer was, in addition to being a Torah scholar, also a renowned scientist, and on this Hirsch states: "and the heretics into whose hands ר"א [Rabbi Eli'ezer] had fallen must have despised all things religious in general, because they believed there was an irreconcilable conflict between science and religion . . . We have here an ancient prototype of the מינות [heresy] which prevails in our own day and which also proclaims the notion that there is a conflict between science and religion."[29]

This stance derives from Hirsch's view that there can be only one truth; it cannot be divided into a religious realm of heaven and a secular realm of Earth (as maintained by Christianity) just as God himself, from whom all things stem, cannot be divided. Therefore, one finds in Hirsch's statements sharp criticism not only of the Reform to his left but also of the Ultra-orthodox, who invalidate anything innovative, to his right:

> The richer the minority's cause, the more will the minority treasure it. But then it may easily come to regard all other knowledge in "outside" domains as unnecessary, or even as utterly worthless. It may reject all intellectual activity in any field outside its own as an offense against its own cause, as an inroad upon the devotion properly due to that cause and an infringement on its prerogatives. Such a one-sided attitude does not stop at mere disregard for other intellectual endeavors. Once this attitude has taken hold in a Jewish minority, that minority will be unable to form a proper judgment and a true image of those intellectual pursuits which are not cultivated

---

28 *Writings*, 8:9–10.
29 Ibid., 6:285–286, in the note there.

in its own ranks but pursued mainly by its opponents. Then, as a result of simple ignorance, the minority will begin to fear that which at first it merely neglected out of disdain. Consequently the minority will begin to suspect the existence of an intrinsic close relationship between these "outside" intellectual pursuits and those principles to which the Jewish minority stands in opposition... Rather, it has cause to regard all truth, wherever it may be found on the outside, as a firm ally of its own cause, *since all truth stems from the same Master of truth.*[30]

In other words, even the benefit of the devout, closed attitude, is outweighed by its cost.

As I have demonstrated above, generally speaking, Hirsch employs the Torah as the standard to examine the statements of science and culture. That being said, he believes that it is sometimes necessary and possible to interpret the statements of revelation according to the attainments of human reason and science. This follows his theory of identicality, and that sometimes we require elucidation to truly understand revelation, an elucidation which reason can provide. For example, in his essay on "The Educational Value of Judaism," Hirsch says that Judaism has no problem accepting the Copernican revolution or Darwin's theory of evolution. This is because the Torah is a guide to ethical norms not a book of science:

> [T]he Rabbis have never made the acceptance or rejection of this and similar possibilities an article of faith binding on all Jews. They were willing to live with any theory that did not reject the basic truth that "every beginning is from God." In fact, they were generally averse to speculations about what was in the past and what will be in the future, because, in their view, such questions transgressed the limits of that which is knowable to man, or, at best, they did not enhance man's understanding of his moral function. In the view of our Rabbis, the Book of Books was intended to be

---

30 *Writings*, 2:247–248. See also ibid., 387–388, and Stern, *Ishim Vekivunim*, 52–53. See also Hirsch, *Writings*, 1:322–325; 4:176–177; 5:312, 326–327; his commentary on Num. 25:12. Hirsch emphasizes that it is one's duty to compromise for the sake of peace on matters related to rights to money and property, but one must not compromise and sacrifice other people's rights or the sacred values of divine goodness and truth. This is also the reason why he would not give up the principle of seceding from the Reform community for the sake of peace.

mankind's guide for life on earth as it is at present... Anything beyond that simply did not exist for our Sages.[31]

Judaism has no fundamental problem with the attainments of the sciences. Scientific theories can even be harnessed to attain Judaism's ethical goals, and to teach mankind about the Creator, based on the natural laws he established:

> What Judaism does consider vitally important is the acceptance of the premise that all the hosts of heaven move only in accordance with the laws of the one, sole God. But whether we view these laws from the Ptolemaic or Copernican vantage point is a matter of total indifference to the purely moral objectives of Judaism. Judaism had never made a credo of these or similar notions... This will never change, not even if the latest scientific notion that the genesis of all the multitude of organic forms on earth can be traced back to one single, most primitive, primeval form of the life should ever appear to be anything more than what it is today, a vague hypothesis still unsupported by fact. Even if this notion were ever to gain complete acceptance by the scientific world, Jewish thought, unlike the reasoning of the high priest of that notion, would nonetheless never summon us to revere a still extant representative of this primal form as the supposed ancestor of us all. Rather, Judaism in that case would call upon its adherents to give even greater reverence than ever before to the one, sole God Who, in His boundless creative wisdom and eternal omnipotence, needed to bring into existence no more than one single, amorphous nucleus and one single law of "adaption and heredity" in order to bring forth, from what seemed chaos but was in fact a very definite order, the infinite variety of species we know today, each with its unique characteristics that sets [sic] it apart from all other creatures. This would be nothing else but the actualization of the law of *le-mino*, the "law of species" with which God began His work of creation. This law of *le-mino*, upon which Judaism places such great emphasis in order to impress upon its adherents that all of organic life is subject to Divine laws, can accommodate even this "theory of the origin of species."[32]

---

31 *Writings*, 7:265–266. Here he is basically contradicting his apologetic position that although not always apparent to us, everything revealed by reason is contained in the Torah and statements of the Sages.
32 *Writings*, 7:263–264.

Even if in the future Darwin's theory, which is still only a hypothesis, is proven, it is God who will gain respect not the amoeba or the ape. At that point it will be possible to interpret the biblical law of "according to its kind" (*le-mino*) (Gen. 1:11) according to Darwin's theory.[33] Based on James Barr's theory of fundamentalism, I have referred to this stance as neo-fundamentalism. Barr argues that according to classic fundamentalism, scriptural inerrancy always overpowers hermeneutics, and whenever difficulties or contradictions between

---

33 Lawrence Kaplan notes that besides seventeenth century thinker Joseph Solomon Delmedigo, Hirsch was the first Orthodox philosopher to explicitly accept the Copernican thesis, a sign of daring progressiveness. Similarly he states that Hirsch was the only major Orthodox Rabbi to discuss evolution, and one of the few to publicly declare that an evolutionary theory detached from materialism concords with the fundamental beliefs of Judaism. See L. Kaplan "Tora Umadda in the Thought of Rabbi Samson Raphael Hirsch," B.D.D. 5 (1997), 12, 22. It should be noted that Rav Kook also (*Orot Ha-Qodesh*, [Jerusalem 1985], 2, *ma'amar ḥamishi, hit'alut ha-olam*, 511–574) deals with the theory of evolution and says that Judaism can live with this theory which accords with kabbalistic ideas. See also Rabbi Avraham Kook, *Li-Nevukhei ha-Dor*, ed. S. Rahmani (Tel Aviv, 2014), 34–44, and below Chapter Twelve.

Rosenbloom preceded Kaplan in his emphasis of Hirsch's daring acceptance of Copernicus (See Rosenbloom, *Tradition in an Age of Reform*). In his review of Rosenbloom's book Breuer criticizes this also, arguing that Hirsch was preceded in this by others such as Judah Loewe ben Betsalel (Maharal) and his student David Ganz (sixteenth century) who was a friend of Johannes Kepler (see Breuer, "Rosenbloom").

The above excerpt demonstrates that Hirsch was one of the only observant, Jewish scholars in the nineteenth century who did not create a dichotomy between accepting religion and science. Instead he argued that one can and must accept them both and create a harmony between them. Hirsch is almost unique in his levelheadedness towards the conclusions of science in all its components, and he believes that science (including the theory of evolution) even supports religion's claims about a God, the creator of nature and its laws and the beginning of life, and the one who orchestrates its processes. On this subject see M. Avraham, *Elohim Mesaḥeq Bequbiot* (Tel Aviv, 2011), specifically 17–19, 166–167, 192–194, 226–228, 355–359, 414–431. Avraham is not aware of this entire nineteenth century middle stream, which accepted and taught the achievements of science and also diligently observed the commandments, which I discussed in my book *The Middle Way*. Its participants are also scattered throughout H. Gafni's book, *"Peshuta shel Mishna": Iyunim Beḥeqer Sifrut Ḥazal Ba'et Haḥaddasha* (Tel Aviv, 2011). In this passage Hirsh essentially summarizes the main points of Avraham's supposedly new arguments which he dubs "modern physico-theological theory" or "evolutionary creationism." Avraham thus joins Hirsch, Rabbi Mordechai Breuer and his biblical "aspect theory," Nathan Aviezer and his harmonization of the big bang and Genesis and David Hanshke who all maintain the illusory, neo-fundamentalist apologetic approach of the nineteenth century, for better or for worse. Although Avraham exposes the shortcomings of Richard Dawkins' evolutionary atheism, he does not offer a plausible solution to the contradictions between science and religion. Even Maimonides did not think that God manages the world every second. Rather, he maintained that God created the world, established its laws and ever since the world has continued to operate on its own.

philosophy and science arise, it is the statements of science which are rejected. New fundamentalism however is apologetic and incoherent and it allows Hirsch to adopt strategies of scriptural interpretation according to his needs—in some cases interpreting Scripture in the light of proven scientific theories, but in all other cases using Scripture to examine and qualify science.[34]

Because the Torah and Jewish religion are identical to science and human culture and complement each other wherever they are lacking, any education system must include them both. Hirsch introduces such a program loudly and clearly:

> Why not employ the age-old principle of תלמוד תורה עם דרך ארץ (אבות פ"ב מ"ב) [*Talmud Torah im Derekh Erets*, Mishna Avoth 2:2] which weds religious and secular education to one another in mutual interdependence? If you will do so, you will see even in your own lifetime how יגיעת שניהם [the toil of both of them], how the careful, simultaneous cultivation of both these elements of education, משכחת עון [keeping sin out of one's mind] will guard your children against error on both sides. You will see with what zest and devotion your children will take to their "Hebrew studies" and drink in the spirit of the Law of God and the wisdom of our Sages, and how nevertheless, or perhaps precisely because of the special education they have received, they will be capable of competing on an equal basis with their contemporaries in the acquisition of all the knowledge, talents and skills that are part of their general education as members of the larger society.
>
> The realm of Jewish learning is not insular, remote from nature, from history, from the world and from the realities of life. On the contrary, it calls upon its disciples to study the heavens and the earth, to reflect on the connections that link the events and developments of history, to take an active part in every phase of physical, intellectual, moral and social life, and to gain the clearest, sharpest possible insight into all things and their relationship to one another...
>
> And so these two areas of learning do not hamper one another, are not mutually detrimental. Rather, they can strengthen and reinforce one another. [...] Equipped with the best of all *truly* humanistic training and

---

34 See Barr, *Fundamentalism*, 40, 93–96, 273–274. For a detailed discussion of Neo-Fundamentalism according to James Barr in Hirsch thoughts, see Chamiel, *The Middle Way*, 288–291. For an explanation on Fundamentalism in general according to Barr see idem, 149–154, in the discussion of whether or not Luzzatto was a fundamentalist.

> guided by the Jewish Law of God and the heritage of our Sages that will constantly give them new strength, light, counsel, admonition, consolation and inspiration, they will be able to meet the challenges that life will hold for them.[35]

Hirsch occasionally emphasizes that the inclusion of secular studies into the curriculum is a religious obligation, arguing that such studies have intrinsic value which contributes breadth and new dimensions to the religious worldview. In his essay on "The Relevance of Secular Studies to Jewish Education" he writes:

> Now if the Judaism for which we are educating our young need not shrink from contact with the intellectual elements of any *other true culture*, it is essential for the future of our youth as citizens, and therefore it is a true *religious duty*, for us to give them a secular education. A secular education is a most beneficial help to our young in understanding the times in which they live and the conditions under which they will have to practice their life's vocation; hence, it is most desirable also from the Jewish religious viewpoint and consequently deserving of warm support. But at the same time, and even more important, a good secular education can give our young people substantial new insights, added dimensions that will enrich their religious training.[36]

But Hirsch does not stop there. In his essay "The Role of Hebrew Study in General Education" (cited in the last chapter) he takes a step further in defining the essence of combined secular and religious studies:

> From the very beginning, our school has been aware that, in carrying out the task it has set for itself, it has combined two distinct elements that are considered mutually exclusive by prejudiced outsiders with a superficial point of view. One, they claim, must of necessity limit the other by virtue of the time and energy required to do justice to both. Our school, by contrast, has been of the opinion from the outset that these two elements, although commonly viewed as mutually limiting antitheses (and even considered by some as nullifying one another), are, in fact, related,

---

35 Hirsch, *Writings*, 7, in the essay "Religious Education," 23–24.
36 Ibid., in the essay "The Relevance of Secular Studies to Jewish Education, 1867," 87–88.

> mutually complementary parts of *one greater, integrated educational unity*. In practical life, this unity produces a Jew with moral and spiritual training in the general culture of mankind, a man and a citizen with a moral and spiritual education in the values of Judaism. As a consequence, the school, which should be the nursery for practical life, should promote both these elements in such a manner that they will complement and support one another to form one harmonious whole.[37]

That is to say, in Hirsch's system, a school should combine both elements to create a dialectical process, resulting in a final product larger, more harmonious and more complete than the basic sum of its parts.

That being said, Hirsch's first tendency—acknowledging the Torah's superiority, considering it the criterion for all truth and good—is heavily emphasized in his writings and it is these statements which are selectively quoted by Haredim. Hirsch cites the *midrash* in *Torat Cohanim* on Lev. 18:4, "to walk in them," which discusses the topic of Torah study and secular studies, and which appears to forbid the study of gentile wisdom: "make them the main thing and do not make them secondary... So that your negotiations will only be in them [...] so that you will not intermingle other things in the world with them." He writes on this:

> It appears that the opening sentence of this statement, ["make them the main thing and do not make them secondary"]... is designed to keep us from a misunderstanding. We should not understand—from the subsequent sentences of the statement—that we must completely ignore all knowledge gained from non-Jewish sources; that we must abstain from any knowledge that has no direct bearing on Torah. For ["make them the main thing and do not make them secondary"]... implies that we are permitted to occupy ourselves with other realms of knowledge also—only that we should make the Torah our principal concern, and the knowledge we gain from Torah should be regarded as absolute and unquestionable.
>
> Other disciplines are to be regarded as auxiliary; they are to be studied only if they are capable of aiding Torah study and are subordinated to it as the טפל [subordinate] to the עיקר [essence]. The Torah's truths must remain for us what is absolute and unconditional, the standard by which to measure all the results obtained in other branches of knowledge. Only that which accords with the truths of the Torah can be accepted by us as true. [...] Accordingly, we will not adapt ideas that are not in consonance

---

37 Ibid., 63, originally published in 1866.

with this perspective; we will not accept conclusions derived from other premises and mix them with words of Torah.

The Torah is not to be considered an equivalent of the other sciences, as though the Torah is just one branch of knowledge among others. We should not imagine that just as there is Jewish knowledge and truths, there is also non-Jewish knowledge and truths of equal importance and authority...

Rather, just as we are sure that the Torah comes from God, and all other branches of knowledge discovered by man are merely human products containing results of man's limited insight into the nature of things, so we are sure that there is only one truth, only one discipline that can serve as our yardstick and evaluator of all the other disciplines, which are valid only conditionally.[38]

As I have shown, these statements, in my opinion, are not intended in principle but in practice—when one is faced with apparent dilemmas and contradictions and when science, philosophy and culture have yet to be purified. The limits of scientific research are similar to the limits of reason in Hirsch's system of ethics. Human reason, despite its divine source, is incapable of adjudicating perfect morality because it is limited by sensuality. This leaves man no choice but to rely on the morality of revelation. The same is true in the case of science. Before being adopted, metaphysical, philosophical and scientific theories attained from human understanding, should first be purified by being subjected to the litmus test of revelation. Only afterwards can we accord them inherent value as truths which can assist Torah study.

Already in Chapter One I have shown the error in the Haredi view, which maintains that Hirsch's decision to include secular studies into the curriculum was a compromise to the time and place in Germany. Hirsch was aware of this erroneous and misleading interpretation of his approach and rejected it explicitly in his essay "The Relevance of Secular Studies to Jewish Education."[39]

It should be stressed that Hirsch, a typical Orthodox traditionalist, maintains that the concept of combining the tradition of Judaism with the culture of the time represents the traditional wisdom of our Sages. This combination has always allowed Judaism to withstand the test of time and has allowed Judaism in our day to be reborn and prove itself within the modern stream. He writes

---

38   Hirsch on Lev. 18:4–5. See also his commentary on Deut. 6:7. Similar priorities can be found in *Horeb: A Philosophy of Jewish Laws and Observances*, translated from the German original by Dayan Dr. I. Grunfeld. (London, 1962), v. 2, 408–409.
39   The article appears in Hirsch, *Writings*, 7. See note 4 in the first chapter.

about this at the height of his dispute with Bamberger over secession from the larger German-Jewish community, which was managed by leaders from the Reform movement. Hirsch argues that despite Bamberger's reservations about the principle of "Torah im Derekh Erets," he must realize that this principle is

> [...] the one true principle conducive to "truth and peace," to healing and recovery from all ills and all religious confusion. The principle of תורה עם דרך ארץ ["Torah im Derekh Erets"] can fulfill this function because it is not part of troubled time-bound notions; it represents the ancient, traditional wisdom of our Sages that has stood the test everywhere and at all times. These Sages, and they alone, have always been, and still are, our חכמים באמת [true sages].[40]

Once again, Hirsch voices his neo-fundamentalist apologetics. Because secular studies for all students was already a *fait accompli* in Germany, and not open to challenge, Hirsch turned it into part of tradition, imputing it into the Sages' statements about "Torah im Derekh Erets" even when this was clearly not their intention. This is the place to note that M. Breuer, a balanced researcher, criticizes Hirsch as well but from the right, claiming that Hirsch exaggerated the identicality between humanist, secular culture and the Judaism of revelation, an identicality which Breuer believes does not exist.[41]

BETWEEN PARTICULARISM AND UNIVERSALISM

The second issue debated by Hirsch's interpreters is his attitude towards the Return to Zion. This debate is linked not only to the extent of his theological fundamentalism but also to differences of opinion concerning his place on the spectrum between particularism and universalism. That is to say, to what extent was he influenced by the ideals of the Haskalah in regard to the importance of equality and the centrality of the individual as a possessor of reason—ideals which oppose the Jewish idea of chosenness?

The more the idea of universalism features in a Jewish philosopher's thought, the more the concept of national chosenness tends to be downplayed to make space for humanity; the more he stresses the idea of universalism, the more he will eschew the idea of a real Return to Zion.

---

40 In the "Open Letter to Rabbi Seligmann Baer Bamberger," *Writings*, 6:221.
41 See Breuer, *Eda*, 75.

The Haredi interpretation of Hirsch's views on these issues is consistent and resolute. Researchers, however, are divided, usually along ideological lines, either overtly or implicitly. Haredim maintain that Hirsch is a Jewish particularist, faithful to his religion. According to him the question of choseness is not up for debate. That being said they believe that Hirsch was not a political nationalist, only a religious one, and that in Hirsch's view any form of Zionism is a rebellion against the three oaths that God adjured the Jewish people upon their exile. Consequently an active return to Zion in an organized and institutional manner is forbidden; it is a matter for the End of Days, utopian and supra-historical.

One exceptional Haredi viewpoint deserves special discussion: that of Rabbi Isaac Breuer (1883–1946), Hirsch's grandson. Breuer developed a form of national-religious messianism and in the wake of a growing Jewish presence in the Land of Israel, began to anticipate a messianic upheaval, which would result in the establishment of a Torah state in the Land of Israel, a process occurring within history. Breuer sought to harness Hirsch's views to support this messianic, Haredi vision:

> We must realize: the deeper significance of Hirsch's project was the return of the Jewish people to the embrace of its history, with no other end-goal before it but the reestablishment of the state of God, [...] a state of God which will rise again, centered in Zion, the location of God's temple, according to God's promise. This State of God represents the spread of the Torah's sovereignty over the entire diverse abundance of human life, reaching the pinnacle of its development in the national state. [...] The past comes to life once again in the aspect of *vayehi* [it will be]—and the future becomes the past in the aspect of *vehaya* [it was]—and from such a past and such a future the form of the new Jewish person will be molded, opening before him a new era of Jewish historical activism. [...] Hirsch was the first modern, Jewish nationalist.[42]

Researchers, however, grapple with the tension between the Jewish and human in Hirsch's thought, and tried to draw him closer to their own sides. Shalom Rosenberg does not consistently deal with Hirsch, but admires him as a Romantic, someone who considers Judah Halevi, the man of ethical

---

42 I. Breuer, "Rashar Hirsch Kemore Derekh Ledoro Veladorot Habaim," in *Bemagalei Shana, Kitvei Rabbi Shimshon Rafael Hirsch*, vol. 2 (Bnei Brak, n.d.), 16–17.

Judaism, his cultural hero. Hirsch, who learned his admiration of Judah Halevi from his teacher Haham Isaac Bernais in Hamburg, certainly tends to agree with Judah Halevi's Neo-Platonist approach to the rationalism of Saadya Gaon (died in 942) and his philosophical disciples. Like Judah Halevi, Hirsch eschewed allegorical-rationalist interpretations of the Torah, philosophical elitism (which after Judah Halevi was most strongly represented by Maimonides) and the conception of intellectual study as man's ultimate goal. Hirsch, like Judah Halevi, prefers an ethical interpretation of the Torah, the simplicity of the masses, and the observance of the commandments as man's ultimate goal, leading to holiness and morality. The truth of the Torah is not proven by reason but by the nation's empirical experience of the Exodus and the public revelation at Sinai, events transmitted by tradition. That being said, I believe that this admiration stops short in places where Hirsch had internalized the Haskalah, a movement which aspires to strengthen emancipation and believes in the mission of the Jewish people to the gentiles, a mission beginning to bear fruit. He does not share Judah Halevi's mystical approach regarding the essential, immanent sanctity of the Jew as chosen to be a prophet and the Land of Israel sanctified for prophecy. Hirsch actually prefers Maimonides's opinion that all humans possess equal potential, and that the sanctity of a people or a land is a function of human activity, not a matter of inherent nature. Rosenberg however disagrees. In his opinion Hirsch's adoption of Judah Halevi's doctrine of mission indicates that he also adopts Judah Halevi's doctrine of chosenness. Rosenberg deals with this issue at least twice. In his article "Lev Usegulah"[43] he considers Judah Halevi's position on chosenness a dialectical one: uniqueness on the one hand—heart and shells—and mission, on the other hand—heart and organs. In his opinion, both Hirsch and a young Luzzatto follow Judah Halevi's path, adopting his doctrine of mission. In his book Rosenberg states this again, without delving into detail, arguing that Hirsch adopted Judah Halevi's position on the subject of chosenness.[44] I, however, maintain that there is no need to see a dialectic here. Judah Halevi believed that the Jewish nation is inherently unique and this uniqueness affords it a responsibility and a calling towards the rest of mankind. Hirsch and Luzzatto, however, do not accept the unique chosenness maintained by Judah Halevi and therefore cannot be considered his ideological successors. They certainly accept Judah Halevi's

---

43 S. Rosenberg "Lev Usgula Ra'ayon Habehira Bemishnato Shel Rihal Uvafilosofia Hayehudit Haḥadasha," in *Mishnato Hahagutit Shel Rabi Judah Halevi*, ed. H. Schwartz (Jerusalem, 1978), 109–119.
44 Rosenberg, *Be'iqvot Hakuzari*, 62–63.

doctrine of mission but not on the basis of uniqueness. They conceive the Jewish people as first in a temporal sense, its task bringing the entirety of humanity into its fold, but not a superior in terms of spiritual rank.⁴⁵

Hirsch's writings indicate that he believed that the distinction between humanity and the Jewish people is based solely on receiving the Torah (like Maimonides). This distinction is explicitly technical and time-bound, and is not a consequence of inherent uniqueness. The Jewish people only have precedence in time; they are first among equals in God's plan to educate mankind. Hirsch thus divests the idea of chosenness of its particularist overtones, replacing it with more universalistic significance. After the first attempt at revelation failed a number of times (the Garden of Eden, the generation of the Deluge, the generation of the tower of Babel) providence decided to create a new nation from the descendants of Abraham, using it as a medium to educate the rest of humanity in the light of the Torah's guidance. At first, this nation was a people dwelling in its own land. Afterwards, when this experiment failed, it became a people scattered among the nations. "Hence, when God says בני ברכי ישראל [Israel is my firstborn son], this means: With Israel, the womb of humanity will be opened; with Israel, the dance will begin; all the people are obligated to join him as My sons. I come to you in your own name and in the name of all humanity. Israel is My first but not My only child; Israel is only the first people that I have won as Mine [...] Israel is not the first in rank, but the first in time."⁴⁶

---

45 Rosenberg correctly claims (ibid.) that only in his youth did Luzzatto maintain a doctrine of mission, but as he got older abandoned this position. See excerpts of Hirsch's position below. For examples of Luzzatto's approach, see his commentary on Exodus 20:3 where he discusses (based on his understanding that the Torah is a book of ethical guidance and is not meant to teach philosophical truths) the Torah's emphasis on Israel's uniqueness and their closeness to God, a doctrine not purely true, because all people are equally God's children. The Torah's providential cunning tells the Jewish People that they are God's unique nation, and therefore God draw them closer to Him. It thus guarantees that they remain loyal to him and continue to bear the yoke of the Torah. This is for the sake of the nations of the world who are destined to have equal status to the Jews. The Jews precede the nations in their unification of God and their superior ethical qualities only in terms of time but not in terms of essence. Compare Rosenberg's view to that of D. Schwartz, *Hara'ayon Hameshiḥi Behagut HaYehudit Biyemei Habeinayim* (Ramat Gan, 1997), 56–59. He explains there Judah Halevi's doctrines of chosenness and mission, and it seems that he agrees that Judah Halevi's view is not dialectical, and at the end of the process the unique distinctions between the Jews and the gentiles will continue to exist. On ethics in Judah Halevi's thought see the *Kuzari*, 3:5, 7, 11, 17.
46 Hirsch on Ex. 4:22–23.

Explaining the verse "which a man shall do and live thereby" (Lev. 18:5), Hirsch writes:

> It does not say here אשר תעשו אותם ותחיו בהם [which you shall do and you will live thereby], but rather, אשר יעשה אותם האדם וחי בהם [which a man shall do and live thereby]; and it does not say אדם [a man], but האדם [the man]. The inference is that Scripture here refers to anyone who exemplifies the spiritual and moral character implied by the term האדם (see Commentary, Bereshis [Bereshit] 1:26)—and attainment that can be reached only through fulfillment of God's laws. Thus, *Toras* [Torat] *Kohanim* infers: [...] even a non-Jew who keeps God's Law is the equal of a High Priest; for it says: [...] "which a man shall do and live thereby" ... We see, then, that life, the teaching, closeness to God, happiness, and well-being are attained through Torah and mitzvos not only by Israel; rather, any man who draws his worldview and his principles from the Torah, anyone who elevates himself to the heights of pure humanity by fulfilling the Torah's חוקים [laws] and משפטים [ordinances], is ensured of attaining the highest level of perfection and happiness in nearness to God. . . The חוקים, which—from a spiritual and sensual standpoint—govern the life of the individual, and the משפטים, which govern the life of the society, are not designed to boost us to extraordinary, superhuman levels. Rather, they are designed to restore to us the same human level which was the original destiny, and remains the destiny, of man who was created in the image of God. The unfolding of this destiny began with the Jewish family of man, and will end with the whole of mankind. This is the whole purpose of God's guidance in history.[47]

This is an explicit departure from Judah Halevi's notion of uniqueness. Even if we accepts Schweid's reading of Judah Halevi—that the Jew is not superior to other humans in terms of reason or morality but only in terms of prophetic abilities[48]—I still do not think one can consider Hirsch's approach a development of Judah Halevi's view, as Rosenberg proposes, and I prefer Mordechai Breuer's view on this issue.[49]

---

47 Hirsch on Lev. 18:4–5. See also Lev. 20:26. Note that Hirsch writes in terms of mankind's keeping the laws and judgments of the Torah, an important matter treated below.
48 See E. Schweid, *Moledet Veerets Ye'uda* (Tel Aviv, 1979), 59–60.
49 Breuer, *Eda*, 65–66. On the uniqueness of the Jewish People according to Judah Halevi see Gutmann, *Hafilosofia Shel Hayahadut*, 119.

Shlomo Chertok offers a reading diametrically opposed to that of Rosenberg. He attributes to Hirsch a universalist approach, deviating from classic rabbinic interpretation, part of Hirsch's progressive attitudes towards the individual, family, community and humanity. In his doctorate (and afterwards in his book),[50] Chertok argues that Hirsch's interpretation of the biblical word *ger* differs from that of the Sages. He bases himself on Hirsch's commentary to Ex. 23:9 and Deut. 10:19, arguing that Hirsh's interpretation of *ger* as a "foreigner," as opposed to a "convert," represents a transition on Hirsch's part from a Torah standard to a human standard. In Exodus Hirsch says about "you shall not oppress a *ger*":

> Our verse now, once again, places the principles of quality and loving-kindness at the forefront. The real test of these principles will be the Jewish state's treatment of foreigners: they are to enjoy all the rights granted to citizens, and are to be treated with love and kindness (the treatment accorded by a state to the aliens living within its jurisdiction is always an accurate indication of the extent to which justice and humanity prevail in that state).

On the statement "and you shall love the ger" in Deuteronomy, Hirsch writes: "Imitate God in loving the stranger who enters your midst from the outside. In receiving the stranger, show that, in your eyes, pure humanity is the highest distinction."

I read Hirsch differently than Chertok and maintain that he remains loyal to the rabbinic approach. Hirsch is aware of the possibility that his readers may mistakenly read his commentary on these verses in isolation from his general identification of the scriptural "ger" as a "convert," based on the definitive determination of the Sages. He therefore took the effort to refer the reader to his commentary on Ex. 22:2 as an essential introduction. His commentary on that verse maintains axiomatically that the obligation of conversion is a prerequisite for full rights and equality in the Jewish state: "one who was born a heathen is entitled to complete equality and full rights among Jews under Jewish law from the moment he joins the Jewish fold by accepting the basic principles of Judaism and Jewish worship." He adds there that Halakhah also accords reduced rights to a *ger toshav* ("resident alien") who has accepted the seven Noahide

---

50 See S. Chertok, *Hayaḥas Lamoderna Befarshanuto Shel Rashar Hirsch Latorah*, Doctoral Dissertation (Beersheba, 2005) 24; idem, *Qanqan Yashan Male Ḥadash* (Bnei Brak, 2000), 35–38.

commandments. However, while eligible for residence and other additional personal rights, the *ger toshav* is still not considered a full citizen. Hirsch tries to weave the different statements of the Sages into a consistent system, explaining when the word "ger" is read as "foreigner" and when it is read as "convert," but in my opinion he fails in this attempt.[51]

A REAL RETURN TO ZION WITHIN HISTORY: HIRSCH AS A PRECURSOR TO ZIONISM OR ITS OPPONENT

I will now deal with the claims of researchers who maintain that Hirsch's views on this subject are incoherent, inconsistent, and ambiguous. In his writings, they argue, he appears to be both Zionism's precursor and its opponent, a contradiction they seek to resolve. In order to incorporate Hirsh into their own religious-Zionist ideal, they try to argue that his opposition only applies to his own generation but that he did expect a Return to Zion later in history.

Pinhas Rosenblit has written two articles on Hirsch's attitude towards the Land of Israel where he discusses the prominent "duality" featuring in the thought of Hirsch and his disciples in regards to the Land of Israel.[52] He bases this view, among other things, on Hirsch's commentary to the Rebuke in Leviticus, *Parashat Beḥukotai*, where Hirsch describes two paths to redemption: a short path accompanied by miracles and a long, "natural" path with none. According to Rosenblit's reading, Hirsch believes that the redemption will occur within history and without miracles.

---

51 On this failed attempt see Chamiel, *The Middle Way*, in the appendix to Chapter One—"Who is a *Ger*?," 319–326. Hirsch's approach is identical to Rashi's in his commentary on Ex. 22:2, which some have mistakenly interpreted as an expression of humane universalism. It seems to me that Rashi was bothered by the Torah's justification of the commandment not to oppress the *ger* (which is a convert) with the argument "for you were *gerim* in the land of Egypt." The Hebrews were not converts in Egypt but foreigners!? To resolve this difficulty Rashi explains that the term *ger* is a shared term which refers to the foreignness of anyone entering a society from without. That being said, it is clear that Rashi does not deviate from the interpretation of the Sages—that the commandment not to oppress the *ger* is directed only at the convert who accepts the religion of the society which he has joined.

52 P. Rosenblit, "Galut Veerets Yisrael Al Pi S.R Hirsch Uvnei Doro," in *Sefer Zikaron Lemordekhai Viser Pirqei Ma'as Vehagut*, ed. S. Schmidt (Qevutsat Yavna, 1981), 160–169. Idem, "Bein Shnei 'Olamot" in *Torah 'Im Derekh Erets Hatenu'a Isheiha Ra'ayonteiha*, ed. M. Breuer (Ramat Gan, 1987), 33–43.

Rivka Horwitz develops this position further, and in a detailed article presents the duality discussed by Rosenblit.[53] Like him, she bases herself on Hirsch's commentary on *Parashat Beḥukotai*. She cites Hirsch's words about the long, less desirable path to redemption and reads it as a short path to redemption occurring within history. I believe that an examination of this passage must take account of what follows: Hirsch's description of the preferable path to redemption, arriving swiftly and miraculously. According to my reading, even the long, undesirable path to redemption only materializes beyond history and not within it.

As a rule, Horwitz's article is an unorganized and unsystematic collection of excerpts from Hirsch's writings. It therefore contains contradictions and errors, and portrays Hirsch as an incoherent figure. According to Horwitz: there are "two faces" to Hirsch's approach, he has a complex philosophy which allowed many good people to rely upon it (464–465): on the one hand, the Land of Israel lies at the center of Jewish existence (448, 451) and possesses uniqueness (459) "an approach close to the opinion of Judah Halevi" (458). On the other hand, it is an approach which condenses the role of the Land of Israel in favor of the Diaspora (456), focusing on a universal closeness to God—"like the views of Mendelssohn and Maimonides" (459), claiming that the Land's sanctity is not intrinsic" (458).

Horwitz does not distinguish between historical time and utopian time in Hirsch's system. She therefore accepts Rosenblit's view that Hirsch's redemption occurs within history and without miracles (455): "at times he envisioned the return to Zion as closer" (456). However, Horwitz also cites sources which show that the redemption is postponed until the end of days and is linked to the elevation of humanity (451), and that Hirsch (unlike Kalischer) "spoke of a heavenly Land of Israel" (462). The excerpts she uses to demonstrate the uniqueness of the Land of Israel in Hirsch's thought (458–460) do not refer to the intrinsic uniqueness of the land, but as she herself says, to a uniqueness deriving from the observance of the Torah's commandments within its boundaries, its value entirely dependent on the morality of its inhabitants. Horwitz maintains that Hirsch's attitude towards the non-centrality of the land only "applies to his generation" (460) and that "Hirsch's treatment of the real Land of Israel was problematic" (463). In her opinion (similar to Rosenberg's), Hirsch's view is also comparable to that of Judah Halevi in terms of his perception of the

---

53 R. Horwitz, "Yaḥaso Shel Shimshon Refael Hirsch Leerets-Yisrael," in *Erets Yisrael Bahagut Hayehudit Haḥadasha*, ed. A. Ravitzky (Jerusalem, 1998), 447–466.

Jewish people among the nations like a heart among organs (461). She does not however recognize that Hirsch considers this uniqueness a temporary state of affairs. I try to show that when it comes to the uniqueness of the people and the land, Hirsch is far from Judah Halevi's position, and his approach cannot be used as springboard to arrive at a real-messianic-Torah Zionism as proposed by I. Breuer (464).

A close reading of Hirsch's writings reveals his view that the Jewish people and the Land of Israel are only instruments, and their purpose is to allow a nation to live a full Torah lifestyle, an example to humanity, a catalyst for mankind's moral awakening.[54] The Torah is the nation's only essence and purpose. It was and continues to be the Jews' portable homeland, before they ever entered the land and long after they were exiled from it.[55] Corrupted by the bounty of the land, the nation failed at its mission twice.[56] It is actually in Diaspora life that the Jewish people succeeded in educating the gentiles in the light of the Torah's morality, and it is that success which has brought the Jews lives of happiness and fortune in their Diaspora homelands.[57] The Sages of the Talmud stated that God adjured three oaths (two to the Jewish people and one to the nations of the world) which forbid the Jewish people from initiating an

---

54 See Hirsch, Gen. 12:2–3; Ex. 6:7–8; 25:12–15; Lev. 2:1; 18:24–28; Deut. 4:5; 16:9; 27:18–19; 32:9.

55 See Hirsch, Ex. 6:8; idem, *Writings*, 1:122. This is the idea of Heinrich Heine (which is based on inverting the same idea expressed by Spinoza—see Y. Yovel, *Spinoza Vekofrim Aḥerim* (Tel Aviv, 1988), 204–206). For the concept of Torah as the portable homeland of the Jewish People see M. Weiner, *Hadat Hayehudit Bitqufat Haemantsipatsia*, trans. L. Zagagi (Jerusalem, 1974), 105; and A. Ravitzky, "'Hatsivi Lakh Tsiunim' Letsion: Gilgulo Shel Ra'ayon," in *Al Da'at Hamaqom*, ed. idem (Jerusalem, 1991), 70 and the additional source from Hirsch he cites there, Deut. 11:18. See also Hirsch, *Writings*, 6:37: "there has always been only one national territory to protect and defend and that national territory is the תורה!"

56 See Hirsch, *Nineteen Letters*, 79; Hirsch, *Writings*, 1:286; 8:293.

57 See Hirsch, *Nineteen Letters*, 82; *Writings*, 2:223. Within history Hirsch preferred the blessed Diaspora, where the Jewish people fulfills its mission as the nation of the Torah, and he opposed rushing the end and violating the Halakhah. Interestingly, we find refusal to see intrinsic value in the land later on (under Hirsch's influence?) in the writing of Rosenzweig and Leibowitz, too. Rosenzweig (Franz Rosenzweig, *The Star of Redemption*, trans. William W. Hallo [New York-Chicago-San Francisco, 1970], 299–309, 334–335; note that there is some similarity in language to that of Hirsch in the *Nineteen Letters*) believed that the Jewish people does not have a task in history, that it lives in eternity, and it is unified by blood relationships—the nation itself. He was apprehensive about normalization. Leibowitz (see, for example, Y. Leibowitz, *Yahadut, 'Am Yisrael Umedinat Yisrael* [Jerusalem and Tel Aviv, 1975], 404–422) who lived in the sovereign State of Israel, was afraid that the land, as "Holy Soil," would become a focus of idolatry and false messianism, and he regarded the Halakhah as the factor that bound the Jews together as a nation.

organized return to the Land of Israel. With love for their host countries, the Jewish people must wait with passive faith until God reinstalls them in the Holy Land, in a miraculous process, at the end of history:

> But this very vocation obliges us, until God shall call us back to the Holy Land, to live and to work as patriots wherever He has placed us, to collect all the physical, material and spiritual forces and all that is noble in Israel to further the weal of the nations which have given us shelter. [...] It forbids us to strive for the reunion or the possession of the land by any but spiritual means. Our Sages say God imposed three vows when He sent Israel into the wilderness: (1) that the Children of Israel shall never seek to re-establish their nation by themselves; (2) that they shall never be disloyal to the nations which have given them shelter; (3) that these nations shall not oppress them excessively (*Kethuboth*, 111a). The fulfillment of the first two vows is confirmed in the pages of history; about the third, the nations concerned must judge themselves.[58]

What then is the nature of this historical messianic future and what role do the nation and land play in its process? What future is Hirsch preparing for us? Will the nations really adopt the entire Torah or just its theological and ethical truths? Will there really be a need for a Jewish state in this utopian era, when humanity has attained the pinnacle of universal moral unity, acknowledging God's kingdom and his will, and if so what will be its purpose? We find that Hirsch's description of this unreal future is vague, and he vacillates between his neo-fundamentalist traditionalism and his philosophy influenced by the thought of his time. That being said, his attitude towards active, institutional Zionism occurring within history is firm and consistent. Hirsch interprets the verses of the Rebuke in *Beḥukotai*, using them to demonstrate that punishment for sin and the bitter exile need not continue until the end of days. We can change the Diaspora into something favorable, by observing the Torah, and joyfully carrying out the task given to us, fulfilling our divine mission to the nations. Hirsch distinguishes between the long path to redemption and the swift path to redemption, the latter unfolding in three stages. The long path to redemption is thus described:

> בקרי [in opposition]: in all the events of world history—which do not appear at all to be directed toward the return of the exiles—I will walk

---

58 Hirsch, *Horeb*, v. 2, 461.

with them. Their whole experience in the land of their enemies—with all the effects of this experience, which educate through suffering—and the whole course of the development of world history itself will ultimately lead to the result that the exiles will be ripe to return to independence. And the events of the history of the nations—the events themselves—will restore the exiles to their homeland. Thus, the whole long and extended exile "in the land of their enemies"—including all the old and new sins—in essence merely actualizes והבאתי אותם [and I will bring them]. God Who conceals Himself brings them home by long, roundabout paths; He brings them back to their ancient homeland and to their original, eternal mission.

או אז [if... then...]: or, perhaps, the other possibility for the future will come to pass. They will not continue the iniquity of their fathers, and will not augment it with new iniquity born of exile. Rather, או, after all the crushing blows of the initial period of exile, the hearts of הנשארים בהם [those remaining of them], those who survive this difficult period, will be humbled. They will not "rot away in sins old and new"; rather, their hearts will be humbled before God, and will ceased to be "ערל" [uncircumcised] and recalcitrant toward Him (see Commentary, Bereshis [Bereshit] 17:10).

ואז, and then—not only in the end of days—ירצו את עונם [they expiate their iniquity]: They will cheerfully accept their destiny in exile and gladly carry out their mission in exile, regarding this as ריצוי עונם [expiating their sin], a means of redressing the wrong of their past sins. Their destiny and mission will satisfy themselves and also "satisfy" the debt they have incurred. If this happens, the גלות [exile] will assume an entirely new form. Instead of being a grave of decay, exile will become ground for new fulfillment of Israel's God-ordained mission, fruitful soil for a גלות-life directed toward God and bound up with Him.[59]

That is to say, there are two paths to redemption. The path which leads to redemption "in its time"[60] is long and full of suffering, lasting through the whole duration of history, and sins committed in exile serve to prolong it, preventing a swift and openly miraculous redemption. On this path, God will return

---

59 Hirsch on Lev. 26:39–41.
60 See Lev. 26:44. Hirsch uses a rabbinic *midrash* from BT Sanhedrin 98a, on the verse in Isaiah 60:22.

the Jewish people to their land naturally, with concealed miracles, through the tortuous and prolonged processes of history. The End of Days at the culmination of this path, which also lies beyond history, will transpire through divine involvement as if unfolding by itself. It will not be perceived until it happens, and only then will the Jewish people receive the reward promised to them. This is the only time that Hirsch addresses redemption in the form of concealed miracles as opposed to overt ones, and the exception only serves to prove the rule. Hirsch candidly regards this exception as the less desirable option, and prefers the short path, expressed with the words "I will hasten it," on which the Jews submit to God, refrain from committing further sins while in exile, and happily accept the task assigned to them. This kind of behavior begins a process of expiation for Jewish sins in the Land of Israel, allowing a more favorable exile, one in which the Jewish people do not decay in their own grave over the long course of history, as in the first way.[61] The short path of Jewish historical destiny is comprised of three stages which are described here as three covenants. "The covenant of Jacob" is the time of bitter exile, suffering, pogroms and martyrdom, serving to expiate sin; "the covenant of Isaac," follows in our own day, a new dawn among nations. The Jewish people begin to flourish upon a land which was until now foreign, its fortune growing greatly, and it is then that it will suffer from the jealousy of the nations who will vacillate between envy and humanity. The Jews will utilize their powers which have been liberated and enriched to fulfill their task in exile, observing the Torah in fortune and health, with greater perfection and diversity. Once they have withstood this trial then the "covenant of Abraham" will arrive:

> Like Abraham, they will observe the Torah, which has been entrusted to them for the salvation of mankind, and they will actualize the full goodness and truth of the Torah in the midst of many peoples. Ultimately, the nations will tolerate and respect Israel—not even though they are the people of the God of Abraham, but because they are the people of the God of Abraham; because they know and observe God's Torah, which brings salvation to mankind. [. . .] They will overcome all the obstacles over which they stumbled while dwelling in their own land, and only then—והארץ אזכר [I will remember the Land]: When they have become "Abraham," I will restore them to the land, so that they should fulfill their mission as the people of the Torah on the land of the Torah.

---

61 See Horwitz, "Yaḥaso Shel Shimshon Rafael Hirsch," 456.

We see then that [the Covenant of Jacob, the Covenant of Isaac, and the Covenant of Abraham] are the three stages in which they are to perform their task in the גלות [exile]. When they have gone through these three stages, their sin will be atoned for, and at the same time they will be ready to return forever to the land of their independence.

'והארץ וגו 43 [And the land...] When the people will be ready for their mission, the land, too, will be restored to its mission. For the mission of the land is to be the soil of Torah observance for God's people. But until the people are ready for this, the land will await them in desolation. The land will not be given to another people, and its soil will not promote the development of strangers. In its desolation it will atone for its Sabbaths—as long as the people in their exile must atone for their sin.'[62]

Hirsch offers no details about the Jews' ultimate purpose in the Land. He only says that it constitutes a prize for successful atonement and will be a means of observing the commandments in their entirety. These are both simple Haredi goals, which do not mesh with any kind of redemptive, worldly zenith in a land repopulated by its inhabitants. It is an eventuality the reader would expect after this long historical odyssey. He describes the Land of God for the people of God—nice words which he fails to give substance. He never sets an end-date for the third stage—the return to the land—nor does he explain how we will know that the time is ripe to return to the land—assuming that the return is a real event within history—in spite of the oaths and dangerous temptations of the land's bounty.

Elsewhere, Hirsch describes the shrinking gap between the Jewish people and the nations over the course of human history. During its history, the Jewish people reveals the one God, orchestrator of history. Its activity also constitutes a divine revelation of sorts in that the Jewish people submits its actions to God's laws. In the case of the gentiles, however, only their histories attest to divine revelation, not their actions. They act according to their nature, and submit only to their own impulses and preferences, not to the will of their creator:

> But *this contrast diminishes more and more*. Under the influence of Israel's mission and under the influence of the example that Israel quietly sets among the nations, this contrast becomes smaller and smaller. [...] The seventh day [of the Succot sacrifices] is the goal of the development of

---

62 Hirsch on Lev. 26:42–43.

mankind and of Israel's mission for it, and on this day the contrast will cease to exist. Israel and all of mankind will be united in their acknowledgement of God and in the life-service of deeds. [...]

However, as regards the historical guidance and their role in fulfilling the mission of mankind, the special standing of Israel amidst the nations will not be discontinued. For Israel and the nations differ in their historical development and in their ability to realize the purposes of mankind; hence Israel and the nations, the nations and Israel, will continue to be separate and distinct, even though they will be equal in their value. Both will be close to God in His direction of their history, and both will lead the world for the achievement of mankind's purposes, but they will continue to be seven *and another* seven כבשים [sheep], one and another איל [ram].

Nonetheless, they will be identical in rendering homage to God by fulfilling the commandments given to each respectively; the Sinaitic Teaching given to Israel, and the general Teaching given to mankind. *In rendering homage to God by doing His Will, Israel and mankind will become one.* The active life of all people will bear the stamp of faithfulness to moral duty, just like the active life of Israel…

בַּיּוֹם הַהוּא, יִהְיֶה יְהוָה אֶחָד—וּשְׁמוֹ אֶחָד וְהָיָה יְהוָה לְמֶלֶךְ, עַל-כָּל-הָאָרֶץ ["And the LORD shall be King over all the earth; in that day shall the LORD be One, and His name one"] (Zechariah 14:9).[63]

Hirsch never states explicitly when this unification is meant to be realized, and also gives no substantial meaning or justification for the Jews' continued separate existence in its own land in an age of Jewish unity with the rest of humanity, an era in which Jews and Gentiles are identical in terms of history and activity.

The second, shorter path is nothing more than an idealization of exile. Hirsch does not follow Maimonides who completely denies the exile, and who believes that its persecutions and suffering are the cause of the nation's spiritual decline. Nor does he follow Judah Halevi's view that the nation in exile plays the role of God's servant, bearing the sufferings of mankind as a passive messenger of progress, continuing to yearn for a real return to its land as soon as possible, its extended languishing in exile a disgrace. Hirsch certainly does not

---

63   Hirsch on Num. 29:13. In his commentary on Psalms 25:4, he distinguishes between forbidden foods and sexual relations, most of which apply only to the Jews, whereas the laws of justice and truth, honesty and compassion, and the social obligations of the Torah will be observed by all mankind.

follow Nachmanides who accords no ideal value to commandments observed outside the Land of Israel, regarding them as nothing more than an exercise to ensure that the commandments are never forgotten. These three thinkers yearned for a Zion within history. Judah Halevi and Nachmanides believed that the Land has inherent value, distinct from the impure ground of the Diaspora (a stance Hirsch refuses to accept), and even implemented and realized (or at least attempted to realize) their dreams within their own personal lives. Hirsch's view is similar to that of Mendelssohn—exile as a mission to the nations, serving as a personal and communal example of a people nursing from the two sources of culture. However, they still disagree on several points: the relationship between these two sources, human progress, and the active pursuit of their mission. Mendelssohn believes that the two sources of culture are two separate realms, each dealing with its own domain; Hirsch believes they are identical. Mendelssohn rejects Gotthold Ephraim Lessing's (1729–1781) ideas of human progress; Hirsch adopts it. Mendelssohn believes that Jews are forbidden from being active and taking initiative in their passive mission; Hirsch believes that the task must be undertaken actively within the midst of humanity.

One can read these descriptions of the different stages of redemption like Hirsch's grandson Isaac Breuer,[64] who was a Haredi, Zionist-Messianist. As I explained, he sees in Hirsch's descriptions of redemption identification with Zionism and Torah messianism, a religious vision of Zionism preceding the secular vision of Herzl. It is also possible to read these descriptions like Rosenblit[65] and Horwitz,[66] who were aware of Hirsch's reservations about an active Return to Zion in his time, but who, as I have shown, limited this to his own generation, and regard Hirsch's description of the future as a final stage taking place within history. They thus try to keep him within their own general consensus: their yearning for a real Return to Zion. It seems to me that this reading is mistaken and is captive to a Religious-Zionist perception hiding behind the apparent "duality" of Hirsch's statements. I prefer the

---

64 Breuer, "Rashar Hirsch Kemore Derekh," 16–21. It is not surprising that the essay does not contain even one excerpt from Hirsch. There were some who thought like Breuer, that Hirsch preceded Herzl in a vision of the future establishment of a real Jewish State. In my opinion, wherever Hirsch discusses a "Jewish state" in his Torah commentary he has one of two things in mind: (1) the state—operating according to the laws established by Moses received from the mouth of God—which Joshua was meant to establish; and (2) the state which will be established at the end of history, miraculously created by the hand of God.
65 See Rosenblit, "Galut Veerets Yisrael," 37–38.
66 See Horwitz, "Yaḥaso Shel Shimshon Rafael Hirsch," 455–456.

balanced reading of M. Breuer.[67] In my opinion, the future described by Hirsch is utopian, lying beyond history. Within history the Land and the temple are neutralized, replaced by the fatherland of Germany, replaced by the Torah, and replaced by the hearts and homes of halakhically observant Jews. Only beyond history will the sins of the Jewish people be fully expatiated allowing it to return to the Land of Israel, free of the sensual temptations posed by its goodness. Only beyond history will mankind achieve unity, proclaiming the oneness of God. In his essay "The Educational Value of Judaism" from 1873 (which was only published in his collected writings, in 1937 for unknown reasons), Hirsch expresses some unusual opinions about Torah and science which perhaps the editors wished to conceal. This essay contains an important passage about universalism and the mission of the Jewish people in the messianic future. Hirsch explicitly addresses the miraculous character of the End of Days—a time when the wolf will dwell with the lamb and peace and brotherhood will prevail worldwide—paraphrasing the words of the prophets in their literal meaning without interpreting them as allegory:

> The enlightenment of all the nations on earth was expressly named as the purpose of all the momentous events in the history of the Jewish people. [...] The gathering of all mankind around God was stated as the ultimate objective of the many sorrows that the Jewish people had to endure over the centuries of its history. [...]
>
> The Prophets of Judaism, which has been so unjustly maligned as exclusivist, were the ones who portrayed as the ultimate goal of the history of the Jews, as well as of the rest of mankind, a future era in which all the nations will go to Mount Zion in order to receive the Word of God. On that day, all men will learn to break up their swords and spears and no longer lift up the sword against each other; they will no longer practice the arts of war but will walk, together with the House of Jacob, in the light of the Lord (Isaiah 2:3–4). In that future world, righteousness sill gird the loins and faithfulness will gird the hips, the wolf will dwell together with the lamb and the leopard with the kid, evil and destruction will no longer be practiced, and the earth will be filled with the knowledge of God just as waters cover the bottom of the sea (Isaiah 11:5–9; Micah 4:1–4; Habakkuk 2:14). This will be a world in which God will pour out His spirit upon all flesh (Joel 3:1), the language of the nations will become

---

67 See Breuer, *Eda*, 79–81.

pure, and they all will call upon the Name of the one, sole God and serve Him dutifully as with one voice (Zephaniah 3:9).[68]

If Hirsch really had in mind an event taking place within history, in which the nation is forbidden to participate actively, and which occurs only when God wills it, the obvious question emerges: when and how will we know that this is God's will? Horwitz asks this question and provides no answer.[69] In my opinion, the decisions of divine providence, at least within Hirsch's preferred short path to redemption, will be accompanied by supernatural, miraculous activity, which we will certainly notice. He asserts this again in 1884, in the essay "Talmudic Judaism and Society." There, he states that the talmudic liturgy links the return of the Jewish people to its land to the redemption of mankind as a whole. In order to dispel the claim that Hirsch changed his views in his old age, and drew closer, if only slightly, to the *Hovevei Tsiyon* movement, it is worth looking at this essay in which he says the following:

> The Talmud incorporated into our daily prayers the assurance of our ultimate return to the land of our fathers and the restoration of the Temple in order that the Law of God may then be carried out in its entirety upon the soil of the Promised Land, which this Law has claimed as its own from time immemorial. This restoration will come hand in hand with the dawn of the Kingdom of God on earth, which will bring everlasting peace to the whole world, because at that time all mankind will recognize God and unite to worship Him by living a life of duty, justice and mercy.
>
> According to that same Talmud which proclaims this promise and those hopes as fundamental components of Jewish belief, any self-willed attempt on the part of its adherents to return to the Land would be an act of criminal rebellion against the Will of God; the Jews must leave the fulfillment of the Divine promise to the Will of God, Who alone can sound the call for their ingathering. Until that time, the Jews are expected to endure their exile patiently in the lands to which they have been scattered, to love those lands as their fatherlands, to promote the welfare of those countries, and to conduct themselves as loyal subjects to their fellow citizens, even as Jeremiah (29:1–7) bade them do when they were exiled to Babylonia. [. . .][70]

---

68   *Writings*, 7:267. See also Hirsch on Gen. 22:17, 49:1–2, 11, 26, 27; Deut. 17:14.
69   Horwitz, "Yaḥaso Shel Shimshon Rafael Hirsch," 453.
70   *Writings*, 7:224–225.

Two issues remain unclear, and Hirsch appears to have left them intentionally vague and ambiguous, situated as he was between *maskilic* universalism and the traditionalist fundamentalism of Scripture and the Sages. These issues are related to the substance and meaning of a nation living in its land in a messianic utopia, and which laws mankind as a whole will observe in that age.

As opposed to Rosenblit and Horwitz, Zeev Levi,[71] in his discussion of Hirsch's philosophy of the Land of Israel, argues that Hirsch severed any real connection between Judaism and the Land of Israel, and that Hirsch maintains that affinity to the Land is not nor ever was an essential part of Jewish religious belief. Levi identifies Hirsch's approach with the views of Geiger and Rosenzweig. Levi pulls Hirsch even farther to the left than Rosenblit and Horwitz, turning him, at least in terms of Zionism, into a nineteenth-century Reform Jew. I believe however that Hirsch was unable to estrange himself from canonical Jewish sources and therefore, to avoid duality, transferred the return to the land to an unreal messianic future—an eventuality which the Reform movement of the nineteenth century did not believe could or would transpire.

I believe that Hirsch would have been happy to abolish the need for a separate nation in its land, even beyond history (like the Reform), and would have liked to believe, as much as possible, that the entire Torah would be observed by all of mankind—in complete opposition to the Reform. However, the traditional Return to Zion, appearing already in Scripture, as well as the halakhic distinction between commandments given exclusively to the Jewish people and seven Noahide commandments given to other nations, prevented Hirsch from saying this explicitly, and required him as an Orthodox ideologue to conform to tradition.

Frequently he has difficulty adhering to these boundaries, implying that the entire Torah, or at least large parts of it, are the focus of the Jewish mission to mankind as a whole. Similarly, he does not succeed in providing substance and meaning to the Jewish life in its land in this supra-historical era, confining himself to pleasant, generic words on the matter.

According to the balanced reading, Hirsch's utopian future is indeed imbued with a spirit of universalist humanity, but is also completely infused with Torah Judaism entailing a Return to Zion.

---

71 Z. Levi, "Erets-Yisrael Bamaḥshava Hayehudit Begermania Mehirsch V'ad Rosenzweig," *Kivunim* 4 (Jerusalem 1979), 54–67.

The day will come when Jerusalem and Zion will rise again and nations will make pilgrimages to the mountain of God so they, too, may learn to know the ways of that Law and to walk in its paths.[72]

All the holy ones of Israel serve as Your instruments to this end. Not only Israel but all of mankind will benefit from the educational and moral influence of those among Israel who sanctify their lives through faithful fulfillment of the Torah. They tacitly serve as a light to all mankind, as models showing how man's sacred calling is to be put into practice. [...] Through Israel they will all band together and form a single group to do God's Will and to fulfill His command."[73]

In an essay on "Principles of Education,"[74] Hirsch notes that the nations today have already accepted the practical duties dictated by the will of God, and therefore the observance of commandments discussed here alludes to something more than the commandments of the Torah. In many places in Hirsch's writings, the word "Torah" is used within the context of the Jewish people's mission to mankind, and my view on the matter is based on this usage.

---

72 *Writings*, 2:303. This passage and others like it emphasize the difference between Hirsch and the Reform on the place of the Land of Israel in the Jewish religion. This is as opposed to the opinion Z. Levi.

73 Hirsch on Deut. 33:3. It is interesting to note that Luzzatto writes in a letter that he loved and admired the author of the *Nineteen Letters* because of his Jewish national pride, which he openly bears with honor, but he thought that his positions and opinions were too conservative and inappropriate to the spirit of the age, and therefore could not influence the thinking and actions of the generation. He read the *Nineteen Letters* and attacked the position of its author, which is also expressed in the source just cited, according to which the mission of mankind is to serve God according to the commandments of the Torah. "Since the explicit revelation is not a natural event, but entirely supernatural, it follows from this that obedience to it cannot be regarded as the natural fulfillment of man's mission; for this appears to be something irrefutable, that this perfection must be attainable without any external, supernatural condition. Furthermore, obedience to the explicit revelation cannot be considered as the universal mission of mankind, until a specific revelation (be it what it may) is known to all of mankind and becomes its full belief." See Luzzatto, *Epistolario italiano, francese, latino di S. D. Luzzatto, publicato da suoi figle* (Padova, 1890), 214–218, in a letter to Abraham Randegger of Trieste, 1837. Dita Campagnano translated this letter for me and I later found a Hebrew translation in Luzzatto, *Peraqim Bemishnato Shel Shadal*, trans. M. E. Artom (Jerusalem, 1968). Artom stresses in his introduction to the selected letters that, at the time he read them, Luzzatto apparently did not know the identity of the author of the *Nineteen Letters*, which was published under the pseudonym "Ben Uziel."

74 Hirsch, *Writings*, 7:226–227.

SUMMARY

In this chapter I have attempted to illustrate how many researchers and Rabbis interpreted Hirsch in the spirit of their own views, some drawing him to the left, others to the right. This, once again, demonstrates the fact that interpreters and scholars bring their own personal views into their readings and interpretations of texts, highlighting the need for awareness and self-criticism, with the understanding that some degree of biased interpretation is inevitable, and that interpretation is ultimately the brainchild of the interpreter. A careful reading of Hirsch's writings reinforces the balanced view that (1) his system of "Torah im Derekh Erets" was not a compromise *post-factum*, but the firm stance of one promoting a middle path between Haredism and Reform, deriving from a neo-fundamentalist ideology anchored in modernity and the Haskalah. To understand Hirsch's approach, one must distinguish between identicality, on the theoretical level, between pure revelation and pure reason, and the practical level of purifying and the attainment of reason and science and examining them according to the criterion of revelation. That being said, if an achievement of reason or science has been proven beyond a doubt and still contradicts revelation, the Torah should be reinterpreted in order to suit science. (2) His attitude towards an active return to the land of Israel within real history is far closer to the Haredi view inasmuch as it is not kabbalistic or mystical (with the exception of the universal elements and opposition to chosenness and uniqueness in Hirsch approach) and dissimilar to the messianic religious-Zionist stance, the national religious stance or the classic Reform stance. The next chapter will be dedicated to the philosophy of Samuel David Luzzatto with a focus on his approach of the "dual truth" and its repercussions on his philosophy of divine reward, retribution and providence.

CHAPTER THREE

"Heavenly Reward"—Samuel David Luzzatto's Doctrine of Divine Providence—between Revelation and Philosophy

INTRODUCTION

In 1936 Joseph Klausner published the second volume of his magnum opus *Historia Shel Hasifrut Haivrit Haḥadasha* (History of Modern Hebrew Literature). The fourth lecture in his book is dedicated to Samuel David Luzzatto, portraying him from a perspective of respect and admiration.[1] In this lecture, Klausner reveals the problematic duality he found in Luzzatto's writings.[2] On the one hand, Luzzatto praises philosophy, considers enlightenment and rational research important tools for uncovering the truth, and spurns *naïve* fanaticism, rejecting Kabbalah and mysticism as charlatanism. On the other hand, he often speaks like a Romantic, directing sharp criticism against Rationalist philosophies based on Maimonides, Ibn Ezra and Baruch Spinoza, and attacks Bible criticism and the Reform movement. According to Klausner, this duality can be traced to two factors—the one societal, the other hereditary, psychological, and personal. His age was one of transition, a time when rationalism and romanticism stood side by side. His father was an admirer of Kabbalah and mysticism, a spiritualist detached from reality, and his mother a

---

1   J. Klausner, *Hahistoria Shel Hasifrut Ha'ivrit Haḥadasha*, vol. 2 (Jerusalem, 1937), 2nd Amended Edition (Jerusalem, 1952), 40–121.
2   Ibid., 47–48, 74–75.

rational pragmatist with both feet planted solidly on the ground. Due to these influences, Luzzatto's "complex work is full of riddles," and his personality is one of "contradictions and oppositions, two faced: on the one hand a researcher on the other hand a believer, a rationalist in his scholarship and some of his views [...] a Romantic in his overall Jewish worldview."[3] This complexity, Klausner argues, created Luzzatto's genius character, one that is comprehensive, consistent, and all-encompassing.

Scholars after Klausner agree with his identification of a problem in Luzzatto's approach and personality, but dispute Klausner's explanation of the phenomenon as well as his positive but strange conclusions about Luzzatto's character. Noah Rosenbloom believes that Luzzatto's approach is inconsistent and compromising and considers him similar to his intellectual colleagues: selective, apologetic, and concessionary, willing to use any means available to attain his compromising goals.[4] Rivka Horowitz points to the variety of colors in Luzzatto's personality, and also identifies inconsistencies in his statements.[5] Shlomo Baron gently writes: "two opposing orientations ran about in the depths of his heart,"[6] and Peter Slymovics adopts a similar view adding that Luzzatto's personality is an unresolved paradox.[7] Shmuel Feiner maintains that Luzzatto is a right-wing radical, an "anti-*maskil*"[8] and Zeev Levi ascribes to him a split personality.[9] Recently Hanan Gafni writes that "his multi-faceted and self-contradictory character is a difficult riddle to crack, as is peculiar his ability to combine rational research, devoid of compromises, with his strong Romantic worldview and his tumultuous religious feelings."[10]

---

3 Ibid., 74–75.
4 N. Rosenbloom, *'Iyunei Sifrut Vehagut Mishilhei Hameah Ha Shmone-'Esre 'Ad Yameinu* (Jerusalem, 1989), 121, 160–163.
5 R. Horwitz, "Mendelssohn Veshadal Vehamodelim Shel Dat Bnei Noah, Vedat Avraham Behagutam" in *Avraham Avi Hamaaminim*, ed. M. Halamish et al. (Ramat Gan, 2002) 268–269.
6 S. Baron, "Shadal Vehamahapekha Bishnot 1848–1849," in *Sefer Asaf: Qovets Maamarei Meḥqar.*, ed. M. D. Cassutto et al. (Jerusalem, 1953), 40–63 (quotation from p. 42).
7 P. Slymovics, "Romantic and Jewish Orthodox Influence in the Political Philosophy of S. D. Luzzatto," *Italia* 4 (1985): 94–126.
8 S. Feiner, "Shadal Vehahaskalah Shekeneged," in *Italia: Shmuel David Luzzatto Matayim Shana Lehuladeto*, ed. R. Bonfil et al. (Jerusalem, 2004), 145–165.
9 Z. Levi, *Hermenoitika Bamaḥshavah Hayehudit Ba'et Haḥadasha* (Haifa-Jerusalem, 2006), 35.
10 Gafni,"*Peshuta shel Mishna*," 121. Can a Romantic really not conduct objective and rational research with any kind of intelligence? This is certainly surprising!

In this chapter I will attempt to solve this riddle and offer a new reading and understanding of Luzzatto's views without delving into the recesses of his personality, a task I leave to psychologists. As I understand it, over the course of his life, Luzzatto changed his views several times, in step with the maturation and deepening of his thought. That being said, in every stage of his life—from rationalist youth to neo-romantic maturity—Luzzatto maintained a clear, consistent and uncompromising stance. Without resorting to apologetics, he sought to contend with the contradiction between intellectualism and the belief in revelation, and his different statements stemmed from this challenge. At the end of this process, Luzzatto formulated a position reminiscent of the medieval "dual truth"—a characteristic, uncompromising middle stance.

I will begin by examining developments in Luzzatto's thought in the context of debates with his cousin Samuel Haim Loli (1788–1843) and against the backdrop of Jewish philosophy in the tumultuous nineteenth century, which offered different approaches to the relationship between revelation and reason, and the relationship between the statements of Holy Scripture and the implications of scientific discoveries. I intend to present the stages of Luzzatto's changing approach towards the apparent contradiction between philosophical determinism and the Torah's notion of free will and divine providence. With this analysis, I hope to strengthen my claims about Luzzatto's difficult statements, a problem which led scholars to speak about the "duality" manifest in his views and character.

Everything taken into consideration, I agree with Klausner's conclusion about Luzzatto's greatness but for completely different reasons, related to his bold and revolutionary character. In order to identify different periods and stages of development in Luzzatto's life, I have used all the sources at my disposal, both Luzzatto's writings and his letters,[11] most of which he dated meticulously. It appears that my scholarly predecessors contented themselves with reading one or a few of Luzzatto's sources and therefore reached different conclusions than mine.

Does divine providence really control the world? Does it control human history and a person's actions? Does man really have free will? Is God the source of evil? And how does the system of divine reward and punishment operate? These are the questions which preoccupy Luzzatto his entire life, as they preoccupied many of his Jewish and non-Jewish contemporaries and predecessors.

---

11 He deals with this issue in both his Italian and Hebrew writings and letters. For Italian letters see below notes 41, 42.

He is well acquainted with the views of the medieval Jewish philosophers on these issues—Judah Halevi, Maimonides, Gersonides, Hasdai Crescas and others. As a modern Jewish *maskil,* Luzzatto could not disregard the rational assessment that humans act according to their heredity and environment and that if there is divine justice in the world, it is not readily apparent. That being said, he also possesses a deep religious consciousness of God's divine providence over his creations and the Torah's divine origins—a text providing ethical education based on the principles of free will, divine providence, and divine reward and punishment. Luzzatto studied mostly Jewish and Christian literature which served as a backdrop for deep contemplation, participation in (sometimes heated) debates, and development of his views over the course of his life, until he settled on his final position. This final position maintains, like the medieval "dual truth"—or in modern terminology "the irresolvable dialectic"—that the true philosopher-believer must consciously and paradoxically encompass two contradictory truths, and live a life pervaded with fate and free will, with revelation and reason.

YOUNG PERIOD—A TRADITIONAL RELIGIOUS POSITION

Luzzatto's young views on reward and punishment were never distilled into a written essay, but we know them from letters to his cousin Loli and to the famous scholar from Gorizia, Isaac Samuel Reggio (1784–1855), and from a later exchange of letters with the editor of the annual *Otsar Neḥmad,* Ignaz (Isaac) Blumenfeld of Brody (1857–1864). From these sources we learn that Loli resided in Trieste from 1816 to 1819 during which he and Luzzatto spent many hours together engaged in extended debates over the issue of free will. At that time, Luzzatto was studying the book of Ecclesiastes which also deals with this subject. In 1819 Loli left Trieste but the two continued a written correspondence. In 1820 Luzzatto wrote his commentary on Ecclesiastes and in 1821 composed an introduction. As he never published anything until he had thoroughly confirmed its veracity, these both remained in his drawer for many years. In the end, both introduction and commentary were published years later, after Luzzatto had already changed his opinion about Ecclesiastes's author and views.

It was only in 1860, in *Otsar Neḥmad* 3, that Luzzatto published the introduction to his commentary on Ecclesiastes.[12] He sent the introduction to

---

12 Luzzatto, "Mikhtav Hesber Vehaqdama Leperush Qohelet," in *Otsar Neḥmad* 3 (Vienna, 1860), facsimile edition Jerusalem 1967, 17–25, and in *Meḥqerei Hayahadut* (Warsaw, 1913), vol. 2, pt. 1, 60–69.

Blumenfeld in 1857 attached with an explanatory letter.[13] The body of the commentary and its conclusion were published in *Otsar Neḥmad* in 1864.[14] Before the commentary, he added a long note (written in 1860), in which he discusses the circumstances of the commentary's composition, forty years prior.[15]

According to this account, Loli had adopted the view of Hasdai Crescas in *Or Hashem*—that man has no free will and all his actions are predetermined by God whereas Luzzatto endeavored to prove the existence of free will, based on Maimonides's position. In 1818 he even wrote three poems on the subject, calling them *Beit Habeḥira*, and dedicating them to Loli.[16] In these poems Luzzatto enumerates the praises of the doctrine of free will. It is sign of man's freedom, it emphasizes the superiority of the ethical person over the corrupt, and it impels man to act in hope of reward and fear of punishment.

In this note, Luzzatto admits that he ultimately failed to persuade his cousin. To the contrary, he was actually drawn closer to Loli's views eventually conceding that man's will is indeed subject to internal causes (man's spiritual and physical nature) and external causes (man's experience and the events of his time), all stretching back in a chain of causality to the first cause—God. But unlike his cousin, who believed that human evil should be attributed to God,

---

13 In his explanatory note Luzzatto writes to the editor why he thinks it appropriate to publish his commentary even though in the years since its writing he has completely changed his views on Ecclesiastes and has learned to recognize the book's virtues. He gives two reasons: firstly, the commentary which is revolutionary and at odds with tradition is proof that already in his youth he was a lover of free inquiry, and his attacks against rationalism do not stem from a pious fundamentalist worldview. Secondly, he considers it important to present the gradual intellectual developments of a scholar who has studied thoroughly from his youth until his older age, against the backdrop of the events that have befallen him. This, he believes, is true science. There are many scholars and sages who hide what they believed before they became famous, afraid to damage their reputation. See Otsar Neḥ.mad (ibid.) 15–16.

14 Luzzatto, "Perush Qohelet," *Otsar Neḥmad* 4 (Vienna, 1860), facsimile edition, Jerusalem, 1967, 17–25. In the version of the commentary published in Luzzatto, *Meḥqerei Hayahadut*, vol. 1, pt. 2, there is an attached explanatory letter (70–71) which Luzzatto sent the publisher in 1858 alongside the manuscript. In this letter he notes an additional reason for publishing the commentary apart for the reasons he gave in his letter in 1857 (see previous note); the book of Ecclesiastes and his commentary contain ethical guidance against egoism which is important for his intellectual battle against his nemesis Spinoza and his rationalist, Jewish followers. The ethics of Spinoza are antithetical to the true morality of Judaism which maintains that the true ethical norm is not "seeking our pleasure and wellbeing, or our honor and glory, but rather seeking good for others."

15 Luzzatto, *Qohelet*, 47–54; *Meḥqerei Hayahadut*, vol. 1, pt. 2, 114–122.

16 Luzzatto, *Kinor Na'im* (Warsaw, 1913), 130.

Luzzatto preferred Judah Halevi's view that distinguishes between the first cause which is God and the first intention which comes from man. Nevertheless, this view also had its problems in his opinion, because it turns God into the cause of evil and because it attributes weakness to God by claiming that human intention does not stem from him. Luzzatto therefore was aided by the views of Plato and Gersonides who believed in a primordial matter, pre-existing alongside God, and who maintained that it is this matter which is responsible for the existence of evil. In 1820 Luzzatto writes about this in a letter to Loli. At the beginning of the letter he reminds him how over the last four years he has contemplated a solution to the question of free will with the sincerity of a truth seeker. He admits that it was impossible for him to ignore the fact that every action has a necessary cause, and that man is not free to choose. A person is subject to his intellect and temperament, elements which lie beyond his control. That being said, he does not agree with the notion of absolute predestination and prefers Judah Halevi's view that while all actions are attributed to God in a causal chain, intentions still belong to a person not to God.[17] Reward and punishment are among the causes influencing a person's actions, and their goal is to draw him closer to justice and to dissuade him from corruption. As to why God created matter, the source of all evil, Luzzatto cites the views of Judah Halevi (*Kuzari*, 1:67), Maimonides (*Guide for the Perplexed*, part 2, 25), Ibn Ezra, and Gersonides who believe that this matter is primordial and not God's creation ex nihilo.

Luzzatto recounts that three days after writing this letter, he began to write his commentary on Ecclesiastes, in a storm of emotion and with youthful zealousness for God, to grapple with the book's view that everything, including evil, is decreed by God.[18]

As mentioned, as early as their debate in 1818 (when he was eighteen, and Loli was still in Trieste), Luzzatto began to study Ecclesiastes which deals with the problems of reward, punishment and free will. At first, he tried to harmonize the views of Ecclesiastes with the accepted, traditional Jewish belief in reward and punishment in the World to Come.

In that year, November 1818, Luzzatto writes to Reggio:

> And our friend Samuel David ben Haim Loli asks after you and after your household, with all his heart and soul. Yet it must be surely said

---

17 *Kuzari*, 5:2.
18 Luzzatto, *Meḥqerei Hayahadut*, vol. 1, pt. 2, 70 in the note, and on p. 118.

that he does not know whence you received the notion that he admits that one should doubt whether Rabbi Moses Mendelssohn believes in free will or not, and he insists that in his opinion that that great man denies this belief, which in my opinion and in the opinion of the great Sages is truly the foundation of the entire Torah; the entire world rests upon it, without it there is no judge and no justice, political association would be destroyed and the world would become formless and void. Anyone who denies it curses and blasphemes [God], more than one who denies the Blessed One's very existence. Who can deny that it is greater evil for a person to say: there is a creator, but he forces his creations to sin, afterwards dispatching his wrath against them, than a person who says: I do not know God at all? Did not the atheist Bayle[19] himself write: I prefer a person who says: I am not in this city to a person who says: I am in this city but my actions are evil and sinful. And if this matter is true (which in spite of myself it is) and Rabbi Moses Mendelsohhn denied free will, then this was an error on his part, because he was ensnared in Leibniz's net of dreams which led him to believe in the existence of monads, which that scholar invented, and he therefore also believed in the existence of *armonia prestabilita* (predetermined harmony); his faith in that scholar led him to believe in divine fate, and he was unwittingly guilty.[20]

It is impressive to see the deep and excited religiosity of the young Luzzatto, who accepts the biblical and classic rabbinic belief in a creator who granted man free will, expects him to behave properly, and judges him fairly according to his actions. These principles are anchored in biblical revelation and constitute its foundation. Luzzatto absolutely refuses to accept divine fate—that all is predestined and that man lacks free will—and he opposes this view more than atheism. Such a view sanctions corruption and its implication is complete societal chaos. According to Luzzatto, Mendelssohn was mistaken on this matter, trapped by the Leibnizian system of monads which entails a deterministic worldview. At that time, Luzzatto believed that the Torah and science reach identical conclusions, and although tensions between them exist, these can be

---

19 The French Christian philosopher Pierre Bayle (1647–1706).
20 Luzzatto, *Igrot Shadal*, vols. 1–9 (Przemyśl-Cracow, 1882–1898), 12–13. These letters are a treasure trove of information for every scholar studying the period.

resolved by disputing scientific speculations or by reinterpreting the Torah to harmonize it with science.²¹

---

21 Irene Kajon identifies among earlier European-Christian thinkers an approach similar to that of the young Luzzatto, examining the possibility that some of them may have influenced him. Kajon puts special emphasis on Luzzatto's statement in his autobiography that he spent a great deal of time reading the writings of Italian and French thinkers. She proves that there is a clear link between Luzzatto's methods of thinking in Torah Nidreshet (1818) and those of Catholic philosopher Francesco Soave in his "Institutions of Logic, metaphysics and ethics" (Istituzioni di logica, di metafisica e di etica) which was published in Vienna in 1791, and in a second edition in 1795. Soave, who was loyal to the truths and dogmas of Christianity but also to modern European scientific thinking, argued that modern science does not contradict the existence of God. To the contrary, it absolutely supports his existence and religion and science are identical. According to Kajon the identical conclusions reached by Luzzatto and Soave clearly attest to the Catholic philosopher's influence on the Jewish thinker. Kajon adds to the list of Luzzatto's influences Immanuel Kant and Johann Gottlieb Fichte, who conceived practical reason as the adjudicator of morality. See I. Kajon, "L'influenza di Franceso Soave sul concetto di ebraismo di Samuel David Luzzatto," in *Italia: Shmuel David Luzzatto Matayim Shana Lehuladeto*, 68–70.

Klausner already noted Soave's influence on Luzzatto in lessons he published on Romanticism and philosophy of the era and in his biography of Luzzatto. He claims that Luzzatto was influenced by the precursors of the Romantic movement, and by romantic and practical empiricist philosophers such as John Locke, Jean Jacque Rousseau, Charles-Louis Montesquieu, David Hume, Immanuel Kant, Johann Gottlieb Fichte, Étienne Bonnot de Condillac, Francesco Soave, and Alessandro Manzoni. Klausner notes that in his autobiography Luzzatto says that when he was young (1814–1818), he assiduously read the works of Christian philosophers such as Locke (using the translation of Soave or another philosopher), Condillac, Montesquieu and others, and they greatly influenced him. As to Soave, Klausner writes in a note that it appears that Luzzatto was heavily influenced by him and recommends researching this influence further. He mentions that Luzzatto recounts in his autobiography that in 1814 he purchased Soave's "Ethical Obligations" volume by volume as well as his "Institutions of logic, metaphysics and ethics" (the work examined by Kajon). See Klausner, Hasifrut Haivrit, 9–17 n. 36, 52–53, 75, 85–87. Similarly, Luzzatto writes in his autobiography that reading Soave's works filled him with admiration of their author, and that Locke's ideas and Condillac's system always had some sway over him. See Luzzatto, Pirqei H. ayim, ed. M. Schulvas (New York, 1951), 23. For a discussion of Rousseau's influence on Luzzatto see M. Artom in his introduction to his edition of Luzzatto's writings: Ketavim, vol. 1 (Jerusalem, 1976), 17. Luzzatto was influenced by the doctrine of Rousseau who was a precursor of Romanticism, specifically his preaching of religious tolerance (influenced in turn by Locke), his belief in man's good nature and natural compassion, and his recognition of natural religion and the importance of ethics. Rivka Horwitz notes that in his autobiography Luzzatto discusses his ideological leanings towards the thinkers of his era, John Locke, Condillac and others and like them he prefers positivist empiricism over philosophical metaphysics. See R. Horwitz, "Shadal Uspinoza" in Barukh Spinoza: 300 Shana Lemoto, ed. S. Fuchs (Haifa, 1978), 174–175. On the growing preoccupation with the conflict between the attainments of a developing science and the beliefs and doctrines of religion, a conflict which was amplified in

In a letter to his cousin Loli, a year later, on September 26, 1819, Luzzatto explains his interpretation of Ecclesiastes 7:14–15, as a solution to the problem of reward and punishment:

> On a good day be happy and joyful, and do not be apprehensive that misfortune may befall you, negating that good. For if you do this, all your days will be unfavorable. Likewise, on a bad day do not be overly apprehensive, but rather observe that misfortune will not last forever and in the future it will be replaced by good, or that you have already received your [portion in this] world. In any case your sorrow and anger will abate when you look at the good you have already received, or the good that is still to come, because "this opposite that God has created," good opposite bad, bad opposite good [...] know that this was the intention of Ecclesiastes [...] and this is true, because *portion for portion they shall eat [veheleq ke-heleq yokhelu]* [Deut. 18:8] and there is no reward for the observance of commandments in this world.[22]

In his poem *Ḥeleq Keḥeleq Yokhelu*, written in 1818, Luzzatto also discusses questions of theodicy. There he offers a similar solution to the one he proposed in his letter to Loli, and also discusses the issue of reward in the World to Come.[23] At the beginning of the poem, Luzzatto raises the famous question: "Why have you surely differed between one man and another? This one, why have you made him great? that one, why have you crushed him?" If one tries to argue that this is because one man is good and the other is evil then immediately the second part of the question emerges: "The souls of the righteous, pure of sin, why are they hurled in the hollow of the sling? And in silence sinners rejoice together, they live tranquilly in their homes, confident from fear." To the observer it appears that "there is no order to good, no law or order to bad, they arrive by happenstance. [...] Is it like a wheel turning around

---

> non-Jewish philosophy as well during the modern period, influencing Jewish thinkers, see Rotenstreich, *Hamaḥ shava Hayehudit*, 8, in the chapter about the sovereignty of morality, part of which is dedicated to Luzzatto. Rotenstreich argues that non-Jewish philosophy also tried to overcome this problem using the compartmental approach, and later in the chapter he explains how this position is reflected in Luzzatto's thought. See ibid., 32–34, and see below about the compartmental approach.

22 Luzzatto, *Igrot Shadal*, 47; idem, *Kinor Na'im*, 110, in the note there.
23 Ibid. The poem's name is based on Deut. 18:8. It says there that the Priests and Levites who serve in the Temple equally split the tithes and priestly gifts they receive from the nation, as they did not receive any property in the Land of Israel.

and around with no one driving it?—silence! silence! God forbid!" A young Luzzatto, conflicted between his faith and the conclusions of logic and empirical observation, explains God's methods of providence in the world according to Ecclesiastes. He asserts that no person in the world has an advantage over another. All people according to their status—rich or poor, farmer or king—receive equal portions of fortune and suffering, happiness and sorrow, pleasure and pain, laughter and tears. Nature, on every point on the surface of the globe, operates according to the same principle: over the course of a full year, time is equally divided between light and darkness, "and this is a fitting analogy to our situation in This World, in which light and darkness, good and bad (in my opinion) are present equally in every person, large and small."[24] Someone who does not realize this is only looking at the matter superficially. With youthful *naïveté* Luzzatto adds that wealth does not always bring happiness, which cannot be purchased with money. Someone accustomed to suffering who experiences one moment of happiness is equivalent to someone accustomed to years of good who is suddenly beset by a disaster. Every social class has its own troubles—wealth increases worries and enemies, and a pauper happy with his lot can be content. God bestows upon people qualities and talents compensating those who have lost certain abilities. Luzzatto concludes that there is "one law: a cup of poison and a handful of tranquility; we all will drink from both in the world below." This conclusion may seem surprising as it seems to suggest equality between the righteous and the wicked. Therefore, Luzzatto falls back on the classic Jewish response in Ecclesiastes, in his own words: "every action done, the Lord will bring in judgment, on the day that all dead will live once again." In other words, the reward of the righteous and punishment of the wicked will be in the World to Come. But in the current world "on a day of good fortune you will be joyful and happy, and on a day of misfortune you will reflect, thus said Koheleth, [...] for one opposite the other the Lord has made." At this stage Luzzatto had created a simplistic harmony between the observations of reason (that good and bad are balanced) and the statements of revelation (that the righteous man benefits), by consigning reward to the World to Come.

Only in 1820, after further deliberation, did Luzzatto move closer to Loli's view. He concluded that Ecclesiastes fully accepted the deterministic worldview and at this point began to write his commentary on Ecclesiastes. In the introduction to his commentary, he notes that the book was written by a man named Koheleth, who lived after the time of Ezra and who held opinions invalid

---

24　Ibid., 116 in the note. The poem itself can be found in ibid., 110–129.

and antithetical to Judaism. He argues that Koheleth wrote the book pseudopigraphically, hoping to gain endorsement by attributing it to King Solomon. The sages of his day erased Solomon's name from the book replacing it with the author's true name, to express their loathing of forgery and to mock the author by exposing his shamefulness. As time passed, people began to mistakenly attribute the work to Solomon, and commentators piled stacks upon stacks of exegesis and interpretation on the book. Later interpreters, who inclined towards the *peshat*, explained Ecclesiastes according to its simple meaning, concluding from it that all is predestined and that there is neither free will nor justice in the world. Luzzatto wishes to save Judaism and show that Koheleth is not Solomon and that his views are unacceptable to Judaism. At the end of his introduction he expresses his surprise at Mendelssohn's claim that the book is authentic, even after he had revealed its secret—the secret of predestination. He concludes that this was only because Mendelssohn was ensnared by the deterministic philosophy of Leibniz which is antithetical to logic and the Torah. In this interpretation, written in 1820, there is no allusion to his earlier attempt to interpret Ecclesiastes 7:14–15 in the spirit of tradition.

From 1821, the year he began writing his commentary, until 1857, when he sent it to Blumenfeld to be published in *Otsar Neḥmad*, Luzzatto's views on free will, divine providence, evil's origins, and divine reward and punishment developed and matured. In 1824, he, and his cousin Loli, each sent each other two letters on the subject of dreams. In 1856 Luzzatto sent the four letters to Blumenfeld for publication, and they were published that same year in *Otsar Neḥmad* 1. At the time of their writing in 1824, Luzzatto believed that dreams, happy and sad, are spiritual beings sent at God's behest like divine angels. Fortune and misfortune befall a person, portion for portion, through these agents. In an attached letter to Blumenfeld, he stresses that he has since changed his view on certain issues, including the subject of dreams, but he believes that *maskilic* readers, lovers of the Hebrew language, will nevertheless enjoy and be gladdened by these letters. He writes in his second letter:

> Therefore, those responsible for these accurate dreams must be other, spiritual beings. But who are they and what is their nature? Harken and listen. My friend, you already know how much I believe in individual providence over each and every person, and each and every incident and misfortune; nothing is hidden from God's providence. You also know, my friend, the tremendous faith I have in the matter of good and evil, and my belief that they are all balanced, each and every person opposite the other,

each and every person's number of days half fortune and half misfortune; nothing is missing, and there is no slack on the rope, for it is certainly weighed as silver upon scales [...] However, as it is well known, the kingdom of heaven is like the kingdom of earth, and therefore I will not believe that the Creator, blessed is he, would personally observe the affairs of each and every man and every small movement he makes. Rather I believe that his individual providence is executed by his servants, who perform his will. The exalted king appoints attendants to watch over a man's steps, from the day of his birth until the day of his death, so that his fortune and misfortune will be precisely equal. I believe that each and every person is watched from the day of his birth until the day of his death by two angels whom God has appointed, one for fortune and one for misfortune, a good angel-good fortune, and a bad angel-bad fortune, their power is equal, and by their hands a person lives a life intermingled with exactly half pleasure and half pain [...] they are the masters of terrifying dreams, causing a person sorrow, and they are the masters of accurate dreams, which rescue him from misfortunes, or which consecrate him with good and with a greater or lesser measure of rejoicing; they also perform acts of magic and the like.[25]

These letters show the immaturity of Luzzatto's thought at the time of their writing. Nevertheless, even then it was clear to him that God is the source of evil, misfortune being conveyed to a person through divine agents, the angels of misfortune. He clung to the doctrine of divine providence over individuals and that people receive equal portions of pleasure and pain, a principle he would never abandon.

In addition to Ecclesiastes, Luzzatto also studied the book of Job. In 1831 he wrote a letter to Issachar Blumenfeld of Brody criticizing the latter's commentary on Job which he had received from him as a gift. In his commentary, Blumenfeld brings evidence to prove that Job should be dated to only after the Babylonian exile and the return to Zion. One of his arguments is that accounts of Satan and the Kingdom of Heaven were unknown in Israel and were imported during the Jewish return from exile. Luzzatto argues that already

---

25 *Otsar Neḥmad* (Vienna, 1856), 91–93. On Luzzatto's change in views see ibid., 78. In his letter to the editor Isaac Blumenfeld from 1857, Luzzatto mentions his letter from the previous year which he attached to his letters on dreams, that "I was twenty four when I wrote them, and I did not publish them to teach mysteries of wisdom but to teach the children of Judah writing and eloquence," because "not everything I wrote and believed when I was young is still true in my eyes today."

Micah (in his prophecy in the days of Jehoshaphat, recorded in Kings I, 22:19) describes the kingdom of heaven, as well as Isaiah and even Moses who speaks of a God who came "with myriads of holy ones" (Deut. 33:2). The Satan featuring in the books of Zacharias, Daniel and Job is not Babylonian. The Babylonians were dualists, believing in a god of good and a god of evil, whereas the Satan, described in the Later Prophets and the Writings, is a servant of the one God, executing his will. In other words, Luzzatto had already abandoned his earlier belief in a primordial matter, preexisting alongside God, and constituting the source of evil. He argues further that Satan's appearance in the account supports his view that the statements made by the book's protagonists attest to its non-Jewish author:

> The god of Job is not the God of Israel, for the God of Israel is a compassionate and merciful God, repaying his creations according to their handiwork. He is a God of faith, never false; righteous and upright is he, treating his creatures like a merciful father. But the god of Job is a tyrannical king; when he hears the complaints of the oppressed righteous, how does he respond?—"Be silent, put a hand to your mouth, be shamed before me; look at my might and your weakness, do you have an arm like a god, and can you thunder with a voice like his?" No sir, this is not a portrayal of the God of Israel; this is not the heritage of Jacob, neither before Exile, nor after it. [...] All of this, in my view, clearly indicates that Job's author never saw the light of the true Torah.[26]

MATURE PERIOD

The Compartmental Approach

In 1828 Luzzatto was appointed head of the rabbinical seminary in Padua and in 1832 prepared lessons for his students on Judaism. These were written for educational and instructional purposes for young men preparing themselves

---

26 *Kerem Ḥemed*, vol. 2, ed. S. L. Goldenberg (Prague, 1836), 119. It was reprinted in Luzzatto, *Meḥqerei Hayahadut*, vol. 1, pt. 2, 52–53. See S. Vargon, "She'elat Zeman ḥibburo shel Sefer Iyov KeḤeleq Metfisat Olamo shel Shadal," *Meḥqerei Morashtenu*, vol. 1, 1999, 7–27. In an addendum to his article, Vargon persuasively argues that Luzzatto's insistence on the early dating of Job was due to his fear of the spreading heresy which post-dated the Torah and denied its divinity, and the assimilation which would develop as a result.

for the rabbinate, and it is reasonable to assume that Luzzatto did not reveal the full extent of his philosophical views through this medium. In these lessons, in a discussion of the Jewish morality of the Torah, he includes the subject of reward and punishment. Although natural law is positive and derives from a person's inner emotions (mercy, justice, sociality, and respect), the morality of the Torah is still superior. This is due first and foremost to the difficulty in enforcing natural morality, which is liable to be brushed aside by a person's sensual desires, and which contains no efficient system of sanctions. The sanctions of nature are not apparent, especially to those who ignore them, and natural morality includes no preparatory guidance. However, the morality of revelation explicitly opposes outbursts of human desire:

> Second, it [the law of revelation] gives the law of nature the most effective sanction because reward and punishment heralded by God, cannot, due to his omnipotence, be without effect; nor can the faithful servant of his laws be afraid that he will be ignored, nor the sinner seduce himself into thinking that he will go undetected, due to divine omniscience. Finally, the divine law can and does in fact contain the necessary Propedeutica [preliminary instruction].[27]

Luzzatto uses these lessons in his essay *Yesodei Hatora*, which he began to write in 1838, and published in 1842. His ethical philosophy (which he gave the title *Raḥem Ugemul Shamayim* in his poem *Derekh Erets* from 1840) [28] is more thoroughly developed at this stage. In this article, Luzzatto compares and contrasts all systems of morality to Judaism, concluding that the morality of the Torah is preferable to them all. This is because the morality of the Torah is based on man's natural emotion of compassion, and even works to instill and cultivate this emotion within a person through the guidance of the commandments.

However,

> the power [of compassion] is not enough to give a person dominion over his spirit, to completely overpower his want and desires; therefore look, the Blessed Giver of the Torah saw fitting to add an additional element to the improvement of morals and this is the hope for reward and the fear

---

27 Luzzatto, "Shiurin Beteologia Yehudit Musarit," in *Ketavim*, vol. 1, 113 (first appeared in Italian in Padua 1862 under the title *Lezioni di Teologia Morale Israelitica*).
28 Luzzatto, *Kinor Na'im*, 290.

of punishment; this is because reward and punishment, related as they are to a person's essence and flesh, leave a deep imprint upon his heart, sometimes even stronger than the mark left by his want and desires, preventing him from satisfying his want and desire, out of fear of punishment and hope for reward. The reward and punishment, which he established as the basis of moral improvement, are not from the hand of man, who sees only what is visible, and several matters are hidden from his eyes; it is from the hand of God, who sees into the heart and nothing is concealed from him. [29]

These pedagogical-religious essays do not raise the philosophical questions of Luzzatto's youth, although he did contend with them at that time. The impression created is that a distinction between the truth of philosophy and the morality of revelation had developed and matured in Luzzatto's mind, but was yet to be expressed explicitly. This distinction is reflected in a letter Luzzatto sent on November 8, 1837 to David Morpurgo to Trieste, responding to the latter's questions. In response to a question on prayer (the seventh question), he writes that God is not subject to the influence of emotions, and that ritual activity, including prayer, are for a person's own benefit. But this truth is not beneficial and even causes harm; therefore, religion does not specifically teach it, leaving humans to believe the opposite. Answering a question about reward and punishment (the eleventh question), he writes that knowledge of the truth that there is no divine reward and punishment is not beneficial and even causes harm. Therefore, religion instills the opposite notion.[30] Later in his life, Luzzatto would clarify and sharpen these distinctions.

In 1838, Luzzatto had already begun to express strong opposition to speculative and egoistic rationalism, replacing it with the Jewish morality of compassion embodied in the commandments of the Torah. In that year he added a passage to his poem *Ḥeleq Keḥeleq Yokhelu*. He realized that the principle of "portion for portion" was liable to pose a moral obstacle, dissuading a person from showing compassion to the weak, a consequence of the belief that every person is meted their fair lot regardless. Luzzatto warns his readers about this evil thought, and cautions them to avoid being shrewd and wicked. God instilled within us the quality of compassion so that we would have mercy

---

29 Luzzatto, *Meḥqerei Hayahadut*, vol. 1, pt. 2, 21; Luzzatto, *Al Haḥemla Vehahashgakha*. Bassi Edition (Tel Aviv, 2008), 53.
30 Luzzatto, *Peraqim Bemishnato Shel Shadal*, trans. M. Artom (Jerusalem, 1968), 13–15. The source is letter 154 in Luzzatto, *Epistolario*.

on those suffering, giving them aid as God's messengers. We were not given reason and science to be clever, to act with guile, or to present philosophical explanations to justify our stubbornness. These gifts are meant to teach us the superiority of kindness and peace over hatred and war.[31]

In a letter written in 1840 to the historian Isaac Mordechai Jost (1793–1860), Luzzatto for the first time discusses explicitly his bold distinction between philosophy and revelation, a distinction he wished to keep secret from the public. He concludes that the two are completely separate realms.[32] Philosophy concerned with rational truth, recognizes an eternal world ruled by necessity. The Torah, concerned with morality and good education, teaches about a created world and preaches the principle of reward and punishment, even if these theological principles are not based on absolute truth. Therefore, at least from a philosophical point of view, Luzzatto inclined towards the impossibility of free will, human actions being determined by heredity and environment. That being said, he favored, as empirical-ethical practice, the need to instill a belief in reward for the righteous and punishment for the wicked, as well as a belief in human endeavor as the key to success, even if a person always remains with a sum total of equal parts pleasure and misfortune. He writes as much to Jost:

> Here it is hinted that the entire foundation of my thinking is *that religion is not desirable to God because of its truth but because of its usefulness to improve morality, and therefore there is no need for everything to be true,* and despite all this we should not distance his divinity, *and we should not distance God for saying untrue things,* because it is impossible to tell the power of the creation to flesh and blood, and the maintenance of society

---

31 Luzzatto, *Kinor Na'im*, 126–127.
32 The different approaches to the relationship between the statements of revelation and the statements of reason are presented here according to the model proposed by Shalom Rosenberg, *Torah Umada*, 23–45. Rosenberg distinguishes between two approaches which claim identicality between Torah and science: the first restricts scientific statements; the second reinterprets the Torah to make it suit the scientific statements. Besides these two positions he also discusses the compartmental approach and the dialectical approach. Rosenberg places Luzzatto in the category of the compartmental approach. I however put Luzzatto's later position, that is the "dual truth," in the category of the dialectic approach, in which one must distinguish between a resolvable dialectic and an irresolvable dialectic—the latter the view of Luzzatto. See also Chamiel, *The Middle Way*, vol. 1, 351–357. On the development of Luzzatto's view from an interpretive identicality approach (Maimonides's position) to a compartmental approach, and from there to the "dual truth" approach, see ibid., 447–492.

and man's success is impossible with knowledge of the truth, but [only] with illusion. [...] And greater than that, it is clear that society could not exist without reward and punishment and without belief in the superiority of some things and the condemnation of others, *and indeed in truth all of our actions are only the results of outer and inner causes*, and justice and evil are truth with respect to the action (whether it is beneficial or damaging) but not with respect to the character of the actor. And more than this, is it possible for a person to be a person and not endeavor to attain success? Despite all this, in my estimation, this is vanity, too, because in whatever situation a person may be, it will always be half joy and half a plague, and in my youth, for twenty-three years I gathered together a collection and called it *Ḥeleq Keḥeleq Yokhelu* ["portion for portion shall they eat"](Deut. 18:8) [...] *All of these things I spoke in a whisper to your ear*.[33]

In 1846 Luzzatto retracted his position that Job's author was not Jewish. He writes as much in an addition to his essay *Imqei Safa* dedicated to Hebrew synonyms, a field he researched primarily in his youth. This essay was edited and published in *Beit Haotsar, Lishka B*, in 1888 by his sons. Luzzatto writes that he considers his previous statements about Job's author to be greatly in error. He had ignored the story's conclusion where Job's end is described as surpassing his beginning. That is to say, the author's goal was not only to humble Job with words about God's might:

> but to show that there is no injustice or evil-doing in the world, and that even if a righteous man is oppressed with all manners of torment, nothing can stop God from removing them and rescuing him from his troubles, bestowing more good upon him in his end than in his beginning, and to gladden him [with pleasure] equivalent to his days of affliction. Therefore, whatever the beliefs of Job and his companions (for they were not of the Children of Israel) there is no doubt that the author of the book of Job was of our nation and a believer in our God, a faithful God, never false, righteous and upright is He, [...] one of the early, great sages of Israel wrote this book in the Holy Tongue [...] to teach the nation that God tries the righteous, sometimes with misfortune and troubles, but will never abandon or forsake them, and will once again have mercy upon them, transforming curse into blessing.

---

33 Luzzatto, *Igrot Shadal*, 661.

> Therefore, a person should seize hold of his righteousness and never let go, for his employer is trustworthy to pay the reward of his labor.[34]

Here Luzzatto focuses on the religious realm of Torah, disregarding the philosophical side of the issue. He portrays Job's author as a romantic believer, disappointed by reason and intellect. Luzzatto returns with him to the warm embrace of tradition, to the belief that the suffering of the righteous should at times be seen as a divine trial, and that one who maintains his righteousness will receive his reward already in this world.

In that same year, Luzzatto made a second addition to his poem *Ḥeleq Keḥeleq Yokhelu*. In this romantic addition, he emphasizes that it is an illusion to think that salvation can be attained by relying on reason. Fortune and misfortune are measured out, and therefore new misfortunes are inevitable. A person's only hope is that ethical behavior (kindness, generosity, and charity) is in human hands and that a person is subject to free will and not to divine decree; "all is in the hands of heaven except for the fear of heaven." But Luzzatto does not ignore the philosophical aspect of this issue, distinct from its ethical aspect, and maintains that these are two separate realms—reason and revelation, philosophy and religion, truth and ethical good, intellect and emotion—and they are not to be harmonized. He writes to Shneur Sachs in 1842:

> Philosophy and poetry are rivals, and if we remove the spirit of hatred and jealously from the ground of poetry, "who can stand before its cold?" [Ps. 147:17] [. . .] Maimonides and his friends, who wanted to bring philosophy into the estate of religion, neither knew nor understood that the god of philosophy has no relation or connection to man, and all worship and all prayer to a god who does not respond and does not change is useless and vain—and everything that is in the world (both natural events and the action of people by choice) all is linked back by its causes to the first cause, and the first cause does not change, and the structure of events will not change because of our worship and our prayer. *But the truth is that which guides philosophy is truth, and that which guides religion is the good and the just.* Man is not only reason, for he is also *poesia*, and *poesia* is most of man, it is his life and his soul. Religion was given to man to guide the *poesia* that is in him along with the good and the just;

---

34 Luzzatto, *Beit Haotsar Lishka* B (Przemyśl, 1848), 28–29; Luzzatto, *Meḥqerei Hayahadut*, vol. 1, pt. 2, 53 in editor's note.

"Heavenly Reward" • CHAPTER THREE | 91

and if philosophy comes and guides religion, both religion and *poesia* will be cut off and perish. *And this is sufficient for now, because the matters are lengthy.*[35]

Luzzatto uses this principle to interpret scriptural verses that seem to contradict scientific truth. For example, he explains that the biblical injunction to ostracize an impure leper does not stem from a fear of infection but rather:

> It appears to me that the change in skin color was in the minds of our ancestors a sign of God's wrath, and they believed that the leper was stricken by God as punishment for some terrible sin he had committed. Therefore, they would separate from him as if he was a person castigated by God [...] and because all of this reinforced the belief in divine providence and the belief in reward and punishment, the Torah upheld this belief and commanded that the leper be ostracized.[36]

In other words, the notion of leprosy as a divine sign attesting to one's sinfulness is apparently not true. Nevertheless, the Torah adopted this belief in order to educate us to be ethical and good and to instill within us the belief in divine reward and punishment.

In his full commentary to the Pentateuch, Luzzatto writes in the same vein. He comments on the verse "visiting the guilt of the parents upon the children" (Ex. 20:5) that now in 1845 he has retracted the question he posed in 1834 in *Hamishtadel* against Gersonides. Now he agrees with him:

> For this is the manner of the Torah, to portray fortune and misfortune as purposefully descending from above as reward and punishment even though they proceed and occur naturally according to the world's natural course; [...] and just as the Torah threatens the Children of Israel saying that God is vengeful, jealous and full of wrath, so too it says that he visits the guilt of the parents upon children as if he does this out of vengeance and rage, even though in truth this only occurs naturally and not, God forbid, as vengeance; rather everything is for the benefit of mankind.[37]

---

35 Luzzatto, *Igrot Shadal*, 779–780.
36 Luzzatto, *Hamishtadel* (Vienna, 1847), Lev. 12:2.
37 Luzzatto, Ex. 20:5. Compare to Luzzatto, *Hamishtadel*, on the same verse. This shift in views is also significant in relation to Luzzatto's statements in his work *Yesodei Hatorah*, from 1845 where he argues that the Torah has two purposes: the improvement of morals

The contrast between Luzzatto's interpretation in 1836 and his interpretation in 1845, demonstrates his transition from *naïve* religiosity to a more daring approach, which contends with the tensions between the Torah and philosophy.

Luzzatto uses the same idea to explain the Torah's emphasis on the uniqueness of the people of Israel and its closeness to God, ideas which are not purely true as all humans are equally children of God. The plan of the Torah's providence is to tell the nation of Israel that it is God's unique nation. This is to draw it closer to God and to guarantee that it remain loyal to him and continue to bear the yoke of the Torah. This is for the sake of the nations of the world who are destined to have equal status to the Israelite people. The nation of Israel precedes the nations in their unification of God and their superior ethical qualities only in terms of time but not in terms of essence. Luzzatto is aware how bold this idea is and therefore adds: "it is unbefitting to explain this matter to an ignoramus."[38]

---

and preservation of the religion. These goals are achieved through the three foundations of the Pentateuch: reinforcing the natural moral of compassion; inculcating a belief in reward and punishment; belief in the uniqueness of the Jewish people. Already in *Yesodei Hatorah*, Luzzatto restricted the foundation of uniqueness, stating that this uniqueness is not one of essence but only represents precedence in time. In *Hamishtadel* he adds that the uniqueness is not true and is a divine tactic for achieving certain goals (see the next note). As for the foundation of reward and punishment Luzzatto states in his Torah commentary, cited here, that it is not literally true and reflects God's establishment of the laws of nature (like Maimonides *Guide for the Perplexed*, part 2, 48; part 3, 17—see Chamiel, *The Middle Way*, vol. 1, 490, n. 197) and God's commandments in the Torah are only an educational means of attaining the goals. This new approach of Luzzatto is reminiscent of Maimonides (*Guide for the Perplexed*, part 3, 28) who divided the commandments into true and necessary, in order to explain commandments that do not accord with science and philosophy. The true commandments, such as the unification of God and belief in his preexistence are few, and are meant to lead a person to higher intellectual perfection. The necessary commandments however, such as belief in Divine Providence and reward and punishment, are numerous and are meant to educate the nation and improve society, and are not always purely true. That being said, Maimonides's view stems from a philosophical stance that maintains that the Torah contains an esoteric philosophy for the benefit of an intellectual elite, not to be revealed to the simple masses lest they become heretics, whereas Luzzatto's view derives from a romantic position that the Torah contains no philosophy and no secrets, and is meant for all people, its goal to educate people to perform good, which is their life's purpose. See M. Halberal, *Harambam* (Jerusalem, 2009), 239–241, 291–293. Luzzatto does not hint to a link between his view and that of Maimonides; on this see below, Chapter Six.

38 See Luzzatto, *Hamishtadel*, Ex. 20:3. This source as well as others demonstrate that Luzzatto rejects Judah Halevi's notion of Jewish chosenness, unlike the interpretations of S. Rostovsky-Halprin, *Shadal Vehitnagduto Larambam* (Tel Aviv, 1954), 20; Rosenberg, *Be'iqvot Hakuzari*, 63; idem, "Lev Usegula," 109–119. See Chamiel, *The Middle Way*, vol. 2, 78–81, n. 113, and 423–426. Luzzatto interprets along similar lines the prohibition of conducting a census directly and without good cause out of concern for the evil eye. This idea

The "Dual Truth" Approach

In 1846 Luzzatto revealed for the first time that, due to his lack of success in bridging the gap between philosophy and God's Torah, he was considering the "dual truth" approach. On the one hand, he concluded that both the identicality approach and the compartmental approach are delusional, and they ignore the contradiction between Torah and science. On the other hand, loyal to a divine Written Torah, he had difficulty accepting that revelation contained no truth, and as a *maskil* had difficulty accepting that true philosophy does not lead to the good. According to this approach, these two realms are not separate—one concerned with truth the other with good, standing alongside each other with no contradiction—but two realms, philosophy and revelation, contradicting each other but both true. According to philosophy, all things progress from a first cause—God. According to revelation, man possesses free will and is subject to reward and punishment. We are required to live with these two truths, which cannot be reconciled logically in our world, and can only be resolved in the infinite realm of God. To use modern Hegelian terminology, Luzzatto's system has a thesis and an antithesis. Each one represents a complete truth contradicting the other. However, one cannot create a synthesis out of these two truths, and their relationship is one of irresolvable dialectic.

In in his first commentary on the Pentateuch (published originally as an appendix to Mendelssohn's *Biur*, printed in 1846 in Vienna, and afterwards in 1847 as a separate work entitled *Hamishtadel*) Luzzatto writes on Deut. 6:5:

> However, these two things are *opposites and contraries*, because if a person knows the perfection of God, which has no end, and if he believes in His

---

is mistaken, but because it is difficult to uproot and because it assists in instilling the belief in God and his providence, and dissuades a person from relying on his own strength and wealth, the Torah adopted it. See Luzzatto on Ex. 30:11. He also uses this method to explain animal sacrifice (Lev. 1:2) not as a genuine, intrinsic need but rather a harnessing of the masses' belief in their importance in order to educate them to obey the norms of God greater than them all, and thus to guarantee for the future of mankind as a whole the persistence of the great ideas of Judaism—the unity of God and the unity of mankind. Here also his view is similar to that of Maimonides even though he gives no indication of this fact. According to Maimonides also, the commandments of the sacrifices belong to the second order, that is they are not "real" but are required for a pedagogical purpose—abolishing idolatry. Verses in Genesis which do not correspond to the science and theology of our day such as "let there be a firmament in the middle of the waters" (1:6) or "the two greater lights" (1:16) "a sweet scent" (8:21) Luzzatto explains in his commentary as corresponding to the widely-held worldview and cosmology of ancient cultures at the time these words were written, and corresponding to what man sees before of him.

absolute unity as explained by the philosophers, then he will fall in one of these two: if he thinks that He is exalted and raised up too high to supervise individuals, or he will think that everything that is in the world is nothing but His decree, blessed be He; and one way or another it is not possible that he will still think to himself to do what will be pleasing in the eyes of God, because he will think that everything is good in His eyes equally. Thus, I am greatly astonished by the philosophers; how could they not have understood that what the Torah's intention is not that of philosophy, *since philosophy is knowledge and perception of truth, and the Torah is the doing of what is good and just*; and if the Torah teaches us the unity of God and that the world is a new creation, it is not in order to endow us with knowledge of God and perception of His perfection as it is in their saying, but everything is to plant useful faith in our souls to guide us in the paths of righteousness and justice. Therefore, the Torah and the prophets always diminish the image of God and bring Him to the level of man, and they attribute anger and will to Him, love and hatred, joy and sadness, and other emotions and lacks, and this is all done to depict a relation and connection between Him and us; and if on the contrary we picture to ourselves the god of the philosophers, who is perfect in endless perfection, then it is no longer possible to depict any relation or connection between him and human beings, and no religion will be possible in the world anymore. And what is the place of prayer, if God is unmoved? And what is the place of repentance, if God is unchanging?—and perhaps a man might say: if as you state that *the Torah and philosophy oppose each other*, then one of them is a lie, so you are contemptuous of wisdom or repudiate the Torah—know that it is neither one nor the other, but I see man composed of *two opposite forces*, thinking and inner emotions (see the introduction to *Beit Haotsar*), and it is impossible to increase one of these forces and cancel the other, because man is necessarily subject to both of them, therefore the *(true)* Torah and *(true)* philosophy, which is not yet written in a book by itself, but it is scattered in a ten thousand books, always mingled with errors and failures, both are the words of the living God, because both of them agree with human nature, *and both of them are the truth alternatively*. This is not the place to go into this at length.[39]

---

39 See note 43 and 44 below. On the "dual truth" approach, see J. Ross, *Mavo Lesefer Beḥinat Hadat Le-rabbi Elijah Delmedigo* (Tel Aviv, 1987), 49–53. In his introduction to Elijah Delmedigo's work, Ross introduces the "dual truth" approach, defining it, and using it to explain the author's statements. On pp. 49–50 he indicates its source in the Christian

"Heavenly Reward" • CHAPTER THREE | 95

At this stage Luzzatto uses both the compartmental approach as well as the "dual truth" approach, without sensing that the two are mutually exclusive.

One could read my proof texts more moderately, understanding Luzzatto's two realms as two viewpoints of the same truth, and not a shift on his part from the compartmental approach. However, if we delve deeper we can begin to identify a sort of medieval "dual truth," or to use modern Hegelian terminology—an irresolvable dialectic. This reading is supported by Luzzatto's use of expressions such as "opposites and contraries," "two opposite forces," "both are the truth alternatively" as well as "both are true" in the excerpt below (from the period of his old age).

In 1848, still excited by the Spring of Nations' potential for the Jews, and free from all censorship, Luzzatto wrote his essay "The Essence of Judaism" and published it in the journal *Il Giudaismo Illustrato* (Judaism Illustrated) which he published in Italian in Padua. In this essay Luzzatto summarizes his current philosophical system for a broader readership. He states there, that Judaism has two faces, a practical aspect and an intellectual one. The basic principle of the intellectual aspect is providence, and of the practical—compassion. Discussing providence, Luzzatto explains, that this principle has two viewpoints. From a *religious perspective*, providence is understood traditionally: fortune and misfortune befall a person not by happenstance but as a result of divine justice, meted out to man according to his actions. He brings as an example Abraham, who spoke of "the judge of the world" (Gen. 18:25), and Job, whose prosperity is ultimately restored by God. All of Holy Scripture, both its legal and narrative elements, is infused with this principle. Only the Jewish philosophers of the Middle Ages (by which Luzzatto means Maimonides) tried to undermine this principle, arguing that providence is applied generally not to the individual, and that an individual merits providence only by excelling in metaphysical studies. In Luzzatto's opinion, this attempt had failed by the beginning of the sixteenth century, and ever since, the dominant opinion in Judaism is that divine providence is all-encompassing. From another point of view, *the philosophical perspective*, one

---

Averroists (followers of the Muslim philosopher ibn Rushd, known in the West as Averroes), and notes that Padua was one of the places where this philosophy was current. On pp. 50–51 he quotes Delmedigo, and on p. 53 he presents the position of "the disappointed rationalist," which, in his opinion was that of Delmedigo, and a position that he calls "complementarist," which in my opinion, is also Luzzatto's position. See also Rosenberg, *Torah Umada*, 36. On the semantic difference between J. Gutman and H. Wolfson regarding the term "dual truth" see Chamiel, *The Middle Way*, vol. 1, 354 n. 14.

must assume another form of providence. The majority of history unfolds according to established natural laws, formulated by God when he created the world. All natural and historical phenomena and man's actions whether good or bad, are therefore necessary results of these laws:

> If we wish to speak in philosophical terms we could on the other hand, conceive the actions of providence as necessary results of natural laws, established by God during the creation of the world, similar to other laws which guide the physical and ethical world; for if we agree that God foresees the future, there is nothing to prevent the belief that there is some kind of pre-established harmony between our behavior and our fates.[40]

Nevertheless, Luzzatto believes that a small number of events and phenomena are the result of miraculous or super-natural providence and not natural providence. This explains revelation and the miracles of Scripture, and it is revelation which is the source of the covenant with Abraham and the commandments in the Pentateuch.

Luzzatto emphasizes that although the world follows a natural course, biblical language draws no distinction between different forms of providence; everything there is miraculous, and providence operates there upon all nations. Indeed Scripture includes accounts of revelations, miracles, and prophetic dreams for the other nations as well. For reasons known only to him, Luzzatto does not reveal that he is basically close to Maimonides's approach from the *Guide for the Perplexed* and in a note says that Maimonides's position is that even biblical miracles were established at creation. In the next paragraph, Luzzatto proceeds to vigorously attack Maimonides views.[41] Likewise, Luzzatto does not reveal—it seems intentionally—the paradoxical nature of the "dual truth" and with unsuccessful mental gymnastics attempts to bridge the gap between its contradictory worldviews.

Luzzatto articulates a stronger conception of the "dual truth"—maintaining the existence of necessary causality alongside divine providence and free will,

---

40 Luzzatto, "Mahut Hayahadut," in *Ketavim*, vol. 1, 50 and in *Al Haḥemla*, 93–94.
41 Luzzatto detests the philosophical, rationalist and speculative views of Maimonides, arguing that they derive from Aristotelian-Muslim sources foreign to Judaism. Based on his statements in a letter to Giuseppe Besso (see note 43 [see next citation]) it is possible that he did not understand Maimonides's view on this issue.

without resolving the inherent contradiction—in a letter to Giuseppe Besso, written in 1857 in Italian:

> True freedom does not exclude obedience to arguments and logic, but demands it. So if free will follows arguments and traces the internal and external causes operating on human will (without which there is only madness), a perfect knowledge of all of these causes (which can only be found in God) predicts a person's choices without limiting, even slightly, this freedom. The solution of Boethius[42] is similar to the solution of Maimonides and it is more capable of calming the youth than my own solution, for it almost says: worship God and be silent. In conclusion, I will say again, that these issues are not suitable for the youth, or most people for that matter, and generally speaking it is enough for them to recognize human freedom and divine omnipotence and omniscience.[43]

In 1850 Luzzatto made a third and final addition to his poem *Ḥeleq Keḥeleq Yokhelu*, following his disillusionment with short-lived revolution of 1848. Luzzatto mocks the gentiles who believed that their redemption from slavery to the nobility, the church, and the king, was at hand. Their reliance on intellect and their denial of God was their downfall:

> But He who dwells in heaven will laugh at them; both their fortune and misfortune remain as was. In vain was their blood spilled, and to straighten all that is crooked they labored in vain. Soon freedom they will abhor and they will even bend their shoulders under a king. In him they will find glory—God has a scale, all affliction is in his hand, and in freedom and slavery there is pleasure and pain.

That is to say, man cannot overpower God and his intellect cannot help him change his circumstances or broaden his share of fortune in his life. Luzzatto writes along similar lines in a letter in Italian from that time.[44]

---

42 An Aristotelian Christian philosopher who lived in Rome in the sixth century.
43 Published in Italian in Luzzatto, *Epistolario*, vol. 2, letter 592. Translated into Hebrew in Luzzatto, *Peraqim*, 67–68.
44 See Luzzatto, *Episotlario*, 536.

OLD PERIOD—CONSOLIDATION OF THE "DUAL TRUTH"

As mentioned, in a note written in 1860, and published at the beginning of his commentary on Ecclesiastes, Luzzatto wrote about his young views on providence and the book of Ecclesiastes, describing the shift in his views inspired by his cousin. Later in the note, he recounts how, over the course of time, he changed his views once again. After reading the book of the English scholar Samuel Clark (1675–1729), he realized that there is no need to believe in primordial matter. It is the nature of created things to have deficiencies and this is the cause of evil. The word "create" (*bara*) used in the Torah is meant to teach us that this was a supernatural creation of God, not the natural creation of a human. In regards to the contradiction between free will and scientific determinism, Luzzatto states "both fate and free will are, in my opinion, true." On the one hand, he explains, it is impossible to deny that God is the first cause of all that exists and occurs in the world; ever since creation he sees and knows everything. Evil also derives from God for it is only through evil that we can identify good. On the other hand, it is clear that everything a person does derives from his own free will and that a person deserves reward and punishment for his choices, even when they stem from causes rooted in his mind and his nature. And, perhaps, this is exactly why there is reward and punishment, because if actions had no cause then it would be impossible to repay them. In this passage Luzzatto no longer mentions the compartmental approach. It seems that he had finally fully adopted "dual truth" approach, employing it whenever encountering an irresolvable contradiction, even though he was aware that this position is paradoxical and difficult to understand. He writes *"I will not go into detail justifying my opinion which most people lack the power to understand."*[45] As mentioned, he maintains that a contradiction prevails not only between the necessary predestination of philosophy and the free will of Jewish faith, but also generally between the truth of philosophy and the truth of revelation.[46]

---

45 Luzzatto, *Meḥqerei Hayahadut*, vol. 1, pt. 2, 119. In his commentary on Deut 6:5 (see next note) in his discussion of the contradiction between the truth of philosophy and the truth of revelation cited above, Luzzatto says things along similar lines: "and there is no space here to go into detail." Even though he replaced his compartmental approach with the "dual truth," Luzzatto did not make corrections or changes to his commentary on the Pentateuch in verses which contain contradictions between the statements of rational science and the statements of the Torah such as my citations above. It seems that he preferred to interpret along logical-historical lines whenever possible (even when this entailed a daring interpretation) and not to claim that the Torah represents divine truth that cannot always be expressed in human language and which cannot be fully understood.

46 See Luzzatto, *Hamishtadel*, in the introduction as well as his commentary on Gen. 1:1 and Deut. 6:6, cited above. I discussed this in detail in my book *The Middle Way*, vol.

Luzzatto also includes here his explanation for the suffering of the righteous (mentioned above), adding that according to his rational, philosophical observation of the word "the evil in the world is also directed by Him the Blessed One and is not happenstance, but according to quantity and amount, a measure of pleasure and suffering for every head."[47]

Luzzatto concludes his remarks on the "dual truth" explaining that this approach can only be grasped by an experienced and mentally settled person. He uses this to explain his earlier interpretation and criticism of Ecclesiastes in his youth.

Complex ideas such as those he presents in his old age,

> cannot be understood by a young man, his heart aflame with the fire of his youth, his blood boiling in his organs, his spirit roaring tempestuously, his waves and swells surging. Therefore, for forty years, I was incensed at Ecclesiastes. But now that the wrath of youth has ceased, and after much experience, after many hardships and after clearheaded observation, *I maintain with faith and research, [the existence of] fate and free will* and I justify the actions of the creator for all the misfortune that prevails in the world, and for all the misfortune that has befallen me. And I am not (as one journalist wrote) a member of the Stoics, for they say that physical evil is not truly evil, and only imaginary. But I say that it is truly evil, but always measured and weighed, nothing is happenstance, and everything is done with wisdom, and prior providence.[48]

Luzzatto is aware of the dangers of the deterministic approach, and emphasizes that one should not sit idly by, but diligently strive for the good, improve all the

---

1, 482–492. My explanation for Luzzatto's "dual truth" leads to two conclusions: firstly, Luzzatto is not a fundamentalist nor a right-wing radical as is often claimed by scholarship (Lawrence Kaplan and Shmuel Feiner respectively); one cannot say this about someone who maintained both the compartmental approach, which stipulates that the revelation embodied in the Holy Scripture is not always true, and the "dual truth" approach, which stipulates that there is an opposing philosophical approach which is no less true than that of the Holy Scripture. See also the interpretation of P. Mendes-Flohr, *Qidma Venaftuleha* (Tel Aviv, 2010), 96. In his opinion, Luzzatto believes that these are different realms of one greater truth. I believe that he was influenced by Rosenzweig's approach (see below, Chapter Nine, n. 164). The second conclusion is that Luzzatto is not a cryptic, unstable two-faced figure as the researchers whom I cited at the beginning of the chapter have argued.

47 Luzzatto, *Meḥqerei Hayahadut*, vol. 1, pt. 2, 119.
48 Ibid.

means at one's disposal to attain it, and fight the seduction of the evil impulse. Moreover, a person must pray and beseech and never surrender to fate, for it is fate which also determines that the supplicant will be saved.

For many years Luzzatto battled the views of Spinoza and his Jewish followers, and takes the opportunity to do so again in this long note. He cites the view of Hasdai Crescas in *Or Hashem* that revealing the deterministic stance to the masses is dangerous, adding that Crescas's statements about free will may have been the impetus behind Spinoza's heresy. Spinoza uses Crescas's statements in his writings, from which Luzzatto concludes that Spinoza studied Crescas's works. Moreover, the systems of the two scholars are similar to each other with one important distinction: Spinoza maintains that everything is necessarily caused, stretching back into eternity with no beginning, whereas Crescas maintains that everything is necessarily caused but stretches back to a beginning (creation), which the Creator established according to his will.

In summary Luzzatto enumerates the possible solutions to the source of evil, listing them according to the character and value of the solver:

1. The simple believer to the right is not perturbed by philosophical inquiries and lives with his *naïve* faith.
2. The scholar who believes and thinks deeply, living in two worlds, an advocate of "the middle way,"[49] has two possible solutions:
    a. Primordial matter existing alongside God is the source of evil (as I have shown, this is not Luzzatto's preferred solution).
    b. There is no absolute evil, and everything occurs according to divine wisdom. Fate and free will are both true, even though they contradict one another; one must learn to live with this paradox which can only be resolved within the infinite wisdom of God.[50]

---

49 *Haderekh hamemutsa'at* is Luzzatto's expression. See Luzzatto, *Igrot*, 322, 599. The terms "right," "left," and "middle," which are used today to denote Ultra-Orthodox, secular, and Modern Orthodox respectively, were used by thinkers of the period to denote devout Orthodox, Reform, and Modern Orthodox respectively. See the introduction to my book *The Middle Way*, vol. 1, 13–22.
50 Luzzatto even anticipated modern day science. Postmodernist philosophy teaches about different narratives with equal validity, and even science today admits that there is not one truth. For example, according to particle-wave duality, light photons and electrons can exhibit qualities of both waves and particles. This theory is an integral part of quantum mechanics. Chaos theory, which is built into nature, is based on this, and its discussions recognize the existence of free will and determinism at the same time. Determinism is not

3. The superficial atheist to the left—there is no creator, and everything is eternal and happens out of predetermined necessity.

This last philosopher will stumble over his own statements and will be forced to deny what intellect demands: the signs of wisdom in nature attesting to the intelligent design and the causal teleology imprinted into the world. According to Luzzatto, this is the invalid position of Spinoza.

In his expanded commentary on Gen. 1:1, Luzzatto writes explicitly about the impossibility of human wisdom encompassing the contradiction between these two truths:

> And just as the matter of providence and reward was not explained (and it was not proper for it to be explained) philosophically in the Torah, but rather the Torah spoke in the language of man. [...] Similarly the matter of creation was not recounted (and it was not proper that it be recounted) philosophically in the Torah, as the Sages said (*Midrash Hagadol* on Gen. 6:6 and many similar passages): to tell the power of the act of creation to flesh and blood is impossible. Thus, it is not proper for a man of the Torah to remove verses from their meaning to make them agree with natural sciences, nor is it proper for a scholar to deny Torah from heaven, if he finds things in its stories that do not agree with natural research.

In 1864 Luzzatto wrote another letter on the subject of Ecclesiastes in which he explicitly retracts his claim that at the book's basis lies Koheleth's study of Greek wisdom. He now believes that the book was written at the end of the First Temple era by a man who believed in divine providence. Therefore, the book opens and closes with the theme of fear of heaven. He argues that the passages comprising the body of the book do not suit these worldviews but rather represent the doubts and deliberations of a thoughtful believer. In this respect Ecclesiastes can be considered the beginning of an unripe Jewish philosophy, prematurely cut short by the temple's destruction. Luzzatto, therefore, holds the book in high esteem. He says that throughout his life he taught that one should distinguish between pristine Jewish wisdom and foreign wisdom, blessing and upholding the Jewish and rejecting the foreign. The conclusion of Ecclesiastes attests to the author's comprehensive position on the importance

---

unidirectional, and randomness is an inseparable part of it. God plays with loaded dice as it were, so that everything is both random and intended. The argument is that man's limited brain cannot, and never will be able to encompass all these contradictions and paradoxes.

of fearing heaven and maintaining the doctrines of divine reward and punishment. The different essays of Ecclesiastes are intended to educate the nation, teaching them not to stray after futile, material luxuries, but to find satisfaction in their lot:

> I, who in my youth slandered Ecclesiastes, admit that he was my rabbi and my teacher, instructing me for my benefit; it was he who guided me along the path which I walked all my life: to be happy with my lot, and to realize that there is no profit for man in all his labor; if he does something indecent in order to increase his success, it will not benefit him at all, and if he accumulates money it will add no happiness or peace to his soul.[51]

SUMMARY AND CONCLUSIONS

The issue of divine providence and free will preoccupied Luzzatto for most of his life. Like in other subjects in his philosophy, he is contending with the contradiction between philosophy and religious faith in revelation, between the notion that there is divine providence, all-encompassing and intimate, granting man free will and judging him according to his choices, and the notion that man's actions are necessarily determined by his heredity and environment and only remotely by God. I have presented the different stages of his developing conception of evil and divine providence which stem from his attempts to contend with this problem. I have shown that he concludes that fate and providence (like revelation and philosophy) should be considered contradictory—a "dual truth," or an "irresolvable dialectic" (also paradoxical), which should be happily accepted in its entirety. This position, besides being difficult to explain and understand, is also extremely daring and was not an accepted position among believing halakhically observant scholars in the nineteenth century, the era of romantic idealism. The modern period was characterized by a firm belief in a grand, super-narrative and a single overarching truth. It was only in the twentieth century that cracks began to appear in this position, and towards the

---

51 A letter to H. Z. Halberstam, printed in *Yeshurun* 4 (1864), 77–82; Luzzatto, *Meḥqerei Hayahadut*, vol. 1, pt. 2, 124–125. See also S. Vargon, "Mihutu Uzemano shel Sefer Qohelet al Pi Shadal," in *Iyunei Miqra Uparshanut*, vol. 5 (Ramat Gan, 2000), 365–384.

second third of that century it was already considered *naïve*.[52] Even Luzzatto's contemporaries, like Samson Raphael Hirsch and Maharats Chajes, accepted western culture only on the condition that revelation be used as the criterion to evaluate and confirm its particulars. In the realm of theodicy, Luzzatto also developed a unique position based on the doctrine of the "dual truth." Non-speculative philosophy maintains that every person receives equal portions of pleasure and pain in this world—according to his class and level. According to revelation, however, a person must consciously plan his actions to be ethical and in accordance with God's will, as he will be rewarded or punished accordingly.

Luzzatto's different positions—the "dual truth," the "irresolvable dialectical approach," and even the compartmental approach which he maintained prior to this—all of these explain, in my opinion, the ambiguity and enigma that Klausner and other researchers sensed in Luzzatto's writings.

According to the compartmental approach, there are two perspectives of the truth, each dealing with a completely separate realm, and when both are purified, they emerge as two sides of the one truth, with no contradiction between them. According to the daring and inclusive "dual truth," philosophy and revelation, even when purified, still represent two truths which contradict

---

52 Its seems that Elijah Delmedigo, father of the Jewish "dual truth," as well as Samuel Hugo Bergman maintained views similar to those of Luzzatto, who believes that the two poles of the dialectic are irresolvable. As to the position of Rabbi Nahman of Breslov, researchers are divided as to whether he even though in terms of a dialectic. As to Rabbi Joseph Ber Soloveitchik, researchers are divided as to whether he believed the dialectic to be resolvable or not. Nahman Krochmal and Rav Avraham Yitshak Kook, following the philosophy of Hegel and his disciples, dispute the notion of an irresolvable dialectic and believed in the possibility of harmonization in the world. Scholars who studied Rabbi Soloveitchik and Rav Kook dealt at length with their indecisiveness, a consequence of the dialectic and contradiction in which they lived, as the solutions they offered were only solutions for a short time. Nevertheless, Luzzatto makes peace with the contradiction, accepting it with serenity, and his system seems the boldest of them all. On Rav Kook, see Chapter Twelve below. In my opinion, Luzzatto developed a unique dialectical approach different than the kabbalistic-Hassidic system (Judah Loew ben Bezalel, Habad Hasidism) as well as the systems of Hegel and Schelling and their Jewish disciples. According to those other dialectical approaches each pole represents part of one overarching truth, and therefore one should make a dialectical effort to unite them, and one who fails suffers. As mentioned, Luzzatto adopts the well-known medieval "dual truth." According to this system, philosophy and science, when they are purified of errors, and revelation, purified of fundamentalism, each constitute their own complete truths, and in man's world they contradict one another and cannot be united. This is an inherently irresolvable dialectic. We must live fully and peacefully with these two truths without invalidating even one of them, in spite of the contradiction, knowing that in the world of God they unite to one identical truth. See Chamiel, *The Middle Way*, vol. 1, 482–489 and in the notes there.

one another. In this manner, one can explain different attitudes in Luzzatto's writings to these two realms or truths: praise when they are purified and criticism when they are intermingled with improper dross.

Philosophy mixed with immoral speculative or egoistic rationalism, which negates pure revelation (Torah from Sinai) as irrelevant and removes it from discussion ("Atticism" in Luzzatto's terminology), is invalid and contemptible. Similarly contemptible is Judaism mixed with zealotry and mysticism, which rejects philosophy, pure research and study, considering these dangerous heresies (in Luzzatto's terminology "fanaticism"). On the other hand, Luzzatto praises all who attempt to live in both realms, in their purified forms, at the same time, even when they continue to contradict each other (in Luzzatto's terminology "Judaism" [יודאיסמוס]). Accordingly, there is no need to explain Luzzatto's position with pseudo-psychological explanations which do not suit his true character, as was done by scholars quoted at the beginning of the chapter.

Indeed, we have before us an impressive and special character, possessing an uncompromising middle approach, ahead of its time.

I will dedicate the next chapter to delving into another important position of Luzzatto, on the evolution of Halakhah in the Mishnah and Talmud called the "Oral Torah." Luzzatto believes that the majority of this body of law was not transmitted at Sinai and I will try to show how his position on this issue developed.

CHAPTER FOUR

Development of Halakhah: Luzzatto's Evolving Views

In my previous book, *The Middle Way*,[1] I discussed Luzzatto's evolving views about the origins of mishnaic and talmudic law and the circumstances which drove the Sages to interpret biblical verses against their simple meaning (*peshat*). Due to the confines of space in an already very large text, I was forced to discuss the issue there concisely.

In this chapter I will fully describe each stage of Luzzatto's developing treatment of classic rabbinic literature, specifically his views on rabbinic understandings of Scripture and the origins of laws appearing in tanaitic (Mishnah, Baraita, Tosefta, *Midrash Halakhah*) and amoraic (Babylonian and Palestinian Talmud) literature.

Scholarship on this topic has recently been enriched considerably by the publication of Hanan Gafni's book, *Peshuta Shel Mishna*.[2] Gafni presents the views of nineteenth-century scholars in Eastern and Western Europe on the amoraic interpretation of the Mishnah: whether or not they deviated from the Mishnah's literal meaning and if so why? The author describes the bitter controversies between Orthodox fundamentalists and researchers. These researchers—most of them rabbis, and influenced by Europe's academic air of historical-critical research—had difficulty (some more, some less) ignoring the errors and contradictions they observed in tannaitic and amoraic sources, and struggled to paint a harmonious picture. Gafni presents the views of fifteen scholars hailing from five geographical areas. While such an overview obviously does not allow a detailed, in-depth discussion of any single scholar's comprehensive methodology, the

---

1   Chapter Two. Chamiel, *The Middle Way*, vol. 1, 314–326.
2   H. Gafni, *"Peshuta Shel Mishnah": Iyunim Beheqer Sifrut Hazal Baet Hahaddasha* (Tel Aviv, 2011).

author stands up well to the task he has set for himself. He presents the views of scholars who cast doubt on the value of the talmudic interpretation of the Mishnah, and who argued that such interpretations, for a variety of reasons, do not capture the Mishnah's simple meaning. According to them, this leaves open the possibility to offer alternative interpretations of the Mishnah. In the third chapter, dedicated to the scholars of Italy, he briefly discusses the views of Isaac Samuel Reggio and Samuel David Luzzatto.

Gafni seldom links scholars' attitudes on the rabbinic interpretation of the Bible to their views on the rabbinic (amoraic) interpretation of the Mishnah nor does he connect these to their views regarding the divine origins of the Written and Oral Torah. Nonetheless, he accurately demonstrates the clear ideological-religious distortions that infected nineteenth-century scholarship; twentieth-century scholarship, having disconnected itself from the world of Torah-observance, had far less difficulty presenting its findings without pangs of guilt or fear.

Gafni's accurately portrays Luzzatto's views on the amoraic interpretations of the Mishnah; Luzzatto's did not modify his views on this issue. By contrast, Luzzatto's position on the more general subject of halakhic development would change over the course of his life—a process inadequately described by Gafni's model. In this chapter I will fill in the blanks left by Gafni, describing Luzzatto's views on the development of Halakhah (from the Bible, Mishnah, *Midrash Halakhah* until the Talmud), and demonstrating that his position was not static (as implied by Gafni's portrayal) but grew in sophistication over time.

Moshe Halbertal, Shalom Rosenberg and Avi Sagi[3] propose models to explain different medieval opinions regarding the Oral Torah, answering questions such as: what precisely did Moses receive at Sinai? what was included in the "Oral Torah"? what role did the Sages play? and what caused disputes between them? To very briefly summarize: according to the Geonim, while the majority of laws appearing in the Mishnah and Talmud were transmitted at Sinai, some of these were forgotten due to war and oppression, and had to be recovered by the Sages, using the thirteen hermeneutical principles (also transmitted at Sinai). According to Maimonides, only the 613 commandments directly related to the Written Torah were transmitted to Moses

---

3   Halbertal, Al *Derekh Haemet: Haramban Viyetsirata Shel Masoret*. (Jerusalem, 2007), 21–79; Rosenberg, *Lo Bashamayim Hi*, throughout the book; A. Sagi, *Elu Vaelu* (Tel Aviv, 1996) throughout the book. For an overview of these models see Chamiel, *The Middle Way*, vol. 1, 158–172. Harris in his book *How Do We Know This?* (Albany, New York, 1995) also presents a model on the same topic, explaining various nineteenth century views on the topic. I criticize this model in my book, *The Middle Way*, vol. 1, 167, n. 11.

and the remainder represents rabbinic creation. According to Nahmanides and his disciples, Moses received the entire spectrum of halakhic opinions on every law and the task of the Sages was to uncover and constitute proper halakhic rulings for us from this gamut of options. The appearance of the Reform movement—which claimed, on the basis of biblical criticism, that the Written Torah and certainly the Oral Torah are human creations—initiated an extensive debate among Jewish scholars, who were split along ideological lines. The devout Orthodox, led by the Hatam Sofer, invalidated all new positions. The Neo-Orthodox led by Rabbi Samson Raphael Hirsch, upheld the view of the Geonim. Members of the historical-positivist school (later known as the Conservative movement) and their predecessors led by Luzzatto, maintained a position similar to that of Maimonides, arguing that the halakhic codex in the Mishnah and Talmud is an evolving corpus.

THE BEGINNING

1829 marked the official opening of The Rabbinic Seminary of Padua. Luzzatto was appointed one of the seminary's co-heads and was also entrusted responsibility for its Bible studies. In his first year, in preparation for the role, he wrote an essay for his students describing the origins of the Bible, its text, and the methods of its interpretation. Originally written in Italian, this essay was later published as the introduction to Luzzatto's Italian translation and Hebrew commentary on the Pentateuch (published in five volumes, Padua 1871). The second part of the essay was translated into Hebrew by Gad Tsarfati. Pinchas Schlesinger incorporated this translation into his edition of Luzzatto's commentary on the Pentateuch (1966). Menahem Emanuel Artom translated the entire essay into Hebrew in 1976, in the second volume of his *Kitvei Shadal*, and gave it the title *Mavo Lebiqoret Uparshanut Hatorah* ("Introduction to the Criticism and Interpretation of the Pentateuch"). In this essay Luzzatto examines for his students rabbinic interpretations of Scripture, exegesis which often conflicts with the text's primary, simple meaning, clarifying his own method of biblical interpretation as well. He writes:

> We therefore should rely on that which our theologians unanimously accepted, and that is that our ancient Sages often used the scriptural text to support laws and principles which they received from the infallible tradition of their predecessors; their intention was not to say that this was the text's precise meaning, but only to fix these traditions in the memories

of their pupils, or to accord them the importance they deserved, an importance the people may have denied had they not felt that they derived from the Sacred Text. And in this sense the Talmudists themselves frequently conclude that this is "merely an *asmakhta*."[4]

We have here a short, broad explanation of a comprehensive system already lying in Luzzatto's drawer, which he would later develop and expand further. Luzzatto speaks about the Sages as a single body and writes about an ancient chain of tradition, conveying laws not recorded in the Torah. However, he does not indicate the beginnings of this transmission and at this point he was yet to explicitly claim that the Sages created their own laws. The Sages employed verses as *asmakhtaot* (textual support) to bolster the laws of the Oral Torah, traditions they had received from their predecessors, even though this was not the intention of the biblical text. They did this to meet two needs: to ensure students would remember unwritten laws and to reinforce the validity of the ancient Oral Law, anchoring it in the written text to imbue it with importance comparable to that of the Written Torah.

FIRST PRESENTATION OF LUZZATTO'S POSITION: THE ORAL TORAH IS NOT FROM SINAI

The first time Luzzatto drew a detailed model of the relationship between the laws of the Oral Torah on the one hand and tannaitic interpretation of Scripture and amoraic interpretation of the Mishnah on the other was a year prior. This was in an essay he wrote on the disputes between Beit Shammai and Beit Hillel, part of a larger project to elucidate the language of the Mishnah. This project was cut short after he was appointed joint head of the rabbinical seminary in 1829. He attached this essay to paragraph 5 of a letter he sent to his friend Solomon Juda Rapoport on July 7, 1831.[5] Seven years later, Luzzatto published the essay as a letter, in *Kerem Ḥemed*, volume 3, 1838. The essay was printed again posthumously in a collection of his essays and letters, *Meḥqerei Hayahadut*, and was given the title "Beit Shammai and Beit Hillel".[6]

---

4   Luzzatto, *Ketavim*, vol. 2, 123. See, for example, Ibn Ezra, Ex. 21:8, Lev. 19:20; Judah Halevi, *Kuzari*, 3:72–73; Maimonides, Introduction to his *Perush Hamishnah*.
5   Luzzatto, *Igrot Shadal*, 195.
6   *Kerem Ḥemed*, vol. 3 (1838), 219–223; Luzzatto, *Meḥqerei Hayahadut*, vol. 1, pt. 2, 154–155. See Luzzatto, *Igrot Shadal*, 195. Luzzatto and Rapoport would continue to correspond regarding this issue. See Luzzatto, *Igrot Shadal*, 226.

In a note Luzzatto writes:

> The words of the Sages are like the spurs used to drive an animal—and it is known that the masses are for the most part like horses and donkeys, lacking understanding. Therefore, when the Sages would make a decree they would not announce its rationale for twelve months, lest some be displeased by a law's reasoning, leading them to disparage it (BT Avoda Zara 35a). Similarly, we find that the rationales of three commandments were explained in the Torah, and the wise King Solomon stumbled over all three of them. And because the Sages were careful not to publicize the rationales of their decrees, this led to them being mostly forgotten, and the decrees remained, no one knowing their source or their reason. And when the Sages of Talmud wished to interpret the rationales of the Mishnah, in most cases they lacked a tradition regarding the reasoning of these rulings and would create their own explanations. Sometimes they would give a law a logical rationale, and sometimes they would link a law to scriptural statements, employing *derashot* [exegetical derivations], distant from the [Torah's] simple meaning. This led to the numerous opinions of the talmudic authors in providing a rationale for a single ruling. Therefore, one who is wise and insightful will judge without a doubt, that the gate is not closed before us in seeking rationales for the laws of the Mishnah, besides those rationales provided by the Talmud. And I have done this here with my own explanation of the prohibition of [levirate marriage to] a relative's co-wife [*tsara*], which the talmudic authors based on the word *litsror*. And from this it is clear how far from the truth are those scholars who forced Scripture to accord with Halakhah; they overturn the words of the living God in order to uphold interpretations which are merely an *asmakhta*. This also caused great damage to the Oral Torah, many of its statements being loathed by the masses and the intellectuals of the nation (certainly by the gentile scholars), as they thought that these were entirely based on the *asmakhtaot* mentioned in the Talmud. But in truth, the words of the early Sages are all sensible to those who understand them, and were established on foundations of deep wisdom for the good of the nation, and according to the needs of the time and the vicissitudes of the generations. But in their deep wisdom they knew that it was inappropriate to reveal the rationales of these matters to all their disciples, only a minority of them, and not in the study hall which was open to all, but in the secrecy of their tents—as is the case with other secrets of the Torah. And because

few disciples received these secrets this led to them being forgotten. Later generations tried to retrieve them using their logic-chopping, but they did not always succeed.

And behold, our forefathers left us a wide space in which to conduct our inquiry: First, we must interpret the Torah according to the depths of its true intention; afterwards we must interpret the rationales of the Mishnah and Halakhah, explaining why they [the Sages] saw fit to adjudicate in opposition to Scripture's simple meaning. And I have already worked on this task in my commentary on *Parashat Mishpatim*. Second, we must give the Mishnah an innovative interpretation, which is not entirely based on the statements of the Talmud; rather the interpreter should weigh the statements of the Amoraim with scales of wisdom, adding to them on his own. And these matters are broad and deep; this is not the place to clarify them; I have only opened for the enlightened a door, small as the eye of a needle, a gift to the wise man and he will be yet wiser.[7]

The main principles of the young Luzzatto's view of the Oral Torah are as follows:

1. Most of the laws in the Mishnah are products of rabbinic legislation, based on the Sages' own insight and their serious, profound assessment of the good of the nation and the changing needs of the times. Therefore, the laws of the Tannaim, and certainly those of the Amoraim, were never transmitted alongside the Written Torah to Moses at Sinai.

---

7   Luzzatto, *Meḥqerei Hayahadut*, vol. 1, pt. 2, 156–157. Luzzatto cites there the dispute between Beit Shammai and Beit Hillel regarding levirate marriage to a relative's "co-wife". The case is as follows: there are two brothers. The one marries two women, the other brother's relative (for example, his daughter) and another woman (who becomes the co-wife of the second brother's daughter). The married brother dies without children, and both wives are eligible for levirate marriage to the living brother. Bet Shammai maintains that the brother must marry the co-wife, while his daughter is free to remarry without performing ḥalitsa. Beit Hillel however maintains that both women—both the living brother's daughter and her co-wife— are free to remarry without ḥalitsa. Luzzatto explains the reasoning of the peace loving Beit Hillel: they forbade marrying a co-wife because such a relationship would not be successful. It would only lead to strife due to the ensuing hatred and jealousy between the living brother's new wife, his relative (in this case his daughter), and his current wife. Luzzatto considers the *derasha* from the word *litsror* an *asmakhta*. Gafni, *Peshuta*, 121–130, focuses primarily on this text. Luzzatto's views on the talmudic interpretation of the Mishnah—Gafni's focus— did not change since his discussion of Beit Hillel and Beit Shammai. However, as I will show, his larger view of halakhic development did change.

Development of Halakhah: Luzzatto's Evolving Views • CHAPTER FOUR | 111

2. Luzzatto distinguishes between two time periods: the period of the tannaitic Mishnah and the period of the amoraic Talmud. The Tannaim created new laws and consciously refrained from publicizing their rationales for a complete year. They did this fearing the public would disapprove or question the applicability of a law's rationale, and eventually come to disparage it.
3. Therefore, the true rationales were transmitted only to a small chosen few, and were taught privately and not in the study hall. This same system was also used to transmit the "secrets of the Torah," which were given to Moses at Sinai, and subsequently transmitted from great sage to worthy disciple. Luzzatto does not clarify here the nature of these secrets.
4. For these reasons, the rationales of the Mishnah's new laws were eventually forgotten.
5. The Amoraim wished to understand the rationales behind the Mishnah's laws but, possessing no tradition on the matter, they provided their own explanations. These were based on logic or *derashot* of the Written Torah. These diverged from the *peshat* of the Torah as they were meant to support laws which differed from the Torah's commandments. For this reason the Amoraim of the Talmud were divided over the rationales of mishnaic laws. This also led intellectuals, the masses, and gentile scholars to despise the words of the Amoraim, which seemed strange and inconsistent with the text's simple meaning. Luzzatto does not mention here that rabbinic *derashot* represent mere scriptural mnemonics—nor does he explicitly mention the necessity of anchoring orally received laws to the text of the written Torah to reinforce their validity. He would, however, revisit these explanations again.
6. Bible commentators, who wished to suit the Bible to Halakhah, and turned the loose exegesis of the Amoraim into the text's primary reading, distorted the biblical text and turned mere *asmakhtaot* into the word of God.
7. The amoraic Talmud's interpretation of the tannaitic Mishnah is not definitive, and every scholar is allowed to provide his own explanation and rationale for the tannaitic statements and rulings appearing in the Mishnah.
8. The scholars in every generation after the Talmud (and in our era as well) have a double task. They must first interpret Scripture to the best of their abilities according to the depths of *peshat*. Likewise, they must interpret the rationales of tannaitic rulings in the Mishnah according to their simple meaning, explaining the motivation behind rabbinic legislation which conflicts with the *peshat* of the

Bible. After this, following a critical, rational analysis of amoraic interpretations, they themselves should provide a new comprehensive interpretation of the Mishnah, sifting out statements which do not suit a literal reading.[8]

It is not surprising that Luzzatto refrained from widely publicizing these bold views, as he feared the ire of the religiously devout who adhered to the doctrine of an Oral Torah transmitted at Sinai.

While Luzzatto's system seems consistent and comprehensive, a number of problems emerge upon further consideration. First, Luzzatto's distinguishes between Tannaim who provided no rationales for laws and Amoraim who did. Yet the Tosefta, *baraitot*, and halakhic *midrashim*, which were contemporaneous with Mishnah, do provide rationales for laws—primarily *derashot* from verses. Moreover, only a minority of the *derashot* cited in the Talmud, are attributed to Amoraim, most being attributed to Tannaim. Second, why did the Amoraim not share the Tannaim's concern about publicizing the rationales for laws? Third, by what authority did the Tannaim create innovative laws which were not given at Sinai and what gave them the right to take measures to ensure their public acceptance? Fourth, Luzzatto's reliance on unknown "secrets of the Torah" is inconsistent with his statements in his 1826 work *Vikuaḥ al Ḥokhmat Haqabbala*, in which he claims that the entire mystical system of Kabbalah derives from an act of charlatanism meant to combat the dangerous, speculative system of philosophical esotericism. Finally, how will Luzzatto respond to the religiously devout who consider belief in the Sinaitic origins of the Oral Torah a fundamental principle of Judaism? The bridge of the "secrets of the Torah" does not seem to be enough to connect tannaitic creation to revelation.

It seems that Luzzatto sensed these difficulties and therefore continued to refine his system.

---

8   Gafni demonstrates that Luzzatto regarded himself the first to argue that every scholar has the right to attempt to interpret the Mishnah divergently from the interpretation of the Amoraim because they did not know the rationales of laws created by the Tannaim, the Tannaim hiding the rationales of their decrees so they would not be disparaged, and the Amoraim only guessing them using their own logic or interpretations of verses. See Gafni, *Peshuta*, 124. See there n. 77 about Luzzatto's wish that Schorr continue his work of interpreting the Mishnah, an interpretation not based on the explanations given in the Talmud, and that he research textual variants in the Mishnah and the Tosefta "according to the door I opened in *Kerem Ḥemed*, vol. 3, 222 [in the notes]." See also ibid., 125, on the debate between Luzzatto and Hirsch Mendel Pineles in 1864. Later I will show that Luzzatto would eventually change his position. Nevertheless, he would continue to maintain that interpretation of the Bible and the Mishnah remains open to us and that rabbinic interpretations are not from Sinai.

SOURCE OF AUTHORITY AND
THE POSITION OF THE DEVOUT ORTHODOX

Seven years after he had formulated the first version of his system, Luzzatto once again dealt with this issue in a letter to Reggio (June 15, 1837), responding to his request that he publicize his views on Jewish belief. This letter was also published in *Kerem Ḥemed*, volume 3, and was given the title "Ḥaqirot Shonot" ("Miscellaneous Investigations"). It was printed again in *Meḥqerei Hayahadut* under the title "Ketivat Hamishna Veharambam" ("The Writing of the Mishnah and Maimonides").[9] This letter includes criticism of Geiger's essays published in his journal on Jewish theology, in which he claimed that Rabbi Judah Hanasi wrote the Mishnah and that it is possible, even today, to change the rulings of the ancient Sages. The letter also includes fierce and daring criticism of Maimonides, condemning his attempt to introduce alien philosophy into Judaism, and attacking his decisive halakhic rulings in his *Mishneh Torah* which were unaccompanied by sources. This marked the beginning of Luzzatto's comprehensive polemic against Maimonides which is beyond the scope of the current chapter. Discussing Geiger's statements about the laws of the Tannaim and the Amoraim, Luzzatto writes:

> Behold, I was most astonished and shocked to see that this scholar [Geiger] maintains that our holy rabbi [Rabbi Judah Hanasi] wrote the Mishnah and that other Tannaim before him also wrote *mishnayot*. For forty years I have written to you, my friend, of the evidence supporting my opinion (which I wrote in *Ohev Ger*) that our holy rabbi did not write the Mishnah nor Rav Ashi the Talmud; only in the days of the Savoraim was the entire Oral Torah committed to writing. [. . .] So long as we do not know that the Sages refrained from writing the Oral Torah in a book, so that a court in every single generation would be able to correct and change according to the need of the place and time, we will not know the foundation of the Oral Torah. [. . .] Because individual dissenting opinions were also recorded in the Mishnah, so that men in a later generation should know both opinions together, and they will investigate them and rule on the Halakhah according to this one or that one, as they see fit and according to the need of the time. [. . .] If it had occurred to Rav Ashi and his court that their words would be

---

9   *Kerem Ḥemed*, vol. 3 (1838), 61–76; Luzzatto, *Meḥqerei Hayahadut*, vol. 1, pt. 2, 159–160, 164–165, 169, 172, 174.

written in a book, they would have expurgated quite a few things, that were good and appropriate at the hour they were spoken, but not to the credit of him who said them if they were written in a book and read in every place and time. [...] I have been told that the sentence, "a court cannot annul the words of its fellow court unless it is greater than it in wisdom and number," is a new ruling, instituted by our holy rabbi (for reasons known to him). [...] And perhaps our holy rabbi foresaw that the Jews would be dispersed outside of the Land of Israel, and the Children of Israel would no longer have a place that would be like a center for them, from which the Torah would go forth for everyone. [...] So that if every single court were permitted to annul the words of earlier ones, the bond of the nation would dissolve, and the unity would be lost.[10]

In 1837 Luzzatto maintained that the early Tannaim derived their authority from a court, in which judges were split into majority and minority opinions, Halakhah being adjudicated according to the majority. These rulings were never written down, and both opinions continued to be studied orally. This allowed courts in subsequent generations (if changing circumstances justified this) to review previous rulings. The *mishnah* in *Eduyot* states that a court in any generation is allowed to rescind earlier rulings or create new ones on the basis of a new majority vote—on the condition that they rely on a previous minority opinion recorded in the Mishnah. This is the source of the Sages' authority.

Luzzatto argues that Geiger in his essay tries to negate this understanding of the Mishnah in *Eduyot*. According to Geiger, the *mishnah* only stipulates one condition—if a court adopts a minority opinion, overturning the previous majority ruling, another court in that *same* generation cannot revoke this new ruling unless it is greater in wisdom and number. Luzzatto claims that Geiger interpreted this *mishnah* according to predetermined goals to suit his needs, thinking that he could thus ensure the freedom of a court in any generation to overturn rabbinic rulings with a majority vote. According to Luzzatto, the *mishnah*'s two sections are disconnected from each other: the second is the explanation of the first and not part of the same passage as maintained by Geiger. The first *mishnah* discusses a case in which a court bases its ruling on a minority opinion from a previous generation, using it as a precedent for change. The second *mishnah* is a separate statement about the relationship between two courts in *different* generations. If a later court wishes to change a ruling without having a minority opinion as precedent, it would need to be greater than its predecessor in wisdom and number—

---

10   Ibid., 159–174.

Development of Halakhah: Luzzatto's Evolving Views • CHAPTER FOUR

practically speaking, impossible. Luzzatto thus situated himself between the Reform who argued that one could make sweeping changes to Halakhah, and the devout Orthodox who maintained that no changes could be made at all. Luzzatto adds that in his opinion, Geiger had accomplished nothing with his interpretation, as even according to him, the *mishnah* still demands a previous minority opinion on which to base a halakhic change.

Luzzatto adds that it seems that the statements of the *mishnah* in *Eduyot* are those of Rabbi Judah Hanasi himself. Until the time of Rabbi Judah Hanasi a court in any generation could rescind the rulings of its predecessors with a majority vote. After the Jews were dispersed throughout the world, Rabbi Judah Hanasi ruled that a court could no longer rescind a previous court's ruling (i.e., his court) unless it based itself on a previous minority opinion or was greater in wisdom and number. This effectively blocked any halakhic reform which lacked precedent ever since the time of Judah Hanasi. Consequently, the Amoraim ceased to create new laws, and were only interpreters of the Mishnah, offering interpretations based on logic or their own *derashot* of the Bible. Luzzatto mentions here for the first time the issue of tannaitic sources besides the Mishnah, arguing that these were studied in secrecy alongside Judah Hanasi's Mishnah, dissenting from his rulings. Nevertheless, Luzzatto still does not clarify by what authority the tannaitic courts created new legislation which was not transmitted at Sinai.[11]

A year later, on June 27, 1838, in the heat of the controversy over Maimonides led by Nahman Krochmal, Maharats Chajes and other Galician *maskilim*, Luzzatto wrote to Joshua Heschl Schorr (1818–1895), telling of Isaac Reggio's request and his response, which had been published a year prior in *Kerem Ḥemed*, volume 3. He planned to publish this letter to Schorr in *Kerem Ḥemed*, volume 4, but decided to shelve it, presumably because of the bold, revolutionary claims it contained. It was only published twenty-five years later in *Otsar Neḥmad* (1863) under the title "Mikhtav" ("A Letter") and again in *Meḥqerei Hayahadut* under the title "Tamtsit Deotav Shel Shadal" ("A Summary of Luzzatto's Views").[12] In this letter Luzzatto once again elucidates the content of his response to Reggio but adds here details which answer two questions he had left unresolved in previous letters. He writes:

> For our ancient Sages did not derive rulings by distorting verses and by interpretations far from the literal meaning of the Bible, but they were

---

11 This claim also seems to be original to Luzzatto. It was later adopted by Joshua Heschel Schorr and Avraham Krochmal. See Gafni, *Peshuta*, 151–155. See also Luzzatto's letter to Schorr from 12.3.1840 on the same subject, Luzzatto, *Igrot*, 677.

12 *Otsar Neḥmad* 4, 108–131 (see also note on p. 108); Luzzatto, *Meḥqerei Hayahadut*, vol. 1, pt. 2, 237–249.

rulings received by them from their ancestors, one man to another, or regulations that they ordained with deep and wondrous wisdom, according to the need of the times, and according to what we were commanded by the Torah to obey the judge who will be in our days, and the interpretations that stray from the literal meaning are merely corroboration. [. . .] And if innocent and honest men, who cling to the Talmud and the legal authorities say to me: "take your goodness and throw it back," because even if your intention was acceptable, your actions are not acceptable, because with the intention of raising up the written Torah you bring down the Oral Law, or with the intention of honoring our Sages of blessed memory, you say that their words were with wisdom and not received, and to bring down the crown of Greek wisdom, you throw down from heaven to earth the pride of our strength, Maimonides of blessed memory—I say to them: my words were not directed to you, but to those who love free inquiry, and I see that which is useful to them is not useful to you, but in the end my words will not harm you, because your faith has deep roots in your hearts, and it will never sway; it might only harm the young students, because their loyalty to logic-chopping of the Talmud and halakhic decisions will be weakened slightly; but this is a danger that has a remedy—prevent your sons from perusing *Kerem Ḥemed*, volume three, which, aside from my letter, also contains other matters that will be an obstacle and impediment to young pupils; and when the young boys grow up and their bellies are full of meat and wine [Talmud and Posqim], then place it in their hands, and I promise you that it will not harm them, because either they will remain in their former faith, and they will throw the book away, the way you threw it away, or their heart will lean toward my words, and then they will begin to acquire Jewish faith like mine, based on intellect and wisdom, not on Greek philosophy, but on Jewish wisdom, and then you will be happy and the people will be happy, for their flocks will have pasturage.[13]

Luzzatto's letter begins with the issue of authority. He no longer bases tannaitic authority on the court system, and now states that there were two types of rabbinical legislation. One was based on ancient tradition transmitted from master to disciple (Luzzatto refrains from stating that this chain of tradition began with Moses at Sinai). The other (which he had already discussed eight years prior) was the Sages' own independent legislation which was introduced

---

13 Ibid., 242–248.

"with deep and wondrous wisdom according to the needs of the times." Using Maimonides's approach (but without saying so), he explains that the authority for this latter type of legislation was of a second-order—a biblical commandment: "and you shall appear before the levitical priests or the judge who will be at that time... observing all of their instructions" (Deut. 17:9–11).[14]

In this letter Luzzatto also discusses the views of the devout Orthodox. They could be expected to accuse him of disparaging Maimonides under the pretense of invalidating Greek philosophy and disparaging the Oral Torah under the pretense of elevating the prestige of the Sages —claiming that they legislated their own laws, undermining the basis of Torah Judaism and its belief in an Oral Torah from Sinai, compromising its only firm source of authority. To this Luzzatto responds that his statements are not directed at them and are only meant for lovers of free inquiry. He even recommends that the devout keep their young children from studying maskilic writings published in journals like *Kerem Ḥemed*, until they have studied Torah and Halakhah and have consolidated their views. At that point they will regardless be exposed to his views, and one of two things will happen: they will either cast aside his writings and not be swayed by them, like their fathers before them, or they will accept his writings, alter their views, and adopt a Jewish faith based on reason and not the foreign philosophy of Maimonides—and this will be for the greater glory of the Jewish people.

THE SECOND SYSTEM: RE-DIVISION OF ORAL TORAH'S HALAKHIC STRATA

Six years later, in 1847, Luzzatto published a collection of his essays entitled *Beit Haotsar*. In the introduction to the book, he explains that publishing his articles alongside unworthy writers in various journals, agitates him like a thorn in his side and he has therefore decided to collect the remaining essays from his archives and publish them in books of his own. He says that Brody resident Joshua Heschel Schor (Luzzatto's affluent friend) had lent him all the money needed to publish the first book. Luzzatto planned to publish further volumes and therefore called this book *Lishka Alef* ("Chamber A"). These anthologies were dedicated to poetry, biblical interpretation, Hebrew, Jewish history, and studies of and excerpts from ancient texts.

---

14 On Maimonides's system of an accumulative halakhic codex see Chamiel, *The Middle Way*, vol. 1, 160–164.

The first essay in the book, apparently written in the thirties, is called "Imqei Safa" (Depths of Language). Written as a letter to a friend, it discusses Hebrew synonyms, specific Hebrew verbs (תור, רגל, ירא), and the praises of the Hebrew language. In 1846 Luzzatto added an addendum to this essay, which was printed alongside it in *Beit Haotsar*. In this addendum Luzzatto presents corrections and additions to his earlier views on the development of Halakhah, answering questions which he had left unresolved in 1828. The topic reemerges in a discussion of Saadya Gaon's contributions to the Hebrew language. Among other things, he discusses Saadya's battle against Karaism, and tries to prove that this rebellious Jewish sect was unknown to the Sages of Talmud, as opposed to the claims of the Leiden University professor Jacob Tringland (1652–1705) who, along with others, argued for Karaism's antiquity. Luzzatto claims that the Sadducees of the talmudic era were worse than their successors the Karaites. While the Sadducees pursued Greek culture, the early Karaites adhered to the Pentateuch and its morality. Nevertheless, the students of the early Karaites erred:

> They did not plumb the depths of the Oral Law, and they did not understand that the Scribes (from the time of Ezra on) made regulations for the benefit of the nation according to the need of the generation, and they explained and defined everything that was unexplained and undefined in the Torah of Moses according to their wisdom, with the power given to them from Sinai, according to the foundations and secrets of the Torah received by them from Sinai, and thus did Sages and Scribes in every single generation, and the Torah in their hand was not like books of the dead and something that has no vital spirit, but it was in their hand like the words of the living God, and as something that is always living and existing, and good and beneficial at all time, according to the need of every single generation. Therefore, they did not wish to record their teachings in a book, so as not to lock the door before those who would come after them, but they, too, could institute regulations according to the need of the times. And behold, the Scribes, they are the first Sages who arose after Ezra, and their names are not known to us, but their regulations are known by the name of *divrei sofrim* [words of the Scribes], and they did not fear to force the words of the Torah so that they would agree with their regulations, because there was no one among the people who would open his mouth and chatter against them, but everyone obeyed the judge who was in their time, as written in the Torah of Moses; and only for the need of the hour, when the Sadducees raised

arguments against them, did the Sages produce evidence from the Torah. [...] But at the close of the Temple period, with the end of the Hasmonean dynasty, the [beginning of] Herod's reign and the decline of morality, and strongmen took over, and the honor of rule was taken from the Sages, and they were no longer as before the judges and magistrates of the people, but their Sages and teachers, then they began to attach the laws and judgments, which had been received by them, to verses from the Torah, and they invented some ways and principles by which the Torah was interpreted, and they began to teach the interpretation of verses to their students (*Mekhilta*, *Sifra*, and *Sifri* [compendia of *midrash*]), but to the greatest of their disciples, they would confide in secret (with other Torah secrets) that these were merely references (*asmakhta be'alma*), and that the Bible is not to be removed from its simple meaning. And from that time on, *midrash* began in Mishnah and Baraita, and then it proliferated in talmudic logic-chopping, especially among the Babylonians, who were sharper of wit. [...] Then the Talmud was sealed and recorded in writing, but the Torah secrets were not written. Perhaps they were forgotten, because they were only transmitted to outstanding individuals, and perhaps they were not written intentionally, because it is not worthy to communicate them to everyone. And then the references, which had been secondary, became primary.[15]

---

15 Luzzatto, *Beit Haotsar, Lishka* A, 13–14. As is well known, Spinoza claimed that Ezra wrote the Torah, and it was he who introduced Ezra the Scribe into the minds of researchers of Jewish Scripture. See Spinoza, *Theological-Political Treatise*, Michael Silverthorne and Jonathan Israel, trans. (Cambridge, 2007), 127–128. Luzzatto was well-versed in Spinoza's views and combatted them with ferocity. The status of Ezra and the Scribes is discussed in the third volume of I. M. Jost's *Geschichte der Israeliten* (History of the Israelites) published in 1822. Likewise, the status of the Scribes is discussed in Krochmal's *Moreh Nevukhei Hazman* printed in 1851, 194–217, and in the works of the first members of the historical-positivist school Zacharias Frankel, *Darkhei Hamishnah*, 1859, 3–20 and Heinrich Graetz, *Geschichte der Juden*, vol. 2, published in 1876 (in Hebrew *Divrei Yemei Yisrael* [Warsaw, 1893], 157–195). Frankel, who wrote essays on the subject as early as 1841, declared his historical-positivist approach in the second rabbinic gathering of 1845, explaining the basis of his thought—the evolving nature of Halakhah. See Chamiel, *The Middle Way*, vol. 1, 230–231 and n. 119 ibid. Luzzatto was well aware of Jost's works in which he argued that Ezra and the Scribes gathered fragments of Scripture which had survived and redacted them into the books we know. Luzzatto fiercely criticized this stance. However, Jost adds that the Scribes also interpreted the books of Scripture anew, in order to make their views and the views of their teachers accord with the contradictory views of Scripture. This is

The main principles of Luzzatto's approach in its new formulation are as follows:

1. The rulings of the Scribes, from the time of Ezra onward, are the first layer of rabbinic legislation—predating the layer of the Tannaim.

---

how the views of the Scribes came to be regarded as holy. It follows that this theory—that the Scribes and their status constitute the first stage in the evolution of Halakhah—was brought up for discussions during the period in which Luzzatto incorporated it into his own theory. Michael Reuben in his book *J. M. Jost* (Jerusalem, 1983) summarizes the historical evolution of Judaism and its holy texts according to Jost. He describes Rapoport's positive attitude towards Jost's important studies and Luzzatto's negative attitude towards Jost's adoption of the documentary hypothesis, which maintains that the Torah is human not divine, a theory Jost had learned from Eichhorn and Ilgen. See Luzzatto in a letter to Rapoport from January 1831, *Igrot Shadal*, 178. That being said, as time passed Luzzatto would come to appreciate Jost's profound research, even his study of the evolution of Halakhah, praising it in a letter from January 24, 1840): "I see in your books profound research which is lacking in the books of all the aforementioned (Zunz, Rapoport, and Reggio). Therefore, you are more precious in my eyes than everyone else, and I hope that your heart also knows this, and only out of modesty and etiquette would you say the opposite" (*Igrot Shadal*, 660). See Michael, *Jost*, 27–31, 36, 79–81; Chamiel, *The Middle Way*, vol. 1, 59–63, 232–235.

On January 29, Luzzatto sent a letter to Leopold Löw, editor of *Ben Chananja*. He added to the letter a short response essay, which Löw published in the sixth volume of the journal, February 1863, 150–151. The letter and the essay were printed again in *Igrot Shadal*, vol. 9, 1403, and in *Meḥqerei Yahadut*, vol. 1, pt. 2, 185–187 (without the letter). In this essay Luzzatto quotes Mordechai Gumpel Schnaber's "Maamar Hatorah Vehaḥokhma," (printed in London in 1771) as an important source for his notion of an evolving Oral Torah, created from innovative rabbinic legislation based on the thirteen hermeneutical principles. Luzzatto does not disclose when he read this essay.

Luzzatto would revisit the Sages' invention of the thirteen principles in 1854 in a letter to Shneur Sachs (1815–1892) the new editor of *Kerem Ḥemed*. Sachs printed the letter in the eighth volume of the journal (1854), 5–9, with the title "Al Inyan Qadmut Ḥelqei Hatanaḥ." This letter was reprinted in *Meḥqerei Yahadut*, vol. 1, pt. 2, 56–59 with the title "Zeman Ḥibburam shel Aḥadim Memizmorei Hatehilim." Among other things, Luzzatto writes: "the Sages of the Mishnah would interpret the verses in various fashions, and invented the thirteen principles in order to base their decrees and the decrees of their predecessors on one of the verses." (ibid., 57). This sentence summarizes Luzzatto's entire system. Luzzatto held this model in high esteem and refers the reader to it in the introduction to his first commentary on the Torah, *Hamishtadel*.

2. The Scribes explained and defined the laws of the Written Torah wherever it lacked instruction or provided insufficient detail. They also created new laws of their own, for the good of the nation, suiting the changing needs of the time.
3. The Scribes' authority to create new laws derived from two factors: the power given to them at Sinai by the commandment "observe to do according to all they teach you," and their knowledge of the principles and secrets of the Torah—transmitted at Sinai and passed down from generation to generation.
4. The Scribes did not commit this legislation to writing lest it hinder future generations from reforming the legislation of their predecessors as new needs arose.
5. The Scribes from Ezra's time and onward did not need to support their laws by distorting biblical verses, even when their laws conflicted with the *peshat* of the biblical text. Because of their great power and influence as judges and officials, the nation did not question their authority, and adhered to the biblical commandment to obey the judge of one's era. It was only seldom, when combating the claims of the Sadducees, that the scribes were impelled to cite verses.
6. With the decline and deterioration of virtues in the days of Herod, the Sages lost the power and the respect of the nation, becoming mere teachers and wise-men. At that point the Tannaim began to use Scripture to support the laws they had received from the Scribes, wishing to ensure their continued acceptance. To do this they created and employed the thirteen hermeneutical principles, teaching their disciples *Midrash Halakhah—Mekhilta, Sifra* and *Sifri*. That being said, they did their best to teach handpicked disciples (to whom they also transmitted the secrets of the Torah) that these *midrashim* were not the true rationales for the Halakhah but mere support-texts, and that Scripture should be understood and interpreted only according to its simple meaning.
7. The Amoraim continued to discuss the Mishnah and the *Midrash Halakhah* of the Tannaim. However, especially in Babylonia, they overanalyzed these *derashot*.
8. The Talmud was eventually sealed and even committed to writing when the Sages were forbidden from teaching and adjudicating. From that time onward the Sages are referred to as Savoraim. Naturally the secrets of the Torah were never written down and as time passed were forgotten. Thus, the *midrash* of verses, which was of secondary importance to the Tannaim and Amoraim, in time, came to be considered the primary rationale for the commandments.

Luzzatto thus adds an additional layer to his model: the stratum of the Scribes. Due to their power, the early Scribes did not need to give reasons for the laws they created. Ever since the reign of Herod, this power sharply declined, and already the Tannaim began to resort to *midrash*, twisting Scripture's simple meaning to ensure obedience. According to this reason, the Tannaim feared to divulge the rationales of their laws not because the nation might not obey them (if they did not agree or did not consider them applicable, Luzzatto's explanation in 1828) but rather because they feared that their laws would be denigrated due to the decline of their powers of deterrence. The tannaitic *Midrash Halakhah* is a reflection of this trend. Luzzatto also attributes the creation of the thirteen principles to the Tannaim. The Sages thus derived their authority from three factors: their knowledge of the secrets of the Torah, the biblical commandment to obey their rulings, and from scriptural verses they interpreted using the thirteen hermeneutical principles (their own invention) to suit their needs. All aspects of Luzzatto's original system of 1828, which were not revised or replaced, remained in force (see above in the description of his system in 1828) including his statements about the amoraic interpretation of tannaitic statements and rationales for their laws in the Mishnah and the *midrashim* in the Talmud.

Luzzatto does not explain in this essay, why the Tanna Rabbi Judah Hanasi did not cite rationales for laws in his Mishnah. This can be explained by a letter Luzzatto sent to Reggio in 1837. There Luzzatto argues that Judah Hanasi wished to guarantee the supremacy of mishnaic ruling, barring future legislation and preventing halakhic change—presumably a good reason for not divulging rationales. Luzzatto argues that this is exactly what Maimonides did in his *Mishneh Torah*: not citing sources and dissenting views to guarantee the supremacy of talmudic Halakhah or his preferred halakhic rulings, and in that same letter Luzzatto harshly criticizes Maimonides for this.[16] With great anger, Luzzatto links Maimonides's action in the *Mishneh Torah* to the erroneous view (shared by both Maimonides and Geiger), that Judah Hanasi committed the Mishnah to writing. Luzzatto explains that only Judah Hanasi's opponents provided rationales for their statements in the *Midrash Halakhah* and it is clear that Luzzatto believed that this was due to the weakness of their position. That being said, Luzzatto excuses Judah Hanasi's activity for a number of reasons: he did not commit the Mishnah to writing, he presented minority opinions to still allow future change, and his hand was forced by the difficult circumstances facing the Jewish people in his day. Luzzatto believes that Judah Hanasi's power

---

16 See note 10 above; Luzzatto, *Meḥqerei Hayahadut*, 165.

was very strong, and like the Scribes in their time, he felt confident enough to refrain from providing rationales for his laws.[17]

This answers the first three questions I raised above in my discussion of Luzzatto's system as articulated in 1828: why rationales for laws are provided in tannaitic sources besides the Mishnah; why the Amoraim publicized the rationales of laws, and what was the source of the Tannaim's authority. The question of the source of authority, which is relevant to those who considers a Sinaitic Oral Torah a primary foundation of Judaism, was already resolved in Luzzatto's letter to Schorr in 1838.

One question still remains: my question regarding the secrets of Torah and this in turn raises a new question: did Luzzatto abandon his position from 1828 that the Tannaim created their own laws, now attributing this role to the Scribes instead? Or perhaps, he now believed that the Tannaim continued the practice of the Scribes—by virtue of their knowledge of the secrets of the Torah, their invention of the thirteen principles and the commandment "observe to do according to all they teach you" which applied to them as well?

On Purim of 1847 Luzzatto completed his system as he explicitly made clear. The Tannaim used *Midrash Halakhah* not only to support laws inherited from the Scribes, but also to support their own independent legislation. In his first commentary on the Pentateuch (*Hamishtadel*, printed in that year for the first time), writing on Lev. 7:18, Luzzatto explains that according to verse's simple reading, if one brings a *shelamim* offering, fails to burn its remains by the end of the second day, instead leaving it for himself or for others to be eaten on the third day—his sacrifice is not accepted and is *pigul* (invalid). Once the sacrifice is thus invalidated, anyone who ate from it, even on the first and second days, retroactively incurs guilt. In Luzzatto's opinion, it is extremely stringent to consider equally culpable one who eats of the sacrifice on the first and second days, when the flesh of the offering was still permitted, and one who ate on the third day, when it was already forbidden. The Tanna Rabbi Eliezer, wondering how the Torah could retroactively invalidate something which had previously

---

17 It is possible that this model espoused by Luzzatto represents a precursor to the system later developed by Rabbi David Zvi Hoffmann in his 1882 work *Die erste Mishnah und die Controversen der Tannaim* (The First Mishnah and the Disputes of the Tannaim). Perhaps the early stratum of the Mishnah discovered by Hoffman is analogous to Luzzatto's stratum of the Scribes—the rationales of their laws the subject of dispute between Judah Hanasi's Mishnah and the *midrashei halakhah* of other Tannaim. The primary difference between Hoffman and Luzzatto is that according to Hoffman no stratum ever created new laws, and all the Sages were merely trying to understand the words of their predecessors which all ultimately originated at Sinai.

been permitted, explained that the verse should be interpreted against its literal meaning as follows: a sacrifice that was eaten on the third day is invalid on the first and second days as well only if at the time of the offering the owner already *intended* to leave over meat until the third day. If others know of his intention then they too cannot eat of it, and if they do so, they will incur guilt even if they eat from the sacrifice on the first two days. Luzzatto writes that until now he had not understood why Rabbi Eliezer had displaced the literal meaning of the verse and annulled the stringency emerging from it, against the Torah's will:

> After some years when I was surprised by the Sages, why (as in the words of Rashbam [Rabbi Samuel ben Meir]) they removed a certain verse from its simple meaning, today (Purim 1847) I was privileged to understand what they were after. Indeed, in every place where the Sages deviated from the simple meaning of the verse, when the matter is not a single man's opinion, but something agreed upon without demurral, this is not an error that they made, but it is a regulation they instituted, because of the need of the generations, and who is a reformer like them? But their regulations were with deep wisdom, and fear of God and love of man, not their own pleasure or honor, and not to find favor in the eyes of flesh and blood.

Luzzatto does not accept the Orthodox position that rabbinic exegesis represents the primary meaning of the biblical text. Conversely, he does not accept the Reform position that the Midrash is at worst a falsehood contrived by the Sages, contrary to the good of the nation and at best a terrible interpretive failure in understanding the Bible and the Mishna—a view maintained by (those Luzzatto considers) irresponsible researchers of Judaism in all un-devout streams (whom Gafni quotes at length in his book) including Geiger and Schorr. In Luzzatto's opinion, *Midrash Halakhah* represents tannaitic innovation. The Tannaim wished to anchor the laws of the Scribes to the text and to add new decrees of their own, sometime conflicting with prior rulings. They did this for the good of the nation according to the needs of the time, ensuring obedience by basing their laws on Scripture.

Luzzatto sensed that his discovery was a dangerous one, which was liable to cause the religious deterioration of those who accept it, leading them to initiate their own religious reforms. Therefore, he stressed the broad difference between the innovations of the Scribes and the Tannaim and the modern innovations of the Reform in his own day, saying that until there are people on the level of the Sages, no reformation is possible. He was careful to note that one can only speak of errors in the words of the Sages when a *midrash* is the individual opinion of one sage whose opinion was not accepted.

In summary, according to Luzzatto, the halakhic codex of Judaism is comprised of four strata: the first is the Sinaitic stratum including the Written Torah and the secrets of Torah.

The second is the stratum of the Scribes from Ezra onwards. They elucidated and elaborated commandments which were transmitted, only in general terms, at Sinai, and also created new laws which oppose the *peshat* of the Torah. They did this by virtue of the authority granted to them by the Written Torah in the law of "observe to do according to all they teach you" (Deut. 17:1–11) and were also aided by the secrets of Torah which were only transmitted to unique individuals.

The third stratum is that of the Tannaim beginning at the end of the Second Temple period. The Tannaim continued to teach the laws formulated by their predecessors and also created new laws of their own. However, due to their weakened authority they also created the thirteen hermeneutical principles and employed scriptural *midrash* to reinforce their legislation.

The fourth stratum is that of the Amoraim. They continued to deeply analyze the laws of their predecessors and cited scriptural *derashot* in the names of the Tannaim, anchoring tannaitic laws to the biblical text. They also interpreted verses themselves (sometimes using peculiar *derashot*) to anchor laws which otherwise lacked a scriptural basis, though they ceased to use Midrash to legislate new laws of their own. In this way, they guaranteed observance, as the nation accepted the Midrash as the authentic interpretation of the text. Only unique individuals were given the secrets of Torah, and only they were informed that Midrash is nothing more than textual support, and not the text's simple meaning. As time passed, the secrets of Torah were forgotten, and the *asmakhta* and Midrash became primary.

Only the first layer of the Torah is from Sinai, and the majority of Jewish law is rabbinic. Luzzatto's invention of the secrets of Torah, for which he provides no textual support (as it was always kept esoteric), allowed him to give obligatory authority of the first order to the non-Sinaitic innovations of the Scribes and Sages and non-obligatory authority to scriptural Midrash. Thus, Luzzatto remains loyal to the rabbinic Halakhah, while still adhering to the simple meaning of Scripture—at odds with the rabbinic Midrash (which is merely an *asmakhta* and sometimes even foreign to the text's true meaning). Luzzatto does not see fit to explain the appearance of several *derashot* in the Talmud used to anchor amoraic laws, nor does he explain innovative amoraic laws which are justified by using thirteen hermeneutical principles. Geiger, Zacharias Frankel, Heinrich Graetz and Isaac Hirsch Weiss (1815–1905) took this step without qualms, contributing additional layers to research of halakhic literature and its development, maintaining that the Amoraim did create new laws.[18]

Did Luzzatto remain loyal to his views regarding the secrets of the Torah? Perhaps this can be answered by a letter Luzzatto sent on December 16, 1857 to Eliezer Zilberman, the editor of the weekly *Hamagid*, printed there a month later.[19] In this letter Luzzatto explains that although his name appears alongside other scholars in an album issued in honor of Geiger (blessing him on the twenty fifth anniversary of his appointment as a communal rabbi), this does not mean that he agrees with the claims of Geiger's book *Urschrift und Übersetzungen der Bibel* ("Texts and Translations of the Bible," Breslau, 1857).[20] He cites a letter he sent at the time to the editor of the album for publication (although it was, presumably, not published), which he opens with a short poem dedicated to Geiger:

> Blessed be Avram from God Most High.
> May he succeed in all his endeavors.
> May his years be long, and his loins be girded.
> And that which he destroyed, may he build again.

Luzzatto continues to sharply criticize Geiger. He recounts that five years prior he sent Geiger a summary of his views on the historical development of Judaism and its literature, fifteen years worth of writing and reflection. The subjects he researched, in order, were: changes made by Onkelos's Targum, the vowelists, the accenters, and the Sages—in their work of interpreting the *peshat* in order to remove obstacles and for the sake of the people. Luzzatto argues that Geiger used these statements as the basis of his own argument that the Sages went as far as editing and correcting the text of Scripture. Geiger argues

---

18 See, for example, Z. Frankel, *Darkhei Hamishnah*, ed. I. Nissenbaum (Tel Aviv, 1959), 336. Frankel's position, which was published in this book from 1859, is similar to that of Luzzatto's regarding the derashot of the Tannaim and Amoraim. See ibid., 17–18. On academic views regarding the relationship between Halakhah, the *derashot* of the Scribes, and the *derashot* of the Tannaim and Amoraim, see Y. Gilat, *Peraqim Behishtalshelut Hahalakhah* (Ramat Gan, 1992), 374–376.
19 *Hamagid* 2.2 14 January 1858.
20 Translated into Hebrew in Geiger, *Hamiqra Vetargumav*, trans. Y. L. Baruch (Jerusalem, 1940).

Development of Halakhah: Luzzatto's Evolving Views • CHAPTER FOUR | 127

that the Sages did this to reform laws for the good of the nation according to the needs of the time. Now, Luzzatto wishes to prove that Geiger was mistaken in accusing the Sages of falsifying Scripture:

> And as time passed I observed (or thought) that these strange interpretations—at odds with the simple meaning of the verses, scattered throughout the Talmud, the *Mekhilta*, the *Sifra* and the *Sifri*—were also not products of ignorance but were done intentionally to support the decrees they [the Sages] would make to meet the needs of the times. Therefore, it is not our obligation to distort verses to make them accord with Halakhah; rather, our obligation is to follow Halakhah, as it says "according to all they teach you."

Luzzatto discusses here the *derashot* of the Tannaim which appear in the *Midrash Halakhah* and the Talmud (as mentioned, the Mishnah does not generally include *derashot* and does not provide explanations for its laws). He reiterates his statements from the previous year: the Sages did not misunderstand the text and were fully aware that their interpretations diverged from the Torah's literal meaning. The Tannaim intentionally interpreted verses in this manner (from a position of weakness) in order to underpin the laws they had created, according them validity and giving them textual support. The Amoraim continued to rely on these interpretations for the same reason. Luzzatto does not specify when he conducted research on this subject, but according to my analysis here, he dealt with the issue of *Midrash Halakhah* between 1828 and 1847.[21]

---

21 If Luzzatto is being precise in his dates, it seems that the letter he sent to Geiger fifteen years prior (1842–1843) reached its destination even before Geiger published his essay on the relationship between the peshat and rabbinic interpretation of Scripture and his reader of mishnaic language from 1844. That being said, the only inspiration Geiger received from Luzzatto's letter was regarding the innovation of laws by the ancients, for the needs of the time, which deviated from the simple meaning of the Torah. However, when discussing the treatment of the Bible and the Mishnah by the Tannaim and Amoraim he is critical, claiming they had erred in their understanding, conducting strained and inadequate exegesis of the Bible to anchor the laws of their predecessors (and we can therefore ignore their interpretations). After Graetz published sharp criticism of Geiger in 1845, Geiger changed his approach, and actually praised the Sages, utilizing additional ideas of Luzzatto. In a response essay to Graetz that same year, Geiger wrote what he seems to have learned from Luzzatto—that the Midrash Halakhah of the Tannaim and the midrashim of the Talmud, cited by the Amoraim, were not attempts to interpret Scripture or the statements of their predecessors but only attempts to support laws created by the Tannaim (Geiger adds the Amoraim as well)

If most Scribal and tannaitic laws represent independent innovation on their part, then they were not transmitted to Moses by the Almighty. If so, what authority obligates us to observe these laws? Why not to overturn or alter them according to the needs of the nation and changing times? Why not modify laws as already done by the Reform and as advocated by the historical-positivist school?

Luzzatto answers that the authority to innovate laws derives from the biblical commandment "observe to do according to all they teach you," an explanation already provided in 1828. According to Luzzatto—unlike Geiger, Frankel and Graetz—this commandment remained in force until the time of Judah Hanasi, and the authors of the tannaitic *midrashei halakhah* (who secretly disagreed with Judah Hanasi). The permission to adjudicate, teach and rely on the minority opinions of the Mishnah ceased with the sealing of the Talmud and the beginning of the Savoraic period. It is important to note that Luzzatto does not reiterate here his claim that chosen sages possessed the secrets of Torah. It seems that this is due to the impossibility of demonstrating the existence of such secrets and to his growing opposition to mysticism and its Hasidic adherents. The thirteen principles are also not mentioned here. According to Luzzatto, while these were used as explanations by the Sages in their own time, in our day, they are no longer relevant. Nowadays we clearly know that the thirteen principles were not transmitted at Sinai, as was claimed by earlier generations. They were the invention of the Tannaim, a means of strengthening their authority, a method allowing them to read verses exegetically in a manner far from their literal meaning.

In the same letter, Luzzatto discusses the occasional contradictions between the statements of the Torah and the conclusions of scientific research:

> And after time I observed (or reflected) that the Torah itself spoke in human language and it was impossible to explain the secrets of creation and the wonders of wisdom to flesh and blood, in any generation, and especially not to those who left Egypt. Therefore, it is improper to distort the Bible to make it agree with science, or to force science to agree with everything that appears in the Bible, and all the more so one should not deny the divinity of the Torah. Rather we should believe that God spoke the entire Torah to Moses, according to what His blessed wisdom saw was good and beneficial to flesh and blood. And this idea is what makes

---

themselves according to the needs of the time. It follows that in our day too we can do as they did, something Luzzatto never proposed. See Gafni, *Peshuta*, 228–240 and n. 50 there.

me faithful to philosophy, free in all my investigations, and also faithful to belief in the Torah's divinity.[22]

Unlike some of his contemporaries, who maintained that the Tannaim did not understand Scripture, that the Amoraim did not understand the Mishnah, and that both erred out of ignorance and misunderstanding, Luzzatto maintains that they were men of great stature, with a clear goal in mind, fully aware of the nature of the texts they were interpreting. He writes as much to his disciple and friend Joshua Heschel Schorr on January 1, 1840:

> This I ask of you, my dear brother, that you should be cautious in your words, and not sully the honor of the Sages of the Talmud, to speak of them as lowly men, as when you say that their eyes were blinded—far be it from us to say that. Every person errs, and they, too, erred, and you and I have erred and will err; but in any event the Sages of the Talmud were sharp-witted, they inquired deeply in love of truth for the benefit of their brethren, and it is unworthy of us to depend upon them as a blind man depends on one who sees, but it is also not worthy of us to be contemptuous of their honor [...] and if you reflect that the Mishnah, Tosefta, Sifra and Sifri which are now available to us in print were available to the sages of the Talmud orally, preserved only in their hearts, you will be amazed by their wisdom, and not by their errors[23]

In other words, the sages of the Talmud were intelligent people, who certainly understood the Mishnah just as well as we do, and they should not be disparaged. Quite the opposite: we should honor and thank them for benefitting the nation by delving into the words of the Tannaim, who with deep insight suited Halakhah to their own times according to the needs of the nation. That being said, they were not angels, and like all humans, no matter how intelligent, they also erred. However, their mistakes were accidental and were not sweeping methodological errors.

---

22 Reprinted in Luzzatto, *Meḥqerei Hayahadut*, vol. 1, pt. 2, 21 (first printed in *Hamagid* 2, 2). On Luzzatto's position on the conflict between philosophy and Torah see Chamiel, *The Middle Way*, vol. 1, 474–491.

23 Luzzatto, *Igrot Shadal*, 657. Luzzatto's reprimand was ineffective. Not only did Schorr continue with redoubled energy to invalidate the words of the Sages in the Mishnah and the Talmud, a few years later he also began to criticize the Bible, regarding it a human creation. Luzzatto never forgave him for this and cut off contact with him in disappointment. See E. Spicehandler, "Mavo Leyehoshu'a Heshel Schorr," *Maamarim* (Jerusalem, 1972), 7–37.

Truth be told, Luzzatto's comments on Leviticus, cited above, clearly demonstrate that he considered the Sages our superiors in intellect and virtue. He, therefore, opposes any attempt on the part of his contemporaries to alter Halakhah to suit the needs of the time, as done by the Sages. He explains that the Sages were worthy reformers, their innovative laws benefitting the Jewish people for many centuries to come. The reformers of his time however, are neither learned nor virtuous. In the aforementioned letter to Schorr from 1838, he writes about the reformers of his time, directing his statements to devout, observant individuals who reject him due to his statements about Maimonides and the laws of the Oral Torah:

> And in addition to this, I also believe with complete faith that all those who wish to make new decrees for Israel, they are all like babes and suckling infants compared to our ancient Sages; they with their Jewish wisdom, received from Sinai, succeeded in erecting Israel like an iron post and a bronze wall, against all the events which have befallen us, and all the hatred which has pursued us. But these [the Reform movement] with their Greek wisdom, cause each day the loss of thousands of Jewish souls; our ancient Sages acted to make Israel joyous and goodhearted in times of misfortune while these make their brethren bitter in times of happiness. Therefore, you, my honest and upright brothers, crying and wailing at all the abominations performed in our midst, do not provoke war against me, for I am yours, and not for your adversaries, God forbid! And truly, my heart is resolute and certain, that only the middle faith which I profess is the only will of God, and it will abide forever. So, even if it is assumed that you will stand against me as well, and I will fight a two-front war, with you on my one side, and the heretics on the other, nevertheless it is the counsel of God which will stand. Whether by me or by others, the pure Jewish faith will spread throughout Israel, and shall reign for eternity.

Has the possibility of creating new laws been barred forever? Luzzatto answers in the negative. Already in the aforementioned letter to Reggio from 1837 he writes about Rabbi Judah Hanasi's abundant wisdom, in permitting future courts to create new laws contravening those of the Tannaim, as long as the court in question is greater than Judah Hanasi's in size and wisdom.

> And because our holy rabbi [Judah Hanasi] foresaw the possibility of restored glory, even during exile—for it is possible that all of Israel or a great part of the nation will establish a court for themselves, which all will submit to—therefore he wisely added, that if this later court be greater in size and wisdom than the first one, then it can annul the statements of the former. And based on this consideration, the decree of our holy teacher was full of wondrous wisdom. And how fitting for the scholars of our time to realize this, that is to preserve the unity of the nation.[24]

It should be noted that none of this has ever come to pass, certainly not in the time of Luzzatto, and therefore practically speaking he opposed any change to Halakhah.

SUMMARY

Luzzatto's interpretation of Scripture's simple meaning (*peshat*) detached, on principle, from the interpretation of the Sages, is his primary contribution to Jewish thought and to the study of ancient, canonical Hebrew literature. In this chapter I have tried to show that Luzzatto's position towards halakhic development in the Mishnah and the Talmud which is called oral law—a bold position for its time—underwent a number of changes. Already at a young age, his discriminating eye and analytical mind realized that the laws of the Mishnah, *Midrash Halakhah* and Talmud do not accord with the text of the Torah and perhaps even contradict it. He therefore concluded that these laws could not have been transmitted orally to Moses at Sinai, and do not represent an interpretation of the Bible's primary meaning. That being said, his ongoing attempts to understand the motivations of the Sages in their different eras of activity, and the source of their authority to create new legislation and to derive laws from Scripture, persisted for much time. A reading of his writings demonstrates that the first time he committed these matters to writing, methodically was in 1828. In subsequent years he altered and changed his views, and only formulated a comprehensive theory in 1847.

The next chapter will be dedicated to Luzzatto's biblical interpretation, focusing on his fascinating attitude towards classic commentators considered to be interpreters of the *peshat*—Rashi and Ibn Ezra.

---

24 Luzzatto, *Meḥqerei Hayahadut*, vol. 1, pt. 2, 175.

CHAPTER FIVE

The *Peshat* is One, Because the Truth is One: Luzzatto between Interpretation and Thought

A man of many talents, Samuel David Luzzatto was part of the Haskalah literary movement in Eastern Europe, the sister movement of Wissenschaft des Judentums in the West. His scholarship spanned most areas of Jewish studies. His greatest efforts were consistently dedicated to the study of Hebrew language and grammar (including poetry and liturgy), Bible studies, his commentary on the Torah, and Onkelos's Aramaic Targum (specifically its text and the evidence of its antiquity); he studied other disciplines only intermittently (for instance, Kabbalah, *mussar* literature, medieval Jewish philosophy, Jewish history and the study of historical figures who interested him). Opportunities to engage in matters of philosophy emerged mainly in in his written correspondences with Italian, Galician, and German intellectuals, with whom he debated various issues of ethics, hermeneutics, philosophy, and occasionally current events.

In his sustained project of biblical interpretation, Luzzatto adopted the method of *peshat*—interpretation of Scripture according to its "simple" or literal meaning—maintaining that the biblical text has only one true meaning, which the interpreter should strive to comprehend. The text's one true meaning is the message the author wished to convey to his audience. In the Torah's case, this author was God who communicated his message on a low level appropriate for its ancient recipients. Luzzatto endeavored to arrive at the simple meaning of the text, carefully and assiduously examining the Torah according to immediate literary context, the principles of Hebrew grammar, and all the historical, philological, and archaeological information available to him at the time.

This method of interpretation is completely harmonious with Luzzatto's general attitude towards various philosophical trends that have developed in the history of Jewish thought. Luzzatto rejects the mystical kabbalistic interpretation of the Torah, maintaining that Kabbalah was created by an act of charlatanism, aimed at overthrowing speculative Aristotelian rationalism by using its own tools against it. Likewise, he rejects the philosophical-allegorical method of interpretation, considering it equally mistaken. Like Hirsch, he maintains that the Torah has no secrets and no strata of meaning, either philosophical or mystical. The Torah teaches morality, and the goals and rationales of the commandments are ethical; they are designed to turn those who keep them into better people. In his opinion, the *Midrash Halakhah* and the *Aggada* of the Sages do not represent their interpretations of the text's primary meaning but are merely *asmakhtaot* (textual reference or support) for laws appearing in the Mishnah and Talmud. This includes laws—which they created to fit changing circumstances and the needs of the community—which conflict with or add to the commandments of the Torah as well. Midrashic readings were also used to reinforce ideological messages the Sages wished to convey to their audience.

A review of Luzzatto's attitude towards classical biblical interpreters reveals an interesting phenomenon. In his philosophical writings (primarily his letters) he harshly criticizes the character and views of Abraham Ibn Ezra but praises and admires the character and views of Rabbi Shlomo Yitshaki (*Rashi*). By contrast, it is readily apparent from a review of Luzzatto's commentary on the Pentateuch that his interpretations frequently conflict with those of Rashi. He often supports Ibn Ezra's interpretation, and when there are disagreements between Rashi and Ibn Ezra, he tends to give an interpretation closer to that of Ibn Ezra. How can this phenomenon be explained?

I will attempt to answer this question on the basis of Luzzatto's philosophy and exegetical methodology, comparing and contrasting Luzzatto's biblical interpretations to those of Rashi and Ibn Ezra, and presenting Luzzatto's attitude towards their respective commentaries. I will begin by presenting Luzzatto's criticism of Ibn Ezra and praise of Rashi.

CRITICISM OF IBN EZRA; PRAISE OF RASHI

The disagreement between Luzzatto and Rapoport on the appropriate attitude towards Ibn Ezra is linked to their disagreement over whether or not the book of Isaiah is comprised of two separate works. This began on July 6, 1831. Luzzatto wrote to Rapoport that he is studying the book of Isaiah with his students, and among other things is reviewing with them the commentaries of Ernst Friedrich Karl Rosenmüller (1758–1835) and Heinrich Friedrich Wilhelm Gesenius (1786–1835). As they deny the existence of prophecy, he feels obligated to refute their statements, which are contrary to the truth in our possession.[1] In response, Rapoport noted that even these commentaries contain some truth, for example, their views on the division of the book of Isaiah into two prophets. According to this theory, the prophecies from chapter 40 onwards are those of a different author, a second "Isaiah" who lived in the time of King Cyrus, a view Rapoport believed was already maintained by Ibn Ezra. This theory infuriated Luzzatto, and in subsequent letters he launched a fierce polemic against it, maintaining that it entailed denial of prophecy, thus destroying the foundations of Jewish faith. When Rapoport responded by citing Ibn Ezra's view on the subject, bringing as support his commentary on Isaiah, Luzzatto responded, for the first time, with vehement criticism of Ibn Ezra's character and interpretive method. These letters are not extant, but we can adduce their contents from Rapoport's responses and subsequent letters from Luzzatto. In his response, Rapoport attacks Luzzatto's main arguments one by one and says that Abraham Ibn Ezra deserves to be honored with the maxim "from Abraham until Abraham there was none like Abraham," a formula customarily applied to Maimonides ("From Moses to Moses there was none like Moses"). Luzzatto responded with a harsh letter on November 11, 1832. Luzzatto would use the text of this letter once again in 1838 when the controversy over Ibn Ezra and Deutero-Isaiah re-erupted, this time with Krochmal, Rapoport and Reggio (the recipient of the second letter). From these letters—the first to Rapoport, the second to Reggio—emerge Luzzatto's main arguments against Ibn Ezra and his justifications for praising Rashi as his superior. I have combined the two letters into one text:[2]

---

1 For a full description of these controversies, including detailed and comprehensive excerpts from correspondence between Luzzatto, Rapoport, Reggio, Krochmal, Goldenberg, and Schorr see S. Vargon, "Havikuaḥ bein Shmuel David Luzzatto Le'amitav 'Al Hayaḥas Le R. Avraham Ibn Ezra Keḥeleq Meolama Shel Tenu'at Hahaskalah," in *Italia: Shmuel David Luzzatto Matayim Shana Lehuladeto*, 25–53; idem, "Havikuaḥ bein Shadal Leyashar bedevar Zeman Ketivata shel Hatorah," *Beit Miqra* 52, 1 (2007), 169–184; idem, "Zehuto Shel Meḥaber Yesaa'yahu 56:9—57:13 Uzmana Shel Hanevua 'Al Pi Shadal," *Beit Miqra* 45, 2 (2000), 97–109; idem, "Emdato Shel Shadal Besheelat Aḥduto Shel Sefer Yesaa'yahu," *Mehqerei Morashtenu* I (1999), 7–27. See also idem, *Shmuel David Luzzatto Biqortiut Metuna Beferush Hamiqra* (Ramat Gan, 2013), 402–425; S. Rostovsky-Halprin, *Shadal Vehitnagduto Larambam* (Tel Aviv, 1954), 21–23. On the controversy over Deutero-Isaiah see Chamiel, *The Middle Way*, vol. 1, 141–144.

2 The first part, up until the first set of curly brackets, only appears in the letter to Reggio, *Igrot Shadal*, 232. The curly brackets include additions and changes to the text in a letter

And I say this to retire the saying "from Moses until Moses" and its parallel, which you, my friend, have added: "from Abraham until Abraham"—may the God of Abraham have mercy! Is this the manner of man you choose? A man who speaks duplicitously? Who says of the great grammarian Rabbi Jonah that his book deserves to be burned because he wrote that the Bible contains some corrupted words, afterwards proceeding to break the fence tradition himself, alluding that certain verses were added to the Torah? On every page he says the Sages' knowledge is broader than our own, that tradition is definitive, and other such things, but afterwards permits the eating of *ḥelev* [forbidden animal fat]; what can you say about his statements on the subject of the *sota* [the ordeal of the wayward wife]? Does a man who suspects that the priest would put deadly poison in that water, possess a notion of a divine Torah? And what good did he do for the members of his nation? The fools remained foolish, considering him a holy man and a master of secrets. The philosophers learned from him to be heretical and break the yoke, and found shelter under that holy man's wings. But Rashi is the opposite. Behold this man is upright and righteous; this is the man I will choose. {And my eyes are blurred in anger when I see some scholars of our age exalting the virtues of Ibn Ezra to the greatest heights while they degrade the virtues of Rashi unto the dust. And you can see for yourself the difference between them.} Rashi was the member of a boorish people who had studied no wisdom. He was an expert in *aggadot*, they were his delight every day, and he began to be a mighty one in that land. He said with clarity: you may expound your *derasha*, but I have come to interpret Scripture's simple meaning. {And not only in homiletics, but also in halakhic matters he pursued the simple meaning even when it opposes Halakhah, such as the verse "you shall not follow the many for evil" where he writes "But I wish to explain the verse so it should fit properly, according to its simple sense, and this is its meaning"}; […] And what resulted from his handiwork?—that little by little, the interpreters of the *peshat* proliferated in Israel, such as his grandson Rashbam, and Nachmanides and Radaq; and many would have ranged far and wide and knowledge would have increased, had it not been for the philosophizers, Ibn Ezra and Maimonides, and their disciples. They re-submerged the Torah in the

---

sent on February 28, 1838 to Reggio and printed in *Kerem Ḥ emed*, vol. 4 (1839), 131–147. This part of the letter (133–137) was later reprinted in *Meḥ qerei Hayahadut*, vol. 1, pt. 2, with the title "Rashi Veharav Avraham Ben Ezra," 193–196.

depths of allegory and parable, and brought up gall and wormwood in their hands. They caused the birth of the kabbalists, and strengthened their hands, paving before them the path of parables, allegories and distortions of verses, and removing them entirely from context. And the kabbalists walked their own path, with worthy intentions, to reinforce religion and faith and to seal the breaches made by the philosophizers. And ever since, from the beginning of the sixth millennium [mid-thirteenth century], the wisdom of Israel has continued to decrease.

And let us return to Rashi and Ibn Ezra. Who is not amazed by Rashi? Though he studied no philosophy, he still attained lucid, pure knowledge, and employed refined language, bright like the very heavens in its purity. He does not say too much or too little; he does not reverse order, and he elucidates his thought and the thoughts of those he interpreted, with a clear and wondrous elucidation. None arose like him. But Ibn Ezra, who studied all forms of wisdom, wrote nothing in proper order or in lucid language. Rather he skips from subject to subject, {presenting matters out of order}, his [method] is darkness and not order. Is this not a sign of a confused mind and a man with no restraint to his soul, enslaved to the thought of the hour, writing whatever jumps to mind at first glance? And if he would have contemplated deeply what he was writing, he would have organized his books in a proper, clear order and not as he did. And do not reply that his lack of order {was done with wisdom} to conceal secrets—for indeed there is no place for this {reason} in his books of grammar, which were truly written with neither precision nor balance.

However, I know that some praise the virtues of Ibn Ezra over Rashi, because he pursued free inquiry, unlike Rashi who clung fully to the faith of his fathers. But can we really consider Ibn Ezra free in his inquiry? Behold, his belief in astrology and the magical properties of numbers proves that he too would believe without inquiry, and what difference is there between the two? Ibn Ezra with all the strength of his scholarship was unable to cast doubt on what the scholars of his generation were saying—that the stars move with will—and never considered, like Isaac Arama (*Aqedat Yitshak*, 2) that perhaps their movements were from a natural cause (as explained afterwards by the wondrous scholar Newton). And he never considered to follow Aviad Sar Shalom Basilea (*Emunat Hakhamim*, ch. 21) who said, that the generation after him would invent another philosophy (as it came to be) [...] and if we turn to another aspect and examine Ibn Ezra in terms of the shape of his heart and the righteousness of his actions, what can we say when we see him saying with guile and self-aggrandizement: see, I am pure!—and he turns events with his tricks, and his thoughts are the opposite of his words.³

From these letters and from subsequent letters to Reggio, Rapoport and Schorr we can summarize Luzzatto's criticism of Ibn Ezra as follows:

1. He provides hasty, superficial interpretations, failing to examine matters in depth, resulting in often mistaken and misleading interpretations.
2. He writes unclearly, chaotically, and discursively, skipping from one subject to another, evidence of his unsettled mind and unorganized thought. He writes like an esoteric philosopher, using parables and riddles, even when unnecessary, and writes verbosely and repetitively to raise wages from his sponsors. This type of interpretation, Luzzatto argues, encumbered us with the esoteric interpretations of philosophy and Kabbalah which deviate from the simple meaning of the text, distorting the Torah's message.
3. He expresses heretical opinions, opposed to Halakhah and tradition, raising doubts about his belief in the divinity of the Torah. For example: he believes that there are verses in the Torah which were added after the time of Moses; he believes that the priest would poison the waters of the *sota*; and he states that the Torah allows the consumption of *ḥelev* and it was only the Sages who forbade it. With trickery, cunning, and hypocrisy he conceals his true views, writing duplicitously, a practice his students may emulate. For example: he proclaims his loyalty to the Sages' interpretation of the Torah even when these seem to be opposed to the *peshat*, but then interprets commandments in the Torah in opposition to them, such as the laws of *ḥelev* and the law of shaving one's sidelocks—which he maintains is only forbidden as an expression of mourning (a view Luzzatto shared). Although he declares his loyalty to reading Scripture according to traditional cantillation, he deviates from this method (sometimes rightfully so). In this claim, Luzzatto reaches the peak of his harsh remarks, describing Ibn Ezra's hypocrisy with the phrase "see, I am pure!"—the language used in *Bereshit Rabbah* (65, 1) to describe the hypocrisy of a pig.

---

3 Luzzatto, *Igrot Shadal*, 232–233.

4. He was a man of bad character, who besmirched the honor of scholars. He said that the book of Rabbi Jonah Ibn Janach the grammarian should be burned because it names more than a hundred corrupted words in the Bible which should be corrected, when he himself maintains that the Torah contains verses written after the time of Moses—a far more dangerous view; he should correct his own defects before criticizing others. He also sullied the honor of Rabbi Saadya Gaon when disagreeing with him over whether angels are greater or lesser than mankind, arrogantly and unjustly arguing that Saadya's arguments are flawed, even though he knew very well that his own Aristotelian conception of angels was completely different than Saadya's traditional-Jewish view.
5. He credulously believes in astrology and numerology, maintaining that stars have will, and that numbers bear secret meanings, and that these influence humans, and can be used to foretell the future. These are foolish beliefs which reflect poorly on their believers.

Conversely, based on the previous text and the one I will cite below, one can summarize Luzzatto's praise of Rashi as follows:

> Judah Halevi! That holy name, my heart yearns for him. Rashi and the author of the *Kuzari* are beloved and pleasant to me, precious and honored in my eyes more than the sages of Israel who arose after the sealing of the Talmud. Rashi is the last of the sages of Israel in time, after him there did not arise among us a great Sage, of many achievements, and faithful with Jewish characteristics, without the admixture of Greek and Ishmaelite characteristics. [...] And Rashi, most precious in my eyes of all the Torah scholars who did not deal with foreign books; and Rabbi Judah Halevi is beloved and honored in my eyes among all the Sages who did meditate on the works of the gentiles. He studied Greek and Ishmaelite philosophy and his heart was not seduced by them; and what is most sublime in his strength and exalted in the power of his intellect above Abraham Ibn Ezra and Moses the son of Maimon, and all the young ones who followed in their footsteps![4]

---

4 Luzzatto, *Betulat Bat Yehuda*, ed. J. Hauben (Nevo) (Tel Aviv, 1996), 135–226. First printed in Prague, 1840. See also introduction, 34.

We can enumerate Luzzatto's praises of Rashi as follows:

1. He did not occupy himself with philosophy. He was a righteous and upright man who did not conceal his intentions with trickery and guile.
2. He expresses himself clearly, lucidly and methodically, reflecting his proper intellect and original and deep wisdom.
3. He is faithful to a simple reading of the Torah, even when such an interpretation opposes a *midrash* or ruling of the Sages.
4. His influence is responsible for interpreters of the peshat in subsequent generation, such as his grandson Solomon Ben Meir (*Rashbam*) as well as Nachmanides and Rabbi David Kimhi (*Radaq*).

Reggio, Rapoport, and Krochmal did not sit idly by, and responded vehemently and aggressively.[5] In various letters they castigated Luzzatto for his arrogance, claiming that his arguments do not help students, as he maintains, but harm them—leading them to denigrate all scholars from past generations. He had erred egregiously in his criticism, they claimed. In their opinion, Ibn Ezra was an unprecedented figure of deep wisdom, praised by all of his successors. Unlike Luzzatto's claims, he maintained exemplary organization in his writings. Indeed, Rashi was never hypocritical, and in this he was superior to Ibn Ezra, who with great wisdom took pains to conceal his true opinions from his adversaries to prevent excommunication and book burnings as befell Maimonides. He truly believed that precedence should be given to the Sages' interpretation of Scripture and his integrity should not be impugned, even if he expressed himself differently according to different audiences and different subject matters—as practiced by many others. His statements on *ḥelev* were part of a polemic against the Karaites and were directed at them exclusively (in this case Luzzatto actually would admit to Rapoport that he had been mistaken on this issue). They argue that Luzzatto himself frequently interpreted verses in a manner which conflicted with the Halakhah of the Sages; why then should he complain about Ibn Ezra? Luzzatto had simply misunderstood Ibn Ezra's interpretation of the waters of the *sota*, and they declared that Ibn Ezra was actually the greatest, most original, and most successful interpreter

---

5   The discussion here focuses on Luzzatto's position on the issue; therefore, I am paraphrasing Reggio and Rapoport's responses, concisely and without citations. Rapoport's statements appear in Rapoport, *Igrot Shir* (Przemyśl, 1845), and Reggio's and Krochmal's in *Kerem Ḥemed*. For details and excerpts see Vargon's articles cited in note 1.

of *peshat*—Rashbam, Radaq and Nachmanides learning from him and not from Rashi. While Rashi sometimes declared that he was only interpreting Scripture's simple meaning as opposed to the *midrash* (a declaration which he copied from the Sages in the Talmud), in practice he generally believed that the *midrash* represented the primary meaning of the text, making no distinction between the two. Ibn Ezra's theology is remarkable, they added. It appears that only Maimonides understood it, and in our day Krochmal has succeeded in deciphering its true meaning.

Despite all this, Luzzatto remained loyal to his criticism and offered no retraction. In a letter to Schorr dated to December 31, 1841 he writes:

> Behold, I, with all my familiarity with Ibn Ezra's methods, believed until this day, that what he wrote about the "morrow of the Sabbath" (Lev. 23:11) was intended to reinforce the Sages' interpretation [that the true meaning is the morrow of the first day of Passover]. Only recently has it become clear to me that his words are nothing but an illusion. [. . .] And my righteous and upright parents taught me to hate the trickery of guileful language. And that which I find praiseworthy in the words of Judah Halevi [*Kuzari*, 3:41] who expresses his opinion properly and using clear language, [that the verse means the appropriate Sunday, and as long as Shavuoth is fifty days after, on that day of the week], I find loathsome in the words of Ibn Ezra [who shares Judah Halevi's view] which are written duplicitously.[6]

LUZZATTO'S INTERPRETATIONS

Given Luzzatto's clear preference for Rashi over Ibn Ezra, one would expect his commentary on the Pentateuch to consistently rely on Rashi's interpretations and avoid and reject those of Ibn Ezra. Surprisingly, the reality throughout Luzzatto's commentary is very different. Why does Luzzatto either ignore or reject the interpretations of Rashi whom he loved, and often prefer the interpretations of Ibn Ezra of whom he disapproved?

Below are just some examples of Luzzatto completely disregarding Rashi's interpretation or preferring interpretations of Ibn Ezra:

Gen. 1:2—**and the wind of God hovered above the waters.** Rashi—"the throne of glory was standing in the air and hovering over the surface of the water. . ."; Luzzatto—"as the Targum says [. . .] a great, strong wind."

---

6   *Kerem Ḥemed*, vol. 7 (1843), 72. See also Luzzatto, Lev. 23:11.

Gen. 1:3—**and God said**. Luzzatto—"God is described as a king who commands. Everything comes into being at His word, to show that God's work is not like the work of a man who uses his hands, but it is as if He were commanding others to work, even though in this case there was no one to command (Ibn Ezra)"

Gen. 1:5—**and it was evening and it was morning**. Rashi—"why did it write 'one day' [and not the first day]? Because the Holy One Blessed is He was still the only one in his world, for the angels were not created until the second day, as explained in *Bereshit Rabbah*"; Luzzatto—"'there was evening and there was morning, that is, one day'. The words 'that is' are missing in the Scriptures hundreds, even thousands of times. 'One day': a whole day; evening followed by morning comprises one day."

Gen. 1:31—**the sixth day**. Rashi—"God added the letter *he* [the definite article] to the word 'sixth' at the conclusion of the work of creation, to say: that God stipulated [the endurance of] the creation, on Israel's acceptance of the five [=numerical value of *he*] books of the Torah. Alternatively: 'the sixth day', all [of creation] stood in suspense until the sixth day, that is the sixth of Sivan, which had been prepared for the giving of the Torah; Luzzatto—"with the definite article *he*, this being the last of the days of creation. The form is equivalent to *ha-yom ha-shishi*. [...]"

Gen. 1:16—**the two great luminaries**. Rashi—"they were created equal in size but the moon was diminished because it complained: it is impossible for two kings to wear one crown"; Luzzatto—"the sun and the moon, which illuminate the earth more than the stars do, which is the reason for their being called 'luminaries,' they are larger than the others. Even though the moon is physically smaller than the stars, and even though it has no light at all of its own, the Torah speaks from a human viewpoint. We receive much light from the moon and therefore it is a 'great luminary.'"

Gen. 1:26—**Let us make man**. Rashi—"even though they [the angels] did not assist God in [man's] creation, making room for the heretics to claim supremacy, nevertheless Scripture did not refrain from teaching good conduct and the virtue of humility, that the greater should consult and ask permission from the lesser. And if it had written 'I shall make man', we would not have learned that He was speaking with his [angelic] court, only with himself; and the refutation to the heretics is immediately in the next verse: 'and he created man', and it is not written: 'and they created man'"; Luzzatto—"in my opinion, this too is an archaism analogous to the Aramaic. It does not mean that he consulted with others, such as the angels, for he also said 'in our image' and man is not in the image of angels. Neither is it the plural of majesty but such is the Aramaic idiom, as in 'And we [i.e., Daniel] will tell its interpretation before the king' (Daniel 2:36). Daniel would not have spoken in a self-aggrandizing manner when speaking with the great king (as noted by Ibn Ezra)."

Gen. 2:3—**which God had created to make**. Rashi—"the work which should have been done on the Sabbath, he performed on the sixth day, double the work, as explained in *Bereshit Rabbah*." Luzzatto—"that God had created and made, meaning he ceased creating and making (so Nachmanides and Mendelssohn)."

Ex. 22:1—**there is no blood for him**. Luzzatto is undecided between Rashi's interpretation that the thief has no blood (his death by the owner is not considered murder) and Ibn Ezra's interpretation that the owner of the house has no blood (will not be executed if he killed the thief). Only in 1859 would he decide in favor of Rashi's interpretation. In 1864 his student showed him that in his short commentary, Ibn Ezra had adopted Rashi's interpretation: that it is the thief who has no blood.

Ex. 22:12—**if it is torn to death, he shall bring a witness**. Rashi—"he shall bring witnesses that it was torn to pieces by accident and he shall be freed of liability"; Luzzatto—"he will bring some of the animal's torn limbs as his testimony and evidence that the animal was torn to pieces [...] (Rashbam and Ibn Ezra)."

Ex. 23:1—**do not bear a false report**. Rashi—"like the Targum: do not accept a false report, a warning not to accept slander, and to a judge that he must not listen to the statements of one litigant until his opposing litigant arrives"; Luzzatto—"do not utter a false rumor with the intention of slandering another person (Ibn Ezra)."

Lev. 19:27—**do not destroy the side-growth of your beard**. According to Rashi, the instruction is applicable to every Jew at every time; Luzzatto—"destroying the side-growth of the beard is mentioned in the context of making gashes as a sign of mourning, and similarly in the priestly laws (ibid., 21:5): 'or cut the side-growth of their beards, or make gashes in their flesh' and see Ibn Ezra ad locum. According to the literal meaning all Jews are forbidden from destroying their beards as a sign of mourning, and the priests are even forbidden from shaving their beards, also as a sign of mourning."

Deut. 17:8—**between blood and blood, between ruling and ruling, between affliction and affliction**. Rashi—"between pure menstrual blood and impure menstrual blood (Niddah 19a); between guilty judgment and innocent judgment: between an impure lesion and a pure lesion (see ibid.)"; Luzzatto—"'between blood and blood' a case in which the judges could not determine if a murder was intentional or inadvertent. And the confusion and doubt is between blood and blood—meaning they could not determine the nature of this blood, that is to say how this killing was accomplished, inadvertently or intentionally [...] 'between judgment and judgment'—between claim and claim, meaning they cannot determine if Reuven's claim against Shimon is valid or not. 'Between affliction and affliction'—matters of wounds and injury (like Ibn Ezra and Nachmanides) and we have found *nega* (affliction) used in this sense: 'he [the adulterer] will be met with *nega* [wounds] and disgrace' (Prov. 6:33) its meaning is apparent from the next verse: 'The fury of the husband will be passionate; he will show no pity on his day of vengeance.'"

LUZZATTO'S INTERPRETIVE METHOD

Before attempting to explain the apparent contradiction entailed by Luzzatto's treatment of Ibn Ezra and Rashi in his commentary, I will briefly summarize Luzzatto's methodology of biblical interpretation, the basis of his attitude towards different commentators:

1. He tried to include in his commentary the interpretation closest to the primary sense of the text (*peshat*)—based on grammatical and literary context, based on the ethical message which the divine author wished to convey, and based on the ancient worldviews current in the era in which Moses received the Torah.
2. To accomplish this, Luzzatto examined almost two hundred ancient and modern commentators, Jewish and gentile, from Onkelos to Mendelssohn, and generally selected the first to capture what he considered the text's simple meaning.
3. Therefore, whenever Rashi, one of the first biblical commentators, provided a literal interpretation which Luzzatto deemed correct, he happily adopted it. However, when Rashi clung to a rabbinic *midrash*, which, according to Luzzatto, distorts the intention of the text, he continued his search and would select the next commentator who first captured the text's literal meaning: Onkelos, Saadya Gaon, Rashbam, Ibn Ezra, Maimonides, Radaq (on Genesis) Nachmanides, Gersonides, Abarvanel, Seforno, Mendelssohn and others.
4. When he could not find an interpretation to his liking, he endeavored to offer his own.[7]

---

[7] How does one arrive at the correct interpretation according to Luzzatto? See a summary of his foundations of correct interpretation in Chamiel, *The Middle Way*, vol. 1, 116–121 and in the next chapter.

5. Frequently, when he felt the need to relay to his readers criticism of a certain interpretation, he would cite it, reject it, and explain his considerations.
6. In exceptional cases, when a passage was particularly difficult, he would present a wide spectrum of opinions, explaining which interpretations he preferred, even when uncertain as to their veracity (for instance, Gen. 49:10, 26; Ex. 18:1; 34:6; Num. 19:12; 35:4–5).

THE EXPLANATION

Here I will mention that Luzzatto also harshly criticized Maimonides, as alluded to in his statements above. In his opinion, Maimonides had enslaved the Jews to himself and to Aristotle, and in doing so "was our downfall." It was he who formulated the thirteen principles of faith, beliefs which merit their believers an afterlife, removing the link between ethical actions and divine reward—"and we did not see the snake coiled around the heel of your words."[8] That being said, Luzzatto does adopt Maimonides's interpretations of the Bible more than once.

Luzzatto himself notes that he distinguishes between the personal beliefs and character of a person and the value of a person's biblical commentary, which for him is based on the degree of his deviation from the interpretive tradition of the Sages. In subsequent correspondence with Rapoport he explains:

> I did not cry out bitterly against Ibn Ezra because he deviated from the tradition of the Sages, but rather because of his duplicity, because in many places he elevates the tradition of the copyists unto the stars and says that the words of the Sages will never fall to the ground (Gen. 36:32). And I, though I am not one of his admirers, have already accepted his interpretation (against Halakhah) of the verse "do not round-off the side-growth of your head," that it is only prohibited as a sign of mourning. I have accepted this in practice, although I do not teach it to others, as I am not involved with halakhic rulings.[9]

---

8   Letter to Reggio, 12 Sivan 1837, *Kerem Ḥemed*, vol. 3 (1838), 61–76. On Luzzatto's polemic against Maimonides see Chamiel, *The Middle Way*, vol. 1, 463–466.
9   Letter to Rapoport dated March 25, 1833, Luzzatto, *Igrot Shadal*, 246. See Vargon, *Biqortiut Metuna*, 400–401. Vargon asks why Luzzatto does not explain here the Sages' deviation from the simple meaning and why he abnormally acted against their rulings. He gives no answer. In my opinion, Luzzatto believed that the Sages ruled that a Jew should grow a beard so as to

In other words, despite his scathing remarks against Ibn Ezra, Luzzatto did not refrain from adopting his *peshat* interpretation of the Bible, and applied this understanding in practice himself, even though it diverged from rabbinic law (something extremely rare for Luzzatto).

In another letter, discussing his approach to Rashi, Luzzatto draws the same distinction between a person's character and the value of a person's commentary: "who has loved Rashi like I, with all of his heart and all of his soul, honoring him more than his very body? Nevertheless, I dispute him each and every day."[10]

In the aforementioned letter to Reggio from 1838, Luzzatto explains that Rashi's affinity to the Sages and Ibn Ezra's progressive interpretations can be explained historically:

> However, I know that some exalt the virtues of Ibn Ezra over Rashi, because he pursued free inquiry, unlike Rashi who clung fully to the faith of his fathers. However, if Rashi at times diverged from his predecessors and teachers, this is a sign of his strong intellect, for with his wisdom and strength he steered his own path. But Ibn Ezra, even if he deviated from the faith of his fathers ten times more than Rashi did, this is no source of pride, because his eyes had been opened by his study of philosophy and wisdom. If at times he spoke better than Rashi, how many helpers did he have that Rashi lacked? Rashi saw nothing but the Talmud, the *midrashim*, the *targumim*, the dictionary of Menahem Ben Saruq and the criticisms of Dunash ben Labrat. Ibn Ezra had at his disposal the words of Rashi as well as the books of Saadya Gaon, Rabbi Judah Hiyug, Rabbi Jonah Ibn Janach, Moshe Hacohen and other authors who wrote in the Hebrew language, who were unknown to Rashi.

In other words, Rashi's library was limited and consisted mainly of *midrashim* and *targumim*. Ibn Ezra however, possessed a far more extensive library and also occupied much of his time studying philosophy, which is beneficial for intellectual development. Their respective circumstances explain the distinction between their commentaries. The fact that Rashi boldly interpreted

---

have a dignified appearance, but did not say so, as this justification is based on fashion and not values. It appears that Luzzatto permitted for himself shaving his beard with a razor after categorizing himself as an istenis (a fastidious person) or a mitstaer (someone suffering), people for whom the Sages permitted certain prohibitions.

10 A letter to Rapoport dated July 19, 1836, Luzzatto, *Igrot Shadal*, 343.

verses according to their simple meaning is a sign of his wisdom and ingenuity, whereas Ibn Ezra, who did not excel beyond the accepted wisdom of his generation, had nothing to be proud of.

It is clear that, objectively speaking, Luzzatto considers Ibn Ezra's commentary the more progressive and developed of the two, preferring interpretive methodologies which do not consider rabbinic interpretation of the Bible definitive. As mentioned, Luzzatto believes that the Sages consciously utilized verses as textual support for their laws, and that they sometimes reformed commandments of the Torah, or expounded verses to convey ideological or ethical messages. The *midrash* was never meant to annul the Torah's simple meaning, a fact acknowledged by Rashi.

Luzzatto's only guiding principle was the search for truth. Luzzatto writes that there is only one true interpretation of the text:

> Pride, love of honor and flattery, these alone drove away the hearts of the multitudes of the learned from the way of the simple meaning. The simple meaning is one, because the truth is one, and its place is very narrow, and there is no way of turning to the right or to the left, and he who aims at the single hair will find it, and he who turns from the point this way and that goes astray.[11]

On his method of interpretation, his search for the one true reading of the text, and his position on the rabbinic-midrashic interpretation, Luzzatto says:

> And you should know that in this book, as in all the rest of my writing, I am neither among the elders nor among the innovators, neither traditionally religious nor a philosopher, neither rabbinic nor Karaite. I pursue the truth, and I accept it from whoever states it, even if he is the least of the least and I will not accept a lie, even if the greatest of the great states it. In my interpretation of biblical verses all my effort was directed at understanding for myself and others the intention of the speaker and writer, and far be it from me to distort the texts in order to make them agree with the Halakha. What Rabbi Moses ben Menahem Mendelssohn wrote in the introduction to *Or Linetiva*, and these are his words: "But if the way that appears to us to be the simple meaning of the Bible contradicts and opposes the accepted

---

11 *Bikkurei Haitim* (1827): 94–95. Luzzatto, *Haotsar, Lishka B*, 93. On Luzzatto's method of *peshat* see Chamiel, *The Middle Way*, vol. 1, 131–133.

way of *derash*, taken from the Sages, so that is impossible for both of them to be right, because contradiction must be avoided, then it is our obligation to go in the path of drash, to translate the Bible accordingly, because we have only the tradition of the Sages, and by their light we shall see light." Perhaps, he wrote that for the need of the hour, but Rashi and Rashbam have already instructed us, and before them the Sages of the Talmud, that a biblical verse must not be removed from its *peshat*, and in several places they said, "however, this is from the sages [...], and the verse is merely a reference [*asmakhta*]."[12]

Luzzatto had concluded that while a man's character, virtues, and ethical and philosophical views attest to his nature as a person, they are not criteria in examining the value of a person's commentary. Interpretation should be evaluated not on the merits of the interpreter but on the merits of his words. A person should evaluate a commentary according to his own exegetical criteria—that is in terms of its correspondence with truth as he sees it.

Luzzatto expresses this idea in a letter to Rapoport which was published as an essay on the subject of the two books of Isaiah:

> And I will go back and say that the words and arguments of these last scholars [Rosenmüller and Gesenius] require investigation. Not all that is published in books and said publicly by university lecturers is true. For scholars, books, and university lecturers God has confounded their language as well; one says this, the other that. What is absolute truth in one university is absolute falsehood in another. That which was absolute truth in another generation, is absolute falsehood in this generation. And the man who loves truth will investigate matters with his own eyes and not rely on anyone else [...] and until this day, I stand by my opinion, and am always willing to learn from every person, and to accept the truth from whoever speaks it.[13]

---

12 From the introduction of his book *Hamishtadel*. On the status of the *Midrash Halakhah* and *Aggada* components of the Oral Torah in Luzzatto's though see Chamiel, *The Middle Way*, vol. 1, 314–328.

13 Letter to Rapoport, 1 Elul 1841, *Kerem Ḥemed*, vol. 7 (1843), 214–242. Reprinted in Luzzatto, *Meḥqerei Hayahadut*, vol. 1, pt. 2, 30–48 in the essay "Sefer Yeshayahu." On Luzzatto's search for truth as a free inquirer, see Chamiel, *The Middle Way*, vol. 1, 110–116. Accepting the truth from whoever speaks it is a principle appearing in Maimonides's introduction to his commentary on *Pirqei Avot* (*Shemona Peraqim*). Luzzatto adopted it as a guiding principle even though he emphatically disapproved of Maimonides's method and

SUMMARY

In summary: Luzzatto was fiercely critical of Ibn Ezra and Maimonides for incorporating foreign speculative philosophies into Jewish thought, and for believing in the existence of philosophical strata within the Torah, which were never entertained by the Torah or the Sages. He even went so far as to harshly criticize Ibn Ezra's personal character and virtues. Nevertheless, Luzzatto does not halt his pursuit of truth and therefore his commentary—written according to the *peshat* (which tends not to fit the tradition of the Sages)—incorporates their interpretations, whenever they seemed to correctly capture the author's intention. However, for all his love of Rashi, of his uprightness, his innocent faith, his distinguished qualities, and his wisdom, Luzzatto only incorporated his interpretations into his commentary when they captured the Torah's intention. But in most places Luzzatto ignored Rashi's statements because he had adopted the *Midrash Aggada* and *Halakhah* of the Sages. Luzzatto did not consider these the intention of the biblical author, but distortions done for important reasons unrelated to interpretation.

The next chapter will be dedicated to Luzzatto's special approach to Maimonides's philosophy.

---

philosophical positions, based on the same principle. Similarly, despite what he says about them in this excerpt, Luzzatto brings the views of Rosenmüller and Gesenius a number of times in his commentary, accepting their interpretations even when they conflict with classical commentators, whenever he believed that they had arrived at the truth. See *Igrot Shadal*, 272, in his letter to Issachar Blumenfeld from Brody, and in the next chapter.

CHAPTER SIX

Luzzatto and Maimonides: "Accept Truth from Whoever Speaks It"

INTRODUCTION

Luzzatto was quite possibly the greatest intellectual to emerge from Italian Jewry in the nineteenth century; he was certainly the most famous. As I explained in chapter 3 of my book *The Middle Way*, Luzzatto began his literary and academic career during Europe's transition from Rationalism to Romanticism—a shift which began with the philosophers Kant and Hegel at the onset of the nineteenth century, starting in Berlin and gradually conquering the entirety of Europe. At the beginning of his career, Luzzatto was an advocate of rationalist philosophy, deeming reason the key to individual and communal success. But he soon shifted to a romantic position, considering emotion, the return to nature, and the remarkable experiences of the past as the keys to human success. While Luzzatto is aware of this shift in his approach, he does not attribute it to a wider transition on the part of society. He considers the transformation of his ideology a process of personal enlightenment, initiated by reason's failure to prevent his personal troubles and hardships. Likewise, he was influenced by (what he considered) the dangerous results of Maimonidean and Spinozan rationalism, approaches he witnessed take the intellectuals of Europe by storm, philosophies which he believed threatened the wellbeing of traditional Judaism and its loyalty to historical revelation. He considered cold philosophical rationalism, and its abstract, distant, and alienating God, dangerous to the masses of simple believers. He quickly found himself adopting a reactionary stance against the *maskilim* of Galicia (citizens of the Austrian Empire like himself) who remained loyal to rationalism which in distant Galicia still reigned supreme in the first half of the nineteenth century.

In the early decades of that century, Europe also saw the rise of Jewish movements which anchored their positions in Jewish sources by embracing medieval philosophers. The Reform movement and the historical-positivist school (the early Conservative movement) generally favored Maimonides who had chosen reason as the sole criterion for establishing truth and who believed that apart from the 613 commandments legislated by Moses, the remainder of the halakhic corpus developed over the course of history. By contrast, Orthodoxy favored Judah Halevi and Nachmanides who considered revelation the sole criterion in establishing truth and who believed that all of Halakhah was transmitted in revelation. Luzzatto, who believed in the divinity of the Written Torah, consciously selected as his inspiration Judah Halevi instead of Maimonides, even though he concurred with the latter regarding the nature of the halakhic corpus. It was only a matter of time until Luzzatto revealed his negative opinion of Maimonidean rationalism, immediately arousing a controversy which swept up all the *maskilim* of Europe at that time.

This chapter is divided into four sections. In the first, I will provide a detailed historical description of Luzzatto's polemic against Maimonides, which he initiated in 1837 and which consisted of fierce accusations against Maimonides, leading to shocked and enraged responses from the scholars of Galicia. I will also present Luzzatto's responses to his detractors' arguments. In the second section, I will enumerate those places in Luzzatto's commentary on the Pentateuch in which he proposes Maimonides's interpretation of a verse, citing him by name. I will note whether Luzzatto accepts or rejects the interpretation. In the third section, I will present seven instances in Luzzatto's commentary on the Pentateuch and his other writings, in which he refrains from citing Maimonides by name, even though he maintains a philosophical position akin to his. In the fourth section I will attempt to answer the question (which I will present at the end of the second section): why in these seven cases does Luzzatto avoid mentioning Maimonides by name, when he himself proudly professed the Maimonidean ideal—to accept the truth from whoever says it?

A. HISTORICAL DESCRIPTION OF THE CONTROVERSY SURROUNDING MAIMONIDES—LUZZATTO'S ARGUMENTS AND THE RESPONSES OF THE SCHOLARS OF GALICIA

In a famous letter to Reggio written in 1837 and published in *Kerem Ḥemed* volume 3, 1838, Luzzatto reopened a polemic which had almost completely died down since the end of the fifteenth century—the polemic against the philosophy of Maimonides.[1] Luzzatto published this letter as a response to Reggio who had turned to him (on behalf of all "super-naturalist" *maskilim*, who believe in the divinity of the Torah, divine providence, reward and punishment, prophecy and miracles), requesting he publicize his views on the spread of rationalism across western and central Europe, which poses a danger to the continuity of traditional Judaism.[2] Later, after the controversy had already erupted, Luzzatto would write to Joshua Heschel Schorr that he had kept his critique of Maimonides's philosophy to himself, only publicizing it after years of examination and analysis. He had considered the matter at length and had dedicated much time and thought to its proper articulation.[3] To Luzzatto the final straw was Abraham Geiger's book *Urschrift und Übersetzungen der Bibel*, which included (what Luzzatto considered) the false claim that Rabbi Judah Hanasi wrote the Mishnah. In Geiger's opinion, Rabbi Judah Hanasi even had at his disposal written *mishnayot*, and the Tannaim's goal was to establish Halakhah

---

[1] *Kerem Ḥemed*, vol. 3 (1838), 69, reprinted in Luzzatto, *Meḥqerei Hayahadut*, vol. 1, pt. 2, 159. On the reopening of the polemic see A. Ravitzky, "Sitrei Torato Shel Moreh Hanevukhim: Haparshanut Bedorotav Uvedoroteinu," in *Al Da'at Hamaqom*, ed. idem (Jerusalem, 1991), 142–182. Ravitzky correctly notes there that Luzzatto's criticism was relatively moderate despite his fierce language. It is based on fifteenth century criticism and does not raise earlier, more radical interpretations (such as those who are in favor of such interpretation like Kaspi and Narboni and those who are against it like Judah Alfakhar and Meir ben Todros Abulafia) which maintained that Maimonides concurred with Aristotle on all subjects including the miracles, the eternity of the world and other issues. In a letter to Schorr from 1838 (its publication, canceled in 1838, only happened in 1863), Luzzatto mentions the issue of the world's eternity, referring to it as a view maintained by Maimonides's philosophical contemporaries (but not a view of Maimonides). From that letter it is clear that Luzzatto never entertained the notion that Maimonides also questioned the simple understanding of miracles, prophecy, and the divinity of the Torah—as maintained by his radical interpreters, then and today (see below). It is also worth mentioning Luzzatto's letter to the editor of *Hamagid*, Eliezer Lipmann Zilberman, which was published 8 Heshvan 5621 (1860) in *Hamagid* 4, 41 (written a month prior on 9 Tishrei) and which contains criticism of Solomon Rubin and his work *Teshuva Nitsaḥat*. Rubin argues against Luzzatto on the issue of Spinoza and Maimonides and Luzzatto responds. It clearly emerges from this letter that Ravitzky was correct in saying that Luzzatto truly took the subject of the world's eternity in the *Guide for the Perplexed* at face value, and did not seek deeper layers of meaning, maintaining that Maimonides did not believe in the world's eternity, and that those who think otherwise (like Rubin) are distorting his words and are mistaken. This letter was published again in *Meḥqerei Hayahadut*, vol. 1, pt. 2, "Neged Spinoza," 214.

[2] See Feiner, *Shadal Vehahaskalah*, 156–157. Luzzatto writes about Reggio's request in a letter to Schorr 4 Tamuz, 5598 (1838) which was published in *Otsar Neḥmad* 4 (1863): 108–131, and afterward in *Meḥqerei Hayahadut*, vol. 1, pt. 2, 237–249, under the title "Tamsit Deotav shel Shadal." See ibid., 241. See more about this letter below.

[3] See more about this letter below. These words of Luzzatto appear in ibid., 247.

according to their own method. Luzzatto argues that if Geiger is correct then it follows that the Amoraim invented the principle forbidding committing the Oral Torah to writing and that all the written books of *mishnayot*, previously available to Rabbi Judah Hanasi, must have suddenly became unavailable to them. Luzzatto sees in this a Maimonidean influence, since Maimonides also committed his halakhic rulings to writing in his *Mishneh Torah*, never citing disputes or sources, hoping to compel his readers to rule like him. Leaving no room for future change, he sought to render obsolete the books of Halakhah written before him—even the Mishnah and Talmud. Geiger criticizes the Tannaim for trying to halt halakhic development, criticism which Luzzatto considers wicked and false. According to Luzzatto, the one who really tried to arrest halakhic development was Maimonides, the object of Geiger's admiration.

Luzzatto's letter to Reggio contains fierce and scathing criticism of many of Maimonides's philosophical positions. For example: his claim that only intellectuals merit an afterlife, consisting of absorption into the divinity after death; his rejection of a physical and eternal resurrection of the dead; his invention of the thirteen principles of faith, which guarantee an afterlife for proper beliefs (and not for good deeds or the proper performance of commandments); his literary activity in which he does not cite disputes or sources (also based on Aristotelianism, an activity which could have made us forget the Mishnah and the Talmud and enslaved us to Maimonides and his foreign doctrines); and his hatred and calls to eradicate gentiles and Jewish heretics who oppose Jewish belief. These views, Luzzatto argues, do not fit the worldview of the Bible and the Sages, threaten the completeness of the Jewish people, and constitute a slippery slope already leading the *maskilim* of Europe to ruin. Luzzatto uses expressions such as:

> [Maimonides] has made us a horror to all the nations of the world, through no fault of our own; your [Maimonides's] resurrection of the dead is that of Aristotle and his commentators, not that of our fathers; behold we, of innocent hearts, not experts in the plots and tricks of the philosophizers, accepted your thirteen principles which you commanded us to believe, occupied ourselves with them for several generations, but failed to plumb the depths of your thought, and did not see the snake coiled around the heal of your words; [according to Maimonides] it is explained that even if the intellectual philosopher has committed theft, murder, and adultery he can still acquire life in the World to Come, and the matter is not related to merit, but only to knowledge of truths.

Luzzatto's words immediately aroused a storm of controversy upon their publication. In a letter he later wrote to Judah Wahrmann of Yaroslaw (12 Kislev 5599 [1838])[4] he defended his position, writing that he never expected the controversy that would ensue—an unconvincing claim. The Galician rationalists led by Nahman Krochmal, Solomon Judah Rapoport, and Zvi Hirsch Chajes received the criticism of their cultural hero with shock and anger. Krochmal sent a letter to the editor of *Kerem Ḥemed*, Samuel Leib Goldenberg from Tarnopol, responding to Luzzatto's criticism of Maimonides. The letter was sent in Heshvan 5599 (1838) and was immediately printed in that year's journal (before the publication of Luzzatto's letter to Wahrman).[5]

Jacob Bodek and Nahman Isaac Fishman from Lemberg, two of the three editors of the journal *Haroeh*, sent Luzzatto fuming and critical response letters, which he briefly responded to in Sivan 5598 (1837).[6] In these letters they threatened to publicize their criticisms, submitting this dispute to the judgment of the scholars of Israel, if he failed to give satisfactory response to their arguments. In response, Luzzatto wrote that he has no intention of responding to their arguments, which he believed lacked substance. To the contrary, let them publish their criticisms and submit them to the judgment of the scholars. In his letter to Bodek, Luzzatto writes that he issues his ideas for public review without fear: "my children whom I raised and cared for, you who knew of my sitting and rising, who examined all my ways, have you ever seen me pursue honor? Say to all who see you: *our father accepts the truth from whoever says it*, even the smallest of the small; he fears no one, and will not admit to something that is not true even if he who says it is greatest of the great." In his letters, including a letter to Bodek himself, Luzzatto refers to the editors of *Haroeh* as the disciples of Sammachus (quarrelsome people), the disciples of Balaam, hypocrites, villains, pests, rogues, fools, evil men and deceitful, sinful boors.[7]

In Elul of 5596 (1836), before the eruption of the controversy, Krochmal had written a friendly letter to Luzzatto, calling him "the perfect scholar." He had considered him his comrade in the challenging middle way, a path maligned from two sides—by both the devout, and the Reform. Now he wrote to Goldenburg that he could not understand what had overcome Luzzatto, and why he had suddenly been seized by a spirit of zealotry against the two greats—

---

4   Published in *Kerem Ḥemed*, vol. 4 (1863), 287, and in *Meḥqerei Hayahadut*, vol. 1, pt. 2, 178.
5   Ibid., 260. Reprinted in N. Krochmal, *Kol Kitvei Ranaq*, ed. S. Rawidowicz (Berlin, 1923), 432.
6   Luzzatto, *Igrot Shadal*, 426, 429.
7   See ibid., 431, 477, 487, 488, 656, 705. Luzzatto, *Meḥqerei Hayahadut*, vol. 1, pt. 2, 237.

Maimonides and Ibn Ezra.[8] His superficial complaints against Maimonides lack substance and have already been discussed in the past. Nevertheless, Krochmal responds in detail to each one of Luzzatto's arguments. In his opinion, Maimonides apologized about the resurrection of the dead and admitted that it is a foundation of Jewish belief (though Krochmal agreed that there was more to this subject than meets the eye). He adds that some of Maimonides's principles of faith were already well-known before him and in formulating them he had answered a real need. The Amoraim and Geonim already wrote clear-cut laws, and Maimonides was not the first to do so. Krochmal writes about Luzzatto's criticism: "such a thing should not be in Israel; oh this man has committed a grave sin, and requires repentance and forgiveness; surely he has already done penance."[9]

When Luzzatto received the letter from his friend Judah Wahrmann rebuking him for his attacks against Maimonides, he realized he had gone too far. He sent a more gently worded response to Wahrmann in an attempt to douse the flames. He sent a copy of the letter to the editor of *Kerem Ḥemed*[10] who published it as mentioned. Luzzatto took this opportunity to request from the editor not to publish his more vehement, radical letter to Schorr or his letter to Reggio. Publishing these at this point would exacerbate and fan the flames of controversy. In his moderate letter to Wahrmann, Luzzatto writes that he certainly acknowledges Maimonides's eminence in every subject he applied himself to, and he only opposes him in certain matters in which he believes he erred. How can scholars and righteous men judge him for not emphasizing Maimonides's already famous virtues and only mentioning some of his mistakes? He is surprised at the outbreak of the controversy and believes that those who accused him of disqualifying Maimonides are mistaken and foolish. If Maimonides were to accuse him in halakhic court, certainly he'd be happy that his disciple acts so bravely, bringing forward criticism against him, without fear or flattery. Maimonides knew that sincere criticism is the highest form of honor, and is superior to obsequious agreement. It is evident to every

---

8   For a full description of Luzzatto's polemic against Ibn Ezra on the issue of Deutero-Isaiah, including comprehensive excerpts from the correspondence among Luzzatto, Reggio, Rapoport, Krochmal, Goldenberg, and Schorr see Vargon, "Havikuaḥ"; as well as idem, "Zehuto"; idem, "*Emdato shel Shadal.*" See also Chamiel, *The Middle Way*, vol. 1, 141–144. Luzzatto responded to Krochmal's letter on 21 Shevat, 5597 (1837), and part of his response is quoted in his letter to Schorr from 1838 (mentioned in note 2 above, *Mehqerei Hayahadut*, 238–239).
9   Krochmal, *Kitvei Ranaq*, 432.
10   Luzzatto, *Igrot Shadal*, 560.

intelligent person that the *Mishneh Torah* is a remarkable composition, superior to all its predecessors, written with the purest of intentions—to lighten and simplify halakhic adjudication and to prevent errors. But Luzzatto's criticism remains unchanged. In-depth study of Talmud continued unabated, thanks to Rabad and the majority of Jewish scholars after him, who criticized Maimonides's goals. Today one can study Maimonides alongside the Talmud and the works of other halakhists, and clarify Halakhah without blindly or uncritically following Maimonides. Likewise, it is clear that Maimonides did not wish to eliminate the study of the Mishnah and Talmud, even though this would have happened had his plans succeeded. Luzzatto also does not retract his criticism of Maimonides's conception of the afterlife. He is aware that Maimonides wrote in riddles and parables, shielding his words from the masses and allowing alternative interpretations. But Maimonides's early interpreters, experts in the philosophy of his time (Efodi, Shem Tov, and Abarbanel), interpreted Maimonides on this subject as Luzzatto does. My entire goal, Luzzatto writes, is to enhance the glory of Torah and serve the good of the nation. If other scholars think that this goal would be better achieved by interpreting Maimonides differently—in a manner which harmonizes his words with the traditional beliefs of Judaism—then I will praise this endeavor.[11]

On the 26 Sivan 5598 (1838), immediately after responding to the letters from the editors of *Haroeh*, Luzzatto wrote a short response to Schorr.[12] He writes that he certainly knows about the attack against him in *Haroeh*, and tells of his short responses to the invectives and rebuke of the journal's authors. But he did not stop there. In that same year on the 7 Tamuz, he sent Schorr a detailed letter explaining his attitude toward the philosophers and Maimonides, and apprising him of the series of events that had driven him to publish his original attack against Maimonides in his letter to Reggio. He sent this letter to be published in *Bikkurei Haitim*, but Goldenberg rejected it and asked him to wait for the publication of Krochmal's and Rapoport's responses. When Luzzatto sent Goldenberg a copy of his letter to Wahrmann,

---

11 See also n. 4 above. On the controversy over Maimonides see Klausner, *Hasifrut*, vol. 2, 101–102; Rostovski-Halprin, *Shadal Vehitnagduto*, 38–53; Spicehandler, "Mavo"; I. Barzilay, *Shlomo Yehuda Rapoport and his Contemporaries* (Ramat Gan, 1969), 103–106. Barzilay presents Luzzatto's dispute with Rapoport regarding Maimonides and Ibn Ezra, and points to the polarity of Luzzatto the romantic who opposed Maimonides and Ibn Ezra, and Rapoport the rationalist, who considered them his spiritual teachers. For further discussion of Luzzatto's polemic against Maimonides and Ibn Ezra see Levi, *Hermenoutiqa*, 37–40; Chamiel, *The Middle Way*, vol. 1, 216–220, 463–470.

12 Luzzatto, *Igrot Shadal*, 431.

he thanked him (in a letter from 15 Kislev 5599 [1838])[13] for not publishing the letter to Schorr, and requested that he publish instead his moderate letter to Wahrmann. This is what Goldenberg did. Luzzatto apprised Schorr of all these developments in a letter written on 19 Kislev 5599 (1838).[14] Luzzatto would only publish this letter fourteen years later.[15]

The tone of Luzzatto's letter to Schorr was harsh. It contained more fierce words against accepted traditional views, besides what he had written to Reggio. It revealed things about Maimonides difficult for faithful Jews to accept and criticisms of the *maskilim* of Europe difficult for them to swallow. He begins by quoting his letter to Krochmal written in 5597 (1837),[16] in which he wrote harshly about Polish Jewry, greatly divided between the old-fashioned devout and the radical *maskilim*. The devout are bound by the chains of Kabbalah, and the secrets of the Zohar and R. Isaac Luria, following the whims of drunken Hasidic masters who pretend to perform miracles. The *maskilim* are more extreme than the philosophizers of Maimonides's era—their most radical belief being the eternity of the world. The *maskilim* today go as far as denying God's existence, denying the Torah's divinity, and denying the possibility of prophecy and miracles. The early philosophers at least attributed these to the Active Intellect.

Likewise, Luzzatto mentions his view that parts of the Mishnah and Talmud are irrelevant to later generations—particularly the Aggada which was only relevant for its time—arguing that the writers never intended to create an enduring tradition or an eternal code of laws. The *midrashei halakhah* of the Sages, which are foreign to the simple sense of the biblical text, were merely an *asmakhta* (textual support). They were meant to support laws received from tradition as well as new laws which the Sages created with remarkable wisdom according to the needs of the time; these interpretations were never meant to distort the primary sense of the text. The import of Luzzatto's statement is that many laws in the Mishnah and Talmud are not Sinaitic but the product of human creativity. He argues that the Mishnah also mentions the rejected minority opinion, leaving adjudication open, allowing future sages to change rulings to suit the needs of the times according to the precedent of

---

13   Ibid., 560.
14   Ibid., 564. It seems that Goldenberg decided, after consulting with Rapoport, not to publish Luzzatto's aggressive letter to Reggio.
15   Above, n. 2.
16   See references to the journals in which this letter was printed in full in Luzzatto, *Igrot Shadal*, 370 and in note there.

a minority view. Maimonides, who does not mention minority opinions in order to anchor his rulings, erred and it is good that Rabad rose up against him. Luzzatto adds that in his opinion, there is no harm in believing in divine corporeality, the feast of the Leviathan, the magical names of God, magical amulets and other such beliefs. These reinforce belief in divine providence and reward and punishment, educating man to be ethical and compassionate. But Maimonides and the philosophers—who only believe in divine providence of the enlightened, and who believed that man's ultimate goal is intellectual—reach the conclusion that the common masses (whether or not they behave or rebel) are not subject to divine providence, and receive no reward or punishment for their actions. This view greatly endangers the wellbeing of society. In his opinion, the radical *maskilim* of his day, followers of foreign philosophies, like Maimonides in his own time, truly pursue nothing but honor and money and only seek their own selfish benefit and personal success by participating in the European cultural milieu according to its rules. These students of philosophy do not become better or more intelligent people. Instead they lose their joy for life, sinking into depression and hopelessness, since philosophers failed to pave a clear path to truth, one destroying what the other one had built. In his mind, his rabbinic opponents are unleashing the dogs against him to quell their anger for his praise of the *maskil* Rapoport, who was appointed rabbi of Prague, at their expense. At the beginning of his letter he derides the editors of *Haroeh*, adding that he sees no reason to lower himself to their level, wasting his precious time responding to the folly of fools. In the depths of their hearts they realize he is correct and they are only feigning their sanctimonious zealotry for Maimonides and the Sages.

In time, Luzzatto would admit in a letter to Goldenberg (17 Tevet 5599 [1839])[17] that his letter to Schorr faithfully represented his true views of Maimonides. However, for the sake of peace, he eventually preferred to publish his softer more considerate letter to Wahrmann. Indeed, his hatred and criticism of Maimonides and Ibn Ezra continue unabated, and he continued to obsess over the issue for years to come. He endlessly repeats this in many letters to different correspondents over the course of his life. Thirteen years after the controversy, in a letter to Shneur Zachs (Adar Sheni, 5613 [1843]), editor of *Kerem Ḥemed* in Berlin, he raises another issue he has with Maimonides—his greater project to incorporate foreign philosophies into Judaism, philosophies which abstract God and distance him from man, and which reject out of

---

17 Ibid., 578.

hand belief in prophecy and revelation. He writes to Zachs that he still hopes to renew his battle against Maimonides, hoping to restore the former glory of divine corporeality based on the system of Solomon Ibn Gabirol. He emphasizes that the belief in abstract spirituality preached by Maimonides (and followed by many after him) is responsible for the growing atheism in his day.[18] In his commentary on the Pentateuch, Luzzatto repeats time and time again that the Torah is not a book of science or philosophy directed exclusively at intellectuals or outstanding individuals (as maintained by the rationalists of Maimonides's school). It is a divine guide to moral behavior, meant to educate the nation as a whole to be compassionate and merciful. (See, for example, his commentary on Gen. 1:1; Deut. 6:5, 20:19).

Another one of Luzzatto's opponents was Maharats Chajes, rabbi of the Żółkiew district in Galicia. Chajes was a God-fearing Torah scholar and Talmudist and a rationalist and *maskil*. His cultural hero was Maimonides, and he considered himself the shield of his champion. Responding to Luzzatto's letter in *Kerem Ḥemed*, volume 3, he wrote a detailed essay entitled *Tiferet Lemoshe* (Glory to Moses) containing responses to all of Luzzatto's arguments. This essay was printed in 1840 in his book *Ateret Tsvi*. Chajes—an excellent example of a moderate harmonistic interpreter of Maimonides (both in terms of Maimonides's content as well as his interpretive method)—maintained that complete harmony prevails between Maimonides's views and the accepted religious belief in definitive theological positions. Maimonides's writings contain no real contradictions or strata of meaning.[19] Chajes argues, like Krochmal, that all of Luzzatto's arguments are old ones; they were given adequate response in the past and he does not understand why Luzzatto is re-raising them now. That being said, he considers it important to respond in detail to his arguments for the sake of his readers. He explains (reiterating Krochmal's explanations) that Maimonides did believe in the resurrection of the dead and even wrote as much. Maimonides was humane; he did not hate gentiles and even learned from gentile scholars. Maimonides did not renounce morality; to the contrary, he stressed that without moral perfection a person cannot ascend in his intellectual study. Maimonides did not wish to eradicate the study of Talmud; he considered it a fundamental pillar of Judaism. The thirteen principles of faith

---

18 Ibid., 1195. See also Luzzatto's commentary on Gen. 1:26, which was first published in 1847. For other letters see Luzzatto, *Igrot Shadal*, 599 to Jost; 618 to Schorr; 621–622 to Jost; 603, 656, 675 to Schorr; 693 to Gedalia Brecher from Prosnitz; 698 to Leopold Leib from Vienna; 701 to Leopold Zunz from Berlin; 738, 740, 761 to Rapoport.

19 The wording is that of Ravitzky, "Sitrei," 149–150.

were important and beneficial, but were regardless not Maimonides's invention. Maimonides rejected the Aristotelian belief in the world's eternity, and the entirety of his philosophy concords with traditional Jewish belief, not with Aristotle. Maimonides was not the first to write law codes, and did nothing wrong.[20] Luzzatto expected to receive Chajes's critique essay through his friend Schorr. When the book was delayed in coming he wrote (28 Tishrei 5601 [1840])[21] that perhaps this is for the best, as it would be a waste of his precious time to articulate responses to the fantasies and derisions of the author.

Luzzatto's friend Rapoport was also less than pleased by Luzzatto's criticism of Maimonides. Since Luzzatto's first letter to Reggio on 28 Av 5589 (1829) the two continued to correspond regularly.[22] Rapoport did not spare Luzzatto his concerned rebuke, imploring him to call off his war, taking pains to do this gently but decisively. In a letter written on 17 Kislev 5599 (1838),[23] Rapoport argues that by defending Maimonides and Ibn Ezra Luzzatto is not serving the devout who are purportedly upset at Luzzatto for impugning their hero; to the contrary, they are happy about Luzzatto's criticism of the philosophers! Luzzatto's criticism supports their hatred of *maskilim*, philosophical inquiry, the study of foreign languages and the study of the sciences. Now even the *maskil* Luzzatto is justifying their cause! On 17 Tevet of that same year, Luzzatto received a letter from Goldenburg. Luzzatto responded that there is a contradiction between the statements of Goldenburg and Rapoport.[24] Goldenberg wrote to him that the devout, who in opposition to Luzzatto adore Maimonides, use Luzzatto's disparaging words against Maimonides to battle Luzzatto and all the *maskilim*; Rapoport claims the exact opposite. Luzzatto concludes that he is unable to understand Polish Jewry and decides he should detach himself from it completely. In this letter Luzzatto also argues against his detractors: if as they claim he is merely reiterating old arguments which lack substance why has everyone attacked him with such ferocious anger?

The publication of *Kerem Ḥemed*, volume 4, which Rapoport had overseen as an advisor, was the final straw, spelling the end of Luzzatto's relationship with

---

20   See Chajes, "Sefer Ateret Tsvi" (1841), in *Kol Sifrei Maharats Ḥayut* (Jerusalem, 1958), 397–433. For an analysis of Chajes's answers see Chamiel, *The Middle Way*, vol. 1, 216–220. For a discussion of the polemics between Luzzatto and Chajes see M. Hershkovitz, *Maharats Ḥayut, Toledot Rabbi Zvi Hirsh Ḥayut Umishnato* (Jerusalem, 1972), 313–329.
21   Luzzatto, *Igrot Shadal*, 709.
22   Ibid., 165.
23   Rapoport, *Igrot Shir*, 104.
24   Ibid., 578, mentioned above in note 14.

Rapoport. Luzzatto scoured the journal from cover to cover, examining every detail published. He found offense from Rapoport in every corner. His poem in honor of Rapoport's appointment as rabbi of Tarnopol was published in full against his request, whereas his note of apology, which he had specifically asked be published, was omitted. Rapoport's critique of one of Luzzatto's essays was published. A critique essay by Krochmal against Luzzatto (mentioned above) was also published with no response from Rapoport. Additionally, Betsalel Stern anonymously published sharp criticism of Luzzatto's interpretation of a difficult passage in Ibn Ezra's *Yesod Mora*, in consultation with the mathematician Eichenbaum, Rapoport not lifting a finger to soften this. Deeply offended, Luzzatto sent Rapoport a parting letter on 1 Iyar 5599 (1839).[25] Their falling out continued for nearly two years, until 7 Nissan 5601 (1841) when Luzzatto reestablished their friendship by writing him an emotional letter[26] after reading Rapoport's recently published scholarly essay in *Kerem Ḥemed*, volume 5.[27] Rapoport was very happy to receive this letter but did not desist in his attempts to change Luzzatto's mind. Responding to Luzzatto (28 Nissan 5601 [1841])[28]—after expressing his joy on their reestablished connection, and apprising him of events since their falling out—he continued to argue that even if some of Maimonides's and Ibn Ezra's ideas were influenced by Greek philosophy, did this necessitate the weakening of their belief? Did this detract from their status and greatness? Would Judaism have survived on its own without occasional assistance from gentile wisdom? The Tannaim learned from the Greeks, and the scholars of the Middle Ages studied from Aristotelian writings translated into Arabic. And indeed, some of Aristotle's views were similar to the views of the Torah! The scholars of Spain sought to draw close the very best of Islamic ideas to the worldview of the Torah. How will we appear in the eyes of gentile scholars if we sully the honor of Maimonides, who is responsible for our glory? Luzzatto responded to Rapoport on 1 Sivan 5601 (1841).[29] He writes that he has not changed his mind regarding the philosophical disciples of Ibn Ezra who adopt his shortcomings (impetuousness, hypocrisy, glory-seeking, and self-aggrandizing at the expense of others) and Rapoport should not ask him to cease his battle. Similarly, Luzzatto expresses anger at Rapoport

---

25 Ibid., 615.
26 Ibid., 730.
27 On this exchange see M. Pelli, *Kerem Ḥemed—Hokhmat Yisrael Hi*, "Yavneh Haḥadasha" (Jerusalem, 2009), 72–78.
28 Rapoport, *Igrot Shir*, 105.
29 Luzzatto, *Igrot Shadal*, 738.

for dubbing Maimonides in his letter with the honorific title "our master Maimonides," an expression inappropriate in his opinion for a Jew (better suiting a Christian) or a philosopher (whose spirit is free) and more befitting a Hasidic devotee's adulation of his Hasidic master. In his response (22 Sivan 5601 [1841])[30] Rapoport responds that many great people have applied the term "our master" to esteemed Jewish scholars, and there is nothing invalid in this, even citing a number of examples. Luzzatto's battle is detrimental to his research and study and is a waste of his time; only in past Diasporas in which there was interaction between our scholars and gentile wisdom, and attempts to draw it closer to us and vice versa, did the Jews flourish; all acknowledge Maimonides's and Ibn Ezra's greatness, and no one can move them from the important place they hold in Jewish history.

The Question

It emerges that in his philosophy and biblical interpretation (according to his letter to Wahrmann in which he states that he disagrees with Maimonides only on few matters), Luzzatto has no qualms about mentioning Maimonides's interpretations and views (as he does with Ibn Ezra)—even citing him by name—regardless of whether or not he agrees with him. According to Luzzatto, his criticism of Ibn Ezra is more vehement than his criticism of Maimonides: "for indeed the eminence of Maimonides I never denied, and far be it from me to include him among Ibn Ezra and his companions."[31] That being said, he does not hesitate to cite in his commentary to the Pentateuch many of Ibn Ezra's *peshat* interpretations. This is based on his view (as he writes to Bodek) that there is one truth which should be accepted from whoever speaks it (see chapter 5). An examination of Luzzatto's commentary, letters, and essays, reveals references to many different interpreters and thinkers, Jewish and non-Jewish, ancient and modern, from the greatest of scholars to the lowliest of his disciples. It thus appears that Luzzatto was sincere, not simply utilizing defensive apologetics, when he wrote to Wahrmann that Maimonides was correct in most of his statements. Nevertheless, it should be recalled that his praise of Maimonides in his letter to Wahrmann was for the sake of peace (as he himself admitted), and that he continued to attack Maimonides's and Ibn Ezra's rationalist points of departure at every

---

30   Rapoport, *Igrot Shir*, 109.
31   Luzzatto, *Igrot Shadal*, 675, in his letter to Jost.

opportunity, believing they posed a danger to Judaism. Moreover—while few—his disputes with Maimonides are over fundamental issues which he considered supremely important to the future of Judaism.

I will first briefly present Luzzatto's explicit citations of Maimonidean interpretations of Scripture, which he sometimes accepted and sometimes rejected. After that I will present instances in which Luzzatto expresses views similar or identical to those of Maimonides but without mentioning him by name, even obliquely. This is an interesting break from his usual practice and it invites the question why does he omit mention of Maimonides in these specific instances?

B. LUZZATTO'S BIBLICAL INTERPRETATIONS THAT CITE MAIMONIDES BY NAME

In his commentary on the Pentateuch, Luzzatto cites some of Maimonides's interpretations to Scripture, drawing them from his writings—primarily the *Mishneh Torah* and the *Guide for the Perplexed*. It is clear that these include a respectable amount of halakhic and philosophical interpretations, demonstrating that despite Luzzatto's harsh criticisms he does not refrain from citing Maimonides by name, and then accepting or rejecting his approach. A few examples:

1. Gen. 1:26, **in our image**—he agrees with Maimonides position in the *The Guide for the Perplexed* (part 1, 1) that the word *tselem* (lit. image) does not denote physical description or structure but essence. He does however, dispute Maimonides's understanding of man's essence—intellect according to Maimonides, possessor of various powers according to Luzzatto.
2. Ex. 3:13, **and what if they say to me what is his name**—Luzzatto praises Maimonides's comment on Moses's question but opposes his explanation, offering his own.
3. Ibid. 7:3, **and I will harden Pharaoh's heart**—he accepts Maimonides's explanation that Pharaoh's sins were so grave that the path to repentance was closed before him but offers his own original interpretation.
4. Ibid. 20, 1, **and God spoke all these matters saying**—he cites Maimonides's contradictory statements in different places as to who heard God at Sinai and what precisely they heard. He states that it is

difficult to decipher Maimonides's secret, and "blessed is God who has freed us of that philosophy that gained power in his days, and which Maimonides favored too much—even if his intentions were good." Luzzatto states that the entire nation explicitly heard all of the Ten Commandments.

5. Ibid. 20:2, **I am the Lord your God**—he cites Maimonides's view that this constitutes a tenet of faith. Luzzatto disagrees stating that God is merely recounting events that had transpired.
6. Ibid. 20:11, **for six days**—he cites Maimonides's view that the Sabbath is meant as a day of rest and a reminder of creation. Luzzatto rejects this interpretation and states that the commandment to give rest to the slave and the animal is an act of compassion and the commandment for Jews to rest is so they may gather together in love and friendship occupying themselves with worship and study.
7. Ibid. 21:10, **her clothing**—he fiercely criticizes the attitudes of Maimonides and "those who pretend to be wise" towards women. They consider wives nothing but maidservants to serve them or a medicine to preserve their health (*Hilkhot Deot* 4:19). This is unlike the Sages who maintained that the man and woman are two equal partners assisting each other with love and camaraderie. Luzzatto accepts this latter view.
8. Ibid. 21:20 **his slave**—he accepts Maimonides's position in his laws of murder that a master who strikes his slave with a killing implement is condemned to die even if more than two days or a year have passed since his death.
9. Ibid. 21:37, **If a man steals an ox or sheep**—he accepts Maimonides's explanation that the easier the robbery the more severe the robber's punishment.
10. Ibid. 22:2, **if the sun rises over him**—Maimonides's ruling is correct: even if the thief came in the day, and there are no witnesses, the house owner is permitted to kill him.
11. Ibid. 22:17 **you shall not allow a sorceress to live**—he accepts Maimonides's explanation, based on his findings in the books of the pagan Sabaeans, that most acts of sorcery must be performed by women. Similarly, he accepts his view that every sorcerer is an idol worshiper.
12. Ibid. 27:18 **all who lie with an animal**—he accepts Maimonides's view that this is an idolatrous practice.

13. Ibid. 22:30, **torn flesh in the field**—he rejects Maimonides's position that eating "torn flesh" is harmful to one's health.
14. Ibid. 33:6, **Lord, Lord merciful and compassionate God**—after presenting his own view Luzzatto presents twelve opinions as to how to count God's thirteen attributes of mercy; the seventh view is that of Maimonides.
15. Lev. 1:2, **from the herd**—he opposes Maimonides's view that the centralization of sacrificial rituals was meant to limit animal sacrifice, reducing materialization as much as possible. He argues that the point of centralization is ethical—bringing together the disparate parts of the nation in fraternity and national unity.
16. Ibid. 18:6, **none of you will come near to anyone of his own flesh**—he opposes Maimonides's view that the laws of incest are meant to minimize the time one engages in sexual activity. Luzzatto argues that were this the case then the Torah should have forbade marrying many wives, or having frequent sex with one's partner. The reason for the prohibition is societal and ethical and it is meant to ensure the flourishing of the home and the state.
17. Num. 20:12, **because you did not believe in me**—he cites the views of Maimonides and others and rejects them. Luzzatto maintains that Moses was not punished for becoming angry; he was punished because his anger led him to rebel against God, striking the stone instead of speaking to it.
18. Ibid. 30:15, **from that day to the next**—he cites the tannaitic dispute whether this means twenty four hours or until the evening. Maimonides rules that it means until the evening but the simple meaning of the verse is twenty four hours.
19. Deut. 6:5, **with all your heart**—he cites some of Maimonides's philosophical views, based on Aristotle and Muslim philosophers, rejecting them as deviating from the statements of the Torah and the prophets. They maintain that love of God can only be attained through intellectual comprehension and a comprehensive understanding of existence. Therefore, it is important to teach "the work of creation" (natural sciences, physics). All of Aristotle's statements about the sub-lunar world are correct, and there are ten intellects which move the celestial spheres, corresponding to the names of angels. Luzzatto argues that Maimonides did not take into account the possibility that one day Aristotle's physics would be invalidated.

20. Ibid. 21:4, **to a "strong" wadi**—he rejects Maimonides's interpretation that the meaning is a wadi overflowing with water, maintaining, like Rashi, that "strong" refers to the hard rock in the wadi.

It should be noted that out of these twenty citations, Luzzatto only fully accepts five of them (8–12) and they are all connected to matters of Halakhah from the *Mishneh Torah*. By contrast, he rejects all eight citations related to philosophical subjects (1–4, 14, 15, 17, 19) which are bound up with *The Guide for the Perplexed*.

C. SUBJECTS IN WHICH LUZZATTO EXPRESSES VIEWS SIMILAR TO THOSE OF MAIMONIDES WITHOUT CITING HIM BY NAME

I will now discuss seven topics in Luzzatto's thought (appearing in his commentary on the Pentateuch and his other writings) in which Luzzatto does not mention Maimonides by name despite the significant affinity between their views.

(1) Devotion to Truth

This issue has been raised in our previous discussions. Luzzatto's practice of accepting the truth from whoever speaks it (as he writes to Bodek) is based on a saying he learned from Maimonides. It appears in Maimonides's introduction to his commentary on *Pirqei Avot* (the introduction to the *Eight Chapters*).[32] Responding to his detractors, Luzzatto explains that he favors no man, not even Maimonides. If the truth really lies with Maimonides's opponents, he will flatter neither him nor his modern defenders, and will present the truth as it appears to him. He does not hold great people (or people who affect greatness) in high esteem, and judges for himself with whom the truth lies, even if this conflicts with the views of great or highly esteemed people. Luzzatto turned this maxim into a principle and used it during his polemic against the theory of two Isaiahs, invoking it at the end of a letter to Rapoport written on 1 Elul 5601 (1841). In this letter he disputes his Jewish opponents Rapoport and Krochmal, and his non-Jewish opponents Rosennüller and Gesenius, maintaining the book's unity and opposing the theory that the prophecies from chapter 40 onwards belongs to another prophet from a later time. Having concluded his arguments

---

32 M. Schwartz, *Rabbi Moshe ben Maimon Shemona Peraqim vehem Haqdamat Harambam Leperusho Lemassekhet Avot: Tirgum Mearavit* (Jerusalem, 2011), 5.

and proofs, he adds that in the first edition of his commentary on Isaiah, he dealt with this dispute and brought evidence for his position in the notes. In subsequent editions, however, he left these out because "I wanted to sit on the matter for some days and years. And until this day I maintain my opinion and in any event I am willing to learn from anyone and to accept truth from whoever speaks it."[33] In other words, he does not distinguish between big and small, Jew and non-Jew. If it can be proven that he has erred completely, he will accept as truth the view of his opponent. This maxim appears already in a letter to Rapoport from 5 Nisan 5593 (1833) in which Luzzatto argues with him about the two Isaiahs and Ibn Ezra. There Luzzatto explains his principles. He will persist in his approach, only pursuing real ideas, and never allowing himself to be swept away by baseless imaginings and unjustified theories. This is a position he will never abandon, and he will indeed be stubborn about it. But the details of his research are different: "their nature is to change over time with the increase of knowledge and research, and in these I accept truth from whoever speaks it, be he great or small, first or last, ancient or modern, distant or near, enemy or friend. And in this quality—of accepting truth from whoever speaks it, declaring it with a full mouth and a joyous heart—unto this day I have seen no one comparable to me."[34] In his letter to Issachar Blumenfeld from Brody (3 Kislev 5594 [1834]) he uses this maxim to explain why he sometimes quotes and accepts the views of gentile commentators such as Rosenmüller and Gesenius. Luzzatto would continue to cling to this principle throughout his life, mentioning it again in 1846, in a letter to Joshua Heschel Schorr. He requests that Schorr make no changes to the manuscript he has sent him to be printed in *Beit Haotsar*. He explains that while he is willing to accept words of truth from every man, until he is convinced of his error he will not change what he wrote.[35]

(2) Rationales of the Commandments and the Existence of Reward and Punishment

On this subject Maimonides writes the following:

> It is necessary to bear in mind that Scripture only teaches the chief points of those true principles which lead to the true perfection of man, and

---

33 Letter to Goldenberg in *Kerem Ḥemed*, vol. 7 (1843), 225–242, reprinted in *Meḥqerei Hayahadut*, vol. 1, pt. 2, 30–48, in the article "Sefer Yeshayahu"; see ibid., 45. See also Schorr's letter to Luzzatto in *Igrot Shadal*, 969.
34 Luzzatto, *Igrot Shadal*, 244–245.
35 See ibid., 272.

only demands in general terms faith in them. Thus, Scripture teaches the Existence, the Unity, the Omniscience, the Omnipotence, the Will, and the Eternity of God. All this is given in the form of final results, but they cannot be understood fully and accurately except after the acquisition of many kinds of knowledge. Scripture further demands belief in certain truths, the belief in which is indispensable in regulating our social relations: such is the belief that God is angry with those who disobey Him, for it leads us to the fear and dread of disobedience. [...] I am prepared to tell you my explanation of all these commandments, and to assign for them a true reason supported by proof, with the exception of some minor rules, and of a few commandments, as I have mentioned above. I will show that all these and similar laws must have some bearing upon one of the following three things, viz., the regulation of our opinions, or the improvement of our social relations, which implies two things, the removal of injustice, and the teaching of good morals. [...] Consider what we said of the opinions [implied in the laws]; in some cases the law contains a truth which is itself the only object of that law, as e.g., the truth of the Unity, Eternity, and Incorporeality of God; in other cases, that truth is only the means of securing the removal of injustice, or the acquisition of good morals; such is the belief that God is angry with those who oppress their fellow men, as it is said, "My anger will be kindled, and I will slay [you with sword, and your children shall be widows and your children orphans]" (Ex. 22:23), or the belief that God hears the crying of the oppressed and vexed, to deliver them out of the hands of the oppressor and tyrant, as it is written, "And it shall come to pass, when he will cry unto me, that I will hear, for I am gracious" (ibid. 22:26).[36]

Maimonides divides the Torah's commandments into two categories: true commandments which lead to correct philosophical beliefs (final goals of a first order) and untrue commandments which lead to necessary beliefs which serve ethical needs, maintaining the unified existence of society and the state (second-order goals). He cites as an example the belief in an angry God who

---

[36] Maimonides, *The Guide for the Perplexed*, trans. M. Friedlander (New York, 1904), part 3, 28, 313–315. See A. Ravitzky, *'Iyunim Maimoniyim* (Jerusalem and Tel Aviv, 2006), 62–66; Halbertal, *Harambam*, 239–241, 291–293. According to Halbertal, 292: "This approach determines that the Torah, sensitive to the needs of time and place, and adaptive to human ritual needs, commands the use of fundamentally flawed forms of worship which it rejects in principle. It does so as a necessary compromise so that some ritual may be used in worshipping God..."

punishes oppressors and answers the supplications of the oppressed. The goal of this belief is to instill the people with fear of God, a means of attaining necessary goals.

Maimonides also believes that divine providence, reward, and punishment are not divine responses to human behavior but laws imprinted into nature by the Creator:

> But [I] believe that the Divine Will ordained everything at creation, and that all things, at all times, are regulated by the laws of nature, This occasioned the sages to say that all miracles which deviate from the natural course of events, whether they have already occurred, or, according to promise, are to take place in the future, were fore-ordained by the Divine Will during the six days of creation, nature being then so constituted that those miracles which were to happen really did afterwards take place. Then, when such an occurrence happened at its proper time, it may have been regarded as an absolute innovation, whereas in reality it was not. And the Sages, one of their statements in reference to this matter being: "Everything follows its natural course."[37] In everything that they said, you will always find that the Rabbis (peace be unto them!) avoided referring to the Divine Will as determining a particular event at a particular time. [...] The sum and substance of the matter is, then, that thou shouldst believe that just as God willed that man should be upright in stature, broadchested, and have fingers, likewise did He will that man should move or rest of his own accord, and that his actions should be such as his own free will dictates to him, without any outside influence or restraint. [...][38]

It follows that according to Maimonides divine providence over a specific individual (not necessarily a Jew) is commensurate with his intellectual achievement and does not proceed from heaven to earth:

> Divine Providence is connected with Divine intellectual influence, and the same beings which are benefited by the latter so as to become intellectual, and to comprehend things comprehensible to rational beings,

---

37 *Yalqut Shimoni, Yitro*, Remez 288. See also BT Avoda Zara 54b.
38 Maimonides, *The Eight Chapters of Maimonides on Ethics: Shemonah Perakim*, trans. J. Gorfinkle (New York, 1912), 90–91. See also Maimonides, *Guide for the Perplexed*, part 2, 29, 204–212.

are also under the control of Divine Providence, which examines all their deeds in order to reward or punish them. [...] Due to the will of God, and in accordance with the justice of His judgments, the method of which our mind is incapable of understanding.[39]

Luzzatto writes along similar lines:

> But when they became a great nation, and the time arrived to bring them into the land that God promised their fathers to give them, God saw that they needed teachings and laws and study and direct guidance, both for the correction of moral attributes and the success of the society, and also for perseverance in the religion, so they would not abandon it and cling to the ways of the gentiles around them or be left without religion. Therefore, he gave them this Torah placing it before the Children of Israel. The means God chose to achieve these two goals are [three]: one dedicated to the perfection of moral qualities and two dedicated to the perfection of moral qualities and the wholeness of the religion together. And these are the three foundations of Moses's Torah. The first foundation—the method dedicated to perfecting moral qualities—is compassion. [...] And behold, this Torah, which Moses placed before the Children of Israel, is what guides them on the path of compassion and grace. [...] And behold the second foundation of the Torah of Moses—a means of achieving both goals together (improvement of moral qualities and preservation of the religion)—is belief in providence and reward and punishment from God. [...] The third foundation of the Torah of Moses—a means of improving moral qualities and preserving the religion together—is the belief that Israel was chosen by God to be a special nation, and that He made a covenant with their ancestors that will never be violated. [...] And behold, all the commandments are divided into two large groups: commandments between man and God and commandments between man and his fellow. And commandments between man and his fellow the rationale for all of them is evident: they are for the success of the individual and the community, by improving moral qualities and so that all should treat their fellows with justice and fairness, kindness and mercy, and the sinner

---

39 Ibid., part 3, 17. See also ibid., 18. On Maimonides's meaning in these passages and other matters in part 3, 51 see Halbertal, *Harambam*, 286–288; M. Goodman, *Sodotav shel Moreh Hanevukhim* (Jerusalem, 2010), 116–117.

shall bear his sin, and the entire nation will hear and fear. But, indeed, the commandments between man and God are largely for the preservation of the religion, that is, so they should remember God, and the fear of him should be before him, and they should not forget him (which is the general intention of every religion in the world) and additionally so that the nation should be on the level of priests in relationship to other nations, separated and sanctified with particularistic laws. From this their hearts will be raised and their souls uplifted, believing they are a special nation—a kingdom of priests and a holy people—and they will not intermingle with other nations and idolaters and will not learn from their actions, but cleave all their days to their God and to his upright and holy ways; moreover, these commandments are greatly beneficial to the improvement of moral qualities.[40]

The commandments are divided into two groups: one consisting of commandments which instill fundamental beliefs in God and divine providence (but not speculative philosophical beliefs about what occurs in higher realms, as believed by Maimonides), the other consisting of commandments which preserve ethics and promote the wellbeing of society. Luzzatto mentions instilling belief in reward and punishment and belief in the chosenness of the Jewish people as a means of attaining these goals. Did he believe that these doctrines are true or did he think that they were only necessary and required? In regard to reward and punishment he is even more decisive than Maimonides:

> Here it is hinted that the entire foundation of my thinking is that religion is not desirable to God because of its truth but because of its usefulness to improve morality, and therefore there is no need for everything to be true, and despite all this we should not distance his divinity, and we should not distance God for saying of untrue things, because it is impossible to tell the power of the creation to flesh and blood, and the maintenance of society and man's success is impossible with knowledge of the truth, but [only] with illusion. And greater than that, it is clear that society could not exist without reward and punishment and without belief in the superiority of some things and the condemnation of others, and *indeed in truth all of our actions are only the results of outer and inner causes* [heredity] *and justice and evil are truth with respect to the action* (whether it is beneficial or

---

40 Luzzatto, "Yesodei Hatorah," in *Meḥqerei Hayahadut*, vol. 1, pt. 1, paragraphs 3–41.

damaging) but not with respect to the character of the actor. And more than this, is it possible for a person to be a person and not endeavor to attain success? Despite all this, in my estimation, this is vanity, too, because in whatever situation a person may be, it will always be half joy and half a plague, and in my youth, for twenty-three years I gathered together a collection and called it Ḥeleq Keḥeleq Yokhelu ["portion for portion shall they eat"] (Deut. 18:8)... *All of these things I spoke in a whisper to your ear.*[41]

These words were directed only at the historian Isaac Markus Jost, who leaned towards Reform and Bible criticism, in a letter on 19 Shevat, 5600 (1840). In this letter Luzzatto explains his decision to reduce his publication of unaccepted views to avoid abuse from his right and left. This is an implicit message on Luzzatto's part to the intellectual reader: there are things which should not be revealed to all. As is well known, this is Maimonides's view as well, who wrote the *Guide for the Perplexed* only for intellectuals, concealing his true views from the *naïve* reader. Luzzatto writes similarly in lessons he prepared for his students, and these made their way into his commentary on the Torah (published in 1871, six years after his death):

> For this is the manner of the Torah, to portray fortune and misfortune as purposefully descending from above as reward and punishment even when they proceed and occur naturally according to the world's natural course; [...] and just as the Torah threatens the Children of Israel saying that God is vengeful, jealous and full of anger, so too it says that he visits the guilt of the parents upon children as if he does this out of vengeance and rage, even though in truth this only occurs naturally and not, God forbid, as vengeance; rather everything is for the benefit of mankind.[42]

---

41 Luzzatto, *Igrot Shadal*, 661.
42 Luzzatto, Ex. 20:5. This shift in views (from what was said in *Hamishtadel* to the same verse) is also significant in relation to Luzzatto's statements in *Yesodei Hatorah* cited above. Luzzatto already limited the chosenness of the Jewish people there (*Yesodei Hatorah*, ibid., 37) stating that their excellence is not immanent but merely precedence in time. In *Hamishtadel*, ibid., Ex. 20:3 he adds that this is not truth but a divine plan for the attainment of final results (see below). Maimonides's bold approach stems from the philosophical position that the Torah contains hidden philosophy, assisting the intellectual elite to achieve their goals, secrets which should not be revealed to the simple masses lest they rebel and become corrupt. Luzzatto's approach however, stems from a romantic view. He maintains that the Torah contains no philosophy and no secrets and is meant for all people, its goal educating them to do good, as ethical behavior constitutes man's ultimate purpose. Luzzatto

It is interesting to compare this to Luzzatto's earlier statements to the same verse on the subject in *Hamishtadel*. He writes:

> Therefore, it appears to me that one should not move from the simple meaning of Scripture, and the intention is that great sins which arouse God's wrath and jealousy, will befall the evil man's offspring commensurately—terrible misfortunes which astound onlookers; and this punishment will last for another three or four generation, so that as long as the men of the generation remember the evil man who has already died and the sins he committed, they will see the wrath of God which has stricken his offspring.

The shift in Luzzatto's views in the direction of the Maimonidean position is a fundamental one. It corresponds to his position regarding the rationales of the commandments (which I discussed above) and is bound up with his position on free will (which I will discuss below). Luzzatto wrote more about this subject in his interpretation of the account of the Garden of Eden in Genesis. He maintains that the goal of the story is pedagogical: to teach people not to complain about their misfortunes, appreciating God for granting them the right to free will. The Torah recounts that the misfortunes which befall humans originate from Adam who was seduced to eat from the Tree of Knowledge. By the same token, it instructs mankind that this state of affairs is preferable to its previous state, when it was like animals or children, lacking the ability to distinguish between good and evil. This is all in spite of the fact that "in truth all these [labor, anger, and suffering] occur due to the nature of creation, but God taught him [man] of them through a curse, as if it were a punishment for eating from the Tree of Knowledge." In other words, reward and punishment do not directly proceed from God; fortune and misfortune are the results of the laws of nature put in place by God. But the Torah's goal is not to teach philosophical truths (as claimed by Maimonides) but to teach good, ethical qualities.

---

already wrote that reward and punishment do not truly exist on November 8, 1837 in a letter to David Morporgo of Trieste answering a number of questions he sent to him. In his answer to question 11, about reward and punishment he writes that knowledge of the truth that there is no reward and punishment, is harmful and not beneficial, just like the truth that God is not influenced by emotions (answer to question 7) and prayer and rituals are meant for man alone. Therefore, religion instills the opposite notion. See Luzzatto, *Peraqim Bemishnato Shel Shadal*, 13–15. The source: Luzzatto, *Epistolario*, letter 154.

This explanation does not appear in *Hamishtadel* and Luzzatto did not publish it in his lifetime. It is a bold and untraditional view.[43]

(3) The Election of the Jewish People—Do the Jewish People Really Have Unique Superiority over Other Nations?

In his interpretation of the second of the Ten Commandments, "you shall have no other gods beside me," Luzzatto explains that the rationale of this commandment is ethical; a belief in many gods entails a belief in gods of evil, a belief which legitimizes evil behavior. Moreover, polytheism fosters disunity among different believers, leading them to hate one another, and increasing jealousy and competition. Therefore, the Torah teaches belief in one God, who as father of the entire human race loves all people. The Torah was received at a time when all the nations were submerged in primitive forms of paganism, only Abraham recognizing and choosing God. Therefore, God selected him and his offspring to receive the Torah for the good of mankind as a whole, at a time when humanity was still not ready. It was necessary to ensure that the Jewish People would continue to preserve the Torah for the rest of mankind:

> Therefore, for all of these reasons, God wanted knowledge of His Unity to persist among the Jews, and He threatened them with all those threats, and he pruned them in many ways, so that they would not worship other gods, and all of this was not solely for the benefit of the Jews, but for the benefit of the human race in general, because from Israel will the Torah go forth, and knowledge of the unity of God will spread from them little by little to all human beings, until in the end of days the world will be filled with knowledge of God. [. . .] So you will understand this secret, [alluded to by the *Kuzari* 4:23] which God could not state explicitly in the Torah, because its publication would thwart its intention, because the Jews would not have eschewed the idols of the ancient nations nor kept themselves from resembling them, if God had not brought them close to His worship in all the ways that He saw in His wisdom to bring them close. And now, too, this matter should not be explained to ignorant people.[44]

---

43 In terms of free will, Luzzatto provides a very moderate reading of Maimonides (*Pirqei Avot*, end of chapter 8, 51–53) and maintains that Maimonides evaded presenting the issue to its full extent. See above Chapter Three.
44 Luzzatto, Ex. 20:3.

All of Maimonides's interpreters concur that he disagrees with Judah Halevi who maintains that the Jewish people possess a superior essence to other nations, a quality unique to them and passed down hereditarily. In Maimonides's opinion, prophecy is not unique to the Jewish people. Any person who reaches the maximal level of intellectual reflection has a chance of meriting prophecy. Besides the passage cited above (*Guide for the Perplexed,* part 3, 17) Maimonides says explicitly: "One of the foundations of our faith is that God conveys prophecy to man. Prophecy is bestowed only upon a very wise scholar of a strong moral character etc."[45] In other words, all intellectuals have the same potential to be prophets. He also writes this at the end of his laws of Sabbatical Years and Jubilees: "The chosenness of Israel was only manifested after they had received the Torah and were required to observe its commandments."[46]

That is to say, the unique chosenness of the Jewish people is not in fact true, and the Jews have no immanent excellence *vis-à-vis* other humans. In this matter, Luzzatto agrees with Maimonides, the only difference being that for Luzzatto this idea is included in the Torah as a "prudent plan of Providence" whereas according to Maimonides excellence is the distillation of the Torah and its commandments. In any event, this is a daring and untraditional position, which Luzzatto (like Maimonides) was not eager to publicize.

(4) The Evil Eye—Is it Scientifically True?

Luzzatto in his commentary on the Torah attempts to explain the source of the false belief in the evil eye. The Torah commands that to avoid a plague—the result of a direct census—Israel is to be counted by collecting half a *sheqel* from each individual. Luzzatto writes that in ancient times rulers would count their armies, leading to hubris and complacency. It was only natural that every tyrant would eventually be overthrown and in the ancient world these downfalls would be attributed to the evil eye: "and from this was borne among all nations the belief in the evil eye and it appears that this belief had already spread in Israel in the generations preceding the giving of the Torah. And behold God did not wish to completely abolish this belief, because at its basis is a belief in divine providence which distances man from trusting in his own strength and

---

45 Maimonides, *Mishneh Torah, Hilkhot Yesodei Hatorah,* 7:1.
46 On the chosenness of the Jewish people according to Maimonides see Halbertal, *Harambam,* 182–188; Goodman, *Sodotav,* 232–341.

wealth, and this is the essence of the Torah."[47] That is to say, this is an untrue belief, adopted by the Torah for ethical and pedagogical reasons.

Maimonides also does not believe in the reality of the evil eye and does not think that it can cause any harm. In his *Mishneh Torah* (*Hilkhot Shehenim*, chapter 2, 14–16) Maimonides rules that when dividing a shared courtyard between two owners one must build a fence four cubits high to prevent the damage caused by one's neighbor observing his activity. However, if the courtyard in question is a garden next to the house, then the wall only need be 10 breadths high. In a valley, that is an agrarian field, one need not make this distinction at all. Rabad, in his critique, says that Maimonides made a great error. A garden, like a courtyard, requires a wall four cubits high to prevent the damage from sight. Shem Tov Ibn Gaon in his commentary *Migdal Oz* is surprised at the Rabad and proceeds to prove that he is mistaken. In his commentary, he cites a question posed to Maimonides by the scholars of Lunel: the crops in a garden courtyard belong to one of the neighbors and are therefore liable to be damaged by the eye of the other. Why then is a partition ten breadths high enough? In his *responsum*, Maimonides distinguishes between the damage caused by watching a neighbor's intimate activities in the adjacent yard, and the damage caused by looking at a neighbor's crops with the evil eye. The latter is "pious conduct. And that answer [given by the Talmud] is merely a response [to a challenge] and is not according to Halakhah." Therefore, while a courtyard requires a partition four cubits high, a garden only requires a partition ten breadths high—marking a boundary to ensure a neighbor does not enter the garden without permission.

(5) Impurity and the Laws of Leprosy—A Harmful Physical Reality?

Maimonides rejects the interpretation which considers the impurities of leprosy demonic-magical or medical-health related. He states categorically in the *Guide for the Perplexed* that being in a state of impurity is not harmful (as opposed to the treatment of menstruating woman by the Sabaeans) and is not intrinsically negative. The Torah's goal in mandating the laws of purity and impurity is to limit entry into the Temple to a minimum, preventing it from becoming a matter of routine and habit, raising the people's esteem for the house of God. Maimonides adds that impurities are considered "dirty" and the laws of purity lead to avoiding them. In this matter, the Torah adopted already

---

47   Luzzatto, Ex. 30:11.

accepted practices. However, in actuality, the Torah does not oppose a person entering into a state of impurity. He may be in such a state as long as he wants provided he does not enter the Temple area. "This distinction applies only in reference to the Sanctuary and the holy objects connected with it: it does not apply to other cases." At the end of the passage Maimonides also cites the Sages who speak of leprosy as a punishment for slander, its appearance a miracle of sorts: "the good effect of this belief is evident. Leprosy is, besides, a contagious disease, and people almost naturally abhor it, and keep away from it." I think it is reasonable to assume that Maimonides considers the first interpretation the rationale of the commandment according to scientific truth, and the second interpretation the necessary truth for the purposes of ethical education.[48]

Luzzatto's position is very similar. He writes:

> And behold, many already have thought that the ostracization of the leper is because that disease is transmitted by touch; and it seems to me, that if the Torah was concerned about infection from the disease, then why does the Torah decree no measure about other infectious diseases and how did it command nothing about the plague? [Therefore,] it appears to me that the change in skin color was in the minds of our ancestors a sign of God's wrath, and they believed that the leper was stricken by God as punishment for some terrible sin he had committed. Therefore, they would separate from him as if he was a person castigated by God; similarly, the change in the appearance of a garment or a house was a sign of God's rebuke, as if the stricken garment or house were hated by God due to some great sin that was committed with them. And because all of this reinforced the belief in Divine Providence and the belief in reward and punishment, the Torah upheld this belief. [. . .] And the matter of the leper is similar to the matter of a *niddah, zav, zavah* and *yoledet* [a menstruating woman, a man or woman with a genital discharge, or a woman who has given birth]—these are all considered castigated by God. This is because the (unwilling) emission of blood or semen is the beginning of death, and it alludes to the fact that man and woman are mortal. Therefore, we were commanded to separate ourselves from them and guard ourselves from their touch. [. . .] And indeed, the impurity of semen is for the glory of

---

48 Maimonides, *Guide for the Perplexed*, part 3, 35, 330 (the twelfth class) and in chapter 47, 366–370.

> the Temple, so that a person should not enter the house of God, and eat holy flesh on the same day he has occupied himself with physical pleasure (which is unnecessary, as opposed to food or drink); and this is similar to the commandments before the giving of the Torah (Ex. 19:15) "be ready for three days, do not approach a woman"; and in the minds of the congregation this prohibition will exalt and uplift the glory and splendor of the Temple and its holy objects, and in the minds of priests it will exalt and uplift the glory of the labor which they perform.[49]

That is to say, Luzzatto believes that leprosy is not truly harmful and is not a miraculous sign of divine rebuke—a daring and untraditional stance. The belief that a leper is being castigated by God is used by the Torah for pedagogical and ethical goals, instilling fear of a watchful God, who punishes a person for his sins, marking him for removal from society. This is so a person will act ethically, following the Torah's commandments. The rationale of fostering honor of the Temple—Maimonides's explanation for all forms of impurity—Luzzatto only uses when discussing the impurity of semen, a natural emission which cannot be attributed to divine castigation.

(6) The Temple and Sacrifices—Optimal or Concessionary and for What Purpose?

Maimonides's rationale for the commandments of animal sacrifices is one of the most famous. Maimonides maintains that the Torah commanded animal sacrifices out of an understanding that it was impossible to transform a people immersed in idolatry and sacrifice all at once. Therefore, it adopted the practice but refined it, giving instructions how to properly practice it and limiting it to one central location:

> It is, namely, impossible to go suddenly from one extreme to the other. It is, therefore, according to the nature of man impossible for him suddenly to discontinue everything to which he has been accustomed. [. . .] But the custom which was in those days general among all men, and the general mode of worship in which the Israelites were brought up, consisted in sacrificing animals in those temples which contained certain images, to bow down to those images, and to burn incense before them; religious

---

49 Luzzatto, Lev. 12:2.

and ascetic persons were in those days the persons that were devoted to the service in the temples erected to the stars, as has been explained by us. It was in accordance with the wisdom and plan of God, as displayed in the whole Creation, that He did not command us to give up and to discontinue all these manners of service; for to obey such a commandment it would have been contrary to the nature of man, who generally cleaves to that to which he is used; it would in those days have made the same impression as a prophet would make at present if he called us to the service of God and told us in His name, that we should not pray to Him, not fast, not seek His help in time of trouble; that we should serve Him in thought, and not by any action. ; comp. "And they shall make unto me a sanctuary" (Exod. xxv. 8); to have an altar erected in his name; comp. "An altar of earth thou shalt make unto me" (ibid. 20:21); to offer the sacrifices to Him; for this reason God allowed these kinds of service to continue; He transferred to His service that which had formerly served as a worship of created beings, and of things imaginary and unreal, and commanded us to serve Him in the same manner; viz., to build unto Him a temple, [...] and to have the altar erected to His name, [...] to offer the sacrifices to Him, [...] to bow down to Him and to burn incense before Him. He has forbidden to do any of these things to any other being. [...] He selected priests for the service in the Temple. [...] He made it obligatory that certain gifts, called the gifts of the Levites and the priests, should be assigned to them for their maintenance while they are engaged in the service of the temple and its sacrifices. By this Divine plan it was effected that the traces of idolatry were blotted out, and the truly great principle of our faith, the Existence and Unity of God, was firmly established; this result was thus obtained without deterring or confusing the minds of the people by the abolition of the service to which they were accustomed and which alone was familiar to them.[50]

That is to say, unlike traditional understandings, there is no intrinsic worth to the Temple and sacrifices, and the Temple laws are necessary commandments. The divine plan used existing beliefs and customs—which were mistaken and idolatrous—and combatted them by redirecting them toward the service of God. This was to achieve the true goal—abolishing idolatry and instilling belief in God's existence and unity.

---

50 Maimonides, *Guide for the Perplexed*, part 3, 32, 323–325.

Luzzatto writes along similar lines:

> The sacrifices were not originally commanded, but were human concession, for humans would makes vows to thank God for his kindness toward them, or to bring before him an offering to calm his wrath and to appease him so that he should fulfill their requests, for it is impossible for a person to act towards his God in a manner different than how he acts toward a king of flesh and blood. [. . .] The divine Torah—its purpose not to teach the nation wisdom and knowledge, but to guide them in paths of justice—did not abolish the practice of sacrifices, not because it did not have the ability, but because this custom is not inherently bad, and does not harm people or the improvement of their morals; to the contrary, it benefits them; for if the Torah teaches the nation that God has no wish for offerings, on the morrow they will say: What does God desire that we may be righteous and what gain is there if we lead our lives innocently? And because one of the foundations of the Torah is the belief that God oversees people's actions, and loves those who do good and hates evil, it was necessary that God not be portrayed to the full extent of his exaltedness, according to his true level. Rather it was necessary to slightly lower his excellence (as it were) and to portray him as a great king who knows their actions, hears their cries, and accepts their gifts. And this was necessary not only for that generation, but in every generation equally. And if instead of sacrifices God would have commanded prayer, hymns, Torah readings and ethical preaching, and not sacrifices, then the greatness of God and his fear would not have been imprinted upon the hearts of the masses. For it would seem to them that the gods of the nations, to whom sacrifices are brought by their worshipers, are greater and more respected than our God, whom we only serve with mere words. For thus is the quality of the masses in every generation, and not only the masses, but the quality of most humans. Who is honored in their view? He who honors himself and enlarges his exaltedness; and truly one who forgoes his privileges and does not demand greatness for himself is not esteemed in their eyes. And the God of truth—although he needs not the respect of flesh and blood—it was necessary for our benefit and good to instill his fear in our hearts so that we would not sin; and since in those days it was impossible to instill his fear in the heart of the nation without sacrifices, he commanded them to do so. And behold the fruit of the sacrifices which the public would bring in the Temple was such, that it would be impressed upon the hearts of the masses that a deity and a great king

dwells in their midst and they are beloved to him. He commanded them to perform the services He wishes, and by doing those services at his behest they are favored by him every day and they draw upon themselves his love constantly. And the Torah commanded that not every person can build an altar for himself—the entire assembly must bring their sacrifices in a designated place which God will choose. [...] And the public sacrifices are so that Israel should have a sanctuary and a temple to serve God, so that it should be impressed upon their hearts that God is in their midst, and he is their king and their leader, overseeing their actions and remunerating them according to their ways and their deeds. This would not be impressed upon the hearts of the masses without something tangible to allude to this. Therefore, it was necessary that the Temple be like the structure of a king's palace, and it was necessary that it should have a table and candelabra, and upon the table a bread set and table vessels, bowls and spoons. And because the practice was to offer God a gift of edible things, it was fitting that we bring before our King varieties of food and drink, and the sacrifices correspond to food and the libations to drink. And it was necessary that the king have servants, who work in his house, and who stand before him, and these are the priests. [...] And because its [the priestly family's] labor in the house of God is for the nation as whole, it is fitting that its livelihood be assured by the nation.[51]

Luzzatto thinks, like Maimonides, that there is no inherent value to the Temple, its vessels, its servants, or its sacrifices, and there is nothing intrinsically true about them. The Torah's goal is not to teach us truths but to educate us. The commandments of sacrifices are necessary not true. Therefore, the Torah adopts the existing practices customary for deities and kings to impress the greatness of God upon the masses, causing them to fear him and observe his ethical commandments. This need for tangibility is a human need in every generation. In the middle of this passage, Luzzatto mentions Maimonides only to reject his overall approach—that the reason for concentrating worship in one place was to minimize as much as possible the practice of sacrifices. In Luzzatto's opinion, the reason for centralization is to gather the entire nation together, increasing love and fraternity. The primary difference between Luzzatto and Maimonides is that Maimonides maintains that the main goal of divine providence is to instill belief in God's existence and unity and to abolish idolatry, whereas Luzzatto maintains that the main goal is to inculcate the belief in a watchful and beneficent God, so

---

51 Luzzatto, Lev. 1:1.

that they observe the commandments which lead to the moral lives of individuals and societies. In either case, the daring and untraditional principle is similar.

(7) The Source of the Oral Law—Transmission from Sinai or Rabbinic Innovation

Maimonides presents a bold and exceptional position in dividing the laws of the Mishnah and the Talmud into a number of categories (as I have explained elsewhere). A careful look at Maimonides's classifications reveals that to him the Written and Oral Torah include only the 613 commandments, as enumerated in his *Sefer Hamitsvot*. Only these are biblical obligations. These laws include commandments recorded in the Written Torah as well as laws derived from thirteen hermeneutical principles but explicitly referred to by the Talmud as biblical, meaning transmitted from Sinai. All other laws—the majority of laws in the Mishnah and the Talmud—are rabbinical laws created by the Sages using their own intellect. These include laws designated "a *halakhah* from Moses at Sinai," laws derived from the thirteen hermeneutical principles but not designated "biblical," as well as decrees and customs.[52]

Maimonides writes in the *Sefer Hamitsvot*:

> And the method is this: anything that you do not find in the text of the Torah and you find that the Talmud learned it from one of the thirteen principles, if they explained it themselves and said that this is the body of the Torah or that it is biblical—then this should be counted [in the 613 commandments of the Pentateuch] for the transmitters of the Oral Torah said it was biblical; but if they did not explain this and did not say this explicitly—then it is rabbinical since the text does not indicate otherwise.[53]

Luzzatto formulated his own theory about the laws of the Mishnah and Talmud. Comparing his position to those of his medieval predecessors, it is clear that his view is closest to that of Maimonides. As I showed above in Chapter Four, Luzzatto's position on the sources of Halakhah developed over

---

52 See his introduction to his commentary on the Mishnah and *Sefer Hamitsvot*, *Shoresh* 1–2, his introduction to *Sefer Hamada* in the *Mishneh Torah*, and *Hilkhot Mamrim*, chapters 1–2. Also see Maimonides's responsa (responsum 355); M. Halbertal, *'Al Derekh Haemet: Haramban Veyetsirata Shel Masoret* (Jerusalem, 2007), chapter 1; Halbertal, *Harambam*, 91–118; Chamiel, *The Middle Way*, vol. 1, 160–163.

53 *Sefer Hamitsvot, Shoresh* 2.

the course of the thirties and forties. In the end he would conclude that while the Scribes did elucidate and strengthen ancient laws, they also created new laws of their own according to the changing needs and circumstances of the nation. Due to their powerful status, they saw no need to justify their legislation by providing rationales. The status of their successors, the Tannaim, was weaker, and they did not know the rationales of their predecessors. They therefore were forced to underpin the laws of their predecessors as well as their own new laws with *Midrash Halakhah* (such as *Tosefta, Sifra, Sifri*, and *Mekhilta*). The Amoraim who succeeded them almost entirely discontinued the autonomous creation of laws based on exegesis, but continued to explain the statements of their predecessors (received orally) with scriptural exegesis and continued to make decrees and establish customs.[54] Luzzatto writes about the exegesis of the Tanna Rabbi Eliezer ben Hyrcanus:

> After some years in which I was surprised by the Sages, why they removed a certain verse from its simple meaning, today (Purim 5607 [1847]) I was privileged to understand what they were after. Indeed, in every place where the Sages deviated from the simple meaning of the verse, when the matter is not a single man's opinion, but something agreed upon without demurral, this is not an error that they made, but it is a regulation they instituted, because of the need of the generations, and who is a reformer like them? But their regulations were with deep wisdom, and fear of God and love of man, not their own pleasure or honor, and not to find favor in the eyes of flesh and blood.[55]

---

54 See Luzzatto, *Haotsar*, Lishka A, 13, quoted in Chamiel, *The Middle Way*, vol. 1, 314–315. See there also about Luzzatto's approach until 328. Also see below Chapter Seven, for a full discussion of Luzzatto's view on the issue.

55 Luzzatto, Lev. 7:18. B. Rubinstein (in *Hama'arechet Letiqun Hadat Vesidrei Hah.ayim Beyisrael Bemah.shevet Sifrut Hahaskalah Ha'ivrit Mipulmus Haheichal Ve'ad Shnot Hashishim Shel Hameah Ha19*, Doctoral Dissertation, Hebrew University [Jerusalem, 1958]) examined the views in Haskalah literature regarding the Reform, a measure advocated at that time by some of the *maskilim*. He dedicates the first chapter to Luzzatto, offering a detailed analysis of Luzzatto's view that the *halakhot* in the Oral Law are regulations innovated by the Sages and explaining how this position served as the basis of Luzzatto's ambition to reform Judaism from within, as opposed to employing the methods of Reform, which derived from an entirely different position—the adoption of a foreign culture. Rubinstein brilliantly shows that Luzzatto's attack on Maimonides in his famous letter to Rapoport is entirely connected to his view that the halakhot in the Mishnah and the Talmud are the developing creation of the Sages. Therefore, he opposes Geiger and argues that putting the Mishnah in writing must be dated later, to the period of the Savoraim, and it is impossible to attribute

A consequence of this view is that the Sages' exegesis of Scripture was not the correct interpretation of the biblical text. For example: The Sages say that "an eye for an eye" means money. Maimonides maintains:

> He who mutilated a limb of his neighbor, must himself lose a limb. "As he hath caused a blemish in a man, so shall it be done to him again" (Lev. xxiv. 20). You must not raise an objection from our practice of imposing a fine in such cases. For we have proposed to ourselves to give here the reason for the precepts mentioned in the Law and not for that which is stated in the Talmud. I have, however, an explanation for the interpretation given in the Talmud, but it will be communicated vivâ voce.[56]

Luzzatto writes similarly in his commentary on the verse "an eye for an eye" in Ex. 21:24:

> This mean that anyone who wounds a friend, should be punished with the same blemish he inflicted upon his friend—whether he intended to harm him, or intended to harm someone else, as is the case when striking the woman; the Sages of blessed memory explained that he must pay money (BT Bava Kamma 84a). And this is one of those matters which the Torah left to the hand of the Judges, for indeed if there is a rich man who will not sense the loss of his money and will find satisfaction in harming people, the judges can apply the [literal] ruling of "an eye for an eye."

D. THE SOLUTION

Why does Luzzatto not mention Maimonides as his source when discussing these subjects? I believe that this is directly related to the controversial and daring nature of these positions, which Luzzatto, like Maimonides, was not

---

its writing to Rabbi Judah Hanasi. Another important Bible scholar—who accurately and thoroughly presents Luzzatto's approach to the Sages' interpretation of the Bible, both in terms of Halakhah and literature—is Vargon. See S. Vargon, "Shadal" and "Yahaso Habiqorti Shel Shadal Klapei Perushey Hazal Shelo Bithum Hahalakhah," Mehqarim Betalmud Uvemidrash, 5 (2005), 135–158. See also Chertok, Qanqan, 66, and his reference to Margolis in n. 16 there.

56 Maimonides, Guide for the Perplexed, part 3, 41, 344. Cf. Mishneh Torah, *Hilkhot Ḥovel Umaziq*, 1:3. See J. S. Levinger, *Harambam Kefilosof Ukeposeq* (Jerusalem, 1990), 56–66.

eager to publicize. As I have already demonstrated above and elsewhere,[57] at the beginning of the forties Luzzatto developed an untraditional approach towards the relationship between philosophy-science and revelation. Maimonides and Judah Halevi maintained that Torah and philosophy are identical. Their dispute was only which should serve as the standard. According to Judah Halevi, revelation is determinative; according to Maimonides, reason is determinative. By contrast, Luzzatto believed that reason and revelation are two separate areas, each one possessing a different part of the truth. At the end of the forties Luzzatto took a step further and concluded that these areas represent two complete but contradictory truths, which cannot be reconciled in man's world. In any event, he believes that there is truth in philosophy as well— as long as it is genuine philosophy—and when the truth of the Torah is not readily understood, one should adopt the philosophical stance. This is what Luzzatto does in the subjects presented above. That being said, Luzzatto also realized that his approach was complex and daring, and that it should not be discussed at length in public.[58] How can someone who invalidates the ideas of Maimonides—because they derive from foreign Aristotelian and Muslim philosophy—persist in adopting some of these ideas (primarily from the *Guide for the Perplexed* and the *Eight Chapters*) and claim that even such forms of philosophy contains some truth? How can one who claimed that Maimonides's views "are an invention neither commanded nor spoken by our ancestors, never entertained in their hearts" adopt some of Maimonides most dangerous positions, which were similarly "not inherited at all from our fathers"?[59]

Therefore, on every sensitive topic (such as the seven discussed) Luzzatto takes pains to hide the fact that his controversial and daring stance bears similarities to the philosophical stance of Maimonides. He thus avoided additional attacks from those who had trouble internalizing his complex position. This is also the reason why Luzzatto does not cite Maimonides as the source of the maxim "to accept truth from whoever speaks it." This principle is what drove

---

57 See Chamiel, *The Middle Way*, vol. 1, 474–491.
58 See chapter 3 above. At the end of his letter to Rapoport (mentioned above in note 2, *Meḥ.qerei Hayahadut*, vol. 1, pt. 2, 247–248) Luzzatto recommends that his detractors from the right—*naïve* and upright believers—as well as students at the beginning of their path, refrain from reading his writings which are only intended for mature adults and lovers of free research. This danger will pass when these students will grow in their knowledge of Talmud and Halakhah, after which they will either reject his words, or accept them and then they may become enlightened believers in the truth and worthy teachers for their communities.
59 Luzzatto, *Mehqerei Hayahadut*, vol. 1, pt. 2, 166–168.

Maimonides to accept the invalid positions of Aristotelian-Islamic philosophers. Luzzatto therefore preferred not to draw attention to the fact that Maimonides is the source of this maxim, which also stems from Islamic scholars.[60] Thus, he could avoid attacks and astonishment from his opponents. It is also worth keeping in mind that Luzzatto explicitly adopts Maimonidean interpretations, primarily on halakhic issues from the *Mishneh Torah* (as shown in the above list), while theoretical ideas, which he explicitly attributes to Maimonides, he usually rejects.

SUMMARY

Luzzatto's relationship to Maimonides is ambivalent. On the one hand he attacks the theoretical basis of Maimonidean rationalism—his justification for incorporating foreign philosophies into Judaism. The adoption and wide dissemination of such ideas by his predecessors poses a danger to the wholeness and religion of the nation. On the other hand, as one who had internalized many positions of the Haskalah movement, Luzzatto maintained a neo-romantic approach to Judaism and could neither accept the statements of the Torah as simple scientific-philosophical truths nor adopt the devout position that all Halakhah stems from Sinai. Therefore, he adopts some of Maimonides's more exceptional and controversial ideas, allowing him to explain instructions in the Torah which contradict logic and science, attributing them to "the prudent plan of Divine Providence." This is based on the adage which he adopted—to accept truth from whoever speaks it. Therefore, he also adopts Maimonides's position regarding the historical development of Halakhah (that only the 613 commandments were given at Sinai). But to avoid accusations of inconsistency, Luzzatto did not note the Maimonidean influence of these explanations. That being said, his criticism of Maimonides remained unchanged—and he continued to condemn him for adopting foreign, speculative philosophies, which sever any possible connection between God and man, and for reading verses allegorically as if they hid philosophical truths. The same holds true for Maimonides's attempts to dominate sources, his advocacy of eliminating his theological opponents, his explanations of the World to Come and the Resurrection of the Dead, and his granting an afterlife only to believers in his thirteen principles of faith and not to those who observe ethical commandments.

In the next chapter I will delve into Luzzatto's negative attitude towards Kabbalah.

---

60   For the source of this saying see Schwartz, *Shemona Peraqim*, introduction, 5, n. 9.

CHAPTER SEVEN

Luzzatto on Theosophical Kabbalah: Harmful Invention with Worthy Intentions

BACKGROUND

Jewish society and thought at the end of the twentieth century and the beginning of the twenty-first century are characterized among other things by a strong attraction to Kabbalah and mysticism—part of the world-wide dissemination of the New Age movement. By contrast, in the rationalist eighteenth century, a strong Jewish opposition to Kabbalah and mysticism developed—even in Eastern Europe, the cradle of Hasidism. In the romantic nineteenth century, some Jewish thinkers took this opposition a step further, bringing their opposition to Kabbalah to the point of veritable revulsion. Having internalized the ideals of the Haskalah, these romantic Jewish thinkers had no place for mysticism in their thought—the reason I refer to this period in Jewish history as "neo-romantic." In Luzzatto's writings this sense of revulsion is particularly salient.[1]

From the time he became self-aware, Luzzatto was conscious of mysticism and Kabbalah. His father Hezekiah was a poor woodturner. Joseph Klausner describes him as a naive, righteous man, God-fearing, and extremely devout in his observance of commandments. He was a believer in superstitions, possessing a poetic soul and a delusional personality. He was detached from real life, living in a world of faith and dreams, interspersed with vows and fasts. He would spend his time reading *mussar* literature, reading about asceticism

---
1   See Chamiel, *The Middle Way,* vol. 1, 453–455.

and abstinence. He was a radical idealist with a strong imagination. One of his attempts at writing was a project to compose a kabbalistic commentary on the Bible.[2]

Luzzatto writes in his autobiography that his father began to study Kabbalah from a young age, and even planned to write a book called *Ḥemdat Hanearim*, collecting sources from the Zohar, the Talmud, and their commentaries toward this end. In this book he also wished to include two short compositions: *Ziqnei Bat Tsion*—a list of names mentioned in the Bible and Talmud, and *Piteron Ḥelomot*—an anthology of passages from the Talmud on the subject of dream interpretation.[3] Luzzatto adds that when he was thirteen years old he fell ill. Forced to leave school, he began to study Torah primarily with his father— mainly *Sefer Habrit*, a book beloved by his father for its inclusion of scientific and kabbalistic information.[4] Luzzatto further recounts that in that year, while studying the talmudic Aggadot in the anthology *Ein Yaakov*, he reached the critical conclusion that the traditional vowels and accent (cantillation) marks of the biblical text do not originate from Sinai. Unknown to the Amoraim, these marks must have been instituted only after the talmudic era. This quickly led to his next conclusion: that the Zohar, which contains many allusions to the biblical vowels and accents, was composed after the era of the Mishnah and the Talmud, and not by Tannaim as commonly believed. His conclusions led to disagreements with his father, frequently erupting into disputes. When his mother contracted her final illness in 1814, his father prayed for her recovery using kabbalistic intentions, but his prayers were left unanswered. He hoped that the intentions of an innocent boy would be more effective and turned to his son, seeking to teach him how to perform kabbalistic intentions: banishing all physical thoughts from the mind, raising the soul from the lowly world of *Asiya* to the worlds of *Yetsira*, *Beria* and *Atsilut*, and from there to the ten *sefirot*, to Primordial Man, to the *Ein Sof*, making one's supplications there. Believing in none of this, Luzzatto refused, to his father's great anger. Luzzatto says, however, that in the end his father, who was an upright man of truth, overcame his nature and ceased to study Kabbalah, perhaps even ceasing to believe in it.[5]

In the years 1815–1817, during personal studies and study with his father, Luzzatto penned critical notes on the Zohar's authenticity and documented *peshat* interpretations of difficult words and passages in Scripture that

---

2   See Klausner, *Hasifrut* 2, 44–48.
3   S. Luzzatto, *Pirqei Ḥayim*, ed. M. Schulwas (New York, 1951), 6.
4   Ibid., 19.
5   Ibid., 20–21.

contradict the traditional vowelization and accentation of the text.[6] In 1817 he collected these notes into a small work called *Maamar Haniqud* (The Essay on Vowelization). Luzzatto recounts that his relative and friend Samuel Haim Loli tried to convince him that he was misguided, but his efforts were in vain. Loli wrote a letter to his friend Reggio, requesting his assistance in convincing Luzzatto that his grave conclusions about Kabbalah and the Zohar's antiquity were mistaken. Reggio sent Luzzatto two letters on the subject, but Luzzatto refuted all of his arguments.[7]

From 1817 to 1818, Luzzatto studied the Babylonian Talmud with his father, all the while searching for any evidence for the existence of vowels and accents, but finding nothing. In June of 1818, he began to study the Zohar methodically, jotting down passages that seemed relevant to the Zohar's antiquity while writing definitive proofs against this notion—a project he never completed.[8]

The question of accentation and vowelization continued to occupy the three intellectuals, and it would come up in their letters time and time again after Loli left Trieste in 1819. In 1819 Luzzatto wrote to Reggio that having studied the topic for six years, he no longer has any doubts about his conclusions. The Sages of the Talmud and the classic Torah commentators wrote many interpretations which do not accord with the traditional accentation of the text. They would not have done this had they thought it originated from Sinai.[9] In that same year, in a letter to Loli, who argued on behalf of the kabbalists, Luzzatto initiated a concentrated attack against their position.

In 1826 Luzzatto finished writing his work on the subject entitling it *Vikuaḥ al Ḥokhmat Haqabbalah Veal Qadmut Sefer Hazohar Veqadmut Hanequdot Vehatamim* (A Disputation on the Kabbalah and on the Antiquity of the Zohar and the Vowels and Accents). The work was written in the style of the *Kuzari*: a dialogue between the *meḥaber* (the author, a representation of Luzzatto) who believes in Kabbalah, and the *oreaḥ* (the guest), a wise Polish Jew, who has taken up residence in the author's city—an opponent of Kabbalah. Over the course of the dialogue, he offers proofs against the Zohar's antiquity, and against the antiquity of the vowels and accents, arguments Luzzatto had formulated over the last thirteen years. The disputation begins at the end of the *Tiqqun* of Hoshannah Rabbah eve in 1825, and continues for three days.

---

6   Ibid., 27.
7   Ibid., 31.
8   Ibid., 35.
9   Luzzatto, *Igrot Shadal*, 60–61.

The guest constantly draws the author—against his wishes and despite his protests—into discussions about Kabbalah, during which he methodically disproves the belief that the Zohar and Kabbalah are divinely inspired traditions transmitted to the Tannaim.

Luzzatto kept the work in his drawer until 1851; only a handful of his disciples and friends had the opportunity to read it or receive a copy. In 1851 Luzzatto decided to publish the work, and it was published in Gorizia in 1852. He dedicated the work to Elhanan (Graziadio) Ascoli in honor of his wedding. In an addendum at the end of the work (Kislev 5612) and in an introduction written to Ascoli in French appended to its beginning (December 1851), Luzzatto states that he wrote the work as proof against the positions of Reggio and Loli who in the end had indeed been convinced by his arguments. At the time, he decided to shelve the work, not wishing to humiliate sincere, religious, God-fearing men deserving of honor and respect. In his region, Luzzatto explains, only a few people study books of Kabbalah, only gleaning from them ethics and fear of God. Their actions and intentions are worthy, and therefore he did not think it proper to confuse them with his arguments. Nevertheless, he recently met in Padua a young Jew from Poland who had seen a copy of the work in the hands of one of Luzzatto's disciples. The young man wrote to Luzzatto, pressing him to print and distribute the book, to assist the Polish *maskilim* in their battle against the Hassidim, who, according to him, are "desecrating the honor of the nation and the honor of the Torah with their vanities and evil deeds." In his dedication to Ascoli, Luzzatto adds another reason for publishing his work at the present time: his desire to demonstrate that the purpose of the commandments, as understood by the Sages, is ethical and for the good of society, and not theurgic ("a mystical trade-deal between earth and heaven"). Moreover, he wishes to show that scholars who argue that kabbalistic writings are based on the teachings of the Talmud, and are part of the "religious philosophy of the Jews" betray their ignorance, as kabbalistic writings postdate the Sages by a thousand years.[10]

---

10 Luzzatto, *Mehqerei Hayahadut*, 239–240; idem, *Ketavim*, vol. 1, 171–172; idem, *Vikuah al Hokhmat Haqabbalah Veal Qadmut Sefer Hazohar Veqadmut Hanequdot Vehatamim*, ed. Y. Bassi (Jerusalem, 2013), 135–137. It is evident from a letter Luzzatto wrote in November 1851 to Y. Stern, who then resided in Algiers, that the latter was the young man who prompted Luzzatto to publish the *Vikuah*. Luzzatto informed him in the letter that the book was in the printing press of Gorizia ready to be printed in honor of the Ascoli's wedding (and to be paid for by him). He writes, "if not for you, I would never have been bestirred to publish it, and already twenty-eight years have elapsed since its writing. May it be His will, that the book be beneficial for the members of our nation, and not a stumbling block to sin"

In this chapter I will give a detailed summary of the *Vikuaḥ*, as well as discussing Luzzatto's statements about Kabbalah in the interim between its shelving and publication. From this overview it will become clear that Luzzatto occasionally made small changes to his views—regarding the relationship between the first Kabbalists and the first philosophers as well as the question of the Zohar's author. From this overview also emerge two different facets to Luzzatto's personality: on the one hand, he is a researcher, who ever since his youth sought truth, never recoiling from it—even if it was bold, even if it contradicted the views of his friends or accepted religious tradition. On the other hand as a lover of his nation and religion who is un-eager to publicize his deviant opinions. Liable to damage the wellbeing of Judaism and its adherents, he only publicized such views when his hand was forced, only when doing so was necessary to prevent even greater damage to Judaism.[11]

FIRST STATEMENTS

In 1820, in the aforementioned letter to Loli, Luzzatto wrote for the first time about the dangers of Kabbalah, calling for its destruction and eradication.[12] In his opinion, Loli is wrong to say that Kabbalah, deriving from tradition, is preferable to philosophy, which is alien to Judaism. Kabbalah is actually less worthy than philosophy, as it is based on a corruption and misunderstanding of philosophy on the part of the kabbalists. He proves to Loli, from a number of examples, that the kabbalists themselves are divided over fundamental tenets of Kabbalah, such as the relationship between God (the emanator) and his emanations. To Loli's claim that the kabbalists were God-fearing men who studied many disciplines, Luzzatto responds that overwhelmed by these myriad

---

(Luzzatto, *Igrot Shadal*, 1124). Idel argues that in his dedication Luzzatto is dismissive of Adolph Franck's study from 1843, which sided with Kabbalah and argued for its antiquity. Unlike Scholem and Tishby, Idel maintains that most Jewish researchers in the nineteenth century, including Krochmal, Landauer, Benamozegh, Franck, Munk, and Jellinek, actually admired Kabbalah and understood its importance in Judaism. Unlike Luzzatto, Idel shows that theosophy, theurgy, ecstasy, and myth all existed in various forms within Judaism from the time of the Bible. See M. Idel, *Kabbalah New Perspectives* (New Haven and London, 1988). For Idel's discussion of the relationship between Luzzatto and Franck see 8–11. Liebes shows that myth is an inseparable part of the Bible and rabbinic literature and that Kabbalah actually tends to police and refine Jewish mythology. See Y. Liebes, *Alilot Elohim: Hamitos Hayehudi, Masot Umeḥqarim* (Jerusalem, 2009). See also note 28 below.

11 See below in the paragraph "After Shelving the *Vikuaḥ*".
12 Luzzatto, *Igrot Shadal*, 78.

disciplines they lost their common-sense, walking blindly after their teachers, failing to use their reason as befitting true philosophers. As to Loli's argument that the kabbalists performed miracles and wonders, Luzzatto responds that Pharaoh's magicians also did as much and even pagan priests practice magic, and employ magical names and techniques; these may be efficacious in the hands of sinners, but they do not prove the veracity of their ideas. He adds that it is well-known that the kabbalists are lovers of bribery, and make easy livings at the expense of the public, benefitting no one. Moreover, when Mendelssohn and Naftali Hirz Wessely taught the nation wisdom and knowledge, these devout kabbalists gaped in disapproval. Luzzatto's description of the evil done to the nation by Kabbalah and kabbalists speaks for itself:

> There is no number to those struck dead by the Kabbalah when it eclipsed the splendorous luster of our Torah, and when it made our faith loathsome to every enlightened person who sees their vanities. They think that they [the kabbalists] truly bear a tradition, and they say: if this is our tradition, then our entire Torah is nothing but utter futility! Were not in ancient times many of the sages of Israel philosophers? Faith was strong then in the heart of the Israelite man, and even when beset by much misfortune and tribulation, it could not budge him from his place and could not banish him from his faith. And now, since the majority of the greats of Israel are kabbalists and not philosophers, faith has been lost. And this came to be because the Torah has been left in a corner; no one studies it and no one seeks to understand its words according to the *peshat*. All those who study it deal only with *derash*, allusions, and mysteries—God forbid they occupy themselves with the *peshat* which they call the straw of the Torah (*Tiqqunei Zohar Hadash*, 34). And when they preach the words of Torah in an assembly of people, only mystery and *derash* are heard from their mouths. And when they rebuke the people for their sins, they do not draw their hearts with moral lessons, but castigate them for sins which are not sins, scaring them with baseless matters. And if men who are wise in matters of faith present before them their doubts, they will further bewilder them with illogical answers. And if they teach children Torah, they will not draw its words close to intellect, or even to the splendor of its simplicity, instead turning it into worthless speech, with *derash*, mysteries, and other baseless matters. And all of this necessarily leads people to be sickened by the words of the Living God, and they will scorn the Torah and come to apostasy. Was it not you who counseled me to hold onto the

wisdom of the *peshat*? How then can you rebuke me when I come to fight against those who despise and disgrace it, those who revile anyone who sends his hand to its branches, eating from it and living forever, by the labor of his hands and the sweat of his brow?[13]

THE ESSAY *VIQUAḤ*—THE FIRST DAY: KABBALAH HAS NO TRADITION

Luzzatto's work *Vikuaḥ al Ḥokhmat Hakkabalah* is written as a dialogue between the author and a guest, taking place over the course of three days. At the beginning of the dialogue, at the end of the *Tiqqun* of *Hoshannah Rabbah*, Luzzatto presents, through the mouth of the guest, his view that the Zohar was not written by the Sages of the Mishnah and the Talmud. True, the book claims to be tannaitic, just as the Torah, the prophets and the Sages testify to the sources of their words. But, according to the guest, we do not establish the origins of our sacred books based on self-testimony, but only on an unbroken chain of tradition from the time of their composition—traditions based on ancient testimonies accepted by the entire nation and even other religions. The Zohar, however, was neither mentioned nor known in the time of the Mishnah, the Talmud, or the Geonim, and was not extant in the eras of Rashi, Ibn Ezra, Maimonides, Nachmanides, and Rabbi Asher ben Jehiel. It follows that the Zohar has no reliable basis in tradition, and its provenance and content should be judged with intellectual investigation and not with faith: "For there is no faith in something that has no tradition, and the Zohar has no tradition from the time of its composition unto this day."[14] The author utterly rejects the guest's statements, but at this point the disputation is cut short and they both leave, one to his home the other to his inn.

The next day the two meet again after the morning prayers and resume their disputation. The guest declares that he is a God-fearing man, who adheres to the Written and Oral Torah, in thought and in practice; consequently, his statements about the Zohar contain no heresy. He distinguishes between the forgotten esotericism of the Talmud—"the secrets of the Torah," the Account of Creation, and the Account of the Chariot—and the system of Kabbalah. He states that the kabbalists themselves say that Elijah the prophet revealed

---

13 Ibid., 80. It should be noted that in his youth Luzzatto was a rationalist and an admirer of Maimonides, Mendelssohn, and philosophy.

14 *Vikuaḥ al Ḥokhmat Haqabbalah*: *Meḥqerei Hayahadut*, 116; Bassi edition, 8; Luzzatto, *Ketavim*, vol. 1, 176.

himself to Rabbi David (Abraham ben David's father) and taught him the secrets of Kabbalah, Abraham ben David, Nachmanides and other kabbalists all learning Kabbalah from him. According to the guest, Kabbalah was unknown in the time of the Geonim. Only after the academies of Babylonia were no more, after beliefs were distorted with the advent of Greek and Muslim philosophy, and after the ensuing confusion of the European pogroms which began in 1096, did Kabbalah appear. The guest emphasizes that the *Heikhalot* literature, *Sefer Yetsira*, and other ancient esoteric texts contain none of the statements made by later kabbalists. Unlike the books of the kabbalists, which are written in a confused, hybrid language, *Sefer Yetsira* is written clearly. Judah Halevi in the *Kuzari* (4:25) writes that the ten *sefirot* in *Sefer Yetsira* are nothing but the digits from one to ten, the number of fingers and the foundation of all numbers. Like letters, the numbers are abstract, infinite forms, used by God to create the world, his mind having established the quality of creation with letters and words and its quantity with numbers. When the Talmud says that the Sages miraculously created creatures using *Sefer Yetsira*, the meaning is they entertained thoughts using numbers and letters, and God actualized them. The guest adds that when Saadya Gaon and Ibn Ezra write about "the Sages of the *sefirot*" in the context of the creation of the luminaries, they obviously are referring to astronomers. Saadya Gaon, who knew nothing of the *sefirot* of the kabbalists or their notion of reincarnation [*Gilgul*], writes in his *Sefer Emunot Vedeot* (*Book of Beliefs and Opinions*; at the end of the sixth essay) that reincarnation is a jumble of madness, a belief unaccepted by the nation. In his *Guide for the Perplexed*, Maimonides writes that writing amulets, inscribing and reciting magical names, and performing wonders through them—is madness, falsehood, and foolishness.

After the guest proves from a number of sources that even the kabbalists themselves were divided over the issue of reincarnation, the author counters that the Mishnah and Talmud also contain disputes yet this does not invalidate the tradition they transmitted. The guest responds with his central argument: the Sages were only divided over details which lacked a tradition or which were forgotten. The kabbalists, however, "dispute each other regarding the principle upon which everything is based, that is the matter of the *sefirot*, which some say are the essence of the creator, while other says they are nothing but created vessels. And how could a discipline, its main principle a matter of doubt, be transmitted faithfully from tradition?"[15] The dispute between the kabbalists is related to the very basis of their system: are the *sefirot* the essence of God, Who

---

15 *Vikuaḥ al Ḥokhmat Haqabbalah*: *Meḥqerei Hayahadut*, 140; Bassi edition, 33; Luzzatto, *Ketavim*, vol. 1, 203.

is divided into a number of powers and layers, or is God a simple unity, and the *sefirot* are merely lofty vessels which He created? As an example, the guest cites the dispute between two schools of thought: Rabbenu Bahya, Rabbi Perets Hacohen, Nachmanides, Joshua Halevi Horowits (author of the *Shnei Luḥot Habrit*; the Shlah) who believed the *sefirot* to be God's essence and Joseph Ben Shusan, Menachem Recanati, Judah Hayat, Elazar of Worms, Moses Cordovero, and Menahem Azaria da Fano who believed the *sefirot* to be vessels. This is a fundamental dispute, the one side (those who maintain that they are vessels) considering the doctrine of the other idolatry. The guest cites a long excerpt from Recanati, which shows that Recanati reached his conclusions about the *sefirot* using logic not tradition. Recanati even argues that all the sages before him built their arguments on nothing—an admission on his part that this important matter had no established or accepted tradition. At the end of that day the guest mentions Rabbi Abraham Porto (author of *Ḥavot Yair*) who opposed the study of Kabbalah and who argued that the Mishnah and Talmud contain no secrets of Kabbalah. He also mentions the dispute between Elia Delmedigo and Joseph Solomon Delmedigo of Candia, the former maintaining that words of the Sages contain no secrets, the latter arguing that the secrets existed but were left unmentioned, the Sages not considering such matters pertinent to the halakhic subject-matter of the Mishnah and Talmud. Abraham Porto demonstrated that Joseph Solomon Delmedigo's claim is baseless: the Sages spoke about medicine in the Talmud, a subject similarly irrelevant to the subject-matter of the Mishnah and Talmud.[16]

THE SECOND DAY: KABBALAH'S PHILOSOPHICAL ORIGINS

When the author realizes the poor guest can no longer afford lodging and food, he invites him to his house for the remaining two days of the festival (*Shemini Atseret* and *Simḥat Torah*). After the evening prayer and the festival meal they sit

---

16 On "essence" versus "vessels" see I. Tishby, *Mishnat Hazohar*, vol. 1 (Jerusalem, 1949), 113–117. It is interesting that in 1852, after the publication of the *Vikuaḥ*, Luzzatto obtained a manuscript of *Sefer Heikhalot*. In a letter to Rapoport he mentions this and says that he sees in this the hand of Divine Providence. Now, after I have published the *Vikuaḥ*, he writes, I will merit completion of a *mitzvah* and will also publish *Sefer Heikhalot*, which will clearly show that the secrets of the ancients were not the secrets of Kabbalah, and that *Sefer Heikhalot* makes no mention of or allusion to the Sefirot and other kabbalistic matters. This shows that Kabbalah was unknown to the ancients, that the kabbalists did not receive their beliefs from them, and that the secrets of Kabbalah have no tradition. See Luzzatto, *Igrot Shadal*, 1155.

down to discuss the author's writings on Hebrew synonyms, the guest having agreed to no longer speak about matters of Kabbalah, which are transmitted only to unique individuals. The next day, early in the morning, the guest studies his host's writings until prayer-time, and after prayer and the meal they resume their dialogue.

The author raises a question which has been bothering him, and which seems to be unrelated to Kabbalah: why are there so few commentators who interpret the Torah according to the *peshat*? Even those considered *pashtanim*, such as Rashi, Ibn Ezra, David Kimhi, Isaac Abarbanel, often deviated from the simple meaning—Rashi following the path of *derash* and Aggada, others employing philosophical exegesis. Only Rashbam and Nachmanides, are true *pashtanim*, interpreting the actual text of the Torah. The guest uses the author's question to advance his discussion of Kabbalah. He replies that Aristotelian philosophy—received from Muslim philosophers who sought to reconcile Aristotelianism with Islam—truly inflicted great damage on Judaism. Under its influence, Jews who lived in Muslim lands sought to reconcile the Torah with this Muslim Aristotelianism. They thus deviated from the Torah's simple meaning, distorted the words of the Torah, prophets, and Sages, and interpreted using methods of philosophical parables and allusions, none of which were ever entertained by our ancestors. While the philosophers were useful in banishing the notion of divine corporeality, the gain was outweighed by the loss: the corruption of the Jewish faith. For example, according to the Sages the soul is a separate entity, existing before its entry into the body and after its departure from it. By contrast, Maimonides in the *Guide for the Perplexed* (part 1, 69 [should be 70]) states that before birth the human soul only exists in potentia. The only way one can attain an afterlife is through actualization of this potential—by occupying oneself with the study of intelligible forms. But one who does not engage in intellectual study will be punished, regardless of his sins, his soul ceasing to exist after death. According to the guest, this is also the view of Isaac Arama who in his book *Aqedat Yitshak* (viii) claims that this view was also formulated by the kabbalists and the Zohar. The kabbalists distinguished between the primary soul, the vitality of the body, possessed also by gentiles, and the exalted, complete soul of a Jew. The gentile will merit an afterlife only if he observes the seven Noahide commandments—otherwise his existence will be extinguished—while a Jewish soul is immune to destruction due to its divine source; its status can be enhanced by observing the commandments but never diminished. About the superiority which the kabbalists attributed to the Jew (as opposed to the philosophical view) the guest says:

This is an addition which the kabbalists added to the words of the philosophers, to give honor to the Children of Israel and to flatter the ignoramuses, so that they would not stone them. But what will you say about someone who believes that only *his* nation possesses a living soul? Is he a wiseman or a fool? Or will you think that our rabbis also believed thus, because they said "you [the Jewish people] are called man"? Tell me please, sir, when Antonius asked Rabbi Judah Hanasi, "When then is the soul placed in man; as soon as it is decreed or when it is actually formed?" why did he not respond to him: "When it is a Jew"? But the truth is that the kabbalists took philosophical ideas which were current in their time, and made some inversions to them, making them agree with our Torah and faith, acquiring them with change, attributing them to themselves. And behold the wisdom of the Kabbalah is accepted by the kabbalists, but not from our ancients, only from the philosophers. I will not condemn them for what they did, *for indeed their intention was truly worthy*; and that is because, seeing that most scholars in their times were attracted to the flawed philosophy of the Arabs, they tried to pick some things out of it, and to make a small change in their words, to bring the philosophizers, too, toward faith.[17]

The guest emphasizes that this conception of the soul is what led the philosophers and kabbalists to conclude that reward in the World to Come is not a divine gift for man's good deeds in this world but a natural consequence of human actions. According to the philosophers, reward is the direct result of the wisdom and good morals a person cultivates in his lifetime. According to the kabbalists, reward is causal, the result of observing commandments. This is also the meaning of the theurgic process of Kabbalah. By observing commandments one fixes the divinity; by sinning one "severs the divine roots": causing separation between the *sefirot*.[18] Similarly, Kabbalah's variety of different souls also derives from the philosophical-Aristotelian idea that a person's soul

---

17 Luzzatto, *Meḥqerei Hayahadut*, 161; Bassi edition, 54. This is the first time Luzzatto clearly criticizes philosophy, an attitude which would only become stronger over the years. This argument of Luzzatto is accepted, in part, by research until this day. See, for example, B. Dinur, *Toldot Yisrael, Sidra Shniya: Yisrael Bagolah*, vol. 2, book 4 (Tel Aviv and Jerusalem, 1970) 277–289. Idel, *New Perspectives*, 143, 252–253.
18 On the doctrine of unity and theurgical conception of Kabbalah see Tishby, *Mishnat Hazohar*, vol. 1, 105–107; ibid., vol. 2, 255, 276–280, 433–435.

is comprised of different parts which perform different actions (Maimonides, *Shemona Peraqim*).

The guest continues to enumerate the philosophical influences of theosophical Kabbalah: (1) According to philosophy, when a person dies the wise man's soul unites with the divinity; similarly, the kabbalists believe that only unique individuals merit the elevated souls *ḥaya* and *yeḥida*, which are uncreated emanations from God and which after death return to their source.[19] (2) According to philosophy, there are ten separate intellects which move the heavenly spheres; in Kabbalah there are ten *sefirot* (called the world of *Asiya*) and above these the later kabbalists added additional worlds—*Yetsira, Beria, Atsilut,* and *Adam Qadmon*—based on the philosophical demarcation of the universe into the lower world, the world of the celestial spheres, and the world of the angels; (3) according to the philosophers the intellect which moves the lowermost sphere is the "Active Intellect;" it maintains a connection with humanity and gives them the ability of intellectual apprehension; according to Kabbalah the tenth *sefira Malkhut* or *Shekhina*, the lowest divine power, is similarly connected to man and the lower material world, transmitting to them the divine effluence from up high; (4) in philosophy there is a dispute whether the first mover is God who moves the first sphere (but is distinct from it) or if the first mover is the first sphere itself, moving itself along with the other nine spheres; in Kabbalah there is a comparable dispute as to whether the *Ein Sof* is separate from the first Sefira, *Keter*, the first emanation from the *Ein Sof*, or if *Keter* is the name of the *Ein Sof* itself and the lower nine *sefirot* emanate from it.[20] According to the guest, the upshot of all this is: "do you see how the *sefirot* and the emanated intellects, Kabbalah and Arab philosophy, are all the same dream?"[21]

According to the guest, the kabbalists copied the image of the *sefirot* as embedded in each other like layers of an onion from the philosophers' celestial spheres, and they copied the idea of the *sefirot*'s inner light versus orbiting light from the philosophical idea of intellects apprehending both themselves and what they generate. All of these theosophical theories are meant to distance man from his creator and are all influenced by philosophy. But if the philosophers learned to deny divine attributes, attributing to God perfect unity, the kabbalists sought to distance even names from the *Ein Sof*, stating that all

---

19 On the concept of the soul in the Zohar see ibid., vol. 2, 69–75.
20 On the ten Sefirot see ibid., vol. 1, 131–135. On the *Shekhinah-Malkhut* see ibid., 219–231. On the relationship between *Keter* and the *Ein Sof* see ibid., 107–111.
21 Luzzatto, *Meḥqerei Hayahadut*, 169; Bassi edition, 62.

of God's names (including the Tetragrammaton) are the names of *sefirot* and not the names of the Creator himself. Moreover, according to Cordovero and Menahem Azaria da Fano, who maintain that the *sefirot* are created vessels, it follows that humans direct their prayers not to God but to created beings—no less idolatry than worship of the sun or the golden calf. Judaism always gave the Creator an agreed upon positive name—a means of referring to him, loving him, and fearing him. When we distance Him due to his sublimity, and give Him a negative name—"the non-finite"—we end up worshiping created beings and find ourselves distorting texts such as interpreting "In the beginning, God created" to refer not to the Creator Himself but rather to "the Creator [who] created God"—that is the Creator who created the lower *sefira* which, in turn, created the world. Luzzatto proceeds to have the guest present consequences of kabbalistic panentheism (distinct from Spinozan pantheism), reading to the author from Haim Vital's *Sefer Haqedusha* (beginning of chapter 3) and asking as follows:

> Do you see what Haim Vital says? That before the world was created the *Ein Sof* and all his creations were one, that the flame was encased in the coal. Do you see with your eyes? The Creator and the created are all one! Before the world was created, what was the world? We in our naivety say it did not exist, or that there was nothing. But the kabbalists, with wonderful counsel and great wisdom, said that the world was encased in the bosom of its creator like the flame in a coal. The world—what is it? We—what are we? The rocks and trees—what are they? Everything is part of God up high. Everything is the essence of the Creator. And now, please come with me and I will show you that this matter is written explicitly by the genius and kabbalist Jacob Emden in his book *Mitpaḥat Sefarim* (19a). [...] And what difference is there between this opinion and the opinion of the atheist, heretic Spinoza—may the name of the wicked rot? [...] I will tell you the difference between them. Spinoza says there is no god at all, but that the world as a whole is a single, ancient object, that was, is, and will be, and he calls it god, even though in fact he has no god at all; and the kabbalists say there is a God separate from the world itself, but when He created the world, He did not create it *ex nihilo* and not from ancient matter, but that He emanated some of His blessed essence and separated it from Himself, whereas beforehand it was all the same thing. Thus, in truth, the kabbalists have a divinity, but they make themselves and the entire world parts of that divinity, something that one's mouth may not utter and one's

ear may not hear; and this was already the opinion of the ancient Persian Zoroaster. And do not stammer and say to me: The kabbalists do not all agree upon this. Know, my brother, that Haim Vital takes his words on this matter from the Zohar; you will find it at the beginning of the *Idra Zuta* which you read on Hoshannah Rabbah night.[22]

According to the guest, even the idea of *tsimsum* (divine contraction) is, at its basis, a pagan corporealization of God, as it implies that God is subject to change. The kabbalists sought to explain that the infinite God needed to contract Himself to allow the creation of the finite. But this statement is meaningless and contains nothing new, for all scholars agree that it is impossible for an infinite being to create another infinite being like it, and it can only create something finite. The philosophers used this principle to explain the existence of evil, which is not something created but merely a consequence of the nature of created entities: due to their finite nature they are limited and therefore exposed to harm.

When preparing his work for publication, Luzzatto added a note: not long ago, he realized from Krochmal's book *Moreh Nevuḥei Hazman* that even the names of the *sefirot* are taken from the philosophers and are not original. They come from the gnostic Basilius, who taught in Alexandria, eighty years after the Temple's destruction and who intermingled Christianity with philosophy and other newly invented beliefs. He dealt with the idea of emanation stating that Thought emanated from God, and from it emanated Insight, Knowledge, Wisdom, Might, Justice and Peace. From these seven "*sefirot*" the kabbalists made ten—the number of *sefirot* recorded in *Sefer Yetsira*.[23]

---

22 Luzzatto, *Meḥqerei Hayahadut*, 177–178, Bassi edition, 71. On the Zohar's simile of "a flame in a coal" as the solution to the problem of the ambiguity of unity and the conception of emanation see Tishby, *Mishnat Hazohar*, vol. 1, 104–105.

23 Luzzatto, *Meḥ.qerei Hayahadut*, 184; Bassi edition, 78. According to Gutman, the idea of emanation is rooted in Neoplatonism. See Gutman, *Hafilosofia shel Hayahadut*, 85. According to Tishby, the kabbalists inherited the idea of the hidden *Ein Sof* from Neoplatonism, and the idea of emanated, revealed Sefirot from Gnosticism. This combination was necessary due to the strong influence of the dispute between those who opposed philosophy, and supported the notion of a close God, and the philosophers who supported the notion of a sublime and exalted God. The kabbalists wished to unite the two approaches. See Tishby, *Mishnat Hazohar*, vol. 1, 102–103 and n. 2. See more about emanation ibid., 135–144.

THE THIRD NIGHT: THE ANTIQUITY OF VOWELS AND ACCENTS

That night, after prayers and the Simhat Torah meal, the guest once again directs the dialogue to a subject which seems unrelated to the authenticity of Kabbalah—the antiquity of vowels and accent marks. The author admits that many times he himself (Luzzatto) interpreted the simple meaning of a verse in contradistinction to the interpretation implied by the cantillation marks or traditional vowelization. According to him, all the classic commentators did the same: Rashi, Rashbam, Ibn Ezra, Nachmanides, R. Bahya ben Asher, Abarvanel, R. David Kimhi, Joseph Albo, Hizkuni, Seforno and also modern commentators such as Mendelssohn and Wessely. With many excerpts he demonstrates this trend, adding that he wrote all of this in a special notebook (i.e., Luzzatto's "Maamar Haniqud" from 1817). When the guest asks him what he has concluded regarding the provenance of the vowels and accents according to this commentators, he responds: "To me it seems that they did not believe that they were written with divine inspiration, and did not think that the prophets and those possessing divine inspiration, the authors of the Holy Scripture, added vowels to their books themselves. For had they believed thus, they would not have allowed themselves to utter an interpretation which opposes its [Scripture's] vowels and accents."[24] The guest adds that Ibn Ezra, R. David Kimhi and Judah Hayyuj spoke explicitly about the institutors of vowels and accents, and Judah Halevi and Nachmanides (according to the *Mahzor Vitri*) wrote that the Torah scroll given to the nation of Israel was simple text, devoid of any vowels and accents. It seems that the ancients believed that it was Ezra and the Scribes who instituted the vowels and accents. That is until the grammarian Elijah Levita, who stated that vowelization did not exist before the sealing of the Talmud. This initiated a dispute among the scholars of Israel and the nations of the world, the sides split between those maintaining like R. Elijah and those who believed that the vowels antedated the Talmud, basing their view primarily on the many references to vowels and accents in the Zohar, which they believed was composed by the Tannaim and Amoraim.

R. Elijah Levita's first proof was that the Talmud and Midrash do not mention vowels and accents, nor were they mentioned by Latin translator of the

---

24 Luzzatto, *Mehqerei Hayahadut*, 188; Bassi edition, 82. Luzzatto himself worked many years to document the mistakes that, in his opinion, had crept into the cantillation marks in our possession. He penned 150 emendations in a letter from September 1853, sent to Shneur Sachs, editor of *Kerem Ḥemed*. See Luzzatto, *Igrot Shadal*, 1207–1222. For the publication of his emendations see *Kerem Ḥemed*, vol. 9 (1856), 1–14.

Bible, Jerome. For example, Jerome says that he did not dare translate the book of Chronicles—which consists primarily of rare names—before reading it with one of the Jewish Sages of Tiberias. This is evidence that he was unable in his time to find a Hebrew Bible which contained vowel signs.[25] Various discussions in the Talmud and Midrash, cited by the author and the guest, clearly demonstrate that vowelization was unknown to them. The guest notes that one should be careful about bringing evidence from *midrashim*, some of which, like *Shemot Rabbah* and *Bamidbar Rabbah*, were composed after the Talmud. The traditional Masoretic Text of the Bible, erroneously attributed to the Men of the Great Assembly, was also developed after the sealing of the Talmud. This was the view of Bahya Ibn Paquda and Ibn Ezra. The claim that Ezra instituted the vowels and accents, but they were later forgotten or corrupted, and therefore the Sages could not determine where a verse ended or paused (as seen in the Talmud)—is illogical. It is far more reasonable to say that in the time of the Sages the correct reading of Scripture existed as an oral tradition, susceptible to corruption, and that the sages of Tiberius, who composed the Masoretic Text, deviated from the rabbinic readings of the Midrash and the Talmud whenever they thought such readings did not correspond to the simple meaning of the text. Therefore, subsequent commentators could disregard the traditional vowelization whenever they thought it diverged from the simple meaning of the Bible and therefore Onkelos and Targum Yonatan sometimes translated divergently to our system of vowels. If we say that the vowels came from Ezra, how did they dare to deviate from them? And if from Ezra, how did the Sages of Tiberius dare to deviate? It seems that due to oppression and exile in the wake of the sealing of the Talmud, it was perceived necessary to establish, in writing, the hitherto oral tradition; thus were the vowels and accents born. The guest adds that it is reasonable to assume that the vowelists operated not much later than the sealing of the Talmud; otherwise, they would have had difficulty disputing the authority of the Talmud. He therefore concludes: "It has become clear to us that the beginning of vowelization was shortly after the sealing of the Talmud, in the days of the Savoraim, sometime around the year 4260 [500 C.E.]." This was the opinion of Elijah Levita who chose a date 436 years after the Temple's destruction, although he erred and wrote 3982. According to this date—a time when there were still no books, and a time much earlier than the appearance of the Karaites (200 years after the sealing of the Talmud)—it is

---

25 Luzzatto, *Meḥqerei Hayahadut*, 205; Bassi edition, 100; Luzzatto, *Igrot Shadal*, 75.

understandable why the institution of vowels was never recorded and why the Karaites did not repudiate it.

Unlike Elijah Levita, who maintains that the vowels were established in Tiberius, the guest reckons that they were established in Babylonia, the seat of the Exilarch and the great, authoritative heads of the talmudic academies—not in the Land of Israel, where the Princehood had been abolished even before the sealing of the Talmud. The vowelists and accenters were exalted Sages called *qaraim* ("readers"; not "Karaites"). Supported by the leaders of Babylonia, their work was accepted without challenge or dispute. By contrast, the formulation of the Masoretic Text, a technical task which followed in the wake of the vowels and accents, was accomplished in Tiberius. The guest says in summary:

> It seems that it was the Savoraic rabbis—who committed the Oral Torah to paper and wrote the Mishnah, Talmud and Targum, which heretofore had all been preserved orally—who commanded some talented sages to conceive a plan to make a fence for the reading [of the Bible] so that it would not be forgotten; and thus they did, and they invented the vowels and accents, and dotted the entire Bible. The Savoraic rabbis supported their work, confirmed it, and upheld it, and thus it was accepted by all of Israel.[26]

Luzzatto added here a note before publication: based on new findings, he now tends to think that the vowels were invented in Babylonia and altered by the Tiberians, from whom we received our current system—as Ibn Ezra writes in his *Sefer Tsahut*.[27]

At two in the afternoon, the guest and author retire to their respective rooms, and meet again in the morning before prayers.

THE THIRD DAY: ESTABLISHING THE ARGUMENTS AGAINST THE ZOHAR'S ANTIQUITY

The guest opens the dialogue the following morning with a leading question. He asks the author if he is now entirely convinced that the vowels and accents were developed after the sealing of the Talmud. Without hesitation, the author says yes. The guest tells him that his answer essentially destroys the basis of the

---

26 Luzzatto, *Mehqerei Hayahadut*, 212, Bassi edition, 107.
27 Luzzatto, *Mehqerei Hayahadut*, 213, Bassi edition, 108.

Zohar and Kabbalah's authenticity. Confused by this, the author says that while he knows that the vowels and accents—like the prophet Muhammad and two sets of Tefillin (based on the different views of Rashi and Rabbenu Tam)—are mentioned in the Zohar, this poses no difficulty to one who believes that the Zohar was written with divine inspiration. The guest explains that not only the vowels and accents are mentioned in the Zohar, but their shapes as well—shapes created by men after the Zohar's purported time, inspiring mounds upon mounds of exegesis and esotericism.

In response, the author yields ground and adopts the view of Jacob Emden (1698–1776), who in his book *Mitpaḥat Sefarim* proved that the Zohar indeed contains later passages, as further confirmed by Mendelssohn. The author claims, however, that these interpolations do not detract from the remainder of the book. The guest answers that this oversight discredits Kabbalah as a whole, for these interpolations eluded great kabbalists, including Isaac Luria, who sanctified the Zohar in its entirety, considering it all the words of the Sages! How did their divine inspiration (of which they were so proud) not reveal to them what Emden found—that the Zohar contains 280 late passages, and that the *Ra'aya Mehemna* and the *Tiqqunei Zohar* are forgeries in their entirety!? The author claims that Emden had exaggerated, but the guest responds that Emden should have admitted that the body of the Zohar is also a late forgery. Surprising the author, the guest tells him about the testimony of Rabbi Issac of Acre who undertook to clarify the provenance of the Zohar, and who interviewed together with his wife, a close relative of the kabbalist Moshe De Leon as well as De Leon's wife and daughter. They all told him that De Leon wrote the Zohar himself, but disseminated the manuscripts as if they belonged to Shimon Bar Yohai to earn esteem for his works to raise his pay. The author adds that this testimony is true, for the great sage R. Abrahm Zacuto cites it in the first printing of his work *Sefer Yuḥasin* (Constantinople, 1566), and Emden copied and incorporated it into his work *Mitpaḥat Sefarim*. In subsequent printings of *Sefer Yuḥasin*, the printers intentionally omitted Isaac of Acre's words because they stand as incriminating evidence against the Zohar's antiquity.

The guest claims that the Zohar's language also demonstrates that it is a forgery. It is not the language of the Bible, or of the Mishnah, or of Daniel and Ezra, or of Onkelos, or of the Targum Yerushalmi, or of the Talmuds, or of the *midrashim*, or of the Geonim, or of the commentators, or the philosophers; it is a ludicrous language cobbled together from of all of these. It is very difficult to write a text in the language of the Mishnah or the Midrash without it being identified as forgery, and one who has not spent time studying Talmud will fail to write in proper Aramaic; instead, he will write in a language as ridiculous as that of the Zohar. The guest cites numerous instances of improper Aramaic and Hebrew in the Zohar—words and expressions that the Sages never used, at least not in the sense implied by the Zohar—as well as late, medieval terminology unknown in the time of the Sages. Similarly, he notes that the Zohar often contains mistakes about the dwelling places and biographies of various Sages, evidence that the author of the Zohar did not know who was whose rabbi, or which Sages lived in the Land of Israel and which in Babylonia. His conclusion is that the book as a whole is a forgery, the work of Moshe De Leon:

> Because the Zohar contains so many passages which cannot possibly be attributed to Tannaim and Amoraim, it is un-befitting for a person of intellect to willingly make difficulties for himself and believe that only those passages are interpolations. Rather he should determine that the book in its entirety is a counterfeit, especially, once we have seen that this book was unmentioned and unknown for thousands of years after the men who supposedly wrote it, and after we have seen that one was already suspected of forging this book, as admitted by his wife and daughter.[28]

The guest proceeds to discuss the Zohar's calculations of the End of Days. Although the Sages opposed such calculations, nine dates for the End of Days appear in the various sections of the Zohar. According to the guest, these dates, with the exception of 5500 (1840), have all passed uneventfully, and they all postdate the beginning of the sixth millennium—the Zohar never selects any dates within the thousand years after Rabbi Shimon Bar Yochai. It follows that the author of the book was not divinely inspired, acted against the Sages, and lived at least a thousand years after Rabbi Shimon Bar Yochai. The forgers

---

28 Luzzatto, *Meḥqerei Hayahadut*, 221, Bassi edition, 118. For an extensive discussion of the evidence for dating the Zohar's writing to the end of the thirteenth century (1280–1305), and for attribution to Moshe De Leon, see Tishby, *Mishnat Hazohar*, vol. 1, 28–108. On Luzzatto's criticism of the Zohar's antiquity and on the interesting, yet failed, attempt of his fellow countryman Elijah Benamozegh to refute Luzzatto's arguments in his book *Taam Leshad* (Livorno, 1863) see ibid., 58–59. On Gershom Scholem's systematic studies on the subject see ibid., 65–67. Tishby distinguishes between the researchers of the Haskalah period, including Luzzatto and Graetz (but not Jellinek) who wrote about the Zohar, its author and its contents from a perspective of disapproval and opposition, and Scholem and his followers, who although they understood that the Zohar is a late work, recognized the greatness of the work and its author and its important place in the history of Kabbalah and Jewish thought in general. See above note 10.

of the book (who knew all of this) wrote in the introduction to the *Tiqqunei Zohar*, that the Zohar would not be revealed until the beginning of the sixth millennium, hoping to thus conceal their forgery. The Christians used a similar ruse: they disseminated a story about a Jew from Toledo who in the third year of the sixth millennium, dug up a book from his garden, written in three languages, telling of a son of God, borne of a virgin, who will suffer to save the world. The book says that he will reappear when Ferdinand rules over Castile (who reigned at the end of the fifth millennium and the beginning of the sixth). One might argue that the author of the Zohar—who seems to have been from Spain—heard this story, and decided to emulate the ruse.

Once again the guest blames the Zohar for the Jews not being redeemed—the very reward promised to them for studying it. Moreover it inflicted harm, causing Jews to eschew study of the Torah's simple meaning for the last five hundred years (with the exception of Joseph Albo and Abarvanel who distanced themselves from the esoteric path of Kabbalah). The guest says that it is only in our generation that we have once again merited interpreters of the *peshat* like Mendelssohn, Wessely and Joel Lowe, who all detested the Zohar. But the author counters: the Zohar saved the Jews from the apostasy of the philosophers, followers of Aristotle who denied creation *ex nihilo*, individual providence, and miracles, who claimed that the World to Come is only for the wise, and who said that certain commandments are no longer relevant. To this the guest answers:

> I have already said, that the *early sages who invented the wisdom of Kabbalah from their hearts, intended only good*; but [I will tell you] what indicates that they did more evil than the philosophizers: Is anyone more contemptuous of the Torah than the book of the Zohar, which says that one who regards the simple meaning of the Torah the Torah's essence, his spirit should depart, and he should have no portion in the World to Come (3:152); and in another place it says that the simple meaning is the straw of the Torah (*Tiqqunei Zohar Hadash* 34), and at the beginning of the *Tiqqunei Zohar* its mocks those who study Scripture calling them eggs [as opposed to hatched chicks].[29]

The guest concludes the morning discussion with a summary of the activity of the kabbalists: According to him, the kabbalists cause harm, wasting their

---

29 Luzzatto, *Meḥqerei Hayahadut*, 225, Bassi edition, 121. (Emphasis added—E.C.)

time and intellect on Gematria and acronyms, dreams and vanities, and by distancing the sages of Israel from studying the Torah itself, that is the *peshat* and the Halakhah. He adds that the Zohar's intrusive and audacious discussions of God's essence besmirch His honor. Such activity will:

> Break the yoke of the fear of heaven from the necks of the sages of Israel, until they care not about the honor of their Creator, asking and replying, writing and printing, about what is above and below, what is within and what is without; they speak about the God of gods with hubris and an arrogant heart: How he created his world, how he manages it, how he contracted himself to create it, how he emanated worlds from his essence, how his essence unites with the worlds he emanated, how one is ten and ten is one, how the soul is truly part of God, how all the worlds are part of God, how the actions of flesh and blood have power to damage and disrupt the uppermost worlds, and other similar matters which makes the hair of anyone with a God stand on end when he reads them in a book. And especially when he sees them speaking about these empty things, bereft of logic and of all the studies which are necessary not only for such lofty investigations, but even for the simplest inquiry. And on the whole, one sees that there is no agreement between them about the principles of their wisdom, and they all feel their way around walls like blind men [when engaged] in matters at the basis of everything, striving to maintain two opposites in one subject, saying things that cannot be understood at all—and the enlightened one who understands will find nothing in their words but curses and blasphemy.[30]

It should be noted that throughout the work, Luzzatto has the guest degrade kabbalists with harsh insults: Those whose villainy has been revealed; those who invent things from their hearts to deceive the fools; deniers; liars; forgers; swindlers bereft of knowledge or understanding; vulgar ones who deny God; idol-worshipers; destroyers, who sin and cause others to sin; those who mock with a false gift, saying that the divine spirit has rested upon them and other such things.[31]

---

30 Luzzatto, *Meḥqerei Hayahadut*, 226–227, Bassi edition, 121.
31 In order: *Ketavim*, 183, 184, 202, 218; *Meḥqerei Hayahadut*, 122, 123, 139, 153, 171, 181, 215; Bassi edition, 14–15, 33, 46, 65, 75, 111.

The angry author at this point stops the dialogue, which has once again slid into Kabbalah as the guest wished, and rushes him to synagogue for morning prayers. When they return from synagogue, they sit down for the meal, and the guest immediately resumes their discussion from the morning. He argues that the Sages based their exegesis primarily on the simple meaning of the text, and their strange textual derivations are not interpretation of Scripture but textual support meant to serve as mnemonic or a means of frightening the ignoramuses from disparaging the decrees of the Sages.[32] According to him, the study of the simple meaning became progressively deeper and wide-spread up until the appearance of the Zohar; ever since it has declined, replaced by faulty interpretation, and the vanities and dreams of people who abuse the Torah, honoring themselves by shaming it and its giver. The author interrupts him and invites him to eat.

After the meal, the author opens for the guest the book *Emunat Ḥakhamim* by Avida Sarshalom Basilea, which tells of Joseph Karo's *Maggid Meisharim*, a book containing kabbalistic and zoharic matters which Karo received from a divine spirit. Cordovero, Karo's disciple, in his book *Pardes Rimmonim*, cites the words of the "magid" who revealed himself to Karo; these quotations indeed appear in Karo's book. According to the author, this proves the authenticity of Kabbalah and the Zohar, for one cannot say that Karo and Cordovero were evil and invented this revelation. The guest responds that perhaps this is merely a case of the powerful imagination of someone who had immersed himself in Kabbalah and asceticism, stimulating a dream that simulated the appearance of a speaking divine spirit; moreover, the two did not lie for their own honor but to instill the fear of heaven among the masses, and it is also possible that all their words are meant as allusions and secrets which we do not understand.

In any event, it is clear that this is not a proof. The guest also argues that the various promises that the Magid made to Karo were not fulfilled—such as that he would die as a martyr on a pyre, that his children would be in the Sanhedrin in the Temple, that his son would be a sage exceeding all in his knowledge of Kabbalah, and that he would compose a commentary on the Zohar and a critique of his father's books. Similarly, the Maggid speaks nonsense such as his promise that Karo can drink fourteen cups of wine at Sabbath meals, as alluded to by the last two letters of God's name Shaddai [שדי]—which is numerically equivalent to fourteen. It seems, the guest says, that this is a case of

---

32 On Luzzatto's stance regarding the provenance of the Oral Torah see Chamiel, *The Middle Way*, vol. 1, 314–326, and Chapter Four in the current book.

auto-suggestion and that the Maggid was merely a reflection of Karo's own thoughts, as is indeed written in *Maggid Meisharim*. The book is full of words of hubris and haughtiness with no good purpose. They are nothing more than lies, which Karo contrived from his thoughts and aspirations. The Maggid's words also contain another ambiguity: It is unclear who the Maggid, the speaker, is—God, God's messenger, the Mishnah or the soul. It seems that Karo's Maggid was not meant to be the *Shekhina* or the *sefira Malkhut*, but merely the speech of his own soul; Cordovero even wrote explicitly that while correct, the Maggid represents Karo's own logic.[33]

At this point, the author gives up on the disputation. He realizes that the guest has cleverly drawn him onto a path with no escape. The next day he informs him that he is returning to his (Luzzatto's) studies of Hebrew language and the simple meaning of the text, and he will leave secrets and Kabbalah to those unique individuals who have merited learning them from a true kabbalist.

The guest thanks his host for the three wonderful days he has spent with him, having experienced nothing like them in the last eleven years. The author advises the guest to refrain from discussing matters of Kabbalah with anyone except a true kabbalist who can open his eyes; if he speaks with someone who, like himself, does not understand Kabbalah, he will be like one who seduces others to worship idolatry. The author adds that even if his guest is correct, and Kabbalah is vanity, it does not harm the masses, and it may even strengthen their worship of God and their observance of the commandments. By contrast, if the guest discourages them with his arguments, their observance of commandments will suffer as a result, and the guest will be responsible for their undoing. The tragedy of the philosophers—who disseminate the Maimonidean rationales of the commandments, which give the commandments obsolete reasons, suggesting that, God forbid, the commandments should be abolished—is already enough, the author says. The only way to oppose them and to strengthen the observance of commandments is through secrets of the Kabbalah and the possibility of fixing or, God forbid, damaging the uppermost worlds according to one's level of observance. But the guest does not agree. He argues that this position may have been correct in the past but today, when inquiry is open to all, and people of faith are dwindling as a result, it is best to purify Judaism of the dross which it has accumulated over the years. If this is not done, then learned people who discover the flawed elements of Judaism (such as Kabbalah) will reject Judaism as a whole and say that all of the Torah

---

33 Luzzatto, *Meḥ.qerei Hayahadut*, 228–236, Bassi edition, 124–133; Luzzatto, *Igrot Shadal*, 80–81.

is falsehood. The author counters that "the world should not be destroyed on account of fools." Thus, the two part ways, with their different opinions.

In an addendum which Luzzatto added to the end of the work before submitting it for print in 1852, he mentions two studies on the subject of the Zohar's author, written long after he had completed the work. Meir Heinrich Landauer wrote a study, which was published after his death in installments in *Orient* beginning in 1845. It claims that Abraham Abulafia wrote the Zohar between 1270–1280. This is based on a comparison of the Zohar to Abulafia's manuscripts which Landauer found in the library of Munich.[34] By contrast, Adolf Jellinek, in a work published in Leipzig in 1851, argues that the Zohar was written by Moshe de Leon in collaboration with others, and that Abulafia had no connection to it at all (unless some of the Zohar's authors had Abulafia's books at their disposal and were influenced by him).[35] Jellinek bases his claim on a comparison between phrases and ideas appearing in the Zohar to the contents of De Leon's writings, such as *Nefesh Haḥokhma*. Luzzatto writes further: having realized that the Zohar and Kabbalah are not the work of the Sages, he has stopped studying them. But from a cursory examination of De Leon's books in the possession of his friend Rabbi Mordechai Samuel Gerondi and Joseph Almanzi, he now thinks that De Leon was not a fraud and counterfeiter like Abulafia. It is possible that he really did obtain the Zohar from elsewhere, erroneously concluding that it was an ancient work, studying it and even incorporating zoharic ideas and expression into his own books. That being said, Luzzatto admits that he cannot decide and he leaves it up to other scholars, as there still remain many mysteries in this subject, which men of truth should unravel.[36]

---

34 On Landauer's study, which does not stand up to criticism, see Tishby, *Mishnat Hazohar*, vol. 1, 61; Idel, *New Perspectives*, 7–8.

35 On Jellinek's study, see Tishby, *Mishnat Hazohar*, vol. 1, 62. Tishby regards Jellinek the most important researcher of Kabbalah in the Haskalah period. See also Idel, *New Perspectives*, 8–9. As opposed to Tishby, Idel considers Franck the most important researcher of Kabbalah in that period. See Idel, ibid., 8.

36 Luzzatto, *Meḥqerei Hayahadut*, 239–240, Bassi edition, 135–137. Luzzatto, Jellinek, and Landauer did not know what Idel would later uncover in his studies (based on G. Scholem, Major Trends in Jewish Mysticism [New York, 1941], lecture 4): that Abulafia was not a theosophical-theurgical kabbalist who studied the world of the Sefirot, but rather the main representative of the ecstatic school of Kabbalah, which deals with isolation and letter combinations as practices leading to Unio Mystica with God, a trend which Idel dubs prophetic-messianic Kabbalah. See Idel, *New Perspectives*, xi-xx, 61–62. It is interesting that Dinur, *Toldot Yisrael*, chapter 16, specifically 281, 365–380, 427–428, identified Abulafia's unique views, but unlike Scholem and Idel, did not discern that Abulafia belonged to entirely different school of Kabbalah.

AFTER THE SHELVING OF THE *VIKUAH*

In 1829 Luzzatto began to serve as the co-head of the newly opened rabbinical seminary in Padua. At that time, he composed an "introduction to the criticism and interpretation of the Torah," to be used by students in a course on the Pentateuch.[37] In this work he reiterates, for the first time, some of his ideas first written in the *Vikuah*. At the beginning of the "introduction" he seeks to prove that Moses wrote the entire Torah, as dictated by the mouth of God, and that due to it being treated as a divine and supremely holy book, neither the Scribes nor the Sages made any emendations or corrections to it. Luzzatto explains that the Samaritan version of the Pentateuch is "distorted, corrupt, and counterfeit,"[38] that the Septuagint "should not be trusted,"[39] and that Targum Onkelos is a free translation, not a literal one. All of this is marshaled to reinforce his argument that, ever since it was written by Moses, no changes have been made to the text of the Torah; it has always been as we have it. After this, Luzzatto proceeds to discuss the principles of biblical interpretation which, above all, rely on tradition. Tradition includes the ancient reading of the text and the ancient understanding of its words and their meanings—primarily in regards to commandments which were anchored in the words of the Sages in the Oral Torah. That being said, the Sages also used verses as textual support for oral commandments, even when they knew that this was not the primary meaning of the text. The reading and accentation of the text are also part of the oral tradition. Over the centuries, however, the Sages began to have doubts, disputes, and uncertainties about these details, as attested to in many places in the Talmud. After the sealing of the Talmud this problem was resolved by "vowelists" who instituted a system of vowel signs and cantillation marks. Although they did this wisely and on the basis of tradition, according to Luzzatto and most interpreters it is possible that at times they erred and therefore can be disputed. Luzzatto cites examples from fourteen interpreters, ancient and modern, from the Geonim and Rashi until Mendelssohn, who interpreted the Torah differently from the interpretation suggested by the traditional vowels and accents. He presents this as evidence that these interpreters also maintained that the vowels and accents were instituted by humans, who though possessing deep, admirable understanding, were not divinely inspired like Ezra and the prophets. Luzzatto proceeds to analyze Targum Onkelos, showing that his

---

37 Luzzatto, *Ketavim*, vol. 2, 97–134.
38 Ibid., 113.
39 Ibid., 117.

translations are not literal, and that he diverged from the original text to avoid using expressions which corporealize God or belittle the honor of our forefathers and the Torah, and to elucidate difficult or unclear words and expressions. After an extensive discussion about tradition, the first element of biblical interpretation, Luzzatto reviews the second element—the rules of language and grammar, and the third—proper use of intellect.[40]

In a letter to Rapoport (1830) Luzzatto responds to Rappaport's concerns about publicizing his own interpretations and emendations of biblical verses, which conflict with the Masoretic text.[41] Luzzatto explains that pure reflection on an interpretation which seems correct and true should be publicized, with fear for no one, as our God is a God of truth who does not tolerate sycophants. Moreover—after it has been proven beyond a doubt that the vowels and accents were instituted by experts only after the sealing of the Talmud, and that the Masoretic Text was instituted even later—then certainly the vowelists and cantillationist, and even more so the Masoretes, could have erred. Therefore, already the classical commentators allowed themselves to interpret differently than the vowelists and cantillationists. Luzzatto notes that he has already taught this to his students in an introductory course on the Pentateuch. He does not, however, mention the manuscript of the *Vikuaḥ* in his archives. Luzzatto writes to Rapoport: "We will publicize our proposition and interpretation, and explain that Scripture was indeed preserved better than other ancient text (primarily the Pentateuch, which truly contains no errors)".[42] That being said, no manuscript, or even a printed work, is completely immune from error.

In a later letter to Rapoport (1832) Luzzatto polemicizes against Ibn Ezra, a figure whom Rapoport greatly respected and held in high esteem.[43] Luzzatto writes that the philosophizing Ibn Ezra spoke with duplicity, broke tradition and did nothing to benefit the Jewish people. By contrast, he praises Rashi, who was righteous and upright, who was responsible for the flourishing of literalist Jewish interpreters such as Rashbam, Nachmanides, and R. David Kimchi, and

---

40 Luzzatto dedicated an entire work *Philoxenus* (eponymous with his first born child, born in 1829) to elucidating Onkelos's method in his translation. The first edition of the book was published in Vienna in 1830, and the second, expanded edition in Krakau 1896, after Luzzatto's death.
41 Luzzatto, *Igrot Shadal*, 174.
42 On preserving the text of the Pentateuch according to Luzzatto see ibid., 182–183, 367–368; Luzzatto, *Ketavim*, vol. 2, 102–107; idem, *Meḥqerei Hayahadut*, vol. 2, 56–57.
43 Luzzatto, *Igrot Shadal*, 232–233.

who was responsible for the spread of knowledge in Israel. Unfortunately, this was all ruined by:

> the philosophizers, Ibn Ezra and Maimonides, and their disciples who re-submerged the Torah in the depths of allegory and parable, and brought up gall and wormwood in their hands. And they caused the birth of the kabbalists, and strengthened their hands. For they paved before them the path of parables, allegories and distortions of verses, removing them entirely from context. And the kabbalists followed their path, *with worthy intentions*, to reinforce religion and faith and to seal the breaches made by the philosophizers. And ever since, from the beginning of the sixth millennium [mid-thirteenth century], the wisdom of Israel has continued to decrease.[44]

Luzzatto defends himself later in the letter from Rapoport's suspicion that he is a fundamentalist and not a critical researcher. To prove to Rapoport that he seeks the truth through research even if it opposes accepted tradition, he recounts, for the first time, the daring research he conducted in his youth: "I, with no teacher, and no guide, and without reading the books of non-Jewish scholars ever since I was fourteen or fifteen years old, realized the forgery of the Zohar and the lies of Kabbalah, and when I was about twenty I wrote a long essay on this to prove that Kabbalah was borne of philosophy."[45]

As mentioned, in 1851, in preparation for the publication of the *Vikuah*, Luzzatto wrote that when he began to write the work he was uncertain as to the Zohar's authorship. When he wrote the *Vikuah*, he believed that the Zohar's author was the counterfeiter Moshe De Leon. In 1851, however, he tended to think that it was forged by Abraham Abulafia and that Moshe De Leon, who obtained the manuscript from elsewhere, truly believed it to be ancient. In 1833 Luzzatto wrote another letter to Rapoport, which indicates that ever since he concluded writing the *Vikuah* he was uncertain about the Zohar's author. But in 1833 he returned to his first conclusion:

> I now see that this book [*Mishkan Haedut* which he received from Hillel Cantoni] and Moshe De Leon's *Sefer Hasodot*, which has been in my possession for many years, are almost the same book and the same dream;

---

44 Ibid.
45 Ibid.

and this view I beheld, the book's language, and the foolishness and self-aggrandizement it contains, led me to follow the majority who say that he [De Leon] is the Zohar's author, [the theory] which until now I stuttered about. At the same time, for the last twenty years, I have realized that the book of the Zohar is a forgery.[46]

In 1836 Luzzatto published in Padua his book *Prolegomeni ad una Grammatica Ragionata della Lingua Ebraica* (Prolegomena to a Reasoned Grammar of the Hebrew Language). As the book was about to be published, Luzzatto wrote two letters to Rapoport (December 1835; April 1836) asking if he has evidence to contradict his theory about provenance of the biblical vowels and accents, which would warrant emending his views on this issue.[47] In these letters he delineates the primary elements of his theory (which he already described in the *Vikuaḥ*): that experts in reading the Torah, *qaraim* ("readers," not "Karaites"), instituted the vowels and accents, following the instructions of the Savoraim in Babylonia. The Savoraim, who committed the Oral Torah to writing, requested that these *qaraim* conceive a plan to anchor the accepted reading and chanting of the Bible, so that it would never be forgotten. The absolute authority of the Sages of Babylonia guaranteed that the vowels and accents (which were the innovation of these *qaraim*) were accepted without challenge even in the Land of Israel—where in time the Masoretic text would also be established. In a second letter, Luzzatto tries to refute some of Rapoport's proofs for the vowels and accents being created in the Land of Israel, its sages experts in Bible and Aggada. In another letter from July of that year, Luzzatto summarizes Rapoport's arguments and his own counterarguments and informs Rapoport that only now, having seen that there are no definitive proofs against his view, does he feel comfortable publicizing it. He explains that philological and historical research, unlike geometry, has no definite proofs; every researcher must rely on what his eyes see; disputes increase knowledge. He adds that he does not oppose Rapoport writing and publicizing a critique of his theory in the future.[48]

From time to time Luzzatto would add passages to the *Vikuaḥ* while it remained in his archives. In a letter to Goldberg (1838), the editor of *Kerem Ḥemed*, he mentions that he wrote a work about Kabbalah thirteen years ago,

---

46 Ibid., 257.
47 Ibid., 319, 331.
48 Ibid., 343–347.

and continues to add to it, and if Goldberg is interested he will send him a copy. He adds that the short essay, which he wrote in 1832 and published in *Kerem Ḥemed* in 1836, is from that work. It contained some of Luzzatto's arguments about the Zohar: How it was forged to appear like an ancient work (based on various researchers) and how it caused great damage to Judaism. According to his testimony, it is possible that passages from his works on Onkelos (whom Luzzatto studied at the end of the twenties) and Spinoza (whom he studied in the thirties and forties) were incorporated into the *Vikuaḥ* after it was shelved.[49]

In 1838 Luzzatto published in *Kerem Ḥemed* a letter he had written to Reggio in 1837. It contained a direct attack on important principles of Maimonides's philosophy, initiating the fierce exchange of polemics with the rationalist *maskilim* of Galicia—Krochmal, Rapoport, the three editors of *Haroe* and Maharats Chajes. With its publication Luzzatto made public for the first time his criticism of Maimonides and the philosophers, which had been contained in his shelved *Vikuaḥ*. In 1839 Luzzatto wrote a letter to the historian Isaac Mordechai Jost in Frankfurt, requesting him to thank Michael Creizenach on his behalf for his principled support of Luzzatto's criticism of Maimonides. Responding to Creizenach's claim that Luzzatto should apply his criticism to the kabbalists as well, especially in terms of the philosophical conception of the soul, Luzzatto asks Jost to inform him that he is breaking into an open door and that in his opinion the "sin of the kabbalists in merely the sin of Ibn Ezra and Maimonides."[50] He quotes a passage from the *Vikuaḥ*—which he

---

49 Ibid., 415. For the aforementioned essay see *Kerem H. emed*, vol. 2 (1836), from 154. From Luzzatto's testimony it emerges that Steinschneider and after him Eckstein and Pelli, were mistaken when they attributed this essay-letter, as well as another letter in *Kerem H. emed*, both signed with the penname *Feli*, to Lelio (Hillel) De la Torre, co-head with Luzzatto of the Rabbinical Seminary of Padua. The "anonymous scholar," "master of disputation," who is quoted in that essay is obviously Luzzatto himself. The second essay which was written in Elul 5591 (1831) was also printed there on p. 85. Like the first essay, it also contains criticism of the rulings of recent halakhists, who write using garbled language, over-analyzing and adding new laws and stringencies and foreign practices to show-off their wit. These laws, the author writes, are unprecedented, have no basis, and bring no benefit whatsoever to the nation. Moreover, they are harmful and cause the corruption of morals. See Pelli, *Kerem H. emed*, 47, 52–53, 305–306. These two short essays fit well with Luzzatto's views and his world of research, but not with the views of a Talmudist and halakhist like De La Torre. It seems that Luzzatto refrained from disparaging students of the Zohar, and even feared them, and therefore published using the penname "Feli" or using Gematria. See also in J. Bassie's introduction to his edition of the *Vikuah*. what Luzzatto wrote in the title page of the manuscript from 1844 (14) and what he printed under the explanatory title from 1852 (9).

50 Luzzatto, *Igrot Shadal*, 621.

says has been shelved in his archives for the last thirteen years—to explain this claim.[51] Responding to Creizenach's statement that it is difficult to prove that the Maimonidean doctrine of the soul poses a danger to religion and morality, Luzzatto writes that even the idea that the soul is part of God, reuniting with him after death, could not have been entertained by any Jewish sages before Maimonides and Ibn Ezra. He concedes that the Sages were privy to secrets, but explains that these were very different from the secrets of the kabbalists. Luzzatto explains that the view of the philosophers—that one who has not completed his soul in this world, and has not actualized its potential by attaining intelligible forms, as Maimonides had done, has no afterlife—implies that "he has no soul, and he is like an animal, and we are not commanded to love him or have compassion on him; and if he is an Israelite (such as Creizenach) then it is a commandment to hate him and destroy him. Can Creizensach still say that the Maimonides's view on the essence of the soul is not *gefahrlich* [dangerous]!?"[52]

In 1840 Luzzatto wrote a detailed letter to the scholar and doctor Gideon Brecher of Prosnitz, who had sent him his commentary on the *Kuzari*. Luzzatto made some critical remarks, among other things criticizing Brecher's understanding of the word *sefirot* in the *Kuzari*. Brecher claims in his book that Judah Halevi believed in the *sefirot*, that is, kabbalistic emanations. Luzzatto accuses Brecher of strengthening the kabbalists, who say that their doctrine is ancient, already maintained by the author of *Sefer Yetsira*, the Tanna Rabbi Akiva, and Judah Halevi. Luzzatto dismisses this position entirely. These Sages did not believe in emanation. The *sefirot* of *Sefer Yetsira* are nothing but numbers, as explained by Judah Halevi himself. Luzzatto cites here a long excerpt from his work the *Vikuaḥ*, explaining in detail *Sefer Yetsira*'s account of God's use of letters and numbers to create the world. Later in the letter, Luzzatto explains to Brecher his theory about Kabbalah's beginnings: that the sages of Israel after Ibn Ezra saw how the philosophy he had disseminated was destroying the religion of Israel, and that the doctrines of Saadya Gaon and Judah Halevi were unable to fill the breach. They had no recourse but to:

> adopt some of the opinions of the philosophers, and to somehow invert them, removing the evil and harmful part, and making them sacred to God; and they had to conceal the provenance of these innovative views,

---

51 The quoted passage is the second part of the quotation appearing above next to note 17.
52 Luzzatto, *Igrot Shadal*, 622.

and had to say that they are a tradition they possessed, and that they are secrets of the Torah that our Rabbis of blessed memory would transmit to their disciples in secrecy, or that some of them were revealed to them by Elijah. And behold the *sefirot* of these kabbalists (not the *sefirot* of *Sefer Yetsira*) are the ten causes or intellects of the philosophers. [...] And because Averroes and Avicennna were divided over the matter of the first mover, [...] so, too, the kabbalists were divided over whether or not *Keter* was the *Ein Sof* itself.[53]

Luzzatto proceeds to delineate his ideas about Kabbalah and philosophy, similar to those appearing in the *Vikuaḥ*. At the bottom of this letter Luzzatto adds a surprising note:

The fathers of the kabbalists are distinct from their grandchildren. The ancients were holy men, and all their actions were for the sake of heaven, and only for the last three hundred years did some of them begin to pursue honor, like that one [R. Joseph Karo] whose Mishnah (or soul) would tell him: You are a man and who is like you in Israel etc. etc. and I will purify you so that you complete all your works with no error, and print them and disseminate them throughout the boundaries of my nation Israel, and many things like this.

This paragraph is a real step down from Luzzatto's heretofore harsh criticism of the theosophical Kabbalah of the Spanish kabbalists.

Two years later, in 1842, Luzzatto wrote another letter to Becher, having realized that Becher, who still maintained that Kabbalah was from the era of the Sages, was spending time elucidating the words of the kabbalists, and even expected Luzzatto to retract his own views. In his letter, Luzzatto writes that he now realizes that he had hoped in vain that Brecher would publish the *Vikuaḥ* on his behalf, and he declares that he is determined to one day publicize his work

against all who attributes the views of Kabbalah to our forefathers, the Sages of the Mishnah and the Talmud, and Judah Halevi, peace be upon him, and against all those who say that the *sefirot* mentioned in *Sefer Yetsira* are anything besides numbers. And confident of your wisdom and

---

53 Ibid., 693–694.

the uprightness of your heart, I am certain you will not request me to show favoritism in matters of Torah, nor expect me, out of my love and respect for you, my precious and esteemed friend, to betray the truth of our forefathers and rabbis, to whom the kabbalists (and all those who antedate the time of Kabbalah's beginnings) attributed views which they had never entertained in their hearts.[54]

A close reading of the letters discussed here, demonstrates that as Luzzatto's criticism of philosophy grew in its intensity, so his negative attitude to the kabbalists of the thirteenth and sixteenth century waned and became more moderate.[55] In 1826 he had argued in the *Vikuah* that the damage inflicted by the Zohar and the kabbalists is greater than that of the philosophers, even if he understands their worthy motive—to combat philosophy. In his letter to Rapoport in 1832, Luzzatto continued to attribute worthy intention to the kabbalists (to strengthen religion and faith and to combat philosophy) but now omitted any mention of the damage it inflicted on the nation. In his letter to Brecher in 1840, he presented Kabbalah as a wise plan devised by holy men, for the sake of heaven—judaizing philosophical ideas and sanctifying them to God. The damage Kabbalah caused in his own day, Luzzatto now attributed to the kabbalists of Safed led by the pretender R. Joseph Karo. As mentioned, in 1851 Luzzatto tended to think that De Leon was guiltless, and that he had been misled by Abulafia's forgery.

---

54 Ibid., 793. At the end of his letter to J. L. Dukes of Tübingen (Heshvan 5605 [1844]) he writes: "May these new ones, coming nowadays, be shamed and disgraced, those who say that Kabbalah and pantheism are the inheritance of the assembly of Jacob for all time" (ibid., 922). In Tevet of that same year he wrote to Rapoport that the year 5314 should be marked as an important year because on Rosh Hashana of that year (i.e., the end of 1553) the Talmud began to be burned in Rome. "This decree was the cause of another, more difficult misfortune, which we have yet to be purified from" (ibid., 935).

55 On the development of Luzzatto's attitude to foreign rationalist philosophy, inherited from the Greeks and Muslims, see Chamiel, *The Middle Way*, vol. 1, 466–470. For a discussion of his criticism of the philosophies of Maimonides and Spinoza see ibid., 216–220, 470–474. In all his writings, Luzzatto prefers the rabbinic-halakhic trend over the mystical-kabbalistic trend and the rationalist-philosophical trend. Tishby and Schweid present these three trends in detail. See Tishby, *Mishnat Hazohar*, vol. 1, 102–107; Schweid, *Hehagut Hayehudit ba'et Haḥadasha*, 65–75. For important emendations to this categorization and its development by Idel and Liebes see note 10 above.

SUMMARY

Due to his keen intelligence and his diligent and intensive study, the autodidact Luzzatto acquired exceptional expertise and insight into the Spanish and Safedian theosophical Kabbalah, as in other areas of Jewish studies. Already at the age of thirteen, he concluded that the accents and vowels, which are frequently mentioned in the Zohar, postdate the Talmud. Consequently, he concluded that the Zohar, which is never mentioned before the thirteenth century, is a later work. Since the Zohar and theosophical Kabbalah did not, in his opinion, constitute an ancient tradition, and since the kabbalists could not even agree on the tenets of their own system, Luzzatto considers it obvious that the Kabbalah is not divine. It is a harmful human invention, even if its original purpose was worthy and important—combating philosophy which distances man from his creator. In his opinion the damage of Kabbalah lies in its erroneous tenets, which are essentially philosophical ideas, having undergone Judaization, which distance its adherents from true Judaism. The claim that God is a multi-layered system of emanations, the theurgic principle that human actions influence the relationships between the *sefirot*, the belief that the soul is part of God returning to its source upon death, and the pantheistic claim that the entire world, including humans and inanimate objects, is part of God—all of these Luzzatto regarded as idolatry, opposed to the transcendental monotheism of ancient rabbinic Judaism. The academic study of Kabbalah subsequently would accept some of his and his contemporaries' theories regarding Kabbalah and philosophy. His arguments that the intricate structure of kabbalistic theosophy was only created in the twelfth and thirteenth centuries, and that the struggle against philosophy was one of central factors motivating this creation, are still accepted today. However, Moshe Idel and Yehuda Liebes have already shown that Luzzatto's arguments against the antiquity of mysticism and mythology in Judaism do not stand up to criticism, and that the mystical-kabbalistic system has strong foundations in all ancient Jewish texts—from the time of the Bible, afterward in the Heikhalot literature, in the Talmud and *midrashim*, and finally in kabbalistic literature itself.[56]

In the next chapter I will present another member of the middle way— R. Tsvi Hirsch Chajes, a community rabbi in Galicia, a Maimonidean, and a talmudist. I will analyze his thought, and show he was influenced by thinkers such as Mendelssohn and Krochmal.

---

56 See note 10 above.

CHAPTER EIGHT

Between Reason and Revelation: The Encounter between Rabbi Tsvi Hirsch Chajes and Nahman Krochmal

INTRODUCTION

Rabbi Tsvi Hirsch Chajes (*Maharats*) was born and raised in Brody, Galicia and was appointed rabbi of Żółkiew district in 1829. He brought to the position his vast knowledge of the Talmud and its commentaries as well as his expertise in the writings of his cultural hero, Maimonides. It was in Żółkiew that fate would introduce him to Nahman Krochmal, also hailing from Brody, who at the time of Chajes's appointment served as the Jewish community leader of Żółkiew. At that time, Krochmal was at the height of his power, acting as the leader of the *maskilim* in Galicia. Although their philosophies of Judaism were extremely different, the two soon cultivated a strong friendship, which would endure even after Krochmal returned to his hometown of Brody.

Chajes was a rationalist, Talmudist, and classical fundamentalist, believing that both the written and Oral Torah were from Sinai, reading Maimonides's *Guide for the Perplexed* as moderately and conservatively as possible. He dedicated his life to battling reformers and to using critical tools to prove the authenticity of the oral chain of tradition stretching back to Sinai. Krochmal, by contrast, was a philosopher of history and a rationalist *maskil*, a forerunner of the historical positivism that would come to characterize the scholarship of Frankel and Graetz. He believed that the books of Scripture were not written by their purported authors; that the halakhic codex of the Mishnah and Talmud had undergone evolution, for the most part the product of rabbinic creation; and that certain *aggadot* were not authentic creations of the Sages, and should never have been included in the Talmud at all. He read Maimonides, whom he considered a man of exemplary cultural virtues, radically—far more radically than Chajes.

In this chapter I will focus on examining the reciprocal relationship between these two figures, showing that Chajes and Krochmal were influenced by each other in a number of areas: (1) Krochmal and Chajes both saw themselves as individuals belonging to a "middle" path—situated between radical *maskilim* and reformers to the left, and Hasidim and devout to their right. (2) Chajes absorbed Krochmal's portrayal of human history *vis-à-vis* the history of the Jewish people and made use of it in his own thought; (3) Krochmal remained loyal to the belief in a written Torah from Sinai, in accordance with Chajes's conservative rejection of Bible criticism. (4) Influenced by the views of Krochmal, and in contrast to his usual methods, Chajes expressed untraditional, non-fundamentalist views regarding the provenance of the laws in the halakhic codex, classifying them according to types and strata. He presented this model as the view of Maimonides, even though the views of Maimonides and Krochmal (who both had different goals than Chajes) were far more daring than those of Chajes himself; (5) Chajes and Krochmal both participated in various discussions about the exalted status of the Sages and about the importance of *Midrash Aggada*—even though they disagreed about its origins; (6) Chajes may have been influenced by Krochmal's interpretation of the nature of the revelation at Mount Sinai.

The *maskil* Jacob Bodek (1825–1874) writes about their relationship as follows:

> From the day of his [Chajes's] arrival [in Żółkiew] they became dear and loving brothers. Rabbi Nahman made him his rabbi [in Halakhah] and Rabbi Hirsch Chajes acquired a friend. And almost every night they would sit and discuss various matters of wisdom until midnight and even later. They would exchange their views, the one bringing Torah studies, the other philosophy and logic, and together they clarified and refined them, and in their hands they became one.[1]

---

1   J. Bodek, "*Qorot Nosafot*" *LeQorot Ha'itim Shel A. Tribitsh* (Lvov, 1851) quoted in S. Rawidowicz, "Mavo Lekitvei Naḥman Krochmal," Rawidowicz edition (Berlin, 1924),

In his biography of Chajes, Bodek describes him as the first to seek a new way of understanding the Oral Torah, successfully linking the Torah and the tradition received at Sinai with the logic, interpretations, and research accepted in the study of philosophy—paving a new path in rabbinical studies (*rabbinische Literatur*).[2]

1. WALKING THE MIDDLE WAY—BETWEEN LEFT AND RIGHT

Krochmal seems to have been the first to perceive the new religious balance materializing among Jews in modern Europe, describing it in terms of "right," "left," and "middle"—terms he borrowed from the new discourse created by European revolutionaries to the left and reactionaries to the right in the wake of the French revolution. At the top of the first page of Gate 2 in his book *Hashevilin*, he cites a passage from the Jerusalem Talmud which compares the Torah to two paths—one of fire and one of snow. Those who traverse either will likely die—be it by burning or by freezing and to survive, one must be cautious, taking a middle way between these two extremes. According to Krochmal, the first is the path of faith alone—the stance of the rabbis. The second is the path of reason alone, the path of lovers of inquiry. Both paths lead to death. The path which makes life possible, is not a compromise between these two extremes but another path altogether. Exalted and dialectical, this alternative path resolves the contradictions between reason and revelation with a synthesis, embracing "both extremes together." Thus

---

85. It was reprinted under the title "Keter Torah," when Chajes left Żółkiew to assume his position as rabbi of Kalisch, *Kokhvei Yitzḥaq*, ed. M. Stern, pamphlets 17–20, 1852–1855. See specifically pamphlet 19, 51. Rawidowicz mentions there a work entitled *Even Harosha* authored by Nahman Krochmal's son Avraham Krochmal, which was published in *Hashaḥar*, year 2 and ibid., 57, printed as a semi-fictional dialogue between Chajes and Krochmal, discussing Spinoza. Cf. I. Beit Halevi, *Rabbi Tsvi Hirsh Ḥayut Parashat Ḥayav Ufo'alo* (Tel Aviv, 1957) 52–55; Hershkowiz, *Maharats Ḥayut*, 235–262.

M. Rotenberg, *Rabbi Zvi Hirsh Ḥayut, his Personality and Books*, Doctoral Dissertation, Yeshiva University, 1963, dedicated 111–118 to presenting similar discussion between Chajes and Krochmal in order to demonstrate mutual influence. He proposed, *inter alia*, discussions about the Essenes; the Jews of Alexandria; the difference between *taqana* and *hatqana* in the language of the Sages; law of a secular state versus religious law according to Nahmanides on (Ex. 15:24) "There He made for them a statute and an ordinance" showing the similarities and differences in each discussion. Likewise, he demonstrates how they both based themselves on Maimonides. That being said, he does not mention any of the connections I propose in this chapter.

2   Bodek, *"Qorot Nosafot."*

united, these two poles prove to be identical.³ Krochmal calls the two sides "right" and "left." In a chapter about Aggada, he criticizes the erroneous interpretations of the Aggada by both sides and explains the correct reading in his opinion—essentially, the position of Maimonides:

> Today what will those who love reason and keep the Torah do, being pressed into a narrow path, with no way of turning right or left?! On one side: all those benighted intellectuals, lowly in their degree and virtue, who are abundant today among the small scholars of Torah. They take *derash* [homiletic interpretation] for the *peshat* [literal meaning] of the text [. . .] and even about those strange legends we alluded to recently, they say that these are the secret of God for those who fear Him, sometimes offering an interpretation of it that altogether is akin to idol worship of the worst kind [. . .] and on the other side stand most of the students of many and various sciences in our community, [. . .] and all of them smile and mock the strange legends, leading them to mock the Gemara, and leading them to degrade the honor of the Sages and to hate those who honor them.⁴

In a letter to Luzzatto, dated 1837, Krochmal writes about the changes in attitude among the Jews in various parts of Europe, explaining that it is impossible to satisfy—at the same time—the Jews of Italy, the exiles of Spain, the radical *maskilim* of Germany, and the Hasidim in Poland and Galicia. Krochmal and Luzzatto agree that only the moderate *maskil*, situated in the middle and aware of both sides, can find the correct path—as long as he does not compromise with either side: "Ultimately, those of us who dwell in the center and see what is done and said on the right and on the left, it is proper for us to say that now is the time for action in the name of the Lord; they have violated your Torah on every side."⁵

---

3   See Krochmal, *Moreh Nevukhei Hazman*, ed. S. Rawidowicz (Berlin, 1924), Amir edition (Jerusalem, 2011), 10–17.
4   Ibid., 247–248. See on this Rawidowicz, "Mavo Lekitvei Nahman Krochmal," 155–159.
5   Krochmal, *Moreh Nevukhei Hazman*, 425. See S. Feiner, *Haskalah Vehistoria* (Jerusalem, 1995), 160–161. Rapoport, another one of Krochmal's students, writes in the same spirit—as a warrior standing in the middle, and being attacked from both sides. See his letter to Luzzatto from 1833 in Igrot Shir, 38.

Chajes, Krochmal's friend, also saw himself as standing in the middle. In an article entitled "Tiferet Lemoshe" [The Glory of Moses], printed in 1841, along with another five articles in a volume called *Ateret Tsvi*, Chajes defended Maimonides from the criticism leveled against him by Luzzatto. In the introduction to this article, Chajes cites the same passage from the Jerusalem Talmud as Krochmal, and in the article itself he attacks "those ignoramuses who oppose any rational inquiry"—apparently referring to the Hasidim, who embittered his life. Perhaps he is also referring to Luzzatto (whom he considered devout). Situated in the middle, he also disagrees with those on the opposite side: those who only accept the authority of reason, and do not acknowledge revelation and the chain of reception—referring to the radical *maskilim* and the Reform movement.

Chajes prefers the "middle sect," those who believe in the Torah but look to reason to elucidate the purpose and essence of the commandments. He also uses Krochmal's metaphor of the narrow path and also compares the trends of his day to the trends mentioned by Maimonides in his introduction to *Pereq Ḥeleq* (chapter 11 of Tractate Sanhedrin): "Two sects that oppose one another radically": those who believe in *aggadot* literally, and those who condemn *aggadot* and mock them. Maimonides states that both sides are foolish, and that the correct path is that of those who understand the hidden layer of meaning embedded in the words of the Sages. According to Chajes, the meaning of the passage in the Jerusalem Talmud is "that a person should try to walk only in the middle, because the path of the intellect alone is very dangerous when unassisted by the Torah, as is the second path. Therefore, a person should guide his course, grasping the one but not letting go of the other, and he should see that both of them assist one another."[6]

Hence Chajes, like Krochmal, maintains that he who takes only the path of reason or only the path of *naïve* faith endangers his soul. One must wisely take from both paths, allowing them to assist one another. Unlike Krochmal, Chajes does not use a bold dialectical formulation. He sees no need to find a level above Torah and wisdom, because in any case they are identical. Later in this article Chajes says that those who attack Maimonides are also extremists hailing from these two unacceptable extremes. From the left, Maimonides has been attacked by the "men of Ashkenaz [Germany] who pursue innovations in religion." They oppose Maimonides because he embraced all of the Halakhah

---

6   Chajes, *Ateret Tsvi*, 397.

in the Talmud and built a fortified wall around the Oral Torah, maintaining that even communal regulations and customs are words of Torah. These men point to the ostensible contradiction in Maimonides's words: accepting Aristotle's authority, even on matters that opposed the tradition, while at the same time plugging every breach of Halakhah, refusing to depart even a hairsbreadth from the Talmud. Maimonides has also been criticized from the right by the devout and by mystics such as "the claimants of Italy." Chajes says in summary: "between one thing and another, both of these sects oppose us like two herds of goats [ref. to 1 Kings 20:27], and the space is very narrow before those who stand in the middle."[7]

Both Chajes and Krochmal describe the troubles of their times as symptoms of heresy and superstition. Both declare that they are basing themselves on Maimonides and following in his footsteps. Like Maimonides, they wish to heal the generation of the confusions afflicting it, from both skeptics and the devout, whom they call "the perplexed ones of our time."[8]

---

7   Ibid., 397–398. By "the claimants of Italy" Chajes is referring to Luzzatto, whom he did not know and thought to be devout and a mystic, which is how Krochmal relates to him, calling him "the devout believer" in the controversy over "two Isaiahs." It is important to note that Krochmal also spoke out against Luzzatto's attacks of Maimonides. It is interesting to compare Chajes' polemics with those of Krochmal in his letter to Judah Leib Goldenberg from Ḥeshvan 5599 [1838] which was published in *Kerem Ḥemed*, vol. 4 (1838). Some of Krochmal's arguments are similar to those of Chajes such as: Luzzatto's arguments against Maimonides are flimsy and old; Maimonides already responded regarding the resurrection of the dead; it is impossible to approach God without a high level of morality; Maimonides was tolerant of gentiles. However, Krochmal's response is completely different in terms of its internal content. It is a rationalist response, far from fundamentalism or accepted Orthodoxy, which does not believe in the resurrection of the dead, rejects the belief in the Oral Torah being given at Sinai, and which believes that rational study is the highest purpose of an observant person.

   Chajes wrote about this controversy between right and left in other contexts as well. In his critique of David Friedländer, who proposed collective conversion, Chajes stated that it was impossible to reject the Torah entirely, for "it had struck roots on the tablet of our heart forever, and it has flourished among the Jews, great and small, among the right and among the left." Chajes, *Minhat Kenaot*, 981, in the note. On the Reform custom of changing the place of the Bima [the platform for reading the Torah] and putting it next to the Holy Ark, Chajes wrote: "And in our day the leaders of the congregation of the holy community of Papa in Hungary have already published the answer of some rabbis of the old rightists and of the new leftists, and all of them have written that this is not according to the law." Ibid., 992 in the note.

8   See Krochmal, *Moreh Nevukhei Hazman*, 7–9, 209 and Chajes, *Hatsaah Lesefer Darkei HaHora'ah*, 209–210.

The *maskil* Jacob Bodek (1825–1874), who was Chajes's close friend in the last thirteen years of his life, wrote a biography of him in which he states: "These are his words, more pleasant than gold, which testify to the direct path he chose in his Torah, and this was the middle way, as we were instructed by Maimonides of blessed memory, and the spirit of the God and the spirit of the community were pleased with him."[9]

2. THE HISTORY OF MANKIND AND THE JEWISH PEOPLE

The nineteenth-century advocates of the middle way, believing in full divine providence, personal and general, maintained that history should be studied and taught based on the principle of divine intervention in history. The divine plan must be sought by the student of history, who should study historical events with the aim of understanding the divine plan. In their opinion, the miraculous existence of the Jewish people during history is the result of special divine providence—testimony of the centrality of the Jews in God's plan. This is in contrast to later historiographical conceptions. Yosef Hayim Yerushalmi writes that Spinoza—a man before his time in his removal of God from the study of history—argued that it was hatred towards the segregated Jews (a result of their particularistic customs, especially circumcision), and not divine providence, which kept them in existence over history. Yerushalmi has shown that this view was not accepted by historians until the late nineteenth century, when the belief in divine providence had already waned.[10]

It should be recalled that Chajes was a close friend of the philosopher of history, Krochmal, and he certainly was familiar with the latter's approach to the uniqueness of Jewish history: a series of rises, falls, and renaissances, in recurring cycles. The Jewish people bears with it the absolute spirit, received from revelation, and it will bring humanity to its peak. This is the cause of the Jewish people's recurring resurgences. Other nations experience only a rise and a final fall. This approach is based on (but not in agreement with) Hegel's theory that Christianity will ultimately bring salvation to mankind, in a dialectical process that will do away with all the other religions and ideas and sublate them ("raising them above," Aufhebung). Acquaintance with Krochmal's theory doubtless

---

9 Bodek, *Qorot Nosafot*.
10 See Baruch Spinoza, *Theological-Political Treatise*, ed. M. Silverthorne and J. Israel, trans. (Cambridge, 2007), 54; Y. Yerushalmi, *Zakhor* (Washington, 1982).

reinforced Chajes's esteem for the study of history, as shown in the following passage:

> Behold no sensible person will deny that knowledge of the history of our nation, in general and in detail, is absolutely necessary for any educated man for whom the Torah of his God is his portion, so that he should know what God did for this nation, and how the people of our nation have always risen and declined, led by His special providence, blessed be He. And [so that he should know] that while in every generation they rise up against us to destroy us, the Holy One, blessed be He, raises up a faithful redeemer, who risks his life to save this great multitude; great is the shepherd who saves them. See the book *Mor Uqtsi'a* by the great Rabbi Jacob Emden, *Hilkhot Shabbat* 307, regarding studying books of wisdom on the Sabbath, he wrote: "And therefore I say that it is a commandment for every Jewish person to be familiar with the pleasant book *Shevet Yehuda*, and with other books about the history of the Jews, to remember God's mercy for us in every generation, for we have not ceased to exist, despite the many decrees [against us]. Incidentally, he will also learn sweet and precious things from it and a wise heart will acquire knowledge in the ways of polemics," see there. [...] Though it seems that [Maimonides] went too far in his discussion of those who deal with the chronicles of the kings of Arabia, which were primarily about romance and non-existent things, like the Arabic stories that have been translated for us today. But as for the chronicles of the history of the nations and the history of the states and the ruling dynasties, this is indispensable for the knowledge of the wisdom of divine providence and guidance.[11]

In *Shut Maharats*, in response to question no. 12, on the study of books of secular knowledge on the Sabbath, Chajes also quotes Emden and adds that on the Sabbath it is permissible to study books of Jewish history that do not contain sorrowful matters. Other books may be studied only on weekdays. Books of general history, however, even if they were written in Hebrew by a Jewish author, are not vital, and may only be read during ones free time on weekdays and on days when yeshivot are not in session. Otherwise, they will take

---

11   Chajes, *Ateret Tsvi*, 406 and the note there.

scholars away from their studies. Chajes explains that the benefit of such study is marginal and only helps one to:

> Learn pure and clean language from them, and also so that a Torah scholar will not be denuded of this knowledge of the history of bygone days and changing times, and so that he will know how to respond to his reviler, and will not be thought of as foolish and ignorant in matters of the world, lest they say, only an ignorant nation poor in knowledge is this one. However, sometimes one must peruse these stories that belong to the nations, to learn about them, or to derive from them good advice and wisdom in matters of the world which are also necessary—especially in matters of intercession with the king and ministers.[12]

Of scholars from the previous generation, Chajes chose to quote Emden rather than Wessely; in the traditional Galicia of his day, quotations from *maskilim* were not welcome. Chajes found it difficult to present history, even Jewish history, as having inherent value, as a subject to be studied in a school or *ḥeder*, and contented himself with views from the eve of the educational revolution. In the introduction to his commentary on the Talmud, he claims that the Sages always sought to study contemporary natural sciences and humanities, using them to assist Torah study. He refers to a number of scientific subjects and states that "above all, [the Sages] dealt with matters of the history of the world, especially the history of our nation from the time of the building of the Second Temple until the sealing of the Talmud. [...] And they plumbed the depths of human knowledge and by that means attained many matters touching upon laws and *halakhot*."

In other words, just as the Sages dealt with Bible criticism, they also dealt with the study of history, and there was nothing innovative in this. Chajes also criticized the devout rabbis in Galicia, who refused to acknowledge the importance of studying Jewish history and ignored everything happening to the Jewish people in Germany in their day:

> And as for the rabbis of our country, who do not endeavor to provide themselves with knowledge of the history of our people, I will not preach a sermon [to them] here. From the start I know that they would be

---

12 Chajes, "Sefer Sheelot Uteshuvot Moharats, pt. 1" (1850) in *Kol Sifrei Maharats Ḥayut* (Jerusalem, 1958), 648–649. A detailed description of God's method of leading his nation in history can be found in Chajes, "Sefer Mevo Hatalmud" (1845) in *Kol Sifrei Maharats Ḥayut* (Jerusalem, 1958), 281–350, 328–329 and Chajes, "Sheelot Uteshuvot Moharats," 607.

astounded at the object that I bring in my hand. They would say: Look, this man has brought us matters of much talk and weariness of flesh—a waste of time in their opinion. What is known to everyone is like a sealed book to them, which they cannot read. Therefore, they would raise their voice against me.[13]

Another allusion to Krochmal's approach can be found in the following passage:

You have no more mighty proof of individual providence than the existence of the Jewish nation, which stood fast against the raging times threatening to wipe it from the face of the earth. Several ancient nations, Babylonia, Assyria, Persia, Media, Greece, and Rome, who once ruled with force and pride and high heart, have had their names erased, and their memory forgotten from the world. But as for us—who were always the smallest of nations, persecuted without respite, thrown from the land of our fathers and exiled again and again, ceasing to be an individual nation—behold: nevertheless, the staff of the persecutor only wounded and destroyed the nation's body and exterior. But the spiritual life is the achievement of the intellect and true opinions, and they are still with us, thank the Lord, in purity and glory and splendor. We have borne them with us in all the places of our dispersion. [...] And during the time when the Greeks multiplied and succeeded we had already gone into exile, and when the Romans exiled us completely, they left no remnant in the land of our dwelling. We were mocked and reviled. We were a despised and persecuted nation among our neighbors, and nevertheless, they died out and faded from the face of the earth, and we, an ancient nation, an old and antique people, the smallest of nations, we remained in spiritual life, the father of all the people of the Earth in the study and knowledge of God's existence and other pure beliefs. Who does not know that only the hand of God did this, and that His providence protected us at every time and moment? [...] By virtue of the Torah we are excellent among the nations and just as the intelligibles are eternal, so, too we will always stand against time, and all the natural causes of the destruction of the nation do not act at all upon us.[14]

---

13 Z. Chajes, "Maamar Minhat Qenaot" in *Shut Moharats*, pt. 3 (1849). Published in *Kol Sifrei Maharats Hayut* (Jerusalem, 1958), 816.
14 Chajes, *Ateret Tsvi*, 464–465.

The following passage contains similar ideas:

> For 1800 years we have ceased being an independent nation, and a spoken language. Nevertheless, we have remained splendid and superior in the countries of our dispersion. The staff of the tyrant only wounded us in external matters of the nation's life, but its spiritual and moral life never submitted to the rule of despots. And just as intelligibles are not subject to natural causes, so, too, the people that bears these truths will stand forever.[15]

His proximity to the *maskilim* of Brody and his close relationship with Krochmal influenced Chajes's attitude toward general studies, especially to history. He was knowledgeable about history and quite familiar with the works of Isaac Jost. In the introduction to his book *Imrei Bina*, he sings the praises of Jewish historians, including the Tanna Rabbi Yose, who wrote *Seder 'Olam*, Rav Sherira Gaon, Joseph Ben Samuel Bonfils, Maimonides, Zacuto (*Sefer Yuḥasin*), Azariah Dei Rossi, and others.[16]

Chajes himself wrote historical studies to strengthen his arguments. For example, he examined the history of the Aramaic translations of the Bible[17] as well as the history of the various versions of the prayers in his "Minḥat Qenaot".[18]

According to Haim Gertner, Chajes planned to publish a new revised version of *Seder Hadorot* by Jehiel Heilprin (first published in 1769), and there is evidence of this in the introduction to *Imrei Bina*. However, Chajes died before he was able to actualize such a project.

Chajes was one of the first supporters of an initiative to publish an Orthodox yearbook to be called *Pleitat Sofrim*, as seem from his letter to Joshua Heschel Levin. Here Gertner identifies a wider phenomenon: rabbis of Eastern Europe responding to the biographies written by the scholars of the Wissenschaft des Judentums. Because of the decline of their power and the power of the rabbinate, these rabbis sought to oppose the pantheon of personalities presented by modern Jewish scholarship, offering an alternative, Orthodox pantheon of

---

15 Chajes, "Sheelot Uteshuvot Moharats," 607.
16 Chajes, "Maamar Imrei Binah," in *Kol Sifrei Maharats Ḥayut* (Jerusalem, 1958), 872. See below notes 62–63.
17 See ibid., section 4, 901–928.
18 See Chajes, "Minḥat Qenaot," 978–980.

their own. The goal was that traditionalists no longer needed to feel isolated in history; they were part of an illustrious rabbinic tradition.[19]

3. ATTITUDE TOWARDS THE ORAL TORAH

It appears that more than anything, Krochmal was influenced by Chajes's enthusiastic belief in the divinity of the written Torah and its transmission to the Jewish people at Sinai through Moses. This influence kept Krochmal from being swept away by the critical orientation of the *maskilim*, who questioned even this fundamental principle.

Chajes declares the Torah's absolute divinity, basing himself on Maimonides. He writes in the introduction to his first book *Torat Haneviim* from 1835:

> The great principle instilled in us by our rabbi [Maimonides] is that this Torah will never be changed or emended, wholly or partially, but will endure forever and ever. For even though it is a great and enduring principle maintained by us, that the Torah that is now found in our hands is itself that which the Master of all imparted to Moses at Sinai, in all its details and precisions, and it is impossible to change or add or remove from it even a hairsbreadth either from what is stated explicitly in the written Torah or from the Oral Law. [...] But far be it from us to think, as those sinners in their souls thought, that the Torah relates to a [particular] time and place and can be canceled at some time, as those heretics, wise in their own eyes, claimed. The malignant plague of heresy shines on their forehead, and all day long they think only evil, plotting to turn us away from the straight path trodden by our forefathers for more than three thousand years in eternal glory for us. But we will walk with the name of the Lord our God and the Rock of Israel and his sanctity, and we will set our path and not abandon it. And may He swiftly save us from those hunters of souls, and may a thousand like them perish, and not a single word of our Torah and our tradition be annulled, and this Torah will abide forever in all its parts.[20]

---

19 See on this H. Gertner, "Reshita Shel Ketiva Historit Ortodoqsit Bemizraḥ Eiropa: Ha'arakha Meḥudeshet," *Zion* 67, 3 (2002): 305–307, 323, 329, and in notes 73 and 181. For a discussion of Chajes's attitude to studying history see Chamiel, *The Middle Way*, vol. 2, 332–337.

20 Z. Chajes, "Sefer Torat Haneviim Hamekhune Ele Hamitsvot" (1836), in *Kol Sifrei Maharats Ḥayut* (Jerusalem, 1958), 4–5.

As I will show below, Krochmal's position differs from Chajes's in regards to the Oral Torah. That being said, in terms of the written Torah (the Pentateuch), their views are very similar. In the introduction of his essay "Imrei Bina" (1849), Chajes praises learned Jewish historians—from Rav Shereira Gaon until his own time—for researching the history and literature of the Jewish people, even if their opinions were different than his own. He counts Krochmal among them:

> And on many passages in the Prophets and the Writings, we have found scattered in journals in various places precious matters, and on certain passages of Psalms and the prophecies of Isaiah the great late sage our master Nachman Hakohen wrote in *Kerem Ḥemed* (part 4 and part 5) pleasant things and specifically in his book *Moreh Nevukhim Haḥadash*—while it was still in manuscript—my eye saw essays on the *aggadot* of the Talmud and the methods of the Talmud and the early sects, and on the circumstances of the Nation of Israel: their blossoming, their stand, and their fall, both first and second Temples, wondrous matters.[21]

As mentioned, Krochmal maintained a daily dialogue with Chajes when they lived together in Żółkiew. Chajes was intimately familiar, although doubtless disagreed, with Krochmal's post-dating several chapters in Psalms, with his attribution of Isaiah to two authors, and with his dialectical approach to the evolution of the Oral Torah. Despite his disagreements, he praised Krochmal, and considered him a prominent scholar and a God-fearing man, observant of

---

21 Chajes, "Imrei Binah," 874. See Hershkovitz's explanations of this passage in *Maharats ḥayut*, 240–251. Hershkovitz shows on page 243 in notes 61–68, that in this passage Chajes brings up many topics which he discussed with Krochmal. On some the two were divided—for example, the era of the authors of certain chapters of Psalms; the questions of Deutero-Isaiah and Ecclesiastes; and the status of *aggadot* in the Talmud. In other areas the two agreed, such as regarding Luzzatto's polemic against Maimonides (during which both marshaled similar arguments to refute Luzzatto's criticisms), issues related to early Jewish sects, and the historiosophy of the Jewish people and the gentiles. Hershkovitz there provides detailed references to *Moreh Nevukhei Hazman* and to Chajes's writings on the same topics. In addition, it is clear from this excerpt that Chajes had seen parts of the manuscript of Moreh *Nevukhei Hazman*, which Krochmal had temporarily entitled *Moreh Nevukhim HaHadash*. As is well known, *Moreh Nevukehi Hazman* was published two years after these words were written—in 1851, edited Zunz. On this issue, Hershkovitz references the statements of Krochmal's son regarding his father and his work which were published in Der Orient, literary supplement, 1849, 6–7 and to Y. F. Lachover *Al Gevul Hayashan Vehahadash* (Jerusalem, 1951), 178, n. 7 and 179 n. 8.

all commandments, big and small, and a believer in the divinity of the Torah.[22] Thus, Chajes included in his list men and subjects with which he did not agree, praising them nevertheless because they were sincere in their pursuit of the truth and in their love of wisdom and of the Jewish people. Moreover, due to his great isolation in his town, he wished to participate in the wider modern phenomenon of scientific Jewish scholarship. Therefore, while he certainly could not have agreed with views contrary to the tradition of the Sages, he nevertheless praised Krochmal's higher biblical criticism on Isaiah and Psalms.[23] That being said, with respect to higher criticism on the Pentateuch, the reliability of the text, and the sincerity of its authors, the two share similar opinions. Krochmal wrote that the radical Bible critics were "mad to doubt, for example, the reality of the faithful shepherd, our master Moses, and his giving the Torah, [or to think] that all the books of prophecy and divine inspiration were perhaps written by some deceitful rabbi."[24]

Instead, Krochmal maintains that only the content and spirit of the Torah materialized during Israel's year camped next to Sinai and during their forty-year sojourn in the wilderness. However, Moses only began to commit the

---

22 On the integrity of Krochmal's faith see his letter to Wolf Baer Schif in Krochmal, *Kitvei Ranaq*, 414 and his eulogy by *Rapoport in Kerem Ḥemed*, vol. 6, 41–49.

23 Hershkovitz presents an expansive discussion about Chajes's ambivalent attitude towards Geiger, Luzzatto, Reggio, Jost, and Krochmal. He states that Chajes removed all obstacles when, at the end of his list, he wrote, "this matter is profane for us and practiced only by scholars of the Nations." In my opinion, Hershkovitz did not pay attention to the fact that Chajes actually wrote that comment before composing his list; it refers only to Bible criticism, where we must make do with the examination of the Sages, whereas a large part of the controversy was waged on the chain of reception, rabbinical *midrash*, and Maimonides, and Chajes, nevertheless, identified with and expressed sympathy for the people in his list. Hershkovitz states that Chajes sent his writings to Reggio and sought to engage in correspondence with him in order to draw him into a public controversy and to cope with him and Geiger, in order to draw close to him. He did so while he was being shunned in a small Galician town by his opponents and critics. See Hershkovitz, *Maharats Ḥayut*, 240–255, 298–303. On Chajes's relations with Reform movement and Wissenschaft des Judentums, see M. Benayahu, "Halifat Igrot 'Al Hareforma Bein R. Mordekhai Shmuel Girondi LeR. Tsvi Hirsch Ḥayut," in Z. Falk, ed., *Gevurot Haromah* (Jerusalem, 1987), 271–292. Benayahu does not agree with Hershkovitz' explanation of Chajes's ambivalent relation to Geiger, as he puts it, but in fact he himself offers no explanation and calls the matter "problematic." I agree with part of Hershkovitz's explanation—that Chajes's isolation in facing his attackers from the right led him to identify with proponents of scientific research. I would add the importance that Chajes ascribed to enhancing the reputation of Judaism and to rehabilitating the nation by restoring its literature as factors contributing to his positive attitude toward them.

24 Krochmal, *Moreh Nevukhei Hazman*, 9.

form and externalities of the text to paper in the fortieth year in the wilderness. Afterward, the prophets continued this literary project, which was completed in Assyrian script, with *qeri* (as it is read) *ketiv* (as it is written), and *iturei sofrim* (scribal emendations) only in the time of Ezra and the Scribes.[25]

Chajes disagreed. In his opinion, the Torah was transmitted at Sinai in the same form as we have it today, including its traditional interpretation. Higher or lower criticism of the biblical text is misguided and impossible in our day, and only the Sages could take such interpretive liberties. In the present, one must focus on understanding of the commandments and Halakhah, and applying criticism to the texts of the Mishnah, the *midrashim*, and the Talmud—but not to the *halakhot* themselves.

4. ATTITUDE TOWARDS THE LAWS OF THE ORAL TORAH

As a rationalist Talmudist, it made sense for Chajes to have adopted the Maimonidean conception of the Oral Torah. In the first six chapters of his "Mevo Hatalmud," which he published in 1845, he presents a detailed model of the different components of the Oral Torah, describing "the main divisions included under this term [i.e., Oral Torah] according to the opinion of Maimonides."[26]

The first component in this model are the interpretations of the commandments which were transmitted in a chain of tradition from Sinai, and supported with (sometimes strange and puzzling) *asmakhtaot* (textual supports) by the Sages. The second component is the "law of Moses from Sinai." The third component is the "Laws that the Sages deduced entirely through traditional methods of interpretation [*derashot*]."[27] They did this relying on their own intellect and without a tradition received from Sinai, using

> the principles by which the Torah is interpreted, which were given to Moses by the mouth of God, so that we can know and prove through them the clarification of the commandments, their interpretations, and their details, and these are the thirteen principles that Rabbi Ishmael teaches. [...] By means of these methods of interpretation, once again all of the extrapolations and the branches that the Sages drew from the written

---

25 See ibid., 191, 199–200.
26 Chajes, "Mevo Hatalmud," 284.
27 Ibid., 290. See also Chajes, *Torat Hanevi'im*, 122–123.

Torah, and that which they will draw in the future, all of them stand ready *in potentia* like branches contained in the potential of the root and like fruit contained in the potential of the seed.[28]

Chajes embraces the well-known *midrashim* (which seem to contradict this component of the Oral Torah, and which are not accepted by Maimonides) that say that already at Sinai, God showed Moses the minutiae of the Torah, the *un* of the scribes, and the future innovations of assiduous scholars, giving them an Aristotelian interpretation. The interpretations and laws which the Sages created themselves—and which Maimonides classified as laws of the scribes which are not considered part of the Oral Torah—became for Chajes, based on his understanding of Maimonides, the written Torah itself: "Since the principles of interpretation were conveyed to Moses, everything that was innovated by the Sages in the last generation, by means of these principles, is placed in the Torah itself by the power of these interpretations and principles."[29]

Use of the Aristotelian method enables Chajes to overcome Nachmanides's criticisms and to restore his master, Maimonides, to the warm embrace of the traditional approach of the Geonim: that the entire halakhic codex of the Oral Torah already existed at Sinai. Chajes adds that, in his opinion, the disputes among the Sages—whether the written Torah is greater than or lesser than the Oral Law—are precisely over this point. The one who says that the written Torah is greater learns as Chajes does:

> He means that matters known to us by the accepted principles for interpreting the written Torah, prepared and standing in the Torah itself and indicated therein by repetition of letters and the order of things early and late, they, too, are the written Torah itself. [...] The [term] Oral Torah only applies to those matters (as we clarified above in the second way) which have no distant support in the Torah and are only received orally.

---

28 Chajes, "Mevo Hatalmud," 288–289. See also idem, *Torat Hanevi'im*, 135 and "Divrei Haneviim Divrei Qabbalah," 137. Maimonides's metaphor of the branches—i.e., the distinction between a text where there is a kernel from Sinai and a midrash that derives further conclusions from it, which are not in it (as Halbertal explains in *Haramban*) allows Chajes to combine the two.

29 Chajes, "Mevo Hatalmud," 289. Cf. *Torat Haneviim*, 122: "And certainly Maimonides concedes that these laws are Torah laws," although Maimonides defined them as rabbinical. On the positions of the Geonim, Maimonides, and Nachmanides regarding the division of the Oral Torah see Halbertal, *Haramban*, 21–76; Chamiel, *The Middle Way*, vol. 1, 158–172.

However, he who believes that the Oral Torah is greater, his rationale is that the methods of interpretation, and thirteen hermeneutical principles were not clarified in the [written] Torah and were also only received [orally] at Sinai. Therefore, even something that is deduced through the principles, even though it has support in the Torah, is only called Oral Torah.[30]

The Geonim believed that the entire halakhic codex was delivered at Sinai; part of it was forgotten due to a crisis in the process of transmission. Chajes, however, does not believe that the entirety of the Oral Torah was actually transmitted at Sinai, and does not believe in any such break in transmission. Rather, he maintains that the Torah is a living, organic body, in which things that existed in potentia at Sinai are actualized by the Sages, like branches from a root or fruit from a seed, and are therefore considered part of the written Torah itself.

It appears that Chajes, eager to distance the views of his "protégé" Maimonides from the Reform movement's calls for innovation, pushed him all the way to the other side of the spectrum towards a traditional notion of revelation. He wished for a connection of the first order, a direct link between the word of God and the regulations of the Sages—the view of the Geonim and Nachmanides who maintained that all of the Oral Torah is from Sinai—and was not content with a tenuous link of a second order, the commandment "you may not turn away [*lo tasur*]," which Maimonides erected between the word of God and the regulations of the Sages. In his understanding of Maimonides, Chajes elevates this category (i.e., *halakhot* derived from the thirteen hermeneutical principles, which Maimonides had placed in the third stratum and had not even included in the framework of the Oral Law, and which Nachmanides had placed in the second stratum), to the level of the first stratum: the written Torah.

Chajes, who claims to be merely explaining the words of Maimonides, ends up actually disagreeing with him. According to Maimonides, the Oral Torah is the product of a process of post-Revelation rational halakhic innovation: the Sages used the thirteen hermeneutical principles to determine the Halakhah in new areas that were not contained in either the written or Oral Torah. According to Chajes's explanation of Maimonides however, the Sages use the thirteen principles to uncover elements that while part of the revelation of the written Torah, were not actively transmitted at Sinai. Everything innovative is merely part of a process of revealing and actualizing that part of

---

30 Ibid., 290.

revelation which had previously existed only *in potentia*.³¹ While this process of actualization takes place within history, it is, in essence, supra-historical. A similar approach, which is built on neo-Platonic foundations, can be found in the philosophy of Judah Halevi (who speaks of continued revelation assisted by the Holy Spirit, and is thus somewhat different than Chajes's notion of uncovering the original Revelation by means of reason). Nachmanides and R. Nissim of Gerona also agree that the Sages revealed things that were not determined at Sinai. However, to them the extent of this determination is choosing halakhic truth out of a variety of possible halakhic options explicitly included in Revelation. According to Chajes, no such spectrum of halakhic options was ever conveyed at Sinai, and the Sages bring to light subjects that were hitherto left untreated.³²

Chajes thus gives an entirely new meaning to Maimonides's words. The creative interpretative activity of the Sages, by means of the hermeneutic principles, permeates the text that was given at Sinai, and, with a majority decision, determines the actualization of potential laws (*halakhot* that were not conveyed explicitly), becoming part of the written Torah itself. In my opinion, Chajes may have learned about the Aristotelian process of actualizing potential from Maimonides, or from the writings of the idealistic philosophers, primarily Hegel,³³ but above all from his friend and colleague in leadership of the community of Żółkiew, Krochmal. Though the degree to which Krochmal was a Hegelian is a matter of dispute,³⁴ it seems likely to me that as a philosopher

---

31 Sagi makes a similar distinction between Chajes and Albo, the latter's approach being close, in his opinion, to that of Maimonides—although he does not clarify the Aristotelian process. See Sagi, *Elu Vaelu*, 84. In my opinion, Albo did not necessarily believe, like Maimonides, that most of the *halakhot* were innovations and legislation of the Sages. Therefore, it might be said that Chajes's approach is similar to that of Albo. In any event, Chajes's approach should be included among those who took the logicistic position in Rosenberg's model. See S. Rosenberg, *Lo Bashamayim Hi* (Alon Shevut, 1997), 59–63.

32 It is interesting that elsewhere, in a discussion unrelated to his model, Chajes notes that Maimonides indeed defined these laws as rabbinical, even though they have a basis in the Torah: "Because the Holy One Blessed is He did not transmit the details except through the principles, and the Sages derive these matters. And it is these derivations upon which there are disputes, because one [Sage] will derive from an extra letter and another one will not." See Chajes, *Torat Haneviim*, 122.

33 See Hershkovitz, *Maharats Ḥayut*, 256.

34 The dispute is between Rawidowicz, "Mavo Lekitvei Naḥman Krochmal," 160–201, who denies an influence, and those who maintain such an influence: Zunz, quoted in Rawidowicz, "Mavo Lekitvei Nahman Krochmal," 163; Klausner, *Hasifrut*, 195–208, who maintains that Krochmal, according to his interpretation of Ibn Ezra was a panentheist; and J. Harris, *Nachman Krochmal, Guiding the Perplexed of the Modern Age* (New York and London,

of history, Krochmal was highly influenced by Hegel. I believe that Hegel's method is based on the notion of development and actualization of national ideas and spirit upon the matrix of a nation's history, in a progression toward identification of the finite (the material subject), with the infinite (the absolute spiritual object). Krochmal adopted important philosophical ideas from Hegel, adapting them to the spirit of Judaism.[35]

My conjecture is that these two champions of Maimonides, Krochmal and Chajes, discussed the difficulty of reconciling Maimonides's statements about an innovative rabbinic stratum of interpretation with the Sages' traditional notion of the Oral Torah originating in its entirety from Sinai. Chajes sought to bring Maimonides closer to the Sages, who said, "everything that an assiduous scholar will innovate in the future was said to Moses at Sinai," whereas Krochmal sought to bring the Sages closer to Maimonides.

> The words "what an assiduous scholar will innovate" refer to those things accomplished by observation and logical inference. Behold, he who said [the above statement] realized that complete unity is the nature of the spiritual, and that an intellected intellect [*sekhel muskal*] will include in His beginning all the consequences that are united in Him; from Him they go out and to Him they return. [. . .] However, so long as they are not yet explained, they are still contained in it only *in potentia*. But when some intellect brings them forth through his study they return in relation to him, becoming included in him in actuality. Now there is a source of the aforementioned teaching in relation to the finite recipient as well, but it only exists in potential; while in relation to the blessed Giver within whom there is no distinction between potential and actual, it also exists in actuality.[36]

In other words: that which to God, the lawgiver, exists in actuality, comes to man, and becomes actualized, only when a Sage innovates it with his own intellect. Before that, the law, at least as far as man is concerned, exists only in potential, and requires actualization through intellectual research. For Krochmal this does not mean progressive development from an inferior position to an exalted

---

1991), 70–81, who makes a similar claim. Cf. Guttman, *Hafilosofia shel Hayahadut*, 410, n. 769.
35 As maintained by Klausner and Harris, see previous note.
36 Krochmal, *Moreh Nevukhei Hazman*, 215–216. See Schweid, *Hehagut Hayehudit ba'Et Haḥadasha*, 192–193.

one (Kant, Lessing, Herder), or a dialectical development (Hegel) in which earlier ideas are sublated. These processes are appropriate for other nations, which lack a connection with the absolute spirit, but not for the Jewish people, who forged a direct link with that spirit at Sinai. According to Judaism, the absolute spiritual God is above history in potential and in actuality, and He is not realized in movement from potential to actual. The message of Judaism (the law of the Torah) is also above history. Part of it was revealed at Sinai, and part of it has continued to exist in potential ever since—until it was revealed by the Sages in history in a series of cyclical intellectual processes.

Krochmal retains the Hegelian idealistic concepts, but emends Hegel's conclusions about Judaism: that Judaism has lost its vitality, or had been swallowed up by higher cultures. According to Krochmal, the stratum of the first revelation, which is unique to the Jewish people, is never revoked nor rendered obsolete, and does not progress or improve. Rather is it is eternal, including within it everything that will be produced from any future intellectual process. The *halakhot* of the Torah—which are the message in which the absolute Spirit with personality and will communicates, existing with Him in potential and actuality—are implemented and executed within the Jewish people in a rational intellectual process.

It should be emphasized that, living at the beginning of the modern period, Krochmal became historically conscious of the fact that Halakhah and the opinions of the Jews, like any culture, develop and form from an inner and outer dialogue with various opinions and cultures, reflecting the time and place of its creators. Krochmal looks from above upon earlier ages—in which this process took place unawares—offering criticism mingled with admiration, explaining history as an unconscious process of nations actualizing potential ideas and then making their exit from the stage. Judaism, however, which bears the absolute spiritual idea above history, unites some of these ideas in a dialectical process and thus leads humanity to its redemption.

According to Krochmal, the process began with the creation of the nation in Egypt[37] and continues throughout history until the modern era.[38] Modern research that seeks to understand who we are, how we developed, how we reached this point, and how to continue this process consciously[39] must relate to this process.

---

37 Schweid, *Hehagut Hayehudit ba'et Haḥadasha*, 42–43.
38 Ibid., 36–38.
39 Ibid., 167.

Chajes inherited the idea of Halakhah as a process of actualization from Krochmal and it served as a foundation of his system. In effect Chajes and Krochmal performed a dialectical process. They unified two contradictory extremes—on the one hand the principle of Torah from Sinai, on the other hand, Maimonides's principle of an accumulative halakhic codex, and the modern innovation of historical development. The Aristotelian move made it possible to create a dialectic move and to unify these two extremes. Krochmal's idea enabled Chajes to elevate the stratum of the interpretations derived from the thirteen principles up to the stratum of written Torah. The link joining interpretation to text is the thirteen principles themselves, which were given at Sinai. This idea provided Krochmal with the basis for his conception of Halakhah as an evolving law developed by human agency in history; the chain of reception has no connection to the revelation event at Sinai. Law and revelation are linked by human reason, in which God dwells immanently.[40]

5. *MIDRASH AGGADA* AND THE STATUS OF THE SAGES

The fact that the Sages were entrusted with the execution of the laws possessing the status of written Torah, gives them, according to Chajes, a superlative status. In this matter, Chajes influenced Krochmal, and both of them vigorously defended the status of the Sages from the criticisms of the Reform movement. The latter wished to lower the Sages' status and downplay the quality of their compositions (the Midrash, the Mishnah, and the Talmud). They went as far as

---

40   On the nature of the connection between Krochmal and Hegel and the other idealist philosophers, see S. Tov, *Torat Hegel Bemishnat Naḥman Krochmal* (Tel Aviv, 1954). On Krochmal's thought see Rawidowicz, "Mavo Lekitvei Naḥman Krochmal 17–225; Guttman, *Hafilosofia shel Hayahadut*, 289–308; Schweid, *Hehagut Hayehudit ba'et Haḥadasha*, 172–201, Rotenstreich, *Hamaḥshava Hayehudit*, 52–70; Feiner, *Haskalah Vehistoria*, 157–168. The principle of actualizing potential in the history of the Halakhah was noted in detail by Luz, who also criticized it. See E. Luz, "Nahman Krochmal Uve'ayat Hahistorizatsia Shel Hayahadut," in M. Idel et al., eds., Minha Lesara (Jerusalem, 1994), 249–257. On Krochmal's philosophy of hermeneutics and Hegel's influence on it, see Levi, *Hermenoitika Bamaḥshavah Hayehudit*, 24–53.

As in many other areas, on the subject of historical consciousness, Mendelssohn was a pioneer in the modern period.

See on this D. Sorkin, *Moses Mendelssohn and the Religious Enlightenment* (Los Angeles, 1996), 78–79. All the *maskilim* who followed Mendelssohn acquired and internalized his ideas, directly or indirectly. A comprehensive discussion of Chajes's position regarding the relationship between revelation and reason can be found in Chamiel, *The Middle Way*, vol. 1, 192–204.

portraying the Sages as power-hungry charlatans who wished to dominate the nation by burdening them with a heavy yoke and by pretending to be authentic interpreters of Scripture.

In his essay "Darkhei Hahoraa" of 1843, Chajes devotes the beginning of the second section to the issue of ruling of Halakhah from Aggada, saying: "But ordinary *aggadot*, either from the Talmud or collections of Midrash, are halakhic decisions for us, aside from those *halakhot* that were presented in *midrashim* spoken before a large audience."[41] This position of Chajes's contradicts Maimonides's explicit statements in his responsa (§458) that in Aggada there is "no tradition [Oral Law], prohibitions, permissions, or judgments."

Chajes writes about Aggada in chapters seventeen to thirty two in his essay "Mevo Hatalmud." He unequivocally states that the *aggadot* "were all received by them from Sinai orally [...] from God to Moses our teacher, may he rest in peace."[42] Even if occasionally one finds an aggadic *midrash* that uses the hermeneutic principles, this is merely a mnemonic reference [*asmakhta*]. He deduces this matter a fortiori from the Halakhah. If the Halakhah, which is merely "an obligation of the limbs and a corridor to purify the religion," was given at Sinai, a fortiori matters of faith and the foundations of the religion (such as the immortality of the soul, the World to Come, prophecy, the unity of God, reward and punishment, free will, providence, the human soul, the coming of the Messiah, the revival of the dead) none of which are mentioned explicitly in the written Torah, must have been received faithfully from Sinai.

Aggadic *midrash* is also meant to help decipher obscure verses in the Bible, as the Sages show us, and as Maimonides shows us in the *Guide for the Perplexed*, part 1, 70: "Consider how these excellent and true ideas, comprehended only by the greatest philosophers,[43] are found dispersed throughout the *midrashim*."[44]

Other aggadic *midrashim*, which are meant to teach us matters of behavior and morality, were deduced by the Sages with their knowledge, experience, and learning, and as Maimonides explains, these, too, were said with "divine power."[45] Chajes attributes the strangeness of aggadic *midrashim* to several factors. First, as noted, these *midrashim* are references and scriptural mnemonics, and not the

---

41 Chajes, "Sefer Darkhei Hahoraa" (1842–3), in *Kol Sifrei Maharats ḥayut* (Jerusalem, 1958), 251–252.
42 Chajes, "Mevo Hatalmud," 316.
43 I.e., Aristotle.
44 Chajes, "Mevo Hatalmud," 316.
45 Ibid., quotation from *Shemona Peraqim*.

simple meaning [*peshat*] of the text. Therefore, they sometimes seem strange and bizarre. Second, the Sages adopt all the means at their disposal to achieve their goal—praising the righteous, their good deeds, and their rewards, or condemning the wicked, their sins, and their punishment. For aggadic *midrash* the Sages used, in addition to the thirteen hermeneutic principles of *Midrash Halakhah*, other principles, such as the thirty-two principles of Rabbi Eli'ezer the son of Rabbi Jose Haglili—all received at Sinai. Frequently the use of these principles led to strange and exaggerated teachings. It was the practice of the Sages to exaggerate their interpretations to arouse joy and hope in times of fortune and misfortune, or to encourage repentance and to frighten listeners in times of trouble by speaking of strange and terrifying, supernatural matters. Third, we must believe that the interpretations that appear to deviate from common belief were delivered as esoteric clues, and they refer to matters of high importance, beyond our understanding. In chapter 27,[46] Chajes cites as evidence chapter 2 of Maimonides's introduction to *Pereq Heleq*, where Maimonides describes the different sects in Judaism, a description Chajes already used to defend Maimonides in 1841. Two groups of people err in their understanding of the *midrashim* of the Sages, but a third group of people admire the Sages and realize that their words are not always self-evident. Chajes emphasizes that according to most rabbis, we must regard all the miracles and wonders in talmudic stories as literal and believe that they occurred as written. But there is also a minority opinion that these were simply dreams and not descriptions of real events. Chajes admits that he is unable to decide which of these opinions is true, and that here one must use the standard of rationalist criticism to distinguish those places where we must take things literally from those places where we must regard them as a dream or imagination. Fourth, some *midrashim* are parables and figures of speech, which explains their strange appearance.

Chajes emphasizes here that we must understand literally all matters of evil spirits, ghosts, the evil eye, magic spells, and enchantments in the Talmud—unlike Maimonides who considered these all parable, riddle and allegory. Regarding these matters and regarding the medical advice in the Talmud, he refers the reader to the responsa of Rabbi Solomon ben Aderet (*Rashba*, Barcelona, 1235–1310) (§ 408, 413), who explains that all of these matters are real; we, being weak in spirit, are simply unable to understand them. Elsewhere in his writings, Chajes uses the comments of certain medieval rabbis, who state that all the words of the Sages of the Talmud—including those that seem

---

46 Ibid., 333–335.

contrary to the natural reality known to us—were true in the reality of their time, but that "nature has changed."[47]

In the introduction to his article, "Tiferet Lemoshe" [Glory to Moses], written in defense of Maimonides in 1849, Chajes explains in detail the character of the various sects in Judaism who relate to the *midrashim* of the Sages and who are described by Maimonides: Two invalid sects: the foolish Torah scholars who read *midrashim* literally and the accursed intellectuals who denigrate the words of the Sages; and one valid one: the scholars who combine Torah with reason. Chajes writes about these sects as follows:

> [There are] the ignorant ones among the people, on the one hand, who think that all study and contemplation is heresy, and in their thoughts they imagine that the divine Torah and human reason are two opposites that are against each other from start to finish. They decree and determine that it is forbidden to investigate the divine religion with reason and knowledge. [...] The second sect that opposes it from the opposite extreme is the sect of those who give a heedful ear only to what human reason can grasp, and they believe that aside from that, there is no reality, and they endeavor with all their power to show that the commandments that came from the Torah are only matters that relate to [a specific] time and place and can change from time to time according to the circumstances of the generation. [...] The middle sect are those who guide their ways only on the path of the Torah, and in this way they are similar to the first sect in believing that the written Torah and the Oral Torah both came from the mouth of the Almighty and were spoken to Moses and stand forever. However, they examine and investigate to give reasons for matters of the Torah, according to the foundations of human intellect, both in main points and in offshoots, and also in the commandments. But in those matters that human intellect cannot attain, they accept things in veneration and awe.[48]

A comparison between Chajes and Krochmal's statements on Aggada raises similar discussions, and Krochmal also uses Maimonides's model.

Chajes and Krochmal have similar views mainly regarding the principles that served the authors of Aggada, the explanations of some of its strange features (related to the Midrash's status as textual support [*asmakhta*], and from

---

47 On this subject see Chajes, "Darkhei Hahora'ah," 228–230; Also see Chajes, "Mevo Hatalmud," 331–342. It appears that this is as opposed to Maimonides's opinion in the *Guide for the Perplexed*, part 2, 28.
48 Chajes, *Ateret Tsvi*, 397.

the need to exaggerate and push to extremes in order to impress). However, the gap between the two thinkers is very wide. Krochmal denies those to his right, "benighted experts," who take individual opinions of a particular time for truths that stand forever, and even of foreign stories, saying they are divine secrets reserved for God-fearing men. While he obviously believes that all *aggadot* and the principles of interpretation are human creations, he goes even farther than Maimonides in his treatment of a significant part of the *aggadot* in the Talmud. In his opinion, *aggadot* about evil spirits and spells, slander, condemnations of the Sages, foul language, and superstitions are not the authentic creations of the Sages. Rather, these originate from the masses—buffoons and minor scholars—who collected stories in their own fashion. These stories were included in the Talmud by its later editors, who were on a far lower level than the Amoraim and who, unable to distinguish between substantial and trivial matters, bound everything together in a single volume. Krochmal also does not forget to criticize those on his left: those who act wise and consult non-Jewish sources, a phenomenon exploited by non-Jewish scholars in order to nullify the entire Talmud, belittle the Sages, and mock those who respect them.[49] He concludes his discussion of this subject with a declaration of loyalty to the Sages and to the chain of Halakhah, similar to words written by Chajes:

> In short, we are certain of Heaven's mercy, that this request of ours [to ignore invalid and dangerous *aggadot*] will not be counted against us as sin or rebellion, and that ultimately we will use it to clarify that the Halakhah and Mishnah and their enhancement included in the Talmud were not touched by the masses, and sprouted no thistles, and that of these [works] the Babylonian Talmud is primary—one should not subtract from it— and should rule according to its principles and excellent methods all of which were transmitted by wise teachers to the ears of wise students, and they all heard from the last generation of amoraic yeshiva heads, from the mouths of their teachers who saw each other and learned from them in famous yeshivas [. . .] and the last of the prophets, upon whom rested God's spirit, his word upon their tongues—and such a strong and successive chain is extremely adequate for the loyal believer in his nation and God.[50]

---

49 Krochmal, *Moreh Nevukhei Hazman*, 238–256. See the excerpt about the "mistaken sects," n. 4 above.

50 Ibid., 256. It is interesting to note that M. Rotenberg, *Rabbi Zvi Hirsh Hayut, his Personality and Books* (Doctoral Dissertation: Yeshiva University, 1963), 119, alludes to the influence of *She'arim* 13–14 in *Moreh Nevukhei Hazman* on Chajes's conception of Halakhah and

6. THE NATURE OF THE REVELATION AT MOUNT SINAI AND THE GIVING OF THE TORAH

What exactly happened at the revelation at Sinai? There are a variety of opinions. Some read the Torah's account of Sinai literally: an account of a historical event occurring within time and space. Others, however, seek to refine the Torah's corporeal descriptions into something reflecting a more spiritual and abstract event, related more to reason than the senses. Judah Halevi's view is more similar to the corporealizing approach; Maimonides's more similar to the spiritual approach.

Interpreters are divided over Maimonides's views regarding the revelation at Sinai. More moderate interpreters maintain that according to Maimonides the event consisted of prophetic influence over the intellects of those present—an unrepeatable, direct act of God. More radical interpreters maintain that the event consisted of a one-time instance of rational-philosophical enlightenment on the congregation as a whole, initiated from below, and with no real influence from above. Alternatively, they maintain that the event did not happen at all and is nothing more than an allegory.[51] Chajes stood on the border between European rationalism and romanticism. Influenced by both, he had trouble picking a side. In this matter, he was trapped between the rationalist approach which maintains that Sinai was an event of intellectual enlightenment and the romantic approach which maintains that it was an event of direct prophecy. It is therefore no surprise that his writings demonstrate a combination of both approaches.

As is well known, a simple reading of Maimonides's *Guide for the Perplexed*, part 2, 32–33 raises two possibilities as to his view. The first option is that only Moses received the Ten Commandments, and afterwards he transmitted them to the people. The second option is that only the first two commandments were transmitted directly to the people, whereas the others were transmitted via Moses. The nation heard the first two commandments as an awesome, terrifying, voice—not God's voice but a creation of God—which Moses translated into comprehensible human speech. These first two commandments

---

Aggada in "Darkhei Hahora'ah" and "Mevo Hatalmud." For a comprehensive discussion of Chajes's approach to *Midrash Halakhah* see Chamiel, *The Middle Way*, vol. 1, 194–200.

51   See, for example, the interpretations of Halbertal, *Harambam*, 271–278 and Goodman, *Sodotav shel Moreh HaNevukhim*, 83–84 about Maimonides's statements regarding the theophany at Sinai that it was philosophical enlightenment not prophetic. Cf. Narboni's interpretation in his *Peirush al Moreh Nevukhim* I, 5, 3 and Efodi (who converted to Christianity) *Peirush al Moreh Nevukhim*, I, 5, §30.

included "intelligibles" about God's existence and unity, information which can be reached through either intellect or prophecy. In this the scholar and prophet are equal. The voice which the nation heard at Sinai, besides the sounds of thunder and trumpets, terrified the people. Overcome with fear, the nation requested that Moses intercede. At that point, Moses left the people, and through prophecy received the remaining eight commandments. These consisted of accepted societal conventions, not intelligibles. He then returned to the people and transmitted these to them, while they continued to hear the sounds of the trumpets and thunder. In any event, the nation only heard sounds, and no explicit words. Maimonides emphasizes that everyone present received information according to his own personal level.

That being said, a close reading of Maimonides suggests that he can be interpreted in a variety of other ways—especially regarding the question of what exactly occurred and what those present understood from the voice which expressed the first two commandments. Some argue (as suggested by a first reading of the text), that the nation understood nothing until Moses translated the voice for them. Others argue that the nation merited understanding through prophecy. Yet others argue that the nation's attainments were due to intellectual enlightenment. According to the last two opinions, this was an unrepeated phenomenon of understanding. Maimonides continually stresses how much intellectual effort is required for a man to reach the level of the philosopher-prophet, a level far beyond the attainments of the nation gathered at the foot of the mountain.

Chajes maintained that, according to Maimonides, the nation merited understanding of "intelligibles" at Mount Sinai:

> Behold, Maimonides sets himself the goal in many of his chapters to show that the Torah does not teach us wisdom, but only righteous laws and judgments, and informing us about the way man should behave towards his Creator, in what way and manner we must act righteously with our fellow, and what must be the conduct of kings and judges. All those laws came to us from the blessed Name, by means of those miracles that go beyond nature—changes in the order of Creation. However, the principles of faith, such as the existence of the blessed Name, reward and punishment in the next world, and divine providence—the Torah relied for all of these matters on what had already been confirmed by proof, by the laws of intellect and on what had become clear to the nation at the hour of receiving the Torah, at the hour they reached the level of prophecy, when

they also attained the intelligibles—including the women and children, who were gathered together at the chosen moment, though it is not in their nature to understand these high and exalted matters, which do not [ordinarily] come to us except to one excellent of the select; in any event, this was a special miracle at the hour of the chosen moment, that all of the nation reached the level of prophecy, as the *Guide [of the Perplexed]* says at the beginning of chapter 16 of part two, that the Torah is received in the way of prophecy, which clarifies matters that the eye has not the power to attain; and more than that, he wrote in chapter 38 of part two, that intellectual attainments come to the prophets, and prophecy will complete the power of speech, so that it knows matters that those faithful to reality [natural philosophers] attained from preparatory intellectual work. See there: indeed, our rabbi clarified a new thing for us: that the prophets, though they lack all the necessary and required preparatory work to attain divine wisdom—which only comes to one after effort and weariness, and after he who desires it has gathered handfuls of various studies of the wisdom of nature and logic and studiousness—nevertheless know all the matters of reality, and they are learned in them, and they arrive at the essence of wisdom, as if they had studied them with all the preparatory work that helps to reach the interior. And not only does he know the future from the word of God that comes to him, and not only does he know the elements of wisdom and faith from prophecy, but also in addition to all that the divine wisdom teaches him whatever is needed, and he understands it completely, as if all his days he had dealt with nothing but this wisdom.[52]

Unawares, Chajes incorporates the views of Mendelssohn into his description of Maimonides's stance: that the Torah is not meant to teach philosophy but only norms and ethical behavior. This is despite the fact that Maimonides believed that Aristotelian philosophy is embedded in the Torah. For our purposes, however, Chajes explains that according to Maimonides the Jewish people came to know the intelligibles from two sources: from intellectual reflection and from the revelation at Sinai, in which the entire nation understood the intelligibles through the divine influence of prophecy even though the members of the nation had expended no intellectual effort to reach the level required for such

---

52 In Chajes's "Tiferet Lemoshe," 418 in note. This essay was published in 1841 in *Ateret Tsvi*, in Chajes's collection of essays. It seems that it was written a year prior, as it opens with a letter of approval from Jacob Orenstein, the rabbi of Lwów, written in Nisan 5599 (1839).

apprehension. This one-time miracle had an enduring influence on later history. The nation, having effortlessly attained intelligibles through the medium of prophecy, passed down what they had achieved from generation to generation.[53] The nation of Israel as whole reached the level of apprehension achieved by every prophet—understanding of intelligibles in all their depth without any effort. Chajes ignores Maimonides's statements to the effect that only two intelligibles, which can be apprehended by anyone with intelligence, were attained by the nation as a whole at Sinai. Similarly, he ignores Maimonides's statements that this event happened only once, and that in the future intellectual effort would once again be required to reach a level suitable for such understanding. Maimonides believes that only those who reach an exalted intellectual level can even merit prophecy, attaining through it deeper intellectual apprehension, impossible with reason alone. He writes this later in part 2, chapter 38. Chajes also ignores Maimonides's statements that even at Sinai there were different levels of attainment.

That being said, Chajes continues his discussion and adds that at Sinai the nation perfected its lowly Egyptian state. This is why Moses in Egypt convinced the nation of his calling by performing supernatural miracles perceived by the senses, instead of marshaling intellectual proofs. This process of refinement was completed at Sinai:

> For from that point onward, all prophets would attain matters [regarding] the true reality in prophetic visions and perfection of reflection and intellect, more than can be achieved by scholars after assiduous study. And see *The Guide for the Perplexed*, part 2, chapter 33 [which explains] that which the Sages said: that the first two commandments were heard from the mouth of the Almighty, this means, from the mouth of an ultimate proof. Meaning, that they [the words] reached them just like they reached Moses, and Moses did not need to convey them. This is because these

---

53 According to this argument, Chajes writes (ibid., 420 in the note) that Maimonides maintains in part I, chapter 62, that the intellectual attainment of a philosopher, through the Active Intellect, cannot be forgotten. This is how he explains the "great voice which never ceased" (Deut. 5:19, as translated by Onkelos): "The great and powerful voice that they understood and heard then, on that occasion, never ceased for them, and if intellectual understanding cannot be forgotten, even less so can prophetic understanding be forgotten, which helped then to reach intellectual understanding, and the voice has never stopped with us, because this understanding is impossible to forget at any time, and thereby we negate any challenger and give the lie to everyone who argues and comes to oppose the Torah and what is correct."

two principles—God's existence and unity—can truly only be attainted through human study, and through proofs, and therefore the prophet and the one who knows them is equal, with no advantage of the one over the other. And these two principles are not exclusively known through prophecy. The Torah said, "you have begun to know that the Lord is your God etc." See there: we see that in his opinion, through their chosen status and their prophecy they attained two principles of religion through proof. And a great sage has written that whenever the blessed Name wishes that all people should receive the truth of one matter at one time, He then summons faithful messengers to arouse hearts, and supreme Providence prepares effective ways to make the people fit to reach that height.[54]

In this passage we already see another approach. At first, Chajes had understood that according to Maimonides, the nation really heard, like Moses, the clear words of the first two commandments from the mouth of the Almighty—a deviation from a literal reading of Maimonides. Now, Chajes understands that when Maimonides writes "from the mouth of the Almighty" he is not referring to hearing through sense perception but rather apprehension through "an ultimate proof"—that is philosophical enlightenment. That being said, in Chajes opinion, this enlightenment proceeds from above through a prophetic miracle. In effect, Chajes combines philosophy and prophecy. His quotation on the methods used by God to teach various truths comes from Mendelssohn's *Jerusalem*,[55] and Chajes takes Mendelssohn's statements out of context to serve his own needs. Mendelssohn, as he explains there, offers an explanation entirely at odds with that of Chajes: he believes that the Creator makes available different means for different types of apprehension: necessary eternal truths (like the laws of logic, mathematics, and correct beliefs such as knowledge of the existence of one, eternal, omnipotent God, divine providence, reward and punishment, life after death, and ethical behavior)—are attained solely through reason. Eternal accidental truths (the laws of nature) are attained through the senses and reason. Historical, one-time truths which require preservation (the Exodus, the revelation at Mount Sinai, and laws of the Torah)—are proven by divine speech, writings, or miracles and wonders. That is to say, according to Mendelssohn, there was no philosophical enlightenment at Mount Sinai.

---

54 Ibid., 419 in note.
55 M. Mendelssohn, *Jerusalem*, trans. A. Arkush (Hanover and London, 1983) 89–94, 97–102. The quote is a paraphrase of 93. My thanks to Yehoyada Amir who pointed me to this source.

It is worth noticing that Chajes refers to Mendelssohn as "a great sage" without quoting him by name. It seems that omitting the names of *maskilim*, even when he relied on them, was a common practice of Chajes; his friends and foes would both criticize him for this. In his article "Igeret Biqoret" from 1840, he writes that Onkelos translated the halakhic passages of the Bible according to the laws of the Sages and not according to the apparent *peshat* of the verse.[56] In a note there he adds that when his friend "the great sage" saw this, he challenged Chajes, asking him why the "excellency of his Torah" fails to mention those instances in which Onkelos interprets against the law of the Sages, such as "and they shall spread the garment," (Deut. 22:17) and "you shall cut off her hand," (Deut. 25:11) which he interprets according to the *peshat*? Chajes argues with his challenger and gives an answer. Regardless, it is clear that the challenger is Krochmal, who received from Chajes, by mail, parts of the draft of the essay which he sent him in Ternopil, responding to him on 1 Adar 5600 [1840],[57] including the aforementioned question. Chajes, as was his practice when citing *maskilim*, does not mention Krochmal by name, calling him only the "great sage," to avoid explicitly associating himself with the *maskilim*. This greatly angered Krochmal, when he received the essay in its entirety, including notes, by mail. In another letter dated 8 Iyar, that same year,[58] he comments on his inappropriate treatment of other scholars. Krochmal claims that Chajes sometimes cites Zunz's book *The Sermons of the Jews* but only mentions him by name once, afterwards referring to him several times only as "the author of the book." According to Krochmal, Chajes is at risk of being branded with the statement of Rabbi Shimon: "Who are these, whose waters we drink, but their names we do not mention?"[59] presumably alluding to the fact that Chajes hides Krochmal's name even though he drinks from his waters.[60] Similarly, Krochmal is indignant at Chajes's harsh criticism of other researchers such as Rapoport, the local rabbi of Ternopil. Krochmal writes that he has met with Rapoport many times, even discussing Chajes's essay with him, and he notes Rapoport's great anger at Chajes. Rapoport

---

56 Chajes, "Igeret Biqoret," 511.
57 Krochmal, *Kitvei Ranaq*, 448–450.
58 Ibid., 452–454. See Hershkovitz, *Maharats Ḥayut*, 269–284.
59 BT Horayot 14a. See the omission of Zunz's name in "Igeret Biqoret," 495.
60 See Rawidowicz, "Mavo Lekitvei Naḥ.man Krochmal," 87, notes 2–6; Rotenburg, *Rabbi Tsvi Hirsh Ḥayut*, 109–111; Hershkovitz, *Maharats Ḥ. ayut*, 236–245, especially note 36.

responded in kind, and published a critique of Chajes's essay,[61] attacking his content, his arrogance in not mentioning him and other researchers like Zunz by name, and for competing with him over the rabbinate of Prague. Chajes apologized for all of these in the introduction of his essay "Imrei Bina" in 1849.[62] He mentions Krochmal's criticism of the fact that he did not mention Zunz, "the wise and amazing," by name, and admitted that this contravened decency and etiquette. To Rapoport, who expressed harsh criticism of Chajes for not critiquing his content appropriately among scholars and even made himself his enemy, portraying him as arrogant and copying from others, Chajes responded softly and said that he had already forgiven him. Later in the introduction, he demonstrates his contrition and mentions the names of many contemporary researchers: "The scholar Reggio of Gorizia, the scholar Luzzatto of Padua, my friend Rabbi Girondi of Padua, the scholar Dukes from Pressburg, the great scholar Rabbi Alzari who is known as Fürst, editor of *Der Orient*, the great and famous scholar Solomon Judah Rapoport, the great scholar our teacher Rabbi Zunz of Berlin, the great scholar our master Rabbi Jost, our teacher the author of *Haketav ve-ha-Qabbalah*, the great scholar Zecharias Frankel from Dresden, the great scholar the late Nahman Hakohen" (see above section 3).[63] Zunz is also mentioned by name later in the essay: "The sage Rabbi Yom Tov Lipmann Zunz," "the sage Rabbi Zunz."[64] Nevertheless, Chajes did not entirely forgive Rapoport. In this essay, Chajes castigates Rapoport for suspecting him of copying his quotation of Rif in his *Igeret Biqoret* from Rapoport's book Toledot Rabbenu Nissim "as if only his eye saw Rif's words and the foreigner has no portion or inheritance in them."[65] He does not mention him by name, calling him instead "the great and famous rabbi who critiqued my book *Igeret Biqoret*." Later in the article he seems to have felt remorse, mentioning Rapoport by name in a different context: "The great, famous, sage of all things our master Solomon Judah Rapoport who critiques my *Igeret Biqoret*," "the great rabbi our teacher

---

61 *Kerem Ḥemed*, vol. 6 (1841), 143–147, 204–259. See Hershkovitz, ibid., 410.
62 Chajes, "Imrei Binah," 871–876.
63 By contrast, Chajes was eager to mention Krochmal by name (immediately after his death in 1840 soon after the critique he had sent him)—"my deceased beloved, the rabbi, comprehensive scholar, and researcher our teacher Rabbi Nahman Hakohen"—already in his book Ateret Tsvi from 1841 in the introduction to his essay "Darkhei Moshe" when describing the Essenes, 449.
64 Chajes, "Imrei Binah," 887.
65 Ibid., 895–896 in the note and on p. 913.

Solomon Judah Rapoport."⁶⁶ He also mentions again Krochmal's challenge from Onkelos's deviations from rabbinic Halakhah, this time citing his full name "my friend, the late rabbi and famous scholar of all things our master Nahman Hakohen."⁶⁷ In his last great essay "Minḥat Qenaot," dedicated to his criticism of the Reform movement, he lets himself speak freely and mentions (negatively of course) by name, the leaders of the Reform movement: Dr. Hess, Friedländer, Ben David, Baruch Landau, Jacobson, Lieberman, Horin, Dr. Herzfeld, Geiger, Holdheim, and Philipson,⁶⁸ and once again mentioned positively "the great and famous sage our master Rapoport."⁶⁹

Before he changed his ways, Chajes cited other *maskilic* sources without mentioning them by name: In his essay "Hosafot Ledivrei Neviim" (1837–1838), 193—the enlightened scholar; in his essay "Mevo Hatalmud" (1845), 304—*maskil*; 328—great sage; 345, 349—scholar; in his essay "Misphat Vehoraa" (1840), 390—scholar (apparently referring to Geiger).

That being said, the phenomenon continued even afterwards, albeit only in instances in which he responded to an inquirer whom he did not deem important or when he opposed a position he considered invalid: *Responsa of Tsvi Hirsch Chajes* (1849–1850), 630, 698, 709, 762, 787, 791, 808, 891—a certain scholar; 795—a certain *maskil*; 854—the *maskilic* scholar. According to Jacob Schachter,⁷⁰ Chajes was referring to Krochmal in all four places in his essay "Mevo Hatalmud." According to Rawidovicz,⁷¹ however, he was referring to Rapoport. It seems clear to me, that Chajes does not mention Mendelssohn by name, lest he appear to be basing himself on the symbol of the Haskalah, which was detested by Chajes's hasidic neighbors, whom he feared.

To return to our subject, it seems that in regards to the revelation at Sinai as philosophical enlightenment, Chajes relied less on Mendelssohn and more on his learning partner, Krochmal. Besides studying together, Chajes saw a draft containing fragments of *Moreh Nevukhim Haḥadash* (its temporary name) which Krochmal gave to Chajes for review and comments. In *Moreh Nevukhei Hazman* there is little discussion of the written Torah and specifically no

---

66 Ibid., 945–946.
67 Ibid., 909 in the note.
68 Chajes, "Minḥ. at Qenaot," 981–982 and in the note; 988 in the note; 993 in the note; 999; 1003; 1011; 1015 and in the note; 1020 in the note.
69 Ibid., 1015 in the note.
70 J. Shachter, The Student's Gide Through the Talmud by Z. H. Chajes, translation from Hebrew (New York, 1960), 85, 180, 249, 266.
71 Rawidowicz, "Mavo Lekitvei Naḥ. man Krochmal," 87 n. 5.

discussion of the revelation at Sinai. In Gate 8, Krochmal begins to describe the first of three historical eras, and says about the dawn of the nation at Sinai: "Similarly, God exalted, strengthened and encouraged his connection to the nation by giving them an exceedingly wondrous and sublime path of laws, statutes, and rulings, righteous and comprehensive, completing the individual and the collective in the most excellent way, promising them in exchange for the preservation of their truth that the nation would not be destroyed or eliminated."[72] As mentioned,[73] Krochmal declares his belief that Moses transmitted the Torah to Israel, while he also believes in true prophets who received the contents of their books from divine inspiration. The atheists who think that a deceitful scholar invented these things are insane, and those who cast doubt on a spiritual existence beyond the world, on the traditions of the fathers, on the apprehension of proper intellect and on inner emotions—are mad. Likewise, he states that already during the forty-year sojourn in the wilderness, many details were added to the general laws given by Moses. These were later included in the Torah, and to the body of the Torah were added new laws such as the goat sin-offering, the ruling of the wood-gatherer and the blasphemer, the laws of Second Passover, the ruling of female inheritance, and the marriages of female inheritors. It was Moses who committed the first version of the Torah to writing. However, the shapes of the biblical letters (including those of the Pentateuch) and the current form of the Pentateuch's wording were consolidated later by prophets and the divinely inspired. The "Watchers," the "Scribes," and the "Men of the Great Assembly" finalized the Torah for later generations, transcribing it with ink on parchment in Assyrian script—the Torah's external garb. They also added the *qeri, ketiv,* and scribal emendations. Ever since, the text of the Torah was carefully preserved and, with the assistance of divine providence, no hand was allowed to touch it. Despite these textual emendations after Moses, "in terms of its content and spirituality, nothing was changed at all, and the laws, statutes, rulings, testimonies, and holy stories given to Moses at Sinai are the same as those currently in our hand. And this confirming gift reached us, through the chain of true receivers, whom God selected with his infinite wisdom."[74]

The excerpts from Krochmal were articulated meticulously, and they were designed to portray their writer as a conservative and a traditionalist.

---

72 Krochmal, *Moreh Nevukhei Hazman*, 44–45.
73 Notes 24, 25.
74 Krochmal, *Moreh Nevukhei Hazman*, 199–200. See also 9, 63–64, and 191. Cf. Rawidowicz, "Mavo Lekitvei Naḥman Krochmal," 126–128.

A careful reading, however, demonstrates that Krochmal avoided discussing a direct prophetic transmission of the biblical text, from above to below. He only writes that the content of the text are divine but not its mode of transmission. Krochmal was careful not to seem like an innovator violating the authority of the text. However, he also never said anything at odds with his radical rationalist views which were based also on his reading of *The Guide for the Perplexed*.

Chajes may not have realized Krochmal's view that the revelation at Sinai was an event of inspiration from below and not a national prophecy from above. Nevertheless, inspired by Mendelssohn and Krochmal, he presented a stance which combines the notion of prophecy with the notion of philosophical enlightenment. Were it not for Krochmal's explanation about the nature of the theophany at Sinai, it would have been easier for Chajes to present a more traditional stance—Sinai as direct prophecy. But Krochmal's interpretation (as understood by Chajes) fit, in Chajes's opinion, with the stance of Maimonides, as I have presented above.

SUMMARY

Researchers of Krochmal and Chajes were aware of the mutual influences between the two. Some put more emphasis on Krochmal's influence on Chajes (Rawidovicz), others on Chajes's influence on Krochmal (Hershkovitz), and still others thought that it is difficult to determine who influenced whom more (Rotenberg). Most researchers tended to focus on specific halakhic topics but not topics of principles or philosophy. In this chapter I have tried to show that the influence between them was far deeper and comprehensive than previously assumed, including fundamental, philosophical issues. Overall, it appears to me that the influence of the rationalist, philosopher and theological historian on the talmudist rabbi was far stronger than the reverse. Krochmal is the one primarily responsible for Chajes's transition from being a standard, traditional rabbi, to becoming a rabbi who gave reason more space, both as a source of dogmatic truth, as well as a method of interpreting Maimonides. Therefore, one can see in Chajes, the fundamentalist rabbi, a man of the middle way, and not simply a devout man of the right and therefore, I believe that Chajes had many characteristics of a Neo-Orthodox rabbi. It is true that when analyzing—from a Galician perspective—the different types of rabbis in Europe in the nineteenth century, that Gertner's classification is appropriate, and there is no doubt that he was correct to distinguish between Chajes's *maskilic* rabbinate of Galicia and the Neo-Orthodox rabbis of Germany.[75] However, a comprehensive look at the European rabbinates reveals important similarities between Chajes and the modern religious rabbinate in Germany—which followed a middle way, combining revelation with reason and science. These similarities are less about externalities—such as the rabbi and the synagogue—and more about common ideological trends: seeing reason and the sciences as a source identical to revelation, maintaining that revelation is the criterion in cases of difficulties and contradictions, using secular studies to enhance the structure of a person, universalism, advancing the use of Hebrew and so forth. Chajes never disapproved of the Neo-Orthodox rabbis. Quite the opposite. He expended much effort to become closer to the members of Wissenschaft des Judentums in Germany, even though he disagreed with them in many areas (like Hirsch did) and advocated the customs of these rabbis, personal and communal in the synagogue, such as sermons in the language of the country, distinguished dress, order, discipline, cleanliness and even a choir.[76]

From here I will move to the twentieth century and begin to discuss Hirsch's influence on the Jewish liberal thinkers of that era.

---

75 H. Gertner, *Harav Vehair Hagedola* (Jerusalem, 2013), 302–304.
76 Chajes, "Minḥat Qenaot," 984. See Chamiel, *The Middle Way*, vol. 1, 425–430.

www.ingramcontent.com/pod-product-compliance
Lightning Source LLC
Chambersburg PA
CBHW052016290426
44112CB00014B/2256